Horace's satires, epistles, and art of poetry, done into English, with notes. By S. Dunster, ... The fourth edition, corrected.

Horace

ECCO

PRINT EDITIONS

Horace's satires, epistles, and art of poetry, done into English, with notes. By S. Dunster, ... The fourth edition, corrected.

Horace
ESTCID: T036663
Reproduction from British Library
Parallel Latin and English texts. Titlepage in red and black. With an index.
London : printed by T. W. for W. Mears, F. Clay, and D. Browne, 1729.
[2],iv,[6],477,[7]p. ; 8°

Eighteenth Century
Collections Online
Print Editions

Gale ECCO Print Editions

Relive history with *Eighteenth Century Collections Online*, now available in print for the independent historian and collector. This series includes the most significant English-language and foreign-language works printed in Great Britain during the eighteenth century, and is organized in seven different subject areas including literature and language; medicine, science, and technology; and religion and philosophy. The collection also includes thousands of important works from the Americas.

The eighteenth century has been called "The Age of Enlightenment." It was a period of rapid advance in print culture and publishing, in world exploration, and in the rapid growth of science and technology – all of which had a profound impact on the political and cultural landscape. At the end of the century the American Revolution, French Revolution and Industrial Revolution, perhaps three of the most significant events in modern history, set in motion developments that eventually dominated world political, economic, and social life.

In a groundbreaking effort, Gale initiated a revolution of its own: digitization of epic proportions to preserve these invaluable works in the largest online archive of its kind. Contributions from major world libraries constitute over 175,000 original printed works. Scanned images of the actual pages, rather than transcriptions, recreate the works *as they first appeared.*

Now for the first time, these high-quality digital scans of original works are available via print-on-demand, making them readily accessible to libraries, students, independent scholars, and readers of all ages.

For our initial release we have created seven robust collections to form one the world's most comprehensive catalogs of 18th century works.

Initial Gale ECCO Print Editions collections include:

History and Geography

Rich in titles on English life and social history, this collection spans the world as it was known to eighteenth-century historians and explorers. Titles include a wealth of travel accounts and diaries, histories of nations from throughout the world, and maps and charts of a world that was still being discovered. Students of the War of American Independence will find fascinating accounts from the British side of conflict.

Social Science

Delve into what it was like to live during the eighteenth century by reading the first-hand accounts of everyday people, including city dwellers and farmers, businessmen and bankers, artisans and merchants, artists and their patrons, politicians and their constituents. Original texts make the American, French, and Industrial revolutions vividly contemporary.

Medicine, Science and Technology

Medical theory and practice of the 1700s developed rapidly, as is evidenced by the extensive collection, which includes descriptions of diseases, their conditions, and treatments. Books on science and technology, agriculture, military technology, natural philosophy, even cookbooks, are all contained here.

Literature and Language

Western literary study flows out of eighteenth-century works by Alexander Pope, Daniel Defoe, Henry Fielding, Frances Burney, Denis Diderot, Johann Gottfried Herder, Johann Wolfgang von Goethe, and others. Experience the birth of the modern novel, or compare the development of language using dictionaries and grammar discourses.

Religion and Philosophy

The Age of Enlightenment profoundly enriched religious and philosophical understanding and continues to influence present-day thinking. Works collected here include masterpieces by David Hume, Immanuel Kant, and Jean-Jacques Rousseau, as well as religious sermons and moral debates on the issues of the day, such as the slave trade. The Age of Reason saw conflict between Protestantism and Catholicism transformed into one between faith and logic -- a debate that continues in the twenty-first century.

Law and Reference

This collection reveals the history of English common law and Empire law in a vastly changing world of British expansion. Dominating the legal field is the *Commentaries of the Law of England* by Sir William Blackstone, which first appeared in 1765. Reference works such as almanacs and catalogues continue to educate us by revealing the day-to-day workings of society.

Fine Arts

The eighteenth-century fascination with Greek and Roman antiquity followed the systematic excavation of the ruins at Pompeii and Herculaneum in southern Italy; and after 1750 a neoclassical style dominated all artistic fields. The titles here trace developments in mostly English-language works on painting, sculpture, architecture, music, theater, and other disciplines. Instructional works on musical instruments, catalogs of art objects, comic operas, and more are also included.

The BiblioLife Network

This project was made possible in part by the BiblioLife Network (BLN), a project aimed at addressing some of the huge challenges facing book preservationists around the world. The BLN includes libraries, library networks, archives, subject matter experts, online communities and library service providers. We believe every book ever published should be available as a high-quality print reproduction; printed on-demand anywhere in the world. This insures the ongoing accessibility of the content and helps generate sustainable revenue for the libraries and organizations that work to preserve these important materials.

The following book is in the "public domain" and represents an authentic reproduction of the text as printed by the original publisher. While we have attempted to accurately maintain the integrity of the original work, there are sometimes problems with the original work or the micro-film from which the books were digitized. This can result in minor errors in reproduction. Possible imperfections include missing and blurred pages, poor pictures, markings and other reproduction issues beyond our control. Because this work is culturally important, we have made it available as part of our commitment to protecting, preserving, and promoting the world's literature.

GUIDE TO FOLD-OUTS MAPS and OVERSIZED IMAGES

The book you are reading was digitized from microfilm captured over the past thirty to forty years. Years after the creation of the original microfilm, the book was converted to digital files and made available in an online database.

In an online database, page images do not need to conform to the size restrictions found in a printed book. When converting these images back into a printed bound book, the page sizes are standardized in ways that maintain the detail of the original. For large images, such as fold-out maps, the original page image is split into two or more pages

Guidelines used to determine how to split the page image follows:

• Some images are split vertically; large images require vertical and horizontal splits.
• For horizontal splits, the content is split left to right.
• For vertical splits, the content is split from top to bottom.
• For both vertical and horizontal splits, the image is processed from top left to bottom right.

Horatius Flaccus

1386 bb 9

HORACE's SATIRES, EPISTLES,

AND

ART of POETRY,

Done into ENGLISH,

WITH NOTES.

By *S. DUNSTER,* D. D.
PREBENDARY of *SARUM.*

Sermoni propiora
Lib I Sat. IV. ℣. 42.

The FOURTH EDITION, Corrected.

LONDON:
Printed by *T. W* for W MEARS, F. CLAY, and
D. BROWNE, *without Temple-Bar*
M.DCC.XXIX.

TO THE

RIGHT HONOURABLE

Thomas, **Lord** *Parker*,

Baron of *Macclesfield*,

In the County Palatine of Chester;

Lord High Chancellor of
GREAT‑BRITAIN;

And One of His Majesty's most
Honourable Privy‑Council.

My Lord,

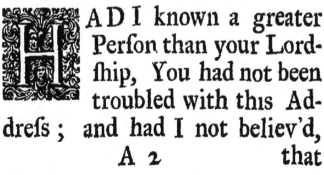

HAD I known a greater
Person than your Lord-
ship, You had not been
troubled with this Ad-
dress; and had I not believ'd,

A 2   that

that the following Performance did, in some Measure, merit your Acceptance, You had been freed from it.

IT is none of the least of Your distinguishing Qualities, that those who have endeavour'd to make themselves useful to the World by their Studies, are sure of Your Protection: The Generous *DORSET* is now no more, and it is not long since the Celebrated *HALLIFAX* was taken from us; and such is our present Situation, that tho' the CLASSICKS may be said to be the Treasures of Knowledge, and as they teach us to think well, are most proper to make a Polite and Finish'd Gentleman (a Character which all Men are ambitious of attaining;) yet both They, and Those who employ Their Time in making them intelligible, are equally neglected.

BUT

BUT how juſt ſoever this Complaint may be, there are ſtill ſome Noble Spirits among us

---Animæ, quales neque candidiores Terra tulit,---

who are altogether free from this Imputation.

AMONG Theſe, Your Lordſhip juſtly claims the Pre-eminence; Your Liberality and Humanity are univerſally admir'd; and what is yet more ſurprizing, a Knowledge of Men, and a profound Intelligence of Things, which but ſeldom, very ſeldom, meet together, are reconcil'd in You.

TO juſtify the Truth of what I ſay, I appeal from Your Lordſhip to the Publick Voice; who, in a juſt Senſe of Your uncommon Vertues, unanimouſly declar'd, at Your late Promotion, that His MAJESTY, whoſe Love to His BRITISH Subjects is beyond Expreſſion, ne-

A 3 ver

ver gave 'em a greater Inſtance of it, than in making You his CHANCELLOR.

Dii dent virtuti tempora longa tuæ.

I am,

My LORD,

Your Lordſhip's

Moſt Obedient

Humble Servant,

S. DUNSTER.

THE
PREFACE.

THE Criticks consider HORACE in a double Capacity, as a Writer of Odes, and a Satirist; *they divide the* Odes *into* Panegyrical, Moral, *and* Bacchanalian: *The Design of which, being rather to raise the Fancy than inform the Judgment, they accordingly consist of Pompous Numbers, Sublime Thoughts, bold and daring Figures and Expressions. This is the Reason that they will hardly admit of a Prose Translation; but this does not hold good as to his Satires and* Epistles; *which were*

The PREFACE.

written, as he himself assures us, for the Instruction of Mankind; they abound with many excellent Rules and Precepts, the Knowledge of which contributes very much to the Improvement of Life, by imprinting in our Minds just and true and lively Sentiments of Moral Honesty and Vertue.

Æque pauperibus prodest, lo-
    cupletibus æque,
Æque neglectum pueris seni-
    busque nocebit.
Fervet avaritia, miseroq; cupi-
    dine pectus?
Sunt verba & voces, quibus hunc
    lenire dolorem
Possis, & magnam morbi depo-
    nere partem.
Laudis amore tumes? sunt cer-
    ta piacula, quæ Te
Ter pure lecto poterunt recreare
    libello.

Invidus,

The PREFACE.

Invidus, iracundus, iners, vino-
    fus, amator,
Nemo adeo ferus eft, ut non mi-
    tefcere poffit,
Si modo culturæ patientem com-
    modet aurem.
        Lib. I. *Epiſt.* I. *v.* 25.

This being the principal De-
ſign of our Poet, *it was neceſſa-*
ry for him to change his Stile;
here are none of thoſe daring
inimitable Flights, for which his
Odes *are ſo juſtly admir'd; he*
is more a Philoſopher *and* Critick *than a* Poet, *his* Satires *and*
Epiſtles *being, as he himſelf*
profeſſes, fermoni propiora, *near-*
er Proſe than Verſe.

This was the Motive which
induc'd me to attempt the fol-
lowing Tranſlation. I am very
ſenſible that the Grace and De-
licacy of the Latin can't be turn'd
into Engliſh; but our Language
is not without its Beauties,
                which

which perhaps are no leß Pleafing and Delightful.

    I have carefully endeavour'd,
throughout the Work, to obferve
a due Medium *between a* Para-
phrafe *and a* Verbal Tranflation;
I have kept my felf clofe to my
Author's Senfe, and have had
fome Regard to the Genius *and*
Spirit *of every particular* Satire
and Epiftle. *This I thought the*
moft likely Way to make him in-
telligible, which is much better
done in Profe *than* Verfe. *The*
Reftraint *of* Rhime *is no ordi-*
nary Difficulty, *it too often forces*
the ingenious Tranflator to aban-
don the true Senfe of the Poet,
and for the fake of a founding
Word, *put in fomething of his*
own. *This is too apparent in*
Mr. Creech's *Performance;* in
Mr. Oldham's *Verfion of* Horace's Impertinent, *and* Art of
Poetry; *but more efpecially in*
our Modern Imitations, *in which*
the

The PREFACE.

the Poets, to make their Compositions the more pleasing and agreeable, have given themselves so great a Liberty, that Horace is little or nothing concern'd in Attempts of that Nature.

'Tis beyond all Question the Busineß of a Translator to have his Author always in his Eye, that the Picture he draws may resemble the Original. If in this Particular he discharges his Duty, tho' the Soil he manures be Barren and Unfruitful in some few Places, let him not fear that his Version will suffer on that Account. He is to consider himself as a Labourer in another Man's Vineyard. An Author can command his Thoughts and Expressions; he can change and vary both as he pleases: But he who Translates has no such Privilege, he is confin'd to his Author's Thoughts, and is consequently under an indispensable

dispensable Obligation to render his Meaning in a happy, easy, natural Manner.

Having given this Account of the following Version, I must advertise the Reader of one thing more, which is, that I have translated nothing which was contrary to the Rules of Decency and good Manners ; insomuch that the most modest Person may now safely read these Satires *and* Epistles, *and not run the Risque of endangering his Virtue.*

Torquet ab obscænis jam nunc
   sermonibus aurem.

Lib. II. Epist. I. v. 127.

HO.

HORACE's

SATIRES,

EPISTLES,

AND

Art of POETRY,

Done into ENGLISH.

B

Q. HORATII

FLACCI SATIRARUM

LIBER PRIMUS.

SATIRA I.

QUI fit, Mæcenas, ut nemo, quam sibi sortem,
   Seu ratio dederit seu fors objecerit, illa
Contentus vivat; laudet diversa sequentis?
   O fortunati mercatores, gravis annis
Miles ait, multo jam fractus membra labore   5
Contra mercator, navem jactantibus Austris,
Militia est potior quid enim? concurritur · horæ
Momento aut cita mors venit, aut victoria læta.

Agricolam

HORACE's SATIRES.

BOOK I.

SATIRE I.

WHENCE comes it to pass, * Mæ-*Men generally* cenas*, that no Man is contented *discontented* with his Condition, whether his *tented* own Reason led him into it, or Fortune threw *with their* it in his Way; but is ever commending the *present* Happiness of those who are engag'd in some *Circumstances.* different Course of Life?

How blest is the *Merchant!* crys the *Soldier*, when loaded with Years, and broken with much Labour and Fatigue The *Merchant*, on the other hand, in a Storm at Sea, thinks the *Soldier* happy; and why? the Battle's fought, and within the Compass of an Hour, he either meets with a speedy Death, or a happy Victory.

* *Mæcenas*, a *Roman* Gentleman, descended from the antient Kings of *Etruria*, of extraordinary Wit and Eloquence, he encouraged Learning and learned Men, which ga e Occasion to *Virgil* and *Horace* to dedicate a considerable Part of their Poems to him. He was in great Favour with *Augustus*

Agricolam laudat juris legumque peritus,
Sub galli cantum consultor ubi ostia pulsat   10
Ille, datis vadibus qui rure extractus in urbem est,
Solos felices viventis clamat in urbe

    Cætera de genere hoc (adeo sunt multa) loquacem
Delassare valent Fabium ne te morer, audi
Quo rem deducam si quis Deus, En ego, dicat, 15
Jam faciam quod vultis et is tu, qui modo miles,
Mercator; tu consultus modo, rusticus hinc vos,
Vos hinc, mutatis discedite partibus eia,
Quid statis? nolint atqui licet esse beatis
Quid causæ est, merito quin illis Jupiter ambas 20
Iratus buccas inflet, neque se fore posthac
Tam facilem dicat, votis ut præbeat aurem?
Præterea (ne sic, ut qui jocularia ridens,
Percurram; quamquam ridentem dicere verum
Quid vetat? ut pueris olim dant crustula blandi 25
Doctores, elementa velint ut discere prima
Sed tamen amoto quæramus seria ludo)
Ille gravem duro terram qui vertit aratro,
Perfidus hic caupo, miles, nautæque per omne

Audaces

THE *Lawyer*, being diſturb'd with the early Viſits of his troubleſome Clients, admires the *Peaſant's* quiet Life; the *Peaſant* again, who, being Surety for ſome Acquaintaince, is forc'd to leave the Country and come up to Town, crys out, that none are happy but the *Citizens*

So many are the Inſtances of this Kind, that to relate all the reſt of them would tire even the long-winded *Fabius*

IF any God ſhould ſay, Well, I'll grant what ye deſire; you *Soldier* ſhall be a *Merchant,* you *Lawyer* ſhall be a *Farmer*; be gone, haſte away to your new Stations Heyday what, do ye ſtand ſtock ſtill? They won't be happy, tho' they have it in their Power What more reaſonable, than that the abuſed *Deity* ſhould revenge himſelf upon them, and for the future, be deaf to their Prayers, ſince they know not what they would be at? * Beſides, (to lay aſide Mirth and be ſerious, tho' Truth and Mirth are not inconſiſtent, it being uſual with *Maſters* to encourage their *Scholars* with Cakes and Sweet-meats, the better to prepare them to receive Inſtruction), if you ask the *Peaſant*, the Retailer of *Law* †, and *Soldier*, or even the daring *Mer-*

---

* *Acron* obſerves, that *Horace* having diſcours'd Men's Inconſtancy or Diſcontentedneſs with their Conditions, begins here another Head of Diſcourſe, *Avarice*

† *Caupo* ſeems to ſignify here *a Retailer of the Law,* one who gives his Advice for Money, and is the ſame with him whom the Poet in *ver* 9 calls *juris legumque peritus.* If *Horace* does not mean this, he does not repeat his four different Conditions of Life with any Exactneſs: And *Caupo* is here metaphorically apply'd to ſuch a Retailer of the Law in the ſame Manner as *Ennius* ſpeaks, in *Cic de Off Lib* 1 *Non cauponantes bellum ſed belligerantes.* And in the ſame Book *Cicero* ſays, That the Practice of the Law is only then honourable, *gratuitò defendentis,* if a Lawyer defends his Client without Fee or Reward.

chant

Audaces mare qui currunt, hac mente laborem   30
Sese ferre, senes ut in otia tuta recedant,
Aiunt, cum sibi sint congesta cibaria. sicut
Parvula, nam exemplo est, magni formica laboris
Ore trahit quodcumque potest, atque addit acervo
Quem struit, haud ignara ac non incauta futuri. 35
Quæ, simul inversum contristat Aquarius annum,
Non usquam prorepit, & illis utitur ante
Quæsitis sapiens   cum te neque fervidus æstus
Demoveat lucro, nec hiems, ignis, mare, ferrum,
Nil obstet tibi, dum ne sit te ditior alter   40
Quid juvat inmensum te argenti pondus & auri
Furtim defossa timidum deponere terra?
Quod, si comminuas, vilem redigatur ad assem
At, ni id sit, quid habet pulchri constructus acervus?
Millia frumenti tua triverit area centum   45
Non tuus hoc capiet venter plus ac meus   ut si
Reticulum panis venalis inter onusto
Forte vehas humero, nihilo plus accipias quam
Qui nil portarit   vel dic, quid referat intra
Naturæ fines viventi, jugera centum, an   50
Mille aret? At suave est ex magno tollere acervo.

Dum

chant himself, who bids Defiance to the Storms and Tempests, to what End or Purpose they undergo these severe Fatigues? They will all tell you, 'tis only to provide themselves a Competency, that in the declining Part of Life they may peaceably and comfortably enjoy themselves. In this they pretend to imitate the laborious Ant, (whom to be sure they always bring in for an Example) who being careful and provident of the Day of Necessity, adds all she can gather to her encreasing Store.

THUS far indeed the Example holds good; but herein is the Difference The Ant in the Winter ceases from her Labour, she stays at Home and wisely enjoys what she had laid up before, but neither Heat nor Cold, Fire nor Sword, Storms nor Tempests, can allay your Thirst of amassing Riches, and all this you do that no other Men may be wealthier than your self Where is the Profit or Satisfaction of hoarding up privately a Mass of Treasure in the Earth, which cannot be done without some Concern? You will possibly reply, should I spend any of it, it would quickly have an End; and unless you do so, where is the Joy of being rich? What Beauty is there in a Heap of Money? Tho' your Barns and Granaries are stor'd with Wheat, yet your Appetite is much the same as mine, the same Quantity of Bread will satisfie us both Suppose you were one among other Slaves, who was pitch'd upon by your Master to carry the Basket of Provisions for the rest, could you therefore eat more than your Companions? Of what Importance is it to a temperate Man, who observes the Bounds which Nature hath prescrib'd him, to have a Hundred, or a Thousand Acres? but, oh the Pleasure of taking from a great Heap! and yet,

Covetousness, the ill Effects of it

Dum ex parvo nobis tantundem haurire relinquas,
Cur tua plus laudes cumeris granaria nostris?
Ut, tibi si sit opus liquidi non amplius urna,
Vel cyatho; & dicas, Magno de flumine malim, 55
Quam ex hoc fonticulo tantundem sumere Eo fit,
Plenior ut si quos delectet copia justo,
Cum ripa simul avolsos ferat Aufidus acer
At qui tantuli eget, quantum est opus, is neque limo
Turbatam haurit aquam, nec vitam amittit in un-
       dis.   60
At bona pars hominum decepta cupidine falso,
Nil satis est, inquit quia tanti, quantum habeas, sis.
Quid facias illi? jubeas miseram esse libenter,
Quatenus id facit ut quidam memoratur Athenis
Sordidus ac dives, populi contemnere voces   65
Sic solitus Populus me sibilat, at mihi plaudo
Ipse domi, simul ac nummos contemplor in arca
Tantalus a labris sitiens fugientia captat

Flumina

if you allow, that my little Stock will supply
me with all the Neceffaries of Life, why fhould
you prefer your Granaries to my Corn-cham-
ber? 'Tis juft the fame, as if wanting a Glafs of
Water, you fhou'd rather choofe to have it from
the River than from a little Fountain Hence it
comes to pafs, that they who extend their Defires
too far, are oftentimes carried away by the Torrent, and ruin'd by their Covetoufnefs ; but he
whofe Defires keep Pace with his Neceffities,
runs no Rifque at all, the Water he drinks is
clear and pure, and he runs no Hazard of pe-
rifhing in the River But, fo it is with the
greateft Part of Mankind, that, being led away
with miftaken Notions, they never think they
have enough A Man, fay they *, is efteemed
in the World in Proportion to his Riches
Now what muft be done in fuch a Cafe? They
deferve to be miferable, who thus induftrioufly
labour to be fo. Like the rich Mifer at † *A-*
thens, who was wholly unconcern'd at what
the Citizens faid of him The *Athenians,* faid
he, hifs me, but when I am at home, and looking over my Money in my Cheft, I clap my
felf 'Tis reported of *Tantalus,* that he was
ready to perifh with Thirft, tho' up to the
Chin in Water ; that when he attempted to

---

* He reproaches the *Romans* who refpected a Man ac-
cording to his Eftate, infomuch that no Man had the
Privilege of being knighted, who was not worth 25000
Crowns, nor could any one pretend to the Honour of
a Senator, unlefs his Revenue was Double that Sum.
Auguftus requir'd that a Senator fhou'd be worth 300000

† *Athens,* the capital Seat of *Attica* in *Greece,* formerly very famous for its Learning and Politenefs · *Plato,*
Ariftotle, Demofthenes and *Sophocles* flourifh'd in this
Place, here it was, that the *Romans* fent their Sons to
be inftructed in Philofophy.

Flumina. quid rides? mutato nomine, de te
Fabula narratur congestis undique saccis   70
Indormis inhians, & tanquam parcere sacris
Cogeris, aut pictis tanquam gaudere tabellis
Nescis quo valeat nummus, quem præbeat usum?
Panis ematur, olus, vini sextarius; adde
Quis humana sibi doleat natura negatis.   75
An vigilare metu exanimem, noctisque diesque
Formidare malos fures, incendia, servos,
Ne te compilent fugientes, hoc juvat? horum
Semper ego optarim pauperrimus esse bonorum.
At si condoluit tentatum frigore corpus,   80
Aut alius casus lecto te adfixit; habes qui
Adsideat, fomenta paret, medicum roget, ut te
Suscitet, ac natis reddat carisque propinquis?
Non uxor salvum te vult, non filius, omnes
Vicini oderunt, noti, pueri atque puellæ   85
Miraris, cum tu argento post omnia ponas,
Si nemo præstet, quem non merearis, amorem?

An,

drink, the Water mov'd from him   You laugh
at this Relation, change but the Name, and
you your felf are the *Tantalus* in the Fable.
You fit gaping o'er your * Money, and dare
no more touch it, than you dare commit Sacrilege; your broad Pieces of Gold are like fo
many Pictures, the Pleafure you take in them,
is juft the fame   What Pity is it, that you do
not better underftand the Ufe of Riches? They The Ufe
were given you to purchafe Bread and Wine, of Riches
and all the other Neceffaries of Life, which
Nature cannot want without Uneafinefs

   To be perpetually kept awake with a Fright;
to be in one continued Fear, left Thieves
fhould break in, or Fire burn you out, or your
Servants plunder you and run away, is this a
Pleafure? If it be, welcome Poverty, may I
never be rich

   BUT what, fay you, if a Fever fhou'd feize
me, or any other Misfortune confine me to my
Bed? How many are ready to offer me then
Affiftance, to call the Phyfician, and to do every thing that is neceffary to re-eftablifh my
Health, and reftore me to my dear Children
and Relations? In this alfo you are mife-
rably miftaken   Neither your Wife nor
Children pray for your Recovery, all your
Neighbours and Acquaintance hate you, and
can you wonder to find your felf fo univerfally
detefted, while you continue fo wretchedly
covetous? Or do you look upon it as nothing

   * Agreeable hereunto is that excellent Defcription
of a covetous Man, which we find in *Lucilius*
   Cui neq; jumentum eft, nec fervus, nec comes ullus,
Bulgam, & quicquid habet nummorum fecum habet ipfe,
Cum Bulga cœnat, dormit, lavit, omnis in una
Spes hominis Bulga, hac devincta eft cætera vita

An, si cognatos, nullo natura labore

Quos tibi dat, retinere velis, servareque amicos,

Infelix operam perdas; ut si quis asellum   90

In campo doceat parentem currere frenis?

Denique sit finis quærendi cumque habeas plus,

Pauperiem metuas minus; & finire laborem

Incipias, parto quod avebas ne facias quod

Ummidius, qui tam (non longa est fabula) dives 95

Ut metuetur nummos, ita sordidus ut se

Non unquam servo melius vestiret, ad usque

Supremum tempus ne se penuria victus

Opprimeret metuebat at hunc liberta securi

Divisit medium, fortissima Tyndaridarum   100

Quid mi igitur suades? vt vivam Mænius aut sic

Ut Nomentanus? Pergis pugnantia secum

Frontibus adversis componere? non ego avarum

Cum veto te fieri, vappam jubeo ac nebulonem.

Est inter Tanaim quiddam socerumque Viselli 105

Est modus in rebus; sunt certi denique fines,

Quos ultra citraque nequit consistere rectum

Illuc,

to be lov'd by your Relations; and that the Money you spend to engage their Affections, is but lost Labour; like attempting to bring up an Ass to the Manage? It becomes you therefore to moderate your Desires The greater your Possessions are, the less Reason you have to be afraid of Poverty You have got what you wanted, do not any longer be your own Tormentor But above all Things, do not follow *Ummidius*'s Example, who was so rich that he measur'd his Money by the Bushel, and withal so sordid, that he always went clad like a menial Servant, and yet this rich, this miserable *Ummidius*, was perpetually in Fear of wanting Bread before he died, at last his valiant and couragious Concubine, like another * *Clytemnestra*, gave him his Death's Wound with the Blow of a Hatchet, and put a Period to his Life and Fears together.

WELL, Sir, what is it that you wou'd have me to do? Shall I live like † *Mænius* or *Nomentanus*? I mean no such Thing, you are all for Extremes. I warn you against Covetousness, must you therefore lead a loose and profligate Life? Is there no Difference between *Tanais*, and the Father-in-Law of *Visellius*? There's a Mean in all Things, even Virtue it self hath its stated Limits, which if a Man falls short of, or goes beyond, it ceases to be Virtue.

* *Clytemnestra*, the Daughter of *Tyndarus* and *Leda*, Wife of *Agamemnon*, whom she slew with an Ax, some time after his Return from *Troy*, her Gallant *Ægisthus*, with whom she had a long time liv'd in Adultery, being assisting to the Murder She was afterwards slain by her Son *Orestes*. See *Juvenal*, Sat vi Lin 656

† *Mænius* and *Nomentanus*, two dissolute young Gentlemen, who were notorious for their Debaucheries.

To

Illuc, unde abii, redeo. nemon' ut avarus
Se probet, ac potius laudet diversa sequentis?
Quodque aliena capella gerat distentius uber,   110
Tabescat? neque se majori pauperiorum
Turbæ comparet? hunc atque hunc superare laboret?
Sic festinanti semper locupletior obstat
Ut cum carceribus missos rapit ungula currus;
Instat equis auriga suos vincentibus, illum   115
Præteritum temnens extremos inter euntem
Inde fit, ut raro, qui se vixisse beatum
Dicat, & exacto contentus tempore, vita
Cedat uti conviva satur, reperire queamus
Jam satis est. ne me Crispini scrinia lippum   120
Conpilasse putes, verbum non amplius addam.

SATIRE

To resume the Argument. Is it so, that no covetous Man is pleas'd, but is ever commending the Happiness of those who are engag'd in a different Course of Life? Does he fret and consume himself with Envy, 'cause another Man's Goat gives more Milk than his? What is the Reason of this Uneasiness? They seldom compare themselves with those many who are poorer than themselves, but are always looking forwards, eagerly aspiring to get before this Man, and that Man, so that as long as there remains One richer than themselves, what Hopes of Satisfaction? They resemble herein the Charioteers, who in a Race are always pressing, always intent on those that are before them, regardless of those they left behind Thus it is with Mankind, and this is the Reason that we seldom or never meet with a Man, who, by his own Confession, has liv'd a happy Life; and who, when his Time is out, can quit Life with as much Satisfaction as a Guest rises from Table when his Belly is full

WHAT has been said is, I think, sufficient; shou'd I detain you any longer, you will possibly suspect me of stealing from * *Crispinus,* to avoid which, I will say no more upon this Argument.

* *Crispinus,* a Stoick Philosopher, who is said to have digested the Opinions of that Sect in very ill Verses

SATIRE

SATIRA II.

AMBUBAIARUM *collegia, pharma-*
           copolæ,
Mendici, mimæ, balatrones; hoc genus omne
Mœstum ac follicitum est cantoris morte Tigelli
Quippe benignus erat. contra hic, ne prodigus esse
Dicatur, metuens, inopi dare nolit amico,   5
Frigus quo duramque famem depellere possit.
Hunc si perconteris, avi cur atque parentis
Præclaram ingrata stringat malus ingluvie rem,
Omnia conductis coemens obsonia nummis.
Sordidus, atque animi quod parvi nolit haberi,   10
Respondet · laudatur ab his, culpatur ab illis.
Fusidius vappæ famam timet ac nebulonis,
Dives agris, dives positis in fenore nummis.
Quinas hic capiti mercedes exsecat; atque

SATIRE II.

FIDLERS, Perfumers, Gipfies, Players, Rope-dancers, or Buffoons, and all that Sort of Cattle, lament the Death of * *Tigellius* the Mufician, and they have Reafon for fo doing, he was very free and generous to them The Reverfe of him is this Man, who for Fear of being called a Spendthrift, won't fo much as relieve a poor neceffitous Friend, though ready to perifh with Cold and Famine.

Nothing more common than for Men to run from one Extream to another.

IF you ask the extravagant Man why he fquanders away thofe Poffeffions which were left him by his *Anceftors,* in taking up Money at exceffive Intereft, to purchafe Dainties for his unthankful Appetite; his Anfwer is, To avoid the Imputation of a fordid Fellow, of one of a mean and narrow Spirit They who profit by his Extravagancies commend him, but others cenfure and condemn his Conduct

THE Ufurer *Fufidius,* who is vaftly rich, both in Land and Money, that he may not be thought a good-for-nothing and extravagant Fellow, lends his Money at 5 *per Cent* Intereft *per* Month; which he deducts at firft from the principal Sum The

---

* A famous Mufician of *Sardinia,* much efteem'd by *Auguftus* for his Skill in Mufick, he was, in other Refpects, a perfect Humorift, and a very debauch'd and extravagant Perfon

more

Quanto perditior quisque est, tanto acrius urget. 15
Nomina sectatur, modo sumta veste virili,
Sub patribus duris, tironum Maxime, quis non,
Jupiter, exclamat, simul atque audivit? At in se
Pro quæstu sumtum facit hic. Vix credere possis
Quam sibi non sit amicus ita ut pater ille, Terenti 20
Fabula quem miserum gnato vixisse fugato
Inducit, non se pejus cruciaverit atque hic.
Si quis nunc quærat, Quo res hæc pertinet? Illuc.
Dum vitant stulti vitia, in contraria currunt
Malchinus tunicis demissis ambulat est qui   25
Inguen ad obscœnum subductis usque facetus.
Pastillos Rufillus olet, Gargonius hircum
Nil medium est.——

SATIRA III.

OMNIBUS *hoc vitium est cantoribus, in-*
    ter amicos
Ut numquam inducant animum cantare rogati;
Injussi numquam desistant. Sardus habebat

Ille

more prodigal any Person is, the more he gripes him He is perpetually enquiring for wealthy Heirs, who, having put on the * *Toga Virilis*, receive but a small and scanty Allowance from their covetous Fathers. Oh! ye Gods! who can forbear exclaiming against such Practices? But perhaps he lives according to his Income: He? you will hardly believe how much this Niggard is his own Enemy, the † old Man in the *Comedy*, whom the *Poet* introduces, weeping and lamenting, and punishing himself for having made his Son run away from him, never underwent half the Severities which he does

Now what is the Moral? 'tis briefly this; while Fools shun one Extream, they run into another There are few or none who observe a due *Medium* This Man has his Coat-sleeves so long as to hang down to his Heels, another thinks it smart to wear a short Jacket that reaches but to his Middle *Gargonius*, by neglecting himself, stinks filthily; *Rufillus*, on the other Hand, smells of nothing but Perfumes.

SATIRE III.

'TIS a prevailing Humour with all Song-The Character ofsters, never to sing when importun'd; but if you let them alone, they chant everlasting-*Tigellius*

* The Sons of Noblemen, and other considerable Persons among the *Roman.*, wore a kind of Vest with Sleeves, which they call'd *Alicata Chlamys*, till they were thirteen Years old, then they put on the *Toga Prætexta*, which they did not change till the seventeenth Year, at which Time they were allowed to wear the *Toga Virilis*.

† See the Character of *Menedemus* in *Terence's Heautontimorumenos*, it has something very tender and moving in it *Act* I. *Scene* I

Ille Tigellius hoc   Cæsar, qui cogere posset,
Si peteret per amicitiam patris, atque suam, non 5
Quicquam proficeret . si conlibuisset, ab ovo
Usque ad mala iteraret, Io Bacche, modo summa
Voce, modo hac, resonat quæ chordis quatuor ima.
Nil æquale homini fuit illi : sæpe velut qui
Currebat fugiens hostem ; persæpe velut qui 10
Junonis sacra ferret · Habebat sæpe ducentos,
Sæpe decem servos · modo reges atque tetrarchas,
Omnia magna loquens, modo, Sit mihi mensa tripes, &
Concha salis puri, & toga quæ defendere frigus
Quamvis crassa queat   decies centena dedisses 15
Huic parco, paucis contento ; quinque diebus
Nil erat in loculis. noctes vigilabat ad ipsum
Mane, diem totum stertebat   nil fuit umquam
Sic impar sibi   nunc aliquis dicat mihi, Quid tu ?
Nullane habes vitia ? Imo alia, & fortasse minora. 20
   Mænius absentem Novium cum carperet : Heus tu,

ly * *Tigellius* was perfectly of this Humour.
Cæsar himself, tho' he could have forc'd him to
it, yet if he only begg'd him by his own, and
by his Father's Friendship, cou'd not get one
Note from him. But, when the Fancy took
him in the Head, he wou'd sing *Io Bacche* † all
Supper-time, one while with a treble Voice,
and another with a bass.

THIS Man was a perfect Emblem of Inconstancy He wou'd often run himself quite out
of Breath, as if an Enemy pursu'd him, then
again he wou'd affect a slow majestick Pace,
like the Priestesses of *Juno*, when they carry in
Procession the holy Vessels to the Temple One
while you might see him with a Retinue of two
hundred Servants, at another time but with ten
One while his Discourse turn'd upon nothing
but Kings and Governors of Provinces, at another time he affected an humble Strain, then a
three-leg'd Table, a little Salt, and a good
Cloth-Coat, no matter how coarse, to keep
out the Cold, was all that he desired, and yet
shou'd you have presented this poor contented
frugal Mortal with five thousand Pounds, he
wou'd have spent it all in five Days It was
his usual Practice to sit up all Night, and to
sleep all Day, never certainly was any Man so
inconsistent with himself

BUT some one may object and say, Pray Men very
what are you, Sir? Are you without your Faults? apt to o-
Why, truly I must confess, that I also have my verlook
Failings, but they are of another Kind, and their own
perhaps not so considerable Failings,
and to
As *Mænius* t'other Day was railing against censure
Novius, one in the Company plainly told him, and condemn the

* See *Tigellius*'s Character in the preceeding *Satire* same
† *Ab Ovo usque ad Mala,* all Supper-time The first Course Faults in
12 the *Roman Entertainments* was *Eggs,* the last *Apples* others

Quidam ait, ignoras te, an ut ignotum dare nobis

Verba putas? Egomet mî ignofco, Mænius inquit.

Stultus & improbus hic amor eft, dignufque notari.

Cum tua prævideas oculis male lippus inunctis, 25

Cur in amicorum vitiis tam cernis acutum,

Quam aut aquila, aut ferpens Epidaurius? at tibi
   contra

Evenit, inquirant vitia ut tua rurfus & illi.

Iracundior eft paulo · minus aptus acutis

Naribus horum hominum. rideri poffit, eo quod 30

Rufticius tonfo toga defluit, & male laxus

In pede calceus hæret. at eft bonus, ut melior vir

Non alius quifquam at tibi amicus . at ingenium
   ingens

Inculto latet hoc fub corpore. denique teipfum

Concute, numqua tibi vitiorum infeverit olim 35

Natura, aut etiam confuetudo mala namque

Neglectis urenda filix innafcitur agris

   Illuc prævertamur, amatorem quod amicæ

Turpia decipiunt cæcum vitia, aut etiam ipfa hæc

Delectant, veluti Balbinum polypus Hagnæ. 40

Vellem in amicitia fic erraremus, & ifti

Errori

that he was forry to find that he was fuch a
Stranger to himfelf, or could think to impofe
upon them, as if they were unacquainted with
his Character O' Sir, fays *Mænius*, I can eafily forgive my felf. What a foolifh and unrea-
fonable Self-love is this, and how deferving of
Cenfure' When you are always blind to your
own Imperfections, why are you fo wonderfully
quick-fighted with refpect to your Neighbours?
An Eagle or a Serpent has not a quicker Eye
than you have, at fpying out their Failings Now
what is the Confequence? Your Friends are
even with you, and reflect on your Vices, with
the fame Severity as you do on theirs

    * This Man, you fay, is paffionate, he is
not fit Company for your fneering Criticks ·
His Hair is in Diforder, his Beard's ill fhav'd,
his Habit clownifh, his Shoes fit like Boots;
and what if all this be true? He is neverthelefs
a good Man, there is hardly his Equal ; befides
he is your Friend, and how indifferent foever
his Appearance may be, his Wit and Parts deferve your Admiration Examine your felf carefully; fome Vices are natural, others again are
contracted by Cuftom; for Fields, when neglected, bring forth nothing but Fern   But of
this hereafter

    I wou'd rather now obferve, how apt Men We ought
are to over-look the Infirmities of thofe they to pafs
love, and fometimes to take a Pleafure in them over the
Of this *Balbinus* is an excellent Inftance, who little
was fo paffionately fond of his beloved *Agna*, Failings
that her *Polypus* feem'd a Beauty to him What of our
is a Fault in Love, when apply'd to Friendfhip Friends,
and to
leffen and
excufe

    * Some Criticks are of Opinion, that *Horace* has here them all
given us a Character of his Friend *Virgil* But others, upon we can
better Authority, affirm, that he here defcribes himfelf

Errori nomen virtus posuisset honestum.

At, pater ut gnati, sic nos debemus, amici

Si quod sit vitium, non fastidire strabonem

Appellat Pætum pater; & Pullum, male parvus 45

Si cui filius est, ut abortivus fuit olim

Sisyphus hunc Varum, distortis cruribus; illum

Balbutit Scaurum, pravis fultum male talis.

Parcius hic vivit frugi dicatur ineptus

Et jactantior hic paullo est. concinnus amicis 50

Postulat ut videatur. at est truculentior atque

Plus æquo liber simplex fortisque habeatur.

Caldior est: acris inter numeretur opinor,

Hæc res & jungit, junctos & servat amicos

At nos virtutes ipsas invertimus, atque 55

Sincerum cupimus vas incrustare probus quis

is a Virtue; and it were much to be wish'd, that Mistakes of this Kind, especially among Friends, were more frequently practis'd, and that some honourable Name of Distinction were given to those who acted in this Manner.

BUT if we cannot ascend this Height of Friendship, let us imitate at least that Kindness and Affection that a tender Father expresses towards his Child, who is so far from being disgusted at his natural Defects, that he labours all he can to conceal or soften them. Is his Son Squint-ey'd? His Father says he winks. Is he * a *Sisyphus* for his Stature? He calls him his Chicken. Do his Legs bend inwards? They are not so streight as he wishes they were. Is he Club-footed? Do his Ancles bunch out? he will tell you, lisping, they are a little too big.

THUS it is that we ought to deal with our Friends. Is your Neighbour parsimonious? say he is frugal. Is he impertinent, and vain? he designs only to divert his Companions. Another perhaps is more fierce, more free than he ought to be; why, let it pass only for Bluntness and Courage. Is he given to Passion? commend him for a brisk and lively Temper. Such a Proceeding as this, is a certain Way of making Friends, and of preserving their Friendship.

BUT such is the great Degeneracy of our Nature, that we give a wrong Turn even to Excellencies themselves, and find a Flaw in a Character where there is none: Does any one

---

* A Dwarf of *Marc Antony*'s, scarce two Foot high; he had a great deal of Wit and Subtilty in him, upon which he was call'd *Sisyphus.*

con-

Nobiscum vivit, multum demissus homo ille
Tardo ac cognomen pingui damus hic fugit omnis
Insidias, nullique malo latus obdit apertum;
Cum genus hoc inter vitæ versemur, ubi acris   60
Invidia, atque vigent ubi crimina pro bene sano
Ac non incauto, fictum astutumque vocamus.
Simplicior quis & est; (qualem me sæpe libenter
Obtulerim tibi, Mæcenas) ut forte legentem
Aut tacitum inpediat quovis sermone molestus   65
Communi sensu plane caret, inquimus eheu
Quam temere in nosmet legem sancimus iniquam !
Nam vitiis nemo sine, nascitur optimus ille est,
Qui minimis urguetur amicus dulcis, ut æquum est,
Cum mea compenset vitiis bona. pluribus hisce   70
(Si modo plura mihi bona sunt) inclinet, amari
Si volet hac lege, in trutina ponetur eadem
Qui, ne tuberibus propriis offendat amicum,
Postulat; ignoscet verrucis illius. æquum est,

converfe with us, who is a modeft * Man? we
fay that he is a bafhful and dejected one. To a
Man of flow Parts we give the Name of a dull,
heavy one: Is he dextrous at warding off Difficulties? does he never leave himfelf expos'd to
any evil Defign, becaufe he lives in a World
where Envy and Malice abound too much? Inftead of calling him a wife and cautious Man,
we brand him for a crafty and diffembling one
Is he fo open and blunt a Man (which I confefs, Sir, you have too often found me) as that
when any one is reading or thinking, he will break
in upon him with his impertinent Difcourfe;
we fay, that he has not common Senfe. Alas!
that we fhould thus inconfiderately make Laws
againft our felves! Every Man has his Failings;
he is the beft who has the feweft When my
Friend compares my good Qualities with my
bad, it is very reafonable, if he defires I fhou'd
love him, that he give his Vote in Favour of
the former, more efpecially if my Virtues are
fuperior to my Vices Upon fuch a fair and
equitable Procedure he may reafonably expect
the like Ufage from me He that expects his
Friend fhould not be offended with his Carbun-
cles, muft forgive his Friend's Pimples. What

---

* *Probus* here fignifies *modeft*, and is oppos'd to
demiffus. So *Quinctil Inft. Lib 1 C III. Probus au-*
tem ab illo fegni & jacente multum aberit So *Tull de*
Orat ufes the Word *fed etiam probitatis commendatione*
prodeffet, Lib 1. C xxvi. So *Quinctil Inft Lib. xi*
C III perfricare faciem & quafi improbam facere And
Saluft fays, that *Pompey* was *oris improbi, animi inicre-*
cundi However, if Dr *Bentley's* Reading be preferr'd,
probus muft fignify a *modeft Man* But I think his Reading
is falfe, for feveral Reafons. That *tardus* is not always a bad Character, may appear from what *Tully,*
Epift ad Lentulum, Ep v fays of *Pompey, Sed nofti ho-*
minis tarditatem & taciturnitatem.

more

Peccatis veniam poscentem reddere rursus   75
   Denique, quatenus excidi penitus vitium iræ,
Cætera item nequeunt stultis hærentia; cur non
Ponderibus modulisque suis ratio utitur? ac, res
Ut quæque est, ita suppliciis delicta coercet?
Si quis eum servum, patinam qui tollere jussus   80
Semesos piscis tepidumque ligurrierit jus,
In cruce suffigat; Labeone insanior inter
Sanos dicatur. quanto hoc furiosius atqve
Majus peccatum est? paullum deliquit amicus,
Quod nisi concedas, habeare insuavis acerbus   85
Odisti & fugis, ut Rusonem debitor æris,
Qui nisi, cum tristes misero venere Calendæ,
Mercedem aut nummos unde unde extricat, amaras
Porrecto jugulo historias, captivus ut, audit.
Conminxit lectum potus, mensave catillum   90
Evandri manibus tritum dejecit ob hanc rem,
Aut positum ante mea quia pullum in parte catini
Sustulit esuriens, minus hoc jucundus amicus
Sit mihi? quid faciam, si furtum fecerit, aut si
Prodiderit commissa fide, sponsumve negarit?   95
Quis paria esse fere placuit peccata, laborant,
Cum ventum ad verum est sensus moresque repug-
    nant,

                                          Atque

more reasonable than that he who would have his own Faults excus'd, should excuse those of others?

BESIDES, since it is impossible to extirpate either the Vice of Anger, or the other Vices, which take such fast Hold of the Minds of Fools, why don't we make Reason use her Weights and Measures, so as always to proportion the Punishment to the Nature of the Crime? If a Man shou'd order his Servant to be hang'd, for licking up the Sauce, or eating the Fish as he took them from the Table, wou'd not all wise Men think him mad? Wou'd it not be much worse in you, if, upon some slight Failure in your Friend (which, without the Imputation of being ill-natur'd, you cannot but pass over) you detest and shun him as a Debtor does * *Rufo*, who, when the Day of Payment comes, if the Money be not ready, no matter how the poor Man comes by it, condemns his Debtors to stand like Captives, with their Necks extended, and hear him repeat his wretched History

The Poet condemns the Opinion of the Stoicks, who asserted that all Crimes were equal

MUST I be angry with my Friend, if after hard Drinking he foul my Room, break a fine Dish that was made by *Evander*, or help himself first with a Chicken which lay before me? What if he steal my Goods, or betray my Secrets, or deny a Pledge that he was entrusted with, is there no Difference to be made? They who assert that all Crimes are equal, find themselves at a Loss to make good their Assertion, when they come to enquire into the Truth of Things The common Notions and Customs, and even

* A famous Usurer, who was a very impertinent Historian

the

Atque ipsa utilitas, justi prope mater & æqui
　Cum prorepserunt primis animalia terris,   100
Mutum & turpe pecus, glandem atque cubilia propter,
Unguibus & pugnis, dein fustibus, atque ita porro
Pugnabant armis, quæ post fabricaverat usus:
Donec verba, quibus voces sensusque notarent,
Nominaque invenere. dehinc absistere bello,
Oppida cœperunt munire; & ponere leges,   105
Ne quis fur esset, neu latro, neu quis adulter.
Nam fuit ante Helenam cunnus teterrima belli
Caussa. sed ignotis perierunt mortibus illi,
Quos venerem incertam rapientis more ferarum
Viribus editior cædebat, ut in grege taurus.   110
Jura inventa metu injusti fateare necesse est,
Tempora si fastosque velis evolvere mundi.
Nec natura potest justo secernere iniquum,
Dividit ut bona diversis, fugienda petendis:
Nec vincet ratio hoc, tantundem ut peccet idem-
　que,   115

Qui

the common Intereſt of Mankind, which is in ſome Senſe the Parent of Juſtice and Equity, are all againſt them

WHEN Mankind firſt crawled out of their Parent Earth, they were (like the Brutes) a baſe and ſpeechleſs Race When they quarrel'd for their *Dens* and *Acorns,* their Fiſts and Nails determin'd the Conteſt, in Proceſs of Time they came to Clubs, afterwards to Swords, which Neceſſity had taught them how to make. Theſe Differences continu'd till the Invention of Words; by which Means every Thing being aſſign'd its proper Name, and Men enabled to communicate their Language and Sentiments to one another, a Peace was concluded Upon which they proceeded to build Cities, and to enact good Laws to prevent Robberies, and put a Stop to Adultery For, long before the Deſtruction of *Troy,* many cruel Wars were occaſion'd by Women; it was then a common and ordinary Thing, for Men to fight and kill one another for the Sake of their Miſtreſſes; they lov'd at large, and enjoy'd whom they pleas'd, like a Bull who lords it o'er the Herd, the ſtrongeſt ſtill prevail'd upon the weakeſt; whoſe Deaths, for want of ſome charitable Poet, are unknown and unlamented

IF we examine the Annals of former Times, and trace Nature to her Cradle, we ſhall then find, that Laws were firſt enacted, to remedy the Evils of Violence and Injuſtice Nature teaches us to diſtinguiſh Things that are profitable from what are not ſo, and Things that are to be avoided, from what is to be deſir'd; but the ſame Nature does not teach us to diſtinguiſh Right from Wrong Nor will Reaſon ever convince us, that a Man who has only
The Reaſon why Laws were firſt inſtituted.

ſtollen

Qui teneros caulis alieni infregerit horti,
Et qui nocturnus sacra Divûm legerit. adsit
Regula, peccatis quæ pœnas inroget æquas:
Ne scutica dignum horribili sectere flagello
Nam ut ferula cædas meritum majora subire 120
Verbera, non vereor. cum dicas esse pares res
Furta latrociniis; & magnis parva mineris
Falce recisurum simili te, si tibi regnum
Permittant homines si dives, qui sapiens est,
Et sutor bonus & solus formosus & est rex · 125
Cur optas quod habes? Non nosti quid pater, inquit,
Chrysippus dicat. sapiens crepidas sibi nunquam
Nec soleas fecit. sutor tamen est sapiens. Qui?

Ut,

only ftolen a few *Colworts, commits as great a Crime as he who hath committed Sacrilege. It is therefore very neceffary, that fome Rule † fhou'd be eftablifh'd to proportion the Punifhment to the Nature of the Crime, that a poor unhappy Criminal, who hath only deferv'd a few Stripes, may not be beaten beyond all Meafure I fay, *beyond all Meafure*; for there is no Fear that you wou'd inflict a lefs Punifhment on a Delinquent than his Crime deferv'd. You who declare Petty-larcenies to be equal to Robberies on the High-way, and threaten that you would punifh the fmalleft Crimes equally with the greateft, if you were King But why, if you were King? Are you not fo already? If, according to your Principles, a wife Man is a rich Man, if he is a good Shoemaker, if he only is a handfome Man, he only a King: Why do you wifh for that, which you are already poffefs'd of? O Sir! you are unacquainted with that Saying of our Father ‡ *Chryfippus*. A wife Man, faith that fage Philofopher, tho' he does not make his Shoes himfelf, is neverthelefs a

---

* The Example which our Poet here makes ufe of, to ridicule the Severity of the *Stoicks*, is taken from the Laws of *Draco*, who exprefly commands that he who fteals a few Colworts, fhou'd be punifh'd as feverely as if he had committed Sacrilege

† The Poet here requires a Rule by which Punifhments may be juftly proportion'd, Crimes be diftinguifh'd among themfelves, Crimes from no Crimes, and Crimes from good Actions This cannot be done without a Rule, and therefore it was well obferv'd by *Cicero*, *Formula quædam conftituenda eft, quam fi fequemur in comparatione rerum, ab officio nunquam recedemus*

‡ A Philofopher born at *Solos* in *Cilicia*, Son of *Apollonius*, and Difciple of *Cleanthes* He was Succeffor to *Zeno* the Author of the *Stoick* Sect, whofe Principles he took upon him to explain, but was fo unhappy in his Expofition, that in Derifion he was call'd *Chefippus*.

D   good

Ut, quamvis tacet Hermogenes, cantor tamen atque
Optimus est modulator; ut Alfenus vafer omni 130
Abjecto instrumento artis clausaque taberna,
Tonsor erat: sapiens operis sic optimus omnis
Est opifex solus, sic rex. Vellunt tibi barbam
Lascivi pueri; quos tu ni fuste coerces,
Urgeris turba circum te stante, miserque   135
Rumperis & latras, magnorum maxime regum.
Ne longum faciam dum tu quadrante lavatum
Rex ibis; neque te quisquam stipator, ineptum
Præter Crispinum, sectabitur; & mihi dulces
Ignoscent, si quid peccâro stultus, amici·
Inque vicem illorum patiar delicta libenter,

Priva-

good Shoemaker. How fo? Juft as *Hermogenes*, when he is filent, is an excellent Mufician, and fings to Perfection. And juft as * *Alfenus*, when he had thrown away his Tools, and fhut up his Shop, was ftill a Barber Thus our wife Man is a perfect Artift in all Profeffions, and thus he is a King too

THE Roguifh Boys pull your Beard, as you walk along the Streets; and unlefs you thrafh them with your Staff, you have a Crowd about you immediately, and you fall a fretting, and raging, and barking, moft mighty King of Kings To be fhort, whilft your Majefty frequents the *Poor's Bath* only, and has no one following you thither in your Retinue, but the impertinent *Crifpinus*, I converfe with fuch good-natur'd Friends, as if I chance to do a foolifh thing, will pardon me, and I fhall be as ready in my Turn to pardon their Failings:

* *Alfenus Varus*, a Barber of *Cremona*, not liking his Bufinefs, went to *Rome*, where he made fuch Improvements in the Study of the Law under *Sulpitius Severus*, that in a little Time he was advanc'd to the moft confiderable Employments. He was at laft made Conful with *Publius Vinicius* in the fecond Year of Chrift. He was a great Friend to *Virgil*, and was very affifting to him in the Recovery of his Eftate near *Mantua*, which *Auguftus* had given to *Arius* the Centurion, in Reward for his Service againft *Brutus* and *Caffius* He is mention'd by *Virgil*, in his Ninth *Eclogue*, ver 27.

Vare tuum nomen (fuperet modo Mantua nobis,
Mantua væ mifera nimium vicina Cremonæ!)
Cantantes fublime ferent ad fidera Cycni

Thy Name, O *Varus* (if the kinder Powers
Preferve our Plains, and fhield the *Mantuan* Towers,
Obnoxious by *Cremona*'s neighbouring Crime!)
The Wings of Swans and ftronger pinion'd Rhime
Shall raife aloft, and foaring bear above,
Th' immortal Gift of Gratitude to *Jove*.

D 2   Thus

Privatufque magis vivam te rege beatus

SATIRA IV.

*E*UPOLIS, atque Cratinus Ariftophanefque
     poetæ,
Atque alii, quorum comœdia prifca virorum eft,
Si quis erat dignus defcribi, quod malus ac fur,
Quod mœchus foret, aut ficarius, aut alioqui
Famofus , multa cum libertate notabant   5
Hinc omnis pendet Lucilius, hofce fecutus,

Mutatis

Thus I enjoy a greater Degree of Happiness, living in my private Station, than your Majesty in yours.

SATIRE IV.

*E*UPOLIS *, *Cratinus*, *Aristophanes*, and all the old Comedians, whenever any Man was notoriously infamous for wicked Theft †, for Adultery, Murder, or any other Villany, were very free in reflecting upon him. ‡ *Lucilius* has closely imitated these Comedi-

* *Eupolis*, *Cratinus*, and *Aristophanes*, three Writers of old Comedy, were Contemporaries, it was usual with them in their Plays, to call Persons by their Names, and to expose their Failings to the Laughter of the People *Aristophanes* had the Boldness to ridicule *Socrates* He was also very free with the Management of *Cleon*, *Nicias*, *Alcibiades*, and other Governors of *Athens* In a Word, that which we call old Comedy, was full of satirical Reflections and scandalous Slanders We have nothing now left of *Eupolis* and *Cratinus*, *Aristophanes* is said to have written Fifty four Comedies, of which we have now but Eleven, he excells in the Force, Purity, Sweetness and Harmony of Stile He flourish'd about the 85th Olympiad.

† *le Malus fur* This Figure of Speaking is called *Hendiadœsis*. Horace in Sat. I has *Formidare malos fures*

‡ A Poet of the *Equestrian* Order, he wrote Satires after the Manner of *Ennius* and *Pacuvius*, but gave 'em a more delicate and graceful Turn, he closely imitated the old Comedy of the *Grecians*, and tho' he did not, like *Ennius*, mingle several Sorts of Verses together in the same Satire, yet he composed several Satires of several Sorts of Verses, one Poem consisted of *Hexameters*, another was entirely of *Iambicks*, a third of *Trochaicks*, as may be seen from the Fragments yet remaining of his Works He liv'd *A. U C* 650

D 3   ans,

Mutatis tantum pedibus numerisque ; facetus,

Emunctæ naris, durus componere versus ·

Nam fuit hoc vitiosus ; in hora sæpe ducentos,

Ut magnum, versus dictabat stans pede in uno   10

Cum flueret lutulentus, erat quod tollere velles.

Garrulus, atque piger scribendi ferre laborem ;

Scribendi recte   nam, ut multum, nil moror Ecce

Crispinus nummo me provocat   Accipe, si vis,

Accipe jam tabulas   detur nobis locus, hora,   15

Custodes   videamus uter plus scribere possit.

Di bene fecerunt, inopis me quodque pusilli

Finxerunt animi, raro & perpauca loquentem :

At tu conclusas hircinis follibus auras,

Usque laborantis dum ferrum emolliat ignis,   20

Ut mavis, imitare beatus Fannius, ultro

Delatis capsis & imagine · cum mea nemo

Scripta legat volgo recitare timentis, ob hanc rem,

Quod sunt quos genus hoc minime juvat; utpote pluris

Culpari dignos. Quemvis media elige turba ;   25

Aut ab avaritia, aut misera ambitione laborat

Hic nuptarum insanit amoribus, hic puerorum ·

Hun.

ans, tho' in a different Kind of Verfe; he had a delicate Turn of Wit, and was very *fatirical*, but his Numbers were rough and unharmonious; his Fault was this, he would throw you out Two hundred Verfes in an Hour, which, as he thought, was very extraordinary When the Stream of his Poetry run muddy, there was fomething in it which was worth the ftooping to take up He was verbofe, and could not fubmit to any Pains in Writing, I mean in writing correctly; for as to writing much, it is a Thing of no Value

CRISPINUS * challenges me to write with him for a trifling Wager " Come, Sir, faith " he, call for Pen, Ink and Paper; let the " Time, Place and Witneffes be agreed on, " and let Trial be made, who can write moft." I thank the Gods, that they gave me a modeft and humble Spirit, I fpeak little, and that but feldom; but you, *Crifpinus*, if you pleafe, may imitate the Blackfmith's Bellows, which never ceafe blowing, till the Iron becomes pliable

HAPPY *Fannius!* who, without being asked, carry'd his Statue and Poems to be plac'd in *Cæfar's Library*, whereas no body reads my Few delight in Sa-Verfes. I am afraid to repeat them in publick, tire, being becaufe the greateft Part of Mankind being confcious confcious to themfelves that they deferve to be that their expofed, there are few or none who take Plea-Actions fure in *Satire* deferve to be repro-

SINGLE any Man out from the Middle of ved. a Crowd, and you will find that he is a Slave either to Covetoufnefs or Ambition This Man runs mad for his Neighbour's Wife, that Man is enflam'd with unnatural Defires, one delights in

* *Crifpinus*, fee Satire I.

burnifh'd

Hunc capit argenti splendor   stupet Albius ære.

Hic mutat merces surgente a sole, ad eum quo

Vespertina tepet regio   quin per mala præceps   30

Fertur, uti pulvis collectus turbine ; ne quid

Summa deperdat metuens, aut ampliet ut rem

Omnes hi metuunt versus, odere poetam

Fœnum habet in cornu. longe fuge. dummodo risum

Excutiat sibi, non hic cuiquam parcet amico :   35

Et quodcumque semel chartis inleverit, omnis

Gestiet a furno redeuntes scire lacuque,

Et pueros & anus Agedum, pauca accipe contra.

Primum ego me illorum, dederim quibus esse poetis,

Excerpam numero. neq, enim concludere versum   40

Dixeris esse satis,   neque si qui scribat, uti nos,

Sermoni propiora, putes hunc esse poetam.

Ingenium cui sit, cui mens divinior, atque os

Magna sonaturum, des nominis hujus honorem.

Idcirco quidam, Comœdia necne poema   45

Esset, quæsivere · quod, acer spiritus ac vis

Nec verbis nec rebus inest , nisi quod pede certo

Differt sermoni, sermo est merus. At pater ardens

Sævit, quod meretrice nepos insanus amica

Filius, uxorem grandi cum dote recuset ;   50

Ebrius & (magnum quod dedecus) ambulet ante

Noctem

burnish'd Vessels of Silver, another in *Corin-thian* Brass This Man trafficks from East to West, and is hurried on from one Danger to another with as much Violence, as Dust with a Whirlwind and all this he suffers through the Fear of not keeping what he has, or the greedy Desire of getting more. What Wonder is it then, if neither Poets, nor Poetry, ever find Acceptance with such as these? A Poet! say they, you may see the Symptoms of Madness about him, have a Care how you come near him; for the Sake of a Jest he'll not spare his best Friend, and then he is so conceited, that whatever he has once written, he will take Care shall be known to all the Boys and old Women that frequent the publick Ovens and Conduits

WELL, Sir, hear a few Words to the contra-ry In the first Place I shall deduct my self from the Number of those whom I allow to be Poets, 'tis not the making a Line to consist of six Feet, which you can call Poetry Nor, if a Man writes, as I do, in a Way little different from Prose, can you think him a Poet He only de-serves this honourable Name who has a Genius, who has a Mind inspir'd with a divine Fury, and whose Stile is pompous and magnificent.

Who may be said to be a Poet.

FOR this Reason it has been disputed, whe-ther Comedy may be said to be a Poem or not, because there is no Vigour and Force of Spi-rit, either in the Subject or the Language of it; and because it differs from meer Prose in nothing but its running in Metre To this, 'tis objected, that Comedy is not wholly destitute of that Sublimity we speak of, a Fa-ther is often introduced in Comedy, who is pas-sionately angry with his profligate Son, who runs roaring about Town with lighted Torches

An En-quiry whether Comedy be a Spe-cies of Poetry or not.

in

Noctem cum facibus.   Numquid Pomponius istis

Audiret leviora, pater si viveret ? ergo

Non satis est puris versum perscribere verbis ;

Quem si dissolvas, quivis stomachetur eodem   55

Quo personatus pacto pater his, ego quæ nunc,

Olim quæ scripsit Lucilius, eripias si

Tempora certa modosque, & quod prius ordine ver-
    bum est,

Posterius facias, præponens ultima primis ;

Non, ut si solvas, Postquam discordia tetra   60

Belli ferratos postes portasque refregit ;

Invenias etiam disjecti membra poetæ.

Hactenus hæc   alias justum sit necne poema,

Nunc illud tantum quæram ; meritone tibi sit

Suspectum genus hoc scribendi. Sulcius acer   65

Ambulat & Caprius, rauci male, cumque libellis ;

Magnus uterque timor latronibus   at bene si quis

Et vivat puris manibus ; contemnat utrumque

Ut sis tu similis Cæli Birrique latronum ,

Non

in the Day-time, and instead of marrying a rich, young Heiress, which the good old Man had provided for him, minds nothing but his Mistresses It may be so, but is this any thing more than what is usual? If *Pomponius*'s Father were now alive, he wou'd accost his Son in the very same Manner In short, that is not Poetry, which, with some little Alteration of the Place of the Words, any one might say on the like Occasion, as the Father in the Comedy. If either mine or *Lucilius*'s Satires were to undergo the like Variations, if the Words were transpos'd, and the Measures diversified, nothing of the Poet wou'd be visible in them, which is quite otherwise in these Verses of * *Ennius,*

> *When Discord, foulest Fiend,*
> *Had open broke the Iron Gates of War*

PUT the Words as much out of their Order as you please, and yet you will find that a Poet is the Speaker But enough of this Subject, at some other Time I will give you my Opinion whether a Comedy be a true Poem or not What I intend at present, is to enquire whether my *Satires* give you any just Reason to be offended with them. When *Sulcius* and *Caprius* appear at Bar with their Rolls of Informations, the whole Gang of Thieves are in Fear of a Discovery; but a just, honest and innocent Man is under no Concern. Suppose you were as great a Villain as *Cælius* and *Birrius,* those

The Poet here offers to justify his Way and Manner of Writing.

---

* *Ennius* was the first that attempted *Satire*, he gave himself the Licence of varying his Numbers at Pleasure, he makes no Difficulty of mingling *Hexameters* with *Iambick Trimeters,* or with *Trochaick Tetrameters,* as appears from those Fragments which are yet remaining of his Works In respect of the Subject and Variety of Matter contain'd in his *Satires,* these of *Horace* are entirely the same.

two

Non ego sim Caprii neque Sulci. cur metuas me? 70
Nulla taberna meos habeat neque pila libellos,
Quis manus insudet volgi Hermogenisque Tigelli
Nec recitem quicquam, nisi amicis, idque coactus;
Non ubivis, coramve quibuslibet. in medio qui
Scripta foro recitent, sunt multi; quique la-
     vantes.   75
Suave locus voci resonat conclusus. manis
Hoc juvat, haud illud quaerentis, num sine sensu,
Tempore num faciant alieno   Laedere gaudes,
Inquit, & hoc studio pravus facis   Unde petitum
Hoc in me jacis? est auctor quis denique eorum 80
Vixi cum quibus? absentem qui rodit amicum;
Qui non defendit, alio culpante, solutos
Qui captat risus hominum, famamque dicacis;
Fingere qui non visa potest; commissa tacere
Qui nequit, hic niger est   hunc tu, Romane, ca-
     veto   85
Saepe tribus lectis videas coenare quaternos;
E quibus unus amet quavis aspergere cunctos,

Praeter

two famous Highway-Men, why should you stand in Fear of me? I am no Informer, as *Caprius* and *Sulcius* are Search all the publick Places of Resort, you will find that my *Satires* are not to be met with, nor are they expos'd on the Booksellers Stalls, to be thumb'd by the common People Nor do I recite my Verses in every Place, and before all Company; in Truth I do it to none but Friends, and even then not without some Reluctance

THERE are many who delight to appear in publick, they recite their Verses in the Baths, which, being vaulted, give a pleasing Eccho to their Repetitions 'Tis impossible to express their Vanity and Ambition, what a Pride they take in reciting their Poems, they never endeavour to inform themselves, whether what they say be Sense or not, or whether the Rehearsal be impertinent and unseasonable

SIR, you take a Pleasure (cries one) in hurting Mens Reputations, and have a Bent of Ill-nature this Way Pray whence had you this Objection which you pelt me with? You are mistaken in the Man. Who of my Companions ever gave me this Character?

HE that backbites his absent Friend, that is not warm and vigorous in his Defence when reproach'd by others; that affects to be the Jester of the Company, and is ambitious of being thought a Wit; that can raise false Reports, and cannot keep the Secrets of his intimate Friends, this is the Man that is to be detested · He ought to be excluded from all Society; he is not fit for civil Conversation. *What Manner of Persons are to be avoided.*

'Tis usual at a Feast, where ten or twelve sit down together, for one Man to rally all the rest, he spares for a Time the Master of the
House,

Præter eum qui præbet aquam · poft, hunc quoque
  potus,

Condita cum verax aperit præcordia liber.

Hic tibi comis & urbanus liberque videtur,　　90

Infefto nigris. ego fi rifi, quod ineptus

Paftillos Rufillus olet, Gargonius hircum,

Lividus & mordax videor tibi? mentio fiqua

De Capitolini furtis injecta Petilli

Te coram fuerit, defendas, ut tuus eft mos　　95

Me Capitolinus convictore ufus amicoque

A puero eft, caufaque mea permulta rogatus

Fecit; & incolumis lætor quod vivit in urbe

Sed tamen admiror, quo pacto judicium illud

Fugerit. Hic nigræ fuccus loliginis, hæc eft　　100

Ærugo mera · quod vitium procul afore chartis,

Atque animo prius, ut fi quid promittere de me

Poffum aliud vere, promitto. liberius fi

Dixero quid, fi forte jocofius, hoc mihi juris

Cum venia dabis infuevit pater optimus hoc me,　105

Ut

House, but by Degrees, as the Wine (which inspires Truth) begins to warm him, he deals as freely with the Master, as with the rest of the Company   You pretend an Abhorrence of all base Fellows, what do you think of such a Man? I'll warrant, with you, he's a lively, facetious, agreeable and free Companion , and yet, if at any time I divert my self with the perfum'd *Rufillus*, or if I rally *Gargonius* for neglecting himself, you immediately say I am envious and satirical.

IF Mention be made of * *Petillius*'s Sacrilege, you defend him after your peculiar Manner O, say you, I have known him from a Child, we have liv'd many Years together, he hath done me a thousand good Offices, and I am glad that he can live here in Town safely, and yet after all, *I cannot but wonder how he got clear of that Matter.*   This is Malice in the highest Degree. I sincerely assure you (and I hope I shall be able to make good my Promise) that nothing of this Nature shall be found in my Writings; but then, if I shall say some Things with more Freedom, and perhaps with more Pleasantry than ordinary, this I think I have a Right to, and in this you ought to excuse me

† MY good old Father, who was surely one of the best of Men, by observing to me the Vi-

He gives an Account of his Education, how his Father inspir'd him with virtuous Principles.

* *Petillius*, Governor of the Capitol, was accus'd of stealing a Crown of Gold, which was consecrated to *Jupiter*, he was acquitted by the Favour of *Augustus*.
† In the same Manner *Damea* in *Terence* instructs his Son.

> *Nihil prætermitto, consuefacio; denique*
> *Inspicere tanquam in speculum in vitas omnium*
> *Jubeo, atque ex aliis sumere exemplum sibi,*
> *Hoc facito, & hoc fugito, &c.*
>
> Adelph Act III Scene III

Ut fugerem exemplis vitiorum quæque notando

Cum me hortaretur, parce, frugaliter, atque

Viverem uti contentus eo quod mi ipse paraffet.

Nonne vides, Albi ut male vivat filius, utque

Barus inops? magnum documentum, ne patriam
    rem

Perdere quis velit. a turpi meretricis amore   110

Cum deterreret   Settani diffimilis fis.

Ne fequerer mœchas, conceffa cum venere uti

Poffem   Deprenfi non bella eft fama Treboni,

Aiebat · fapiens, vitatu quidque petitu   115

Sit melius, cauffas reddet tibi. mi fatis eft, fi

Traditum ab antiquis morem fervare, tuamque,

Dum cuftodis eges, vitam famamque tueri

Incolumem poffum. fimul ac duraverit ætas

Membra animumque tuum, nabis fine cortice   Sic
    me   120

Formabat puerum dictis   & five jubebat

Ut facerem quid, Habes auctorem, quo facias hoc.

Unum ex judicibus felectis objiciebat

Sive vetabat; An hoc inhoneftum & inutile factu

Necne fit, addubites, flagret rumore malo cum 125

Hic atque ille? Avidos vicinum funus ut ægros

Exanimat, mortifque metu fibi porcere cogit

                                                Sic

ces of others, taught me how to avoid them.
When he advis'd me to be frugal, and to live
contented with that small Estate which he had
provided; Do you not see, said he, to what
an Extremity of Misery young *Albius* and *Barus*
have reduc'd themselves? Let their Example be
a Warning to you, let it instruct you to manage
the little Estate you have, with Caution and
Prudence. When he wou'd deter me from the
scandalous running after profligate Women, he
wou'd say, Remember that you be not like
Sectanus To perswade me not to follow other
Mens Wives, when I might have a lawful one
of my own, he would say, the Story of *Trebo-
nius*, who was caught in the very Act, is not
for his Credit

IT belongs to the Philosophers to explain to
you the Reasons of moral Good and Evil; all
that I pretend to, is to train you up in the Way
of your Ancestors, and preserve both your Life
and Reputation, while you are a Minor, when
you come to Age, and are grown strong in
Mind as well as Body, then you are to walk
without Leading-strings

THIS was the Method which my Father
took in my Education; when he advis'd me to
this or that Action, he laid before me some considerable Example, some Senator or other, who
was eminently remarkable for his Virtue and Integrity And then again, when he dissuaded
me from any thing that was ill, can you doubt,
said he, whether what you are doing be honourable and advantagious or not, when such and
such Persons are every where so severely censur'd
for the very same Thing?

As a Neighbour's Death is oftentimes the
Means of making a sick Man more temperate

E and

Sic teneros animos aliena opprobria ſæpe

Abſterrent vitiis. ex hoc ego ſanus ab illis,

Perniciem quæcumque ferunt   mediocribus, & quis

Ignoſcas vitiis, teneor fortaſſis & iſtinc   130

Largiter abſtulerit longa ætas, liber amicus,

Conſilium proprium neque enim, cum lectulus aut me

Porticus excepit, deſum mihi. Rectius hoc eſt

Hoc faciens vivam melius   ſic dulcis amicis   135

Occurram   hoc quidam non belle   numquid ego illi

Imprudens olim faciam ſimile? Hæc ego mecum

Compreſſis agito labris. ubi quid datur oti,

Inludo chartis. hoc eſt mediocribus illis

Ex vitiis unum   cui ſi concedere noles,   140

Multa poetarum veniet manus, auxilio quæ

Sit mihi (nam multo plures ſumus) ac veluti te

Judæi, cogemus in hanc concedere turbam.

and abstemious, so the Examples of such who have ruin'd themselves by riotous Living, are frequently a Means of preventing young Persons from falling into the like Extravagancies.

By this happy Way of Management, I am free from all those Faults which are destructive: Some I have indeed, but then they are of the smaller Size, and such as may be easily pardon'd; and of these a good Number (I think) has been wore off by Length of Time, by the Help of sincere Friends, and even by my own serious Reflections; for I am not wanting to my self either when lying in Bed, or walking in the Portico This (say I to my self) is rightest; if I do this, I shall live more happily: If I take this Way, I shall be more agreeable to my Friends That was not done handsomely: Surely I shall never be such a Fool as to do the same again Thus it is that I employ my Thoughts When I have any Leisure-time, I give it to the *Muses*. This is one of my Faults of the smaller Size, as I said, which if you won't pass over, I'll call the whole Tribe of Poets (and we are a strong Body) to my Assistance, who, like * *Jews*, shall force you to become one of our Proselytes, whether you consent or not.

---

* The *Jews* were the most impudent People in the World in making Proselytes, our Saviour tells us, Mat xxiii 15 *That they would compass Sea and Land to make one* Agreeable to which is that excellent Passage of St *Ambrose*, who gives 'em this Character, *Hi arte* (saith he) *insinuant se hominibus, domos penetrant, ingrediuntur Prætoria, a tres judicum & publica inquietant, & ideo magis prævalent, quo magis sunt impudentes*

SATIRA V.

EGRESSUM *magna me excepit Aricia*
      Roma
Hospitio modico · rhetor comes Heliodorus,
Græcorum longe doctissimus inde Forum Appi,
Differtum nautis, cauponibus atque malignis.
Hoc iter ignavi divisimus, altius ac nos   5
Præcinctis unum · minus est gravis Appia tardis
Hic ego, propter aquam, quod erat teterrima, ventri
Indico bellum, cenantis haud animo æquo
Exspectans comites jam nox inducere terris
Umbras & cælo diffundere signa parabat   10
Tum pueri nautis, pueris convicia nautæ
Ingerere. Huc adpelle trecentos inferis ohe!
Jam satis est Dum æs exigitur, dum mula ligatur,
Tota abit hora mali culices, ranæque palustres

Aver-

SATIRE V.

LEAVING *Rome* with *Heliodorus* the Rhetorician, who without Dispute is the most knowing Man of all the *Græcians,* we came safe to * *Aricia,* where we were but indifferently entertain'd   From thence we went to † *Appii Forum,* which we found fill'd with Sailors and most rascally Victuallers   To render our Journey the more easy and commodious, we made two Days of it, though such as were better mounted than we, might easily have compass'd it in one.   The Water of this Place being very nasty, I could not eat any thing; and was therefore very impatient in waiting for my Friends, whilst they were at Supper.   As Night came on, there arose no small Clamour among the Boys and Bargemen; one call'd for the Barge, another cry'd out, in an angry Tone, oh you Rogue, do you mean to drown us? You have taken in three hundred already   What with wrangling for their Fare, and the Time they spent in harnessing the Mule, it was an Hour at least, before we put off.   The Gnats

A Description of the Poets Journey from Rome to Brundusium

* *Aricia,* now *La Riscia,* a little Town of *Italy* situate on the *Appian Way,* about 20 Miles from *Rome,* it was formerly a very considerable City   Near this Place was a Grove consecrated to *Egeria,* where *Numa,* as he pretended, had frequent Conversation with her

† *Appii Forum,* a little Town about 46 Miles from *Rome,* situate on the *Appian Way* near the Marshes of *Pomptina,* which being drain'd by *Augustus,* a Canal was made which reach'd from thence to *Feronia.*

and

Avertunt somnos. absentem ut cantat amicam 15
Multa prolutus vappa nauta, atque viator
Certatim   tandem fessus dormire viator
Incipit; ac missæ pastum retinacula mulæ
Nauta piger saxo religat, stertitque supinus.
Jamque dies aderat, nil cum procedere lintrem 20
Sentimus   donec cerebrosus prosilit unus,
Ac mulæ nautæque caput lumbosque saligno
Fuste dolat quarta vix demum exponimur hora.
Ora manusque tua lavimur, Feronia, lympha.
Millia tum pransi tria repimus, atque subimus 25
Impositum saxis late candentibus Anxur
Huc venturus erat Mæcenas optimus atque
Cocceius, missi magnis de rebus uterque

Legati;

and Frogs prevented my fleeping; at length the Bargeman, being very bouzy, fell a finging, in Praife of his abfent Miftrefs, and the Paffengers fung againft him in Praife of theirs, till they were tired, and began to fall afleep; the Bargeman feeing this, firft faftned the Boat to a Point of a Rock with the Mule's Traces, who was now fent a grazing, and then laid himfelf quietly down to reft, and fnor'd profoundly

IT was now Day, when we perceiv'd the Barge to be at a ftand, upon which, one in the Company, more paffionate than the reft, leap'd on the Shore, and having firft provided himfelf with a good Willow-cudgel, he exercis'd it upon the Mule and the Bargeman's Head and Shoulders, as long as he cou'd ftand; but notwithftanding this feafonable Correction, it was ten of the Clock before we landed at * *Feronia.*

HERE we immediately wafh'd our Hands and Faces in the holy Fountain, this done, we fat down to Dinner, after which we made a flow Journey of about three Miles to † *Anxur;* which, being fituated upon the Top of a white Rock, is feen from far by the diftant Traveller

HERE it was that *Mæcenas* and *Coccerus* were expected, who were both of them fent by

---

* *Feronia,* a little Village within three Miles of *Terracina* Near this Place was a Grove and Fountain confecrated to *Juno* under the Name of *Feronia* *Strabo* relates, that thofe who facrific'd to her, walk'd bare-foot upon burning Coals, without hurting themfelves, a very pleafant Relation

† *Anxur,* now *Terracina,* a City fituated on a Hill, which reaches along the Sea-fide from *Oftia* to *Naples,* it was called *Anxur,* becaufe *Jupiter Anxurus* was worfhipp'd there

the

Legati; averſos ſoliti componere amicos.
Hic oculis ego nigra meis collyria lippus   30
Inlinere. interea Mæcenas advenit, atque
Cocceius, Capitoque ſimul Fonteius, ad unguem
Factus homo, Antoni, non ut magis alter, amicus.

   Fundos Aufidio Luſco prætore libenter
Linquimus, inſani ridentes præmia ſcribæ,   35
Prætextam, & latum clavum, prunæque batillum.
In Mamurrarum laſſi deinde urbe manemus,
Murena præbente domum, Capitone culinam

   Poſtera lux oritur multo gratiſſima   namque
Plotius & Varius Sinueſſæ, Virgiliuſque   40
Occurrunt; animæ, qualis neque candidiores
Terra tulit, neque quis me ſit devinctior alter.

the Publick upon Affairs of Importance, and who had both made it their Practice to compose Differences among Friends. As I was anointing my Eyes with the usual Remedy, Word was brought me, that *Mæcenas*, *Cocceius*, and *Fonteius Capito*, a most accomplish'd Gentleman, and an intimate Friend of *Marc Antony's*, were just arriv'd. We pursu'd our Journey the next Day, and came to ª *Fundi*, where *Luscus* was ᵇ *Prætor*. We left this Place, as soon as possible, diverting our selves with the Vanity of the Man, who, from a poor Attorney, was so elated with his present Honour, that he ridiculously affected the Dignity of a Senator, and to appear like one of the highest Quality. In the Evening we came to ᶜ *Formia*, where we staid, being much fatigu'd : *Muræna* gave us the Use of his House, and *Capito* invited us to his Table. But the next Day was infinitely the most pleasant Part of our Journey : ᵈ *Virgil*, *Varius*, and *Plotius* met us at ᵉ *Sinuessa*, who are my very good Friends, and certainly the best and sincerest Men upon the Face of the Earth   'Tis

ª *Fundi*, a little City 20 Miles from *Terracina*, famous for its excellent Wine.

ᵇ An Officer created to assist the *Consuls* in administring Justice. There was at first but one, but the Number afterwards was considerably multiplied, the Government of the Provinces being committed to them.

ᶜ *Formia*, a small City remarkable for the Birth of *Mamurra*, who was one of the richest and most considerable Men among the *Romans* *Murena* and *Capito* had each of them a House in this Place

ᵈ *Virgil*, *Varius*, and *Plotius*, three eminent Poets : *Varius* and *Plotius* were employ'd by *Augustus* in reviewing *Virgil's* *Æneids* after his Death.

ᵉ *Sinuessa*, a City situated in *Terra di Lavoro*, near the River *Liris*, it hath long since been ruin'd , in the Place of it is *Rocca di Mandragone*.

impossi-

O qui conplexus, & gaudia quanta fuerunt !
Nil ego contulerim jocundo sanus amico
Proxima Campano ponti quæ villula, tectum   45
Præbuit; & parochi, quæ debent, ligna salemque
Hinc muli Capuæ clitellas tempore ponunt
Lusum it Mæcenas, dormitum ego Virgiliusque ·
Namque pila lippis inimicum & ludere crudis.

　　Hinc nos Coccei recipit plenissima villa,   50
Quæ super est Caudi cauponas nunc mihi paucis
Sarmenti scurræ pugnam Messíque Cicirri,
Musa, velim memores & quo patre natus uterque
Contulerit lites Messi clarum genus Osci ·
Sarmenti domina exstat ab his majoribus orti   55
Ad pugnam venere prior Sarmentus, Equi te

Esse

impoſſible to imagine the Joy and Satisfaction which then poſſeſs'd us ; it was ever my Opinion, that an agreeable pleaſant Friend is ſo great a Bleſſing, that it admits of no Compariſon We lodg'd that Night in a little Village near the Bridge of *Campania*, where the * Commiſſaries brought us Salt and Wood, according to Cuſtom The next Day we arriv'd early at † *Capua* *Mæcenas* immediately went to the Tennis-Court , *Virgil* and my ſelf compos'd our ſelves to Sleep, that Kind of Diverſion being neither good for ſore Eyes, nor an ill Digeſtion From hence we were conducted to *Coccetus*'s Seat, ſituated beyond the Inns of *Caudium*, who regal'd us with Plenty of every thing

HERE I invoke the Aſſiſtance of my Muſe, in relating a famous and memorable Scuffle, which happen'd between *Sarmentus* the Buffoon and *Meſſius Cicirrus* · Say, my Muſe, whence were they deſcended, and what was the Conteſt which they had with each other ? *Meſſius* deriv'd his Pedigree from the ‡ *Oſcians* , *Sarmentus* was a Slave, whoſe Miſtreſs was then living; this was their Origin Being enter'd the Liſts, *Sarmentus* claim'd the Poſt of Honour, and began the Attack, he told *Meſſius*, that his Face

---

* *Julia lex prima*, the Author C *Julius Cæſar* Conſul, with M *Calpurnius Bibulus*, A U C 691 compriz'd under ſeveral Heads , the ſecond of which was, That the Towns and Villages, through which a *Roman* Magiſtrate paſs'd towards the Provinces, ſhou'd be oblig'd to ſupply him and his Retinue, with Salt, Wood, Corn, Lodging, and other Conveniencies

† *Capua*, the Capital City of *Campania*, built upon the *Vulturnus*, two Miles from the Ruins call'd the Seat of Pleaſure, and was compar'd with *Rome* and *Carthage* for Magnificence It is now in a declining Condition

‡ A People of *Campania*, of the moſt infamous Character in all *Italy*.

was

Esse feri similem dico. Ridemus: & ipse

Messius, Accipio   caput & movet. O, tua cornu

Ni foret exsecto frons, inquit, quid faceres; cum

Sic mutilus miniteris? at illi fœda cicatrix   60

Setosam lævi frontem turpaverat oris.

Campanum in morbum, in faciem permulta jocatus,

Pastorem saltaret uti Cyclopa, rogabat:

Nil illi larva aut tragicis opus esse cothurnis.

Multa Cicirrus ad hæc   Donasset jamne catenam 65

Ex voto Laribus, quærebat   scriba quod esset,

Nihilo deterius dominæ jus esse   rogabat

Denique, cur umquam fugisset; cum satis una

Farris libra foret, gracili sic, tamque pusillo.

Prorsus jocunde cenam producimus illam.   70

   Tendimus hinc recta Beneventum; ubi sedulus

     hospes

Pene, macros, arsit, turdos dum versat in igni.

Nam vaga per veterem dilapso flamma culinam

Vulcano,

was like that of a wild Horfe *Meſſius* nodded
his Head, and bad him proceed ; at which the
whole Company burſt out a laughing O! ſaid
Sarmentus, what a dangerous Fellow would you
be if your Horn were on, when you threaten
ſo without it ? (for you muſt know, that *Meſſius* had at that Time the Mark of a Wen in his
hairy Forehead, which had lately been cut off)
he continu'd to jeſt on his botchy Face, and to
rally the common Diſtemper of *Campania* ; at
laſt he deſired him to come out and dance the
Jig of *Polyphemus* Upon my Word, *Meſſius*,
there is no Want of Maſques and Buſkins, your
Air, and Shape, and Meen are the ſame; you are
the *Cyclop* all over To all this *Meſſius* made
ſuitable Returns He ask'd *Sarmentus*, if he had
yet offer'd up his Chains in Sacrifice to the
Houſhold Gods ? Tho' you are now a Scribe,
yet your Miſtreſs's Right over you is ſtill the
ſame : Prithee, Sirrah, continued he, how came
you to run away ? Is not a Pound of Bread a
ſufficient *quantum* for ſuch a little, ſuch a skinny
Wretch as you are ? With ſuch Merriment as
this we diverted our ſelves all the Time we were
at Supper.

LEAVING *Capua*, we went directly to
* *Beneventum*, where our officious Hoſt, being
over-diligent in roaſting ſome poor lean Thruſhes,
almoſt roaſted himſelf; the Fire by Accident
falling down, the Flame immediately ſpread it

---

* *Benevent*, a City in the Kingdom of *Naples*, with the
Title of a Dutchy and Archbiſhoprick It was built by
Diomedes in his Return from *Troy*, and by him nam'd
Maleventum, which the *Romans*, upon their ſending a Colony thither, chang'd into *Beneventum*, which Name it
has retained ever ſince *Orbilius* the Whipping School-
maſter, to whoſe Care *Horace* was entruſted, was born
here.

ſelf

Vulcano, summum properabat lambere tectum.

Convivas avidos cenam, servosque timentis   75

Tum rapere, atque omnis restinguere velle videres.

   Incipit ex illo montis Appulia notos

Ostentare mihi, quos torret Atabulus , & quos

Nunquam erepsemus, nisi nos vicina Trivici

Villa recepisset, lacrimoso non sine fumo,   80

Udos cum foliis ramos urente camino.

Hic ego mendacem stultissimus usque puellam

Ad mediam noctem exspecto somnus tamen aufert

Intentum veneri . tum immundo somnia visu

Nocturnam vestem maculant, ventremq; supinum 85

   Quatuor hinc rapimur viginti & millia rhedis,

Mansuri oppidulo, quod versu dicere non est,

Signis perfacile est   venit vilissima rerum

Hic aqua ; sed panis longe pulcherrimus, ultra

Callidus ut soleat humeris portare viator   90

Nam Canusi lapidosus ; aquæ non ditior urna

[Qui locus a forti Diomede est conditus olim]

Flentibus hic Varius discedit mœstus amicis.

Inde Rubos fessi pervenimus , utpote longum

Carpentes iter, & factum corruptius imbri   95

Postera tempestas melior, via pejor, ad usque

Bari

self through the Kitchen, and before we could tell where we were, was at the Top of the House It was pleasant to observe, how both Guests and Servants were as follicitous to save their Supper as to extinguish the Fire

AT this Place we first discover'd the Mountains of *Apulia*, which were so burnt up by a scorching Wind, (which the Inhabitants call *Atabulus*) that we could not possibly have pass'd them, had we not refresh'd our selves at a Village near [a] *Trivicus*, where our Eyes were almost put out, by the Smoke of some green Wood which was thrown upon the Fire From thence we travell'd in a Post-chaise to [b] *Equotutium*, which was about Four and Twenty Miles; this Place is very remarkable for its bad Water, which is sold in this Village like other Commodities; nor is it less famous for its excellent Bread, insomuch that all Travellers provide themselves here with what they have Occasion for, that of [c] *Canusium* (which was built by *Diomedes*, and no more abounds with Water than the other Place) being gritty and full of Stones Here we had the Misfortune to lose *Varius*, who left us in great Grief; nor were we less disconsolate at his Departure

THE next Day we came to [d] *Rubi*, but tir'd, because the Journey was long, and the Road bad, by Reason of much Rain, from thence

[a] *Trivicus*, a great strong City in the Kingdom of *Naples*, surrounded on all Sides with Water, and therefore of difficult Access

[b] *Equotutium*, a small Village of no Note

[c] *Canusium*, a Town situated on the Side of a Hill, about five Miles from *Canna*, it was formerly of great Esteem for its Gold-colour'd Wool, which made very rich and fine Cloth, it is now call'd *Canosa*

[d] *Rubi*, a small Village 18 Miles from *Canosa*

2

Bari mœnia piscosi   dein Gnatia lymphis
Iratis exstructa dedit risusque jocosque
Dum flamma sine tura liquescere limine sacro
Persuadere cupit. credat Judæus Apella,   100
Non ego. namque Deos didici securum agere ævum;
Nec, si quid miri faciat natura, Deos id
Tristis ex alto cœli demittere tecto.

   Brundisium longæ finis chartæque viæque.

S A=

we continu'd our Courfe to * *Bari*; the Roads were worfe, but the Weather fomewhat better The Sea, which comes up to the Walls of this Place, is very famous for Plenty of good Fifh. Keeping along the Shore, we came to † *Gnatia,* whofe Inhabitants are very foolifh and fuperftitious; and made us laugh with endeavouring to perfuade us, that the Incenfe, which they put at the Entrance of their Temple, diffolv'd of itfelf, without any Fire Let *Apella* the *Jew* believe this, if he pleafes, for my Part I fhall never be fo credulous, for I have learn'd, that the Gods live an eafy and quiet Life, without interpofing in human Affairs, and that, confequently, if any thing extraordinary happens in Nature, they are not to be thought the Authors of it

FROM *Gnatia* we journey'd on to ‡ *Brundufium,* which put an End to our Tour, and to the long Account, which I have here given of it.

* *Bari,* a Town fituated on the *Adriatick,* the Capital of a Province call'd the Land of *Bari*

† *Gnatia,* now *Gnazzi,* or *Nazzi,* a Town fituated on the *Adriatick,* between *Bari* and *Brindes* A Miracle, of much the fame Kind as this, is yet pretended by the *Papifts* at *Naples,* who upon every extraordinary Occafion, expofe the Blood of St *Januarius,* which as they tell you, is liquified at the Approach of the Saints Head, tho' it was hard congeal'd before Mr *Addifon,* in his Remarks on feveral Parts of *Italy* fays, That though he twice faw the Operation of this pretended Miracle, yet he thinks it fo far from being a real one, that he looks upon it as one of the moft bungling Tricks that he ever faw, and yet Monfieur *Pafcal* has, among others, hinted at this very Miracle in his Marks of the true Religion

‡ *Brundufium,* now *Brindes,* a Town fituated at the Beginning of the *Adriatick,* between *Otranto* and *Bari,* it has an excellent Port

SATIRA VI.

NON, quia, Mæcenas, Lydorum quicquid
    Etruscos
Incoluit finis, nemo generosior est te ;
Nec quod avus tibi maternus fuit atque paternus,
Olim qui magnis legionibus imperitarent ;
Ut plerique solent, naso suspendis adunco   5
Ignotos, ut me libertino patre natum.
Cum referre negas, quali sit quisque parente
Natus, dum ingenuus   persuades hoc tibi vere,
Ante potestatem Tulli atque ignobile regnum,

Multos

SATIRE VI.

THO' you, *Mæcenas*, are defcended from Men to be
as noble and antient a Family as any of regarded
the *Lydians*, who are fettled in *Etruria* ; tho' rather for
your Grandfathers, both by Father and Mo- their Vir-
ther, have commanded mighty Armies ; yet, tues than
notwithftanding thefe great Advantages, you do Defcent.
not, like other Men of Quality, contemn a Perfon for the Meannefs of his Origin ; no, not
even me, whofe * Father was only a Slave made
free: When you publickly declare that you do
not fo much regard a Man's Family as the Man
himfelf ; that you never mind what his Parents
were, fo he be an † honeft worthy Man ; you
judge, and that very rightly, that long before
the Reign of ‡ *Tullius*, whofe Mother was a
Captive, there were many Perfons of ignoble

* *Libertinus* is here put for *Libertus*, they who were
free of the City of *Rome*, are generally diftinguifh'd into
Ingenui, *Libertini*, and *Liberti* The *Ingenui* were fuch as
were born free, and of Parents that had always been
fo , the *Libertini* were the Children of thofe who had obtain'd their Freedom, the *Liberti*, fuch as had actually
been made free themfelves But notwithftanding this
Diftinction, it muft be confeffed that *Plautus*, *Tully*, and
others, ufe *Libertus* and *Libertinus* indifferently for a Perfon who had obtain'd his Freedom.

† *Ingenuus* in this Place does not fignify one that was
born free, but has relation to the Morals and good Difpofition of the Perfon to whom it is apply'd

‡ *Servius Tullius*, the Sixth King of *Rome*, he was murder'd by *Tarquinius Superbus*, his Son-in-Law, at the In-
ftigation of his own Daughter *Tullia*, after he had reign'd
44 Years.

Ex-

Multos sæpe viros nullis majoribus ortos   10
Et vixisse probos, amplis & honoribus auctos :
Contra, Lævinum, Valeri genus, unde Superbus
Tarquinius regno pulsus fugit, unius assis
Non unquam pretio pluris licuisse, notante
Judice, quo nosti, populo : qui stultus honores   15
Sæpe dat indignis, & famæ servit ineptus ;
Qui stupet in titulis & imaginibus. quid oportet
Vos facere, a volgo longe longeque remotos ?
Namque esto · populus Lævino mallet honorem
Quam Decio mandare novo Censorne moveret   20
Appius, ingenuo si non essem patre natus ?
Vel merito, quoniam in propria non pelle quiessem.
Sed fulgente trahit constrictos gloria curru

Non

Extraction, who were eminent for their Pro-
bity, and no lefs confiderable for the Titles and
Dignities, to which by their Merits they advanc'd themfelves. And, that on the contrary,
Lævinus (whofe Anceftor *Valerius* deliver'd his
Country from the Tyranny of *Tarquin*) was not
to be valued a Whit the more for that, as the
Common-people themfelves judg'd, whofe Tempers you are well acquainted with · The Common-people, who oftentimes very foolifhly be-
ftow Honours upon fuch as are unworthy of
them, who are always fo unskilful, as to follow
blindly common Fame; and whofe Eyes are
dazled with the Shew of Titles, and of Statues
of Anceftors which fome carry in Proceffion

How then ought fuch as you to act, whofe
Sentiments are fo widely different from the
Vulgar? But, fuppofe that the People following the Bent of their Inclinations, would lay
afide *Decius*, a Man of known Merit, but of a
mean Extraction, and give their Votes in favour
of *Lævinus* (how unworthy foever) to be one
of their Magiftrates, becaufe a Perfon of Condition; and fuppofe that fome rigid * Cenfor,
like *Appius*, would hinder me from ftanding for
any Poft, for not being the Son of a Freeman
Truly, I can't fay but he would be in the right
of it, fince I was not contented with my own
† Condition. To excufe their ambitious Pur-
fuit after Glory, Men generally pretend that the
Chariot of the Goddefs is fo exquifitely tempt-

---

* *Cenfor,* an Officer of great Repute among the *Romans*, his Bufinefs was to furvey the People, and to cenfure their Manners, he had the Power to punifh an Im-
morality in any Perfon of what Order foever, the Senators themfelves not excepted.

† *Quoniam in propria non pelle quiessem,* the Poet alludes
in this Place to the Fable of the Afs in the Lion's Skin

ing,

Non minus ignotos generofis. quo tibi, Tilli,
Sumere depofitum clavom, fierique tribuno ?   25
Invidia adcrevit, privato quæ minor effet.
Nam ut quifque infanus nigris medium impediit crus
Pellibus, & latum demifit pectore clavum ;
Audit continuo ; Quis homo hic, aut quo patre natus ?
Ut fi qui ægrotet quo morbo Barrus, haberi   30
Ut cupiat formofus ; eat quacumque, puellis
Injiciat curam quærendi fingula ; quali
Sit facie, fura, quali pede, dente, capillo :
Sic qui promittit, civis, Urbem fibi curæ,
Imperium fore, & Italiam, & delubra Deorum ; 35
Quo patre fit natus, num ignota matre inhoneftus,
Omnis mortalis curare & quærere cogit.
Tune Syri, Damæ, aut Dionyfi filius, audes
Dejicere e faxo civis, aut tradere Cadmo ?

ing, that the Prince and Peasant are both alike charm'd with its Splendor and Magnificence.

BUT tell me, * *Tillius,* what Advantage was it to you, to resume your former Seat in the Senate, and to be a *Tribune?* The People envy you more now, than they would have done, had you been in a private Condition For when any one affects to appear on a sudden in black Buskins, and in a Senator's Robe, People presently ask, (and 'tis very natural for them to do so) Who is this Man? Who was his Father? As when any one labours under the same Distemper, as *Barrus* did, and wishes for nothing so much as to be thought a handsome Fellow; where-ever he goes, the Ladies examine him from Head to Foot; they immediately ask, Whether he has a good Face, a well-shap'd Leg, whether his Foot be handsome, whether he has a good Set of Teeth and Head of Hair?

'TIS just the same, when a Man pretends to take Care of the City, to govern the Empire, preside over *Italy,* and to inspect the Temples of the Gods; all Men are sollicitous to be appriz'd of his Family, and, of course, enquire what were his Ancestors? Oh! say they, dare you who are the Son of a † *Syrus, Demetrius,* or *Dionysius,* sentence a Citizen to be thrown down headlong from the *Tarpeian* Rock? or to be deliver'd up to the cruel ‡ *Cadmus?* You re-

* *Tillius,* a Person of an obscure Birth and ill Morals, who was oblig'd by *Cæsar* to lay aside the *Laticlave* for having sided with *Pompey Cæsar* being dead, *Tillius* resum'd it, and was sometime after created Tribune, all Things being then in so great Confusion, that the vilest Slaves were made Senators.

† The *Roman* Slaves were for the most Part *Syrians,* and were usually call'd *Demetrius,* or *Dionysius*

‡ *Cadmus,* the Name of one of the *Lictors,* who carried the *Ax* and *Fasces* before the *Consuls*

ply

At Novius collega gradu post me sedet uno · 40

Namque est ille, pater quod erat meus. Hoc tibi
   Paullus,

Et Messala videris? at hic, si plostra ducenta,

Concurrantque foro tria funera, magna sonabit

Cornua quod vincatque tubas. saltem tenet hoc nos.

Nunc ad me redeo libertino patre natum   45

Quem rodunt omnes libertino patre natum ·

Nunc, quia sum tibi Mæcenas convictor; at olim,

Quod mihi pareret legio Romana tribuno.

Dissimile hoc illi est quia non, ut forsit honorem

Jure mihi invideat quivis, ita te quoque amicum; 50

Præsertim cautum * dignos adsumere. pravâ

Ambitione procul. felicem dicere non hoc

Me possunt, casu quod te fortitus amicum.

Nulla etenim tibi me fors obtulit. optimus olim

Virgilius, post hunc Varius, dixere quid essem. 55

Ut veni coram, singultim pauca locutus,

(Infans namque pudor prohibebat plura profari)

Non ego me claro natum patre, non ego circum

Me Satureiano vectari rura caballo,

---

* I am apt to think that this Place should be point-
ed and read thus:
   —— —— dignos adsumere: pravâ
Ambitione procul, Felicem dicere non hoc
   Me possum, casu —— i e. *Without Ambition I may
say, that it was not owing to meer Chance that I have the
Happiness of being one of your Friends* And I like this
Reading the better, because *Horace* speaks almost in the
same Words, *Sat x*
   Ambitione relegatâ, te dicere possum,
   Pollio ——

ply, *Novius* my Collegue is a Degree below me;
he is but what my Father was, and yet he is a
Senator What of that? do you therefore
fancy your self a * *Paulus Æmilius*, or *Messala*
Corvinus? As for *Novius*, his Lungs are so pro-
digiously strong, that in a Stop of two hundred Drays, and three Funerals with their Train
of Horns and Trumpets, his Voice was much
superior to them all; and do you think this nothing?

BUT to return 'Tis objected against me, ~He gives~
that my Father was a freed-Man; this proceeds, ~an Ac-~
partly, from the Honour I have of eating at ~count~
~how he~
your Table; partly, from my having had a ~came ac-~
Share in the Command of a *Roman* † *Legion* ~quainted~
How strangely different are these two Articles! ~with Mæ-~
~cenas, his~
Tho' they might envy my being a *Tribune* in ~Patron.~
Brutus's Army, yet what can they object against
your being my Friend? You, who are careful
to choose none but such as are very far from
Ambition? They can't say, that it was owing
to meer Chance, that I have the Happiness of
being one of your Friends; for it was not good
Luck only that threw me in your Way *Virgil*
and *Varius* were my Advocates in your Favour;
they gave you my Character. When I appear'd in your Presence, I spoke but little, and
that with Hesitation (for I was so dash'd, that
I could not say much.) I did not pretend that
my Father was a Gentleman of a good Family,
or that I had a large Estate, and us'd to ride
about my Manour on a *Barbary* Horse; but told

* *Paulus Æmilius* and *Messala Corvinus*, two illustrious
Romans

† A *Roman Legion* consisted of thirty *Manipuli*, which
made about 6000 Men, who were commanded by six
Tribunes, or *Colonels*.

you

Sed, quod eram, narro · respondes (ut tuus est
 mos)   60
Pauca · abeo & revocas nono post mense, jubesque
Esse in amicorum numero. magnum hoc ego duco,
Quod placui tibi, qui turpi secernis honestum,
Non patre præclaro, sed vita & pectore puro.

 Atqui si vitiis mediocribus ac mea paucis 65
Mendosa est natura, alioqui recta; (velut si
Egregio inspersos reprendas corpore nævos)
Si neque avaritiam, neque sordis, aut mala lustra
Objiciet vere quisquam mihi; purus & insons,
(Ut me collaudem) si & vivo carus amicis; 70
Causa fuit pater his · qui macro pauper agello
Noluit in Flavi ludum me mittere; magni
Quo pueri magnis è centurionibus orti,
Lævo suspensi loculos tabulamque lacerto,
Ibant octonis referentes Idibus æra;
Sed puerum est ausus Romam portare, docendum
Artes, quas doceat quivis eques atque senator
Semet prognatos. vestem, servosque sequentes
In magno ut populo si qui vidisset, avitâ
Ex re præberi sumtus mihi crederet illos 80
Ipse mihi custos incorruptissimus omnes
Circum doctores aderat. quid multa? pudicum

         (Qui

you what I was You gave me your Anſwer in
ſhort, according to your Cuſtom, and I departed. About Nine Months after, you were
pleas'd to ſend for me, and to enroll me in the
Number of your Friends. This indeed is a
conſiderable Advantage, and I cannot but value
my ſelf upon it, that being deſtitute of Birth
and Fortune, my Merit and Honeſty recom-
mended me to your Favour, who are ſo excellent a Judge of Mankind.

IF I am of an honeſt and virtuous Diſpoſition, He gives a farther Account of his E-ducation.
if my Faults are few and inconſiderable, like ſome
little Spots in a beautiful Face, which neverthe-
leſs is charming and agreeable ; if no Man can
juſtly accuſe me of Covetouſneſs, of frequent-
ing Houſes of an ill Reputation, or of doing
any baſe, or diſhonourable Action ; if (to ſay
thus much in my own Commendation) I lead an
honeſt and innocent Life, and am dear to my
Friends, I owe all to my Father ; who, notwithſtanding his ſhort and narrow Circumſtances, diſdain'd to put me to *Flavius*'s School,
(where ſeveral great Men plac'd their Sons, who
carry'd on their Arms, their Counters and Tables of the Monthly Intereſt of ſeveral Sums, of
which they were oblig'd to give in the Compu-
tation.) No! my generous Father had the
Courage and Spirit to carry me to *Rome*, and
to give me a noble and liberal Education, ſuch
as Knights, and even Senators themſelves beſtow'd upon their Children. I was ſo well
dreſs'd, and had ſuch a Number of Servants at
Command, that they who ſaw me cou'd not
but conclude me a Perſon of Condition. My
good old Father, like a faithful Guardian, was
never from me; he was always at hand when
my Maſters inſtructed me. In a Word, he preſerv'd

(Qui primus virtutis honos) servavit ab omni

Non solum facto, verum opprobrio quoque turpi :

Nec timuit sibi ne vitio quis verteret, olim 85

Si præco parvas, aut (ut fuit ipse) coactor

Mercedes sequerer; neque ego essem questus. ad hæc

 nunc

Laus illi debetur, & à me gratia major.

Nil me pœniteat sanum patris hujus · eoque

Non, ut magna dolo factum negat esse suo pars, 90

Quod non ingenuos habeat clarosque parentes,

Sic me defendam. longè mea discrepat istis

Et vox & ratio. nam si natura juberet

A certis annis ævum remeare peractum,

Atque alios legere ad fastum quoscunque parentes 95

Optaret sibi quisque : meis contentus, honestos

Fascibus & sellis nollem mihi sumere; demens

Judicio vulgi, sanus fortasse tuo; quod

Nollem onus, haud unquam solitus, portare molestum,

Nam mihi continuo major quærenda foret res, 100

Atque salutandi plures; ducendus & unus

Et comes alter, uti ne solus rusve peregrève

Exirem, plures calones atque caballi

Pascendi; ducenda petorrita. nunc mihi curto

Ire licet mulo, vel, si libet, usque Tarentum; 105

Mantica

serv'd my Modefty, which is the Foundation of
Virtue, and thereby kept me not only from bafe
and difhoneft Actions, but from all Cenfure on
that Account: He was under no Apprehenfion,
that my felf or others would ever reproach him
for what he did, if afterwards I fhould get no
better an Employment than that of a Crier, or
a Collector of the Cuftoms, as he himfelf was.
For that very Reafon his Praife is the greater,
and fo are my Acknowledgments   While I enjoy the Ufe of my Reafon, I will never be a-
fham'd of fo good a Father, much lefs will I
follow their Example, who, to excufe the
Meannefs of their Birth, are perpetually complaining, that it was not their Fault, but rather
their Misfortune, that their Fathers were not
Men of Quality. For my Part, I muft differ
from them; infomuch that were it permitted
us by Nature, to begin again to live, and to
choofe what Manner of Parents we pleas'd, fuch
as our Vanity wou'd fuggeft unto us; not Con-
fuls, nor Senators fhou'd be my Choice, I wou'd
rather continue contented with my own   The
common People may think me diftracted, but
you, *Mæcenas*, have different Sentiments, you
will think it an Act of Wifdom in me in refu-
fing thofe Titles, which wou'd certainly difturb
my Quiet and Well-being   Were I the Son of
a Conful, or *Prætor*, how follicitous muft I be in
providing my felf with a competent Eftate? How
many more Perfons muft be faluted? I muft never go into the Country unattended, Horfes and
Coaches muft be hir'd, and Grooms and Pages
muft be fubfifted. Whereas, as I am, I can
ride when I pleafe, upon my little gall'd
Mule, with my Wallet behind me, as far as

The In-
conven-
iencies of
Greatnefs.

* *Taren-*

3

Mantica cui lumbos onere ulceret, atque eques armos.

Objiciet nemo fordes mihi, quas tibi, Tilli,

Cum Tiburte viâ prætorem quinque fequuntur

Te pueri, lafanum portantes œnophorumque.

Hoc ego commodiùs, quàm tu, præclare fenator, 110

Millibus atque aliis, vivo. quacunque libido eft,

Incedo folus: percontor quanti olus, ac far:

Fallacem Circum, vefpertinumque pererro

Sæpe forum: affifto divinis: inde domum me

Ad porri & ciceris refero laganique catinum. 115

Cœna miniftratur pueris tribus · & lapis albus

Pocula cum cyatho duo fuftinet: adftat echinus

Vilis, cum paterâ guttus, Campana fupellex.

Deinde eo dormitum; non follicitus, mihi quòd cras

Surgendum fit manè, obeundus Marfya, qui fe 120

Voltum

* *Tarentum.* I pass unobserv'd. and escape the Censure and Reflections of the World, but you, *Tillius*, when as Prætor you appear in the *Tiburtine* Road, with your Equipage of five Footmen, one carrying your Pots, another your Wine, are rail'd at and condemn'd by all Men for your Covetousness: So that all Things consider'd, tho' you are a great Senator, yet my Life is infinitely preferable to yours, and to a thousand others I enjoy my Liberty, and go alone where I please, I ask the Price of Herbs and Barley; I walk one while in the *Circus*, which usually abounds with Quacks and Cheats; then I strole about the *Forum*, and amuse my self with listening to those who pretend to tell Men's Fortune; and from thence I saunter home, where my Pulse, Leeks, and Onions are got ready for my Supper I have three Boys to serve me at Table; on my Side-board stand two Cups and a Bottle; besides these, I have a Bason, Dish, and Ewer, all right *Campanian* Ware Supper being over, I go quietly to Bed, where I sleep securely; free from the Apprehensions of being cited by Break of Day, to make my Appearance before † *Marsyas's* Sta-

---

* *Tarentum, Urbs Salentinorum,* a City of the Province of *Otranto,* in the Kingdom of *Naples* It is now an Archbishop's See, small, but strong and well inhabited, defended by a Castle. *Horace* was so pleas'd with the Sight of this City, that he wish'd it might be one of those in which he shou'd spend the latter Part of his Life For this Corner of the World (saith he) seems to me one of the most beautiful, having Plenty of excellent Honey, delicate Oil and Wine, little inferior to that of *Falernum,* an early Spring and a soft Winter, rend'ring it a pleasant Habitation to an old Man *Lib* II *Ode* VI.

† The Judges us'd to assemble near the Statue of *Marsyas.*

2

Voltum ferre negat Noviorum posse minoris.
Ad quartam jaceo: post hanc vagor, aut ego lecto,
Aut scripto quod me tacitum juvet. unguor olivo,
Non quo fraudatis immundus Natta lucernis.
Ast ubi me fessum sol acrior ire lavatum   125
Admonuit, fugio Campum lusumque trigonem.
Pransus non avidè, quantum interpellet inani
Ventre diem durare, domesticus otior. hæc est
Vita solutorum miserà ambitione gravique.
His me consolor, victurum suaviùs ac si   130
Quæstor avus, pater atque meus, patruusque fuisset.

SATIRA VII.

*P*ROSCRIPTI *Regis Rupili pus atque ve-*
    nenum
Hybrida quo pacto sit Persius ultus, opinor
Omnibus & lippis notum & tonsoribus esse
Persius hic permagna negotia dives habebat

Clazo-

tue, who by his threatning Posture discovers an Uneasiness at the Sight of young * *Novius*.

I lie till Ten, when having wrote or read something for my Diversion, I strole abroad, and am anointed with Oil; but for this Purpose I get the best I can, and do not, like the nasty miserable *Natta*, defraud the Lamps of what I have Occasion for When the Weather is sultry, I refresh my self with Bathing, and refrain from Exercise; I eat no more at Dinner, than what will just allay my Appetite till the Evening; and then I spend the rest of the Day in Leisure at home. This is the Life of those few wise Men, who are free from Ambition, these are my Enjoyments, and with these I live a more happy Life, than if my Uncle, Father, or Grandfather had been a Lord High-Treasurer

* This *Novius* was a very sordid, covetous Wretch.

SATIRE VII.

I SUPPOSE that there is not a sick Man, or a Barber in Town, but has heard how *Persius* the Mungrel reveng'd himself upon that Outlaw *Rupilius*, sirnam'd the *King*, for the foul Language which he gave him This *Persius* was a rich Merchant who traded much to * *Clazomene* .

An Account of a Contest between *Persius* and *Rupilius*, who was sirnam'd the *King*

* *Clazomene*, a Town in *Ionia*, in *Asia Minor*, situated on the *Ægean Sea*, between *Smyrna* and *Chios*, famous for a Temple which was consecrated to *Apollo Grynæus*, and for the Birth of *Anaxagoras*, and several other eminent Philosophers. *Strabo, Lib* XIV

Rupilius

Clazomenis, etiam litis cum Rege moleſtas;   5
Durus homo, atque odio qui poſſet vincere Regem,
Confidens, tumiduſque; adeo ſermonis amari,
Siſennas, Barros ut equis præcurreret albis
Ad Regem redeo. poſtquam nihil inter utrumque
Convenit. hoc etenim ſunt omnes jure moleſti,   10
Quo fortes, quibus adverſum bellum incidit inter
Hectora Priamiden, animoſum atque inter Achillem
Ira fuit capitalis, ut ultima divideret mors.
Non aliam ob cauſam, niſi quod virtus in utroque
Summa fuit duo ſi diſcordia verſet inertis;   15
Aut ſi diſparibus bellum incidat, ut Diomedi
Cum Lycio Glauco   diſcedat pigrior, ultio
Muneribus miſſis   Bruto prætore tenente
Ditem Aſiam, Rupili & Perſi par pugnat, uti non
Conpoſiti melius cum Bitho Bacchius. in jus   20
Acres procurrunt ; magnum ſpectaculum uterque
    Perſius exponit cauſam   ridetur ab omni
Conventu . laudat Brutum, laudatque cohortem ·

Solem

Rupilius and he fell out with one another; as to his Character, he was of a stubborn obstinate Temper, and more troublesome, if possible, than *Rupilius* himself, he was proud and arrogant, and so given to *Satire*, that * *Barrus* and *Sisenna* were not a Match for him

ALL Ways were attempted to accommodate this Difference, but all to no Purpose. When two Warriours fall out, if they once engage, 'tis difficult to part them, so it is with Men of litigious Tempers, they will not hear of a Reconciliation *Hector* and *Achilles* were so enrag'd against each other, that nothing but Death cou'd determine the Difference; and why was all this Passion, but because they were superiour to all others in Valour? The Case is different between two Cowards, or between two Warriours of unequal Courage, such as *Diomedes* and *Glaucus*; when these fall out, the weakest immediately sues for Peace, and is glad, upon any Terms whatever, to make up the Quarrel

THIS Contest commenc'd when *Brutus* the Prætor was in *Asia* *Bithus* and *Bacchius*, two famous Gladiators, were not more equally match'd than these two Combatants. It was a pleasant Scene to see them enter the Hall together *Persius* was the first who open'd the Cause, he no sooner began his Plea, but the Court fell a laughing, he commended *Brutus* and his Army to the Skies, he compar'd the

---

* Two *Satirists*, who made it their Business to rail against others. There goes a remarkable Story of *Sisenna*, who being reproach'd in the Senate upon the Account of his Wife, who was a very leud and infamous Woman, Gentlemen, (said he) I marry'd her by the Advice of *Augustus*, by which he gave them to understand, that he was oblig'd to do so, to conceal the Intimacy that was between her and the Emperor.

General

Solem Afiæ Brutum adpellat, ftellafque falubris
Adpellat comites, excepto Rege : Canem illum, 25
Invifum agricolis fidus, veniffe : ruebat
Flumen ut hybernum, fertur quo rara fecuris.

    Tum Præneftinus falfo multoque fluenti
Expreffa arbufto regerit convicia ; durus
Vindemiator, & invictus, cui fæpe viator   30
Ceffiffet magna conpellans voce cuculum.

    At Græcus, poftquam eft Italo perfufus aceto,
Perfius exclamat : Per magnos, Brute, Deos te
Oro, qui reges confuefti tollere, cur non
Hunc Regem jugulas? operum hoc, mihi crede, tuo-
rum eft.   35

SATIRA VIII.

OLIM truncus eram ficulnus, inutile lignum :
  Cum faber incertus fcamnum faceretne Pri-
apum,

                          Maluit

General to the *Sun,* and his *great Commanders* to propitious *Stars* ; but *Rupilius,* he said, was like the *Dog-star,* which Constellation has a very fatal and malignant Influence on the Labours of the Husbandman

Thus he went on inveighing against him, like a Winter Torrent, which bears down Trees and Forests before it, where the Woodmen seldom appear with their Axes.

In return to this sharp impetuous Raillery, *Rupilius,* like a rude, blunt, surly Vine-dresser, who quarrels with Passengers, and out-rails all he meets, call'd the Merchant all the bitter Names which those Rusticks have very ready at Command *Persius,* at last, was so grievously stung with the *Italian's* Reproaches, that he cry'd out in a Passion, O *Brutus,* 'tis the Prerogative of your Family to deliver us from Kings ; I adjure you by the immortal Gods, that you do not suffer this *Rupilius King* to plague us any longer ; hang him, cut his Throat, do any thing with him, there is nothing that will better transmit your Name to future Ages, than so glorious an Action

SATIRE VIII.

I WAS formerly the Trunk of an old useless Fig-tree; the Carpenter was long in Dispute with himself what to do with me One while he thought of making me a Bench, then again he resolv'd I should be a *Priapus,* after much Deliberation, he made me a *God* From

hence

Maluit esse Deum. Deus inde ego, furum aviumque
Maxima formido . nam fures dextra coercet,
Obscœnoque ruber porrectus ab inguine palus .   5
Ast importunas volucres in vertice arundo
Terret fixa, vetatque novis considere in hortis
Huc prius angustis ejecta cadavera cellis
Conservus vili portanda locabat in arca.
Hoc miseræ plebi stabat commune sepulcrum,   10
Pantolabo scurræ, Nomentanoque nepoti
Mille pedes in fronte, trecentos cippus in agrum
Hic dabat   hæredes monumentum ne sequeretur.
Nunc licet Esquiliis habitare salubribus, atque
Aggere in aprico spatiari, qua modo tristes   15
Albis informem spectabant ossibus agrum.
Cum mihi non tantum furesque feræque suetæ
Hunc vexare locum, curæ sunt atque labori,
Quantum carminibus quæ versant atque venenis
Humanos animos   has nullo perdere possum   20
Nec prohibere modo; simul ac vaga luna decorum
Protulit os, quin ossa legant, herbasque nocentes.

   Vidi egomet nigra succinctam vadere palla
Canidiam, pedibus nudis, passoque capillo,
Cum Sagana majore ululantem. pallor utrasque 25

Fecerat

hence it is that I derive my Divinity, I who am the Terror of the Birds and Thieves; these I fright away with my Staff, and those are so scar'd with my Crown of Reeds, that they dare not come nigh these new Gardens.

To this Place formerly dead Bodies used to be brought, but of the meanest Sort, such whom their Fellow-servants brought hither upon their Shoulders, out of some blind Alley, and on a Hackney-bier. This was the common Bury-ing-place for the most necessitous People, for such as * *Pantolabus* the Buffoon, and *No-mentanus* the Spendthrift

It reaches a thousand Foot in Breadth, in Length three hundred; as we are inform'd by an old Inscription, which expresses the Will of the Testator, to prevent his Heirs laying Claim unto it

This melancholy Place, which was so late-ly full of dead Men's Bones, is now happily chang'd into a healthful Garden, where one may walk upon an airy Terrace

But the Birds and Thieves, which frequent these Walks, are nothing near so troublesome to me, as those who make use of Charms and Poisons to change Men's Affections, the Moon is no sooner risen, than here they flock, to ga-ther Bones and venomous Herbs; nor is it in the Power of my Divinity to prevent them

It was no longer than last Night that I saw *Canidia*, in a short black Gown with her Petti-coats tuck'd up, her Feet naked, and her Hair loose upon her Shoulders; the old Witch *Sa-gana* was with her; they howl'd horribly as

---

* Two young profligate Gentlemen, who had spent their Estates in riotous Living; they were both alive when this *Satire* was written.

they

Fecerat horrendas aspectu scalpere terram
Unguibus, & pullam divellere mordicus agnam
Cœperunt. cruor in fossam confusus, ut inde
Manes elicerent, animas responsa daturas.
Lanea & effigies erat, altera cerea. major   30
Lanea, quæ pœnis compesceret inferiorem.
Cerea suppliciter stabat, servilibus ut quæ
Jam peritura modis Hecaten vocat altera, sævam
Altera Tisiphonen serpentis atque videres
Infernas errare canes, lunamque rubentem,   35
Ne foret his testis, post magna latere sepulcra.
Mentior at si quid, merdis caput inquiner albis
Corvorum; atque in me veniat mictum atque cacatum
Julius, & fragilis Pediatia, furque Voranus.
Singula quid memorem? quo pacto alterna loquentes 40
Umbræ cum Sagana resonârint triste & acutum?

Utque

they went along, and their pale Faces made them look moſt hideouſly.

THEY ſcratch'd up the Earth with their Nails, and having made a little Pit, they fill'd it with the Blood of a black Lamb, which they tore to Pieces with their Teeth This done, they ſolemnly invok'd the infernal Spirits, whom they us'd to conſult upon all Occaſions. They had two Images, one of Wool, the other of Wax; the woollen tormented the waxen, which was much the leaſt, and which ſtood, as it were, in a ſuppliant Poſture, like a poor Slave juſt before his Execution. *Canidia* call'd upon * *Hecate*, *Sagana* implor'd † *Tiſiphone*'s Aſſiſtance At that Inſtant you might have ſeen the Dogs and Serpents of the infernal Regions, running about the Earth The Moon bluſh'd, and modeſtly withdrew her ſelf behind the Sepulchres, that ſhe might not be a Witneſs of their abominable Incantations

IF what I ſay be not true, may the Crows drop down their Dung upon me, nor may *Ju-lius*, *Voranus*, or the ſoft effeminate *Pediatia* uſe me more civilly

THERE is no Occaſion to mention Particu-lars, how theſe Sorcereſſes and the Ghoſts en-tertain'd each other in a very ſhrill and mourn-

---

* *Hecate*, a Goddeſs call'd *Luna* in Heaven, *Diana* on Earth, and *Hecate*, or *Proſerpina*, in Hell. She is re-preſented with three Heads, upon which Account ſhe is call'd *Triceps* in *Ovid*, and *Tergemina* in *Virgil* She is ſaid to detain the Souls of unburied People on this Side *Styx* 100 Years, and was therefore call'd *Hecate*, from the *Greek* Word Εκατὸν: She was very ſkilful in Poiſons, and their Antidotes

† *Tiſiphone*, one of the three Furies of Hell, ſo call'd from the *Greek* Word Τίσις, *Ultio*, and Φόνος, *Cædes*. T' Fiction was invented to repreſent the unhappy Co tion of the Wicked both in this World and the r xt.

ful

Utque lupi barbam variæ cum dente colubræ
Abdiderint furtim terris, & imagine cerea
Largior arserit ignis? & ut non testis inultus
Horruerim voces Furiarum & facta duarum?   45
Nam displosa sonat quantum vesica, pepedi
Diffissa nate ficus. at illæ currere in urbem
Canidiæ dentes, altum Saganæ caliendrum
Excidere, atque herbas, atque incantata lacertis
Vincula, cum magno risuque jocoque videres   50

SATIRA IX.

IBAM ut forte via sacra, sicut meus est mos,
   Nescio quid meditans nugarum, & totus in illis
Accurrit quidam notus mihi nomine tantum;
Arreptaque manu, Quid agis, dulcissime rerum?
Suaviter, ut nunc est, inquam; & cupio omnia
   quæ vis   5
Cum adsectaretur, Numquid vis? Occupo at ille,
Noris nos, inquit docti sumus. Hic ego, Pluris
Hoc, inquam, mihi eris Misere discedere quærens,
Ire modo ocius, interdum consistere, in aurem
Dicere nescio quid puero. cum sudor ad imos   10

Manaret

ful Tone; how they took a Wolf's Beard, and a speckled Serpent's Teeth, and hid them secretly in the Ground, how the Fire blaz'd with the waxen Image; how in a just Detestation of their Villanies, I reveng'd my self upon them, by letting, on a sudden, a thundering Fart, which was as loud as the bursting of a Bladder It was pleasant to see these two old Beldames hurrying towards the City in the utmost Confusion, their Astonishment was so great, that they left their Tools and Charms behind them; *Canidia* lost her Set of Teeth, *Sagana* her Towre, I leave you to judge, if a Man cou'd possibly forbear laughing at a Sight which was so very diverting.

SATIRE IX.

AS I was walking the other Day, in the Way that leads to the Capitol, very seriously meditating upon some Trifle or other, as my Custom is, a Man, whom I only knew by Name, taking me by the Hand very familiarly, ask'd me how I did Very well, Sir, (said I) for the Season, I am your most humble Servant. Perceiving that he followed me, I ask'd him if he had any farther Business; I have a Mind (replies he) that you should be acquainted with me, I am a Man of Letters. Oh Sir, said I, I esteem you the more. I endeavour'd in the mean time, all the Ways I cou'd think of, to rid my self of him; sometimes I walk'd fast, sometimes I stood still, then I whisper'd my Servant, the Sweat all this time

The Description of an Impertinent.

Manaret talos; O te, Bolane, cerebri

Felicem, aiebam tacitus cum quidlibet ille

Garriret; vicos, urbem laudaret; ut illi

Nil respondebam: Misere cupis, inquit, abire,

Jamdudum video. sed nil agis; usque tenebo · 15

Prosequar hinc, quo nunc iter est tibi Nil opus est te

Circumagi. quendam volo visere non tibi notum:

Trans Tiberim longe cubat is, prope Cæsaris hortos.

Nil habeo quod agam, & non sum piger; usque se-
     quar te.

Demitto auriculas, ut iniquæ mentis asellus,   20

Cum gravius dorso subiit onus. incipit ille.

Si bene Me novi, non Viscum pluris amicum,

Non Varium facies. nam quis me scribere pluris

Aut citius possit versus? quis membra movere

Mollius? invideat quod & Hermogenes, ego
     canto.   25

     Interpellandi locus hic erat · Est tibi mater,

Cognati, quis te salvo est opus? Haud mihi quisquam ·

Omnis composui Felices! nunc ego resto

Confice: namque instat fatum mihi triste, Sabella

Quod puero cecinit mota divina anus urna.   30

running down to my Heels Oh! *Bolanus,* said I to my self, how happy are you in breaking loose from an Impertinent. He continu'd talking at Random to me, he extoll'd the Grandeur and Magnificence of *Rome*; then he commended the Streets and Houses, till at length observing that I gave him no Answer, I find, Sir, said he, that you are in Pain to be gone; I have observ'd it for some time; but it must not be, I cannot leave you, where-e'er you go, you shall have me for your Companion Sir (says I) there is no Occasion for you to go out of your Way; I am going to see a Friend that you are not acquainted with, and his House is at a considerable Distance, on the other Side of the *Tiber,* near *Cæsar's Gardens* 'Tis no Matter, Sir, said he, I'll go along with you, I am perfectly at Leisure, and I love to be stirring. At this I hung down my Ears, like an Ass over-burden'd. He proceeds, If I know my own Perfections, neither *Viscus* nor *Varius* deserve your Friendship better than my self. I write more Verses, and am read'er in my Compositions than any Man living, I dance finely and gracefully, and then for singing, my Voice is so sweet, so agreeably charming, that I move the Envy of *Hermogenes* himself

HERE I took an Occasion to interrupt him; Have you, Sir, no Mother, or Relations living, who would be glad to see you in Health? Not one, I have laid them all to Rest The more happy they, said I softly to my self, I am the only remaining Person, O perfect your Work, and do not keep me in Pain any longer; I plainly see that the sad fatal Hour is come, which was foretold me when a Boy, by an old *Sabine* Woman, after she had shook the Fortune-tell-

Hunc neque dira venena, nec hosticus auferet ensis,

Nec laterum dolor, aut tuſſis, nec tarda podagra ·

Garrulus hunc quando conſumet cumque · loquacis,

Si ſapiat, vitet, ſimul atque adoleverit ætas.

Ventum erat ad Veſtæ, quarta jam parte diei 35

Præterita . & caſu tunc reſpondere vadatus

Debebat; quod ni feciſſet, perdere litem

Si me amas, inquit, paullum hic ades Inteream, ſi

Aut valeo ſtare, aut novi civilia jura

Et propero, quo ſcis Dubius ſum, quid faciam, in-

   quit ;   40

Tene relinquam, an iem Me ſodes. Non faciam, ille

Et præcedere cœpit ego, ut contendere durum

Cum victore, ſequor Mæcenas quomodo tecum,

Hinc repetit, paucorum hominum, & mentis bene

   ſanæ?

Nemo dexterius fortuna eſt uſus : haberes 45

Magnum adjutorem, poſſet qui ferre ſecundas,

                Hunc

ing * Urn. This Boy, faid fhe, fhall never
perifh by Steel or Poifon; neither Coughs, nor
Spleen, nor Gout, nor Cholick, fhall prove
mortal to him; no! he is doom'd to fall by the
Tongue of a talkative Man; and therefore if he
is wife, it will concern him, when he comes to
Age, to avoid all great Talkers.

It was Nine of the Clock, when we drew
near to *Vefta's Temple*; as good Fortune wou'd
have it, this impertinent Companion was oblig'd, as he had given Bail, to make his Appearance before the Judge Oh! Sir, faid he,
for God's fake, if you love me, turn in here a
Minute or two May I die, Sir, if I can be
upon my Legs fo long, or if I underftand any
thing of the Law; befides, you know I am
engag'd elfewhere I am in Doubt, faid he,
whether I fhall leave my Caufe, or you Oh!
Sir, me, by all Means. No, fays he, I am refolv'd not to part from you, and fo on he leads
Finding that it was in vain to argue, I march
along with him, when immediately he refum'd
the Difcourfe Pray, Sir, faid he, how ftands
your Intereft with *Mæcenas? Mæcenas*, I anfwer'd, is a Gentleman of great Senfe, and extremely nice in the Choice of his Acquaintance.
He reply'd, You have manag'd your good Luck
as dexteroufly as any Man could do; but you
would have a rare Help in your humble Servant, who would be content with the fecond

---

* *Divina mota anus urna* This kind of *Divination* was
in great Repute among the *Græcians*, and from them
deriv'd to the *Romans*, the Manner of it was this, a
great many Letters or Words were put into an Urn,
which being well fhook together, they turn'd them out,
if they exprefs'd any thing, that was received as an in-
fallible Prediction See *Monfieur Fontenelle's* Hiftory of
Oracles, *Chap.* XVIII.

Hunc hominem velles si tradere: dispeream, ni
Submosses omnis. Non isto vivitur illic,
Quo tu rere modo: domus hac nec purior ulla est,
Nec magis his aliena malis: nil mi officit, inquam, 50
Ditior hic, aut est quia doctior: est locus uni-
Cuique suus. Magnum narras, vix credibile. Atqui
Sic habet. Accendis, quare cupiam magis illi
Proximus esse. Velis tantummodo, quæ tua virtus,
Expugnabis. & est qui vinci possit; eoque 55
Difficilis aditus primos habet Haud mihi deero:
Muneribus servos corrumpam; non, hodie si
Exclusus fuero, desistam; tempora quæram;
Occurram in triviis; deducam. nil sine magno
Vita labore dedit mortalibus. Hæc dum agit, ecce 60
Fuscus Aristius occurrit, mihi carus, & illum
Qui pulchre nosset. consistimus, Unde venis? &
Quo tendis? rogat, & respondet. vellere cœpi,
Et prensare manu lentissima brachia, nutans,
Distorquens oculos, ut me eriperet. male salsus 65
Ridens dissimulare: meum jecur urere bilis.
Certe nescio quid secreto velle loqui te

Aiebas

Place, if you would introduce him to *Mæcenas*'s Favour. Let me die, if I don't think you would supplant all his other Favourites To this I return'd, that he was altogether mistaken in our Way of living There is no Family in *Rome* which is more remarkable for its Integrity than ours, we are perfectly free from those Intrigues and Jealousies with which others are infected; if another there is richer or more knowing than my self, that is no Hindrance to me Every one has his Place there according to his Merits What you tell me, he return'd, is very surprizing, and almost incredible But, said I, it is true Now, cry'd he, I am more desirous than ever of being intimate with him .'Tis but making the Trial, a Person of such rare Accomplishments as your self cannot miss of Success *Mæcenas* is a Gentleman that is easily won upon, and it is for that Reason that he makes the first Accesses to him as difficult as he can I will not, continu'd he, be wanting to my self in this Affair, I will bribe his Domesticks, no Repulse shall discourage me, I will seek out the most favourable Opportunities of addressing him, when he appears abroad, I'll attend upon him, and wait his Motions till he returns You know that there is nothing in Life which we Mortals can attain without Trouble.

While he was upon this, up comes *Fuscus Aristius*, who was my Friend, and who knew him full well. We both stop As soon as the usual Questions of, whence come you? whither go you? were over, I pull'd him by the Arm, and made other Signs with my Eyes and Head, desiring him to release me, he, like an ill-natur'd Fellow, only smil'd, and would not understand me This almost fretted me to Death You hinted the other Day, said I to him, as if

H   you

Aiebas mecum   Memini bene, sed meliore
Tempore dicam   hodie tricesima sabbata. Vis tu
Curtis Judæis oppedere? nulla mihi, inquam, 70
Relligio est. At mî   sum paullo infirmior, unus
Multorum. ignosces   alias loquar Hunccine solem
Tam nigrum surrexe mihi? fugit improbus, ac me
Sub cultro linquit   casu venit obvius illi
Adversarius &, Quo tu, turpissime? magna 75
Inclamat voce, &, Licet antestari? ego vero
Oppono auriculam   rapit in jus. clamor utrimque,
Undique concursus. sic me servavit Apollo

SATIRA

you had fomething to fay to me in private You fay true, I have not forgot it; but another Time will be better : Befides, this is a folemn * Feaft-day among the *Jews*; wou'd you offer fo grofs an Affront to them, as to talk of Bufinefs on fo great a Day? Oh! I have no Scruple in the World about that But I have, Sir, excufe my Weaknefs, 'tis perhaps a Fault in me, but a Fault that many others are guilty of befides my felf, have a little Patience, I will take a more favourable Time of difcourfing with you.

O the fatal inaufpicious Day! He went away in the moft barbarous Manner, and left me (as it were) with the Halter about my Neck; but by good Luck this impertinent Fellow's Adverfary met him and feiz'd him. O you Rogue! faid he, in a menacing Tone, did you think to get away? Sir, will you pleafe to bear Witnefs. I readily confented. Upon this he hurried him away to the Bar; the Clamour was great on either Side, the People flock'd in from all Parts, which gave me an Opportunity of making my Efcape. Thus it was that † *Apollo* preferv'd me.

---

* The *Jews* celebrated the Paffover on the 15th of the Month *Nifan*, which anfwers to our *April*, that Feaft is here call'd *Tricefima Sabbata*, it being juft 30 Weeks from the Beginning of their Year, which commences on the firft Day of the Month *Tizri*, which is our *September*

† He alludes to that Paffage in *Homer*, where *Apollo* is faid to deliver *Æneas* out of the Hands of *Achilles*

SATIRA X.

*N*EMPE *incomposito dixi pede currere versus*
    Lucili quis tam Lucili fautor inepte est,
Ut non hoc fateatur ? at idem, quod sale multo
Urbem defricuit, charta laudatur eadem.
Nec tamen hoc tribuens, dederim quoque cætera
    nam sic   5
Et Laberi mimos, ut pulchra poemata, mirer
Ergo non satis est risu diducere rictum
Auditoris & est quædam tamen hic quoque virtus
Est brevitate opus, ut currat sententia, neu se
Inpediat verbis lassas onerantibus auris   10
Et sermone opus est modo tristi, sæpe jocoso,
Defendente vicem modo rhetoris atque poetæ,

Inter -

SATIRE X.

'TIS true, * I formerly censur'd *Lucilius's* Verses, for their rough and uneven Numbers; and who is so impertinent an Admirer of him as to say the contrary? But then in the same Discourse I commended him for the Fineness of his *Satire*, in which he reproves the *Romans* for their Vices But notwithstanding I allow him this good Quality, I cannot esteem him as an accomplish'd Poet, for at that rate of judging, the pleasant Farces of † *Laberius* the *Mimick*, wou'd have my Vote for finish'd Pieces

He justifies the Character he gave of *Lucilius* in his 4th Satire

To move the Laughter therefore of an Audience is not enough, tho' I grant it to be some Degree of Excellence, but there are other Qualifications which we wish for in a Poet His Language must be concise, so as that the Sentences may run well, and the Ear not be tir'd with too great a Load of Words; it must be sometimes passionate and moving, sometimes lively and chearful One while he must act the Part of an Orator, at another Time of a Poet; and, as

What Qualifications are requisite to form a Poet

---

* The Subject of this *Satire* being the same with the 4th, they will both be better understood if read together

† *Decimus Laberius,* a Poet, who was particularly happy in writing Farces, he was so fortunate in diverting *Julius Cæsar* in one of his Plays, in which he acted himself, that he gave him 500 *Sestertia,* a Gold Ring, and admitted him again into the *Equestrian Order,* which Honour he had forfeited by acting on the Stage We have nothing of his remaining, but some Fragments of his mimical Pieces, publish'd with those of *Publius Syrus,* who was his Contemporary.

Occa-

Interdum urbani parcentis viribus, atque
Extenuantis eas consulto. ridiculum acri
Fortius & melius magnas plerumque secat res. 15
Illi, scripta quibus Comœdia prisca viris est,
Hoc stabant, hoc sunt imitandi: quos neque pulcher
Hermogenes umquam legit, neque simius iste,
Nil præter Calvom & doctus cantare Catullum.

At magnum fecit, quod verbis Græca Latinis 20
Miscuit O seri studiorum! quine putetis
Difficile & mirum, Rhodio quod Pitholeonti
Contigit? At sermo lingua concinnus utraque
Suavior, ut Chio nota si conmixta Falerni est
Cum versus facias. teipsum percontor, an & cum 25
Dura tibi peragenda rei sit caussa Petilli?
Scilicet oblitus patriæque patrisque Latini,
Cum Pedius caussas exsudet Poplicola atque

Corvinus,

Occasion serves, he must put on the Gentleman; he must lay aside Satire, and endeavour to be witty and facetious in Conversation; for it often happens, that to turn Things into Ridicule, is of greater Service, even in the most important Matters, than strongly to inveigh against them

IN this Particular, the antient Comedians distinguish'd themselves; and in this they deserve our Imitation But these are contemn'd by the fine *Hermogenes*, nor will *Demetrius*, that Ape of a Poet, vouchsafe to read them, alas! they relish nothing but what is wrote by * *Calvus* or † *Catulus*

BUT (say they) *Lucilius* was peculiarly happy in mixing *Greek* Words with *Latin* ones. Abominable Ignorance! that any Man shou'd admire *Pitholeon* the *Rhodian*, and imagine that there is any thing difficult or extraordinary in his *Epigrams*

THEY reply again, that a compound Language is more sweet and graceful, as the *Falernian* is more agreeable when mix'd with *Chian*. Tell me thou Poet, if ‡ *Petillius*, when accus'd, were to choose you for his Advocate, would you so far forget that you are a *Roman*, as to reply to the labour'd Speeches of *Poplicola* and

---

* *Licinius Calvus*, an Epigrammatist, and Writer of Love-verses, he was Contemporary with *Catullus*

† *Caius Valerius Catullus*, a facetious witty Writer of Epigrams, he translated into *Latin* Verse whatever was most beautiful and delicate in the *Greek Poets*, upon which Account he gain'd to himself the Title of Learned His Epigrams for the most part conclude with a graceful Turn of Thought, which renders them extreamly entertaining He was born at *Verona*, in the second Year of the 173d Olympiad.

‡ *Petillius*, see Sat IV

H 4 *Corvinus*,

Corvinus, patriis intermiscere petita
Verba foris malis, Canusini more bilinguis?   30
Atqui ego cum Græcos facerem, natus mare citra,
Versiculos, vetuit tali me voce Quirinus
Post mediam noctem visus, cum somnia verâ.
In silvam non ligna feras insanius, ac si
Magnas Græcorum malis implere catervas   35
   Turgidus Alpinus jugulat dum Memnona, dumque
Defingit Rheni luteum caput; hæc ego ludo,
Quæ neque in Æde sonent certantia, judice Tarpa,
Nec redeant iterum atque iterum spectanda theatris.
Arguta meretrice potes, Davoque Chremeta   40
Eludente senem, comis garrire libellos
Unus vivorum, Fundani Pollio regum
Facta canit pede ter percusso forte epos acer,
Ut nemo, Varius ducit. molle atque facetum

Virgilio

Corvinus, in an Harangue of foreign Words mix'd with those of your own Country, such as the Inhabitants of * *Canusium* make use of?

IT was once in my Head, who am an *Italian,* to make some *Greek* Verses. As I was intent upon the Work, *Romulus* appear'd to me after Midnight, when our Dreams are true, and desir'd me to desist, 'tis an unpardonable Extravagance, said he, to attempt to encrease the Number of the *Grecian* Poets, it is like carrying Wood to the Forest Being thus admonish'd, I laid aside my Design

WHILE the Poet *Alpin* in lofty Numbers murders *Memnon* in a barbarous Manner, while the *Rhine* runs muddy in his Description, I employ my Time in writing Verses, which are neither design'd to be acted over and over again in the Theatre, nor to be recited publickly for some Prize in *Apollo*'s Temple, where *Metius Tarpa,* that excellent Critick, sits as Judge

YOU only, *Fundanius,* of all Men living, are fit to write *Comedy,* you best can describe a † knavish Servant and a subtle intriguing Courtesan, contriving together to deceive an old Man *Pollio,* in *Iambicks,* sings the Acts of Kings, which are proper for *Tragedy* The *Epic* Poem owes its Glory to *Varius*; and the *Rural* Muses are indebted to ‡ *Virgil* for their Charms

---

* *Canusium,* see *Sat* V
† He alludes to the *Andria* of *Terence*
‡ *Virgil,* the Prince of the Latin Heroick Poets, born at *Andes,* not far from *Mantua,* in the third Year of the 177th Olympiad, and died in the second Year of the 190th, about 19 Years before Christ He wrote ten *Eclogues,* four Books of *Georgicks,* and twelve *Æneids* These last were not publish'd 'till after his Death He was possess'd of all the Graces of Poetry, no Man ever under-

Virgilio adnuerunt gaudentes rure Camenæ.   45
Hoc erat, experto frustra Varrone Atacino,
Atque quibusdam aliis, melius quod scribere possem,
Inventore minor neque ego illi detrahere ausim
Hærentem capiti cum multa laude coronam.

At dixi fluere hunc lutulentum, sæpe ferentem 50
Plura quidem tollenda relinquendis. age, quæso,
Tu nihil in magno doctus reprehendis Homero?

Nil

Charms and Graces. *Varro,* and others, have attempted *Satire,* but without Succefs. This Kind of Writing fuits my Genius beft; but I do not pretend to equal *Lucilius,* who was the Inventor. Far be it from me to attempt to pluck from his Head that † Garland, which he fo juftly merited, and which he now wears with fo much Applaufe But I am charg'd with comparing his Verfes to a River, whofe Stream was muddy and full of Slime; and with faying, that, tho' there were many Things in them to be approv'd, there were fome to be found Fault with.

But pray, Sir, tell me, fince you are fo knowing, Did you never find Fault with any thing in ‡ *Homer,* that incomparable Poet?

---

understood the Number and Harmony of Verfification like himfelf He is fmooth, majeftick, and wonderfully happy in his Characters and Defcriptions.

* Tho' *Horace* in this Place feems to make *Lucilius* the firft Author of *Satire* in Verfe among the *Romans,* he is only to be underftood, that *Lucilius* had given a more happy and graceful Turn to the *Satire* of *Ennius* and *Pacuvius,* not that he invented a new *Satire* of his own: For, as Mr *Dryden* obferves, the *Roman* Language, in *Lucilius'*s Time, was grown more capable of receiving the *Grecian* Beauties, than it was in the Days of *Ennius* and *Pacuvius* See the Character of *Ennius,* Sat IV Pag 41

† The Statues of the Poets, which were plac'd in *Apollo*'s Temple, were crown'd with Laurel

‡ *Homer,* the moft celebrated of the *Greek* Heroick Poets· He flourifh'd under *Diognetus* King of the *Athenians,* about 23 Years before *Iphitus* and *Lycurgus* inftituted the *Olympian* Games He wrote divers Poems, which are all loft, (two only excepted) the *Iliads* and *Odyffes* In the firft he defcribes the Strength and Vigour of the Body, in the laft, the Subtilty and Policy of the Mind. He was, without Difpute, the vafteft, fublimeft, and moft univerfal Genius that ever was known in the World, as *Virgil* was the moft accomplifh'd See a farther Character of his Writings, in *Book* I. *Ep* 2.

Has

Nil comis tragici mutat Lucilius Acci?

Non ridet versus Enni gravitate minores?

Cum de se loquitur, non ut majore reprensis   55

Quid vetat & nosmet Lucili scripta legentis

Quærere, num illius, num rerum dura negarit

Versiculos natura magis factos & euntis

Mollius, ac si quis, pedibus quid claudere senis

(Hoc tantum) contentus, amet scripsisse ducentos 60

Ante cibum versûs, totidem cœnatus? Etrusci

Quale fuit Cassi rapido ferventius amni

Ingenium; capsis quem fama est esse librisque

Ambustum propriis fuerit Lucilius, inquam,

Comis & urbanus; fuerit limatior idem,   65

Quam rudis & Græcis intacti carminis auctor,

Quamque poetarum seniorum turba sed ille,

Si foret hoc nostrum fato dilatos in ævum,

Detereret sibi multa recideret omne, quod ultra

Perfectum traheretur · & in versu faciendo   70

Sæpe caput scaberet, vivos & roderet unguis.

Has not *Lucilius* made several Alterations in
* *Accius*'s Tragedies? Has he not censur'd some
of *Ennius*'s Verses, as not coming up to the
Dignity of his Subject? when at the same
Time he speaks of himself as not superior to
those whom he finds Fault with

THIS is just my Case. What then shou'd
hinder me when I read *Lucilius*, but that I may
examine whether it was principally owing to
his Want of Genius, or to the crabbed inexpli-
cable Nature of the Things he treats of, that
his Numbers are as rough and unharmonious, as
if a Man should write 200 Verses before Supper, and as many after, not regarding in the
least the Variety of their Measures, so they were
but Verses? Such a fertile Vein was that of
Cassius the *Tuscan*, whose Genius for Poetry (if
we may call it Poetry) was more rapid, if possible, than a raging Torrent. 'Tis reported of
this *Cassius*, that he wrote as many Verses as
serv'd him for his Funeral Pile, both they and
their Author being consum'd together

SUPPOSING that *Lucilius* was a pleasant
and agreeable Writer, that he is smoother and
more correct than *Ennius*, who first attempted
this kind of Verse (which was unknown to the
Grecians) and supposing that he is justly preferable to all the Poets that liv'd before him;
yet I must say, were he now alive, he wou'd
certainly blot out a good many Things; he
wou'd cut off Abundance of Superfluities, and
when he was making Verses, he wou'd often
scratch his Head, and gnaw his Nails to the
Quick, taking Pains in his Compositions

* *Accius*, a Tragick Poet, he liv'd about 50 Years after *Pacuvius* We have yet the Fragments of above
sixty of his Plays, among which are several valuable
Pieces.

HE

Sæpe ſtilum vertas, iterum quæ digna legi ſint
Scripturus   neque, te ut miretur turba, labores,
Contentus paucis lectoribus. an tua demens
Vilibus in ludis dictari carmina malis?   75
Non ego   nam ſatis eſt equitem mihi plaudere. ut
     audax,
Contemtis aliis, exploſa Arbuſcula dixit.
Men' moveat, cimex Pantilius, aut cruciet, quod
Vellicet abſentem Demetrius? aut quod ineptus
Fannius Hermogenis lædat conviva Tigelli?   80
Plotius, & Varius, Mæcenas, Virgiliuſque,
Valgius, & probet hæc Octavius optimus, atque
Fuſcus, & hæc utinam Viſcorum laudet uterque:
Ambitione relegata, te dicere poſſum,
Pollio; te, Meſſalla, tuo cum fratre; ſimulque 85
Vos Bibule, & Servi; ſimul his te, candide Furni;
Compluris alios, doctos ego quos & amicos
Prudens prætereo· quibus hæc, ſunt qualiacumque,
Adridere velim; doliturus, ſi placeant ſpe
Deterius noſtra Demetri, teque, Tigelli,   90
Diſcipularum inter jubeo plorare cathedras.
     I puer, atque meo citus hæc ſubſcribe libello.

Q. HO.

HE that would have his Works deserve to be read a second Time, must be often correcting what he writes; he must not affect the empty Applauses of the unthinking Many, but rest contented, if a few good Judges, Souls of the highest Rank and truest Understanding, vouchsafe to read him

IF you are so vain as to take a Pleasure in repeating your Poems in the publick Schools, I must freely own, that I differ from you. For I say, as *Arbuscula* the Actress did, when she despis'd the common People that hissed her; I am satisfy'd if the Men of Taste and Distinction clap me   Shall such an Insect as *Pantilius* make me uneasy? Shall any thing that *Demetrius*, or the foolish *Fannius* say of me at *Hermogenes*'s Table, disturb my Quiet? May *Plotius*, *Varius*, *Mæcenas*, *Virgil*, *Valgius*, and the good *Octavius* approve my Satires; may *Fuscus* and the *Visci* be pleas'd with what I write, may *Pollio*, whom I do not mention out of Ostentation, and the illustrious *Messallæ* give their Votes in my Favour; may *Bibulus*, *Servius*, and *Furnus* that good-natur'd Critick, with many more of my learned Friends, whom I purposely pass over, vouchsafe to commend and applaud my Poems. I desire nothing more than that these my *Satires*, whatever in themselves, may be acceptable to them, and I cannot but say, that it wou'd much concern me to be disappointed of my Expectations But for *Demetrius* and *Tigellius*, they are not worthy of my Care, I value not their Approbation, let them lament and bemoan themselves among the Female Criticks, their Admirers

Go, Boy, make Haste and transcribe this *Satire*, and place it with those I have already written.   a   Q. HO-

Q. HORATII

FLACCI SATIRARUM

LIBER SECUNDUS.

SATIRA I.

SUNT quibus in Satira videar nimis acer, & ultra
  Legem tendere opus sine nervis altera, quicquid
Composui, pars esse putat, similisque meorum
Mille die versus deduci posse Trebati,
Quid faciam, praescribe Quiescas. Ne faciam, inquis,   5
Omnino versus? Aio Peream male, si non
Optimum erat · verum nequeo dormire Ter uncti
Transnanto Tiberim, somno quibus est opus alto;
Inriguumque mero sub noctem corpus habento.

Aut,

HORACE's SATIRES.

BOOK II.

SATIRE I.

HORACE *and* TREBATIUS.

Hor THE Town is divided in their Opinion of my *Satires*, some say, that I take too great a Liberty; that my Raillery is too severe and cutting; others accuse my Compositions, as wanting Strength and Sinews; a Man, say they, might write a thousand such Verses in a Day Your Advice, * *Trebatius*, what must I do in this Case? *Tre.* Sit still *Hor* Do you mean, that I should write no more Verses? *Tre* I do. *Hor* May I die, if that wou'd not be the best Way; but I cannot sleep *Tre* I have a Remedy for that; anoint your self and swim over the *Tiber* two or three times, drink a Bottle of good strong Wine in the Evening, and take my Word, you will sleep profoundly; but if you needs

---

* A great and learned Lawyer, who was no less eminent for his Knowledge of the Laws, than for his Goodness and Integrity.

I   must

Aut, si tantus amor scribendi te capit, aude　　10
Cæsaris invicti res dicere, multa laborum
Præmia laturus. Cupidum, pater optime, vires
Deficiunt: neque enim quivis horrentia pilis
Agmina, nec fracta pereuntis cuspide Gallos,
Aut labentis equo describit volnera Parthi.　　15
Attamen & justum poteras & scribere fortem,
Scipiadam ut sapiens Lucilius. Haud mihi deero,
Cum res ipsa feret: nisi dextro tempore, Flacci
Verba per attentam non ibunt Cæsaris aurem.
Cui male si palpere, recalcitret undique tutus.　　20
Quanto rectius hoc, quam tristi lædere versu
Pantolabum scurram, Nomentanumve nepotem?
Cum sibi quisque timet; quamquam est intactus, &
　　odit.
Quid faciam? saltat Milonius, ut semel icto
Accessit fervor capiti, numerusque lucernis.　　25
Castor gaudet equis; ovo prognatus eodem,

Pugnis.

muſt write, if nothing can take you off from Poetry, attempt to ſing the Acts of *victorious Cæſar*, and you cannot fail of being liberally rewarded. *Hor* What you adviſe is the Heighth of my Ambition; but, Father, I want a Genius; 'tis not for every Poet to deſcribe great *Cæſar's* Legions horrid all with [a]Darts, or paint the *Gaul* juſt breathleſs and expiring, the broken Spear ſtill reeking in his Wound; or image out the [b]*Parthian* Warriour, when, from his generous Steed, he drops transfix'd and bleeding. *Tre* But, tho' theſe Things are above your Reach, yet you may ſpeak of his Juſtice and Magnanimity; thus it was, that the wiſe *Lucilius* commended *Scipio.* *Hor* I'll not be wanting to my ſelf as Occaſion offers; [c]*Horace* muſt obſerve the ſoft and happy Seaſon of Addreſs, or in vain hopes to ſucceed with *Cæſar,* who hates nothing more than dull groſs Flatterers *Tre* How great ſoever the Danger may be, 'tis infinitely better to hazard the Trial, than to fall foul on the Buffoon [d]*Pantolabus,* or the profligate *Nomentanus.* Every one is conſcious of his own Miſmanagements, and tho' your *Satire* is not directly levell'd at him, ye he fears the worſt, and conſequently hates you. *Hor.* But what would you have me to do? *Milonius,* as ſoon as the Wine is got into his Head, and he begins to ſee Double, falls to dancing. *Caſtor* delights in Horſes, while *Pollux* (tho' his

[a] The *Pilum,* or Dart, was made of a Piece of Wood about three Cubits long, and a Slip of Iron of the ſame Length, hook'd and jagg'd at the End

[b] The Poet alludes in this Place to the Defeat of *Pacorus* King of the *Parthians,* who was kill'd by *Ventidius.*

[c] See his Letter to *Vinnius Aſella, Book* I. *Epiſt* XIII.

[d] See *Sat.* VIII *Book* I.

I 2　　　　　　　Twin-

Pugnis quot capitum vivunt, totidem studiorum

Millia me pedibus delectat claudere verba,

Lucili ritu, nostram melioris utroque.

Ille velut fidis arcana sodalibus olim   30

Credebat libris; neque, si male cesserat, usquam

Decurrens alio, neque si bene quo fit ut omnis

Votiva pateat veluti descripta tabella

Vita senis. sequor hunc, Lucanus an Appulus, an-

    ceps ·

Nam Venusinus arat finem sub utrumque colonus, 35

Missus ad hoc, pulsis (vetus est ut fama) Sabellis,

Quo ne per vacuum Romano incurreret hostis;

Sive quod Appula gens, seu quod Lucania bellum

Incuteret violenta sed hic stilus haud petet ultro

Quemquam animantem, & me veluti custodiet en-

    sis   40

Vagina tectus quem cur distringere coner,

Tutus ab infestis latronibus? ô pater & rex

Juppiter,

Twin-Brother) is diverted with nothing but Boxing As many Men, so many Minds My Inclinations lead me to *Satire,* and in this I follow *Lucilius*'s Example, who was much our Superior in the Art of Poetry It was his Practice to commit all his Secrets to his Papers, as to his intimate Friends ; whatever Accident happen'd to him, whether prosperous or adverse, he never made use of any other Confidents ; so that all the Transactions of this old Man's Life are as clearly and distinctly related in his *Satires,* as if they had been drawn in a * Picture, such as those which Men hang up in Performance of a Vow, for their having been deliver'd from Shipwreck. His Steps I follow, I that am a *Lucanian,* or an *Appulian,* I don't know which ; for *Venusia,* where I was born, borders on both Provinces, and was a Colony sent thither (as old Story says) when the *Sabines* were driven out of it, with Intent that it might hinder the making Incursions upon the *Roman Territory,* thro' that long uncultivated Tract of Land, if the fierce Nation either of *Apulia,* or *Lucania* should wage War against us Be this as it will, I will never willingly employ my Pen against any Man living ; I will keep it, as I do my Sword, in its Scabbard, to be drawn only in my Defence , but which shall be sheath'd as long as no Enemy is

---

* It was a Custom for those who had been sav'd from Shipwreck, to have all the Circumstances of their Adventure represented on a *Tableau,* which they hung up in the Temple of that particular God, by whom, as they suppos'd, they had been deliver'd They likewise represented in *Tableaux* a Detail of their good Success , it being as reasonable to pay God our Acknowledgments for Blessings receiv'd, as to thank him for any signal Deliverance

near

Juppiter, ut pereat positum robigine telum,
Nec quisquam noceat cupido mihi pacis! at ille,
Qui me conmorit, (melius non tangere, clamo) 45
Flebit, & insignis tota cantabitur urbe
Cervius iratus leges minitatur & urnam;
Canidia Albuci, quibus est inimica, venenum;
Grande malum Turius, si quid se judice certes
Ut, quo quisque valet, suspectos terreat, utque 50
Imperet hoc natura potens, sic collige mecum
Dente lupus, cornu taurus petit; unde, nisi intus
Monstratum? Scævæ vivacem crede nepoti
Matrem; nil faciet sceleris pia dextera. minum
Ut neque calce lupus quemquam, neque dente petit bos.
Sed mala tollet anum vitiato melle cicuta 55

   Ne longum faciam: seu me tranquilla senectus
Exspectat, seu mors atris circumvolat alis;
Dives, inops; Romæ, seu, fors ita jusserit, exsul;
Quisquis erit vitæ, scribam, color. O puer, ut sis 60

Vitali

near. Grant, O *Jupiter*, Father and King, that it may rather be confum'd with Ruft, and that I, who, above all Things, am a Lover of Peace, may never meet with any Provocations! But if any one fhall dare to urge my Rage, 'twere better for him that he had not provok'd me, I'll fet him out in his proper Colours, and make him a Jeft to all the City

The Danger of provoking a Poet

Cervius the Informer threatens thofe that offend him, with an Action, or Information *Canidia* has always her Poifons ready to revenge her felf on her Enemies *Turius* threatens thofe whom he is angry with, that they fhall lofe their Caufe, if it comes before him in Judgment 'Tis common with all, to make ufe of their utmoft Strength and Power againft their Adverfaries, and in fo doing, they do but follow the Dictates of Nature, which are not to be refifted. How this comes about, confider a little with me. The Wolves fight with their Teeth; Bulls with their Horns; and whence is it that they do fo, but that they are directed by natural Inftinct?

TRUST the profligate *Scæva* with the Care of his long-liv'd Mother; and to be fure he will do her no Injury with his pious Hands. No Wonder, for a Wolf won't kick, or an Ox bite, but he will do what is as bad, he will take Care to difpatch the old Woman, with putting a Dofe of Poifon in her Honey

To be fhort, Whether I am to expect a quiet old Age, or whether Death be now hovering about me; whether I be poor, or rich, whether I lead my Life at *Rome*, or be unhappily banifh'd from my Country; whatever my Condition or Circumftances be, I muft write *Satires.*

I 4   *Tra.*

Vitalis metuo ; & majorum ne quis amicus

Frigore te feriat. Quid? cum est Lucilius ausus

Primus in hunc operis componere carmina morem,

Detrahere & pellem, nitidus qua quisque per ora

Cederet, introrsum turpis; num Lælius, & qui 65

Duxit ab oppressa meritum Carthagine nomen,

Ingenio offensi? aut læso doluere Metello,

Famosisque Lupo cooperto versibus? atqui

Primores populi arripuit populumque tributim;

Scilicet uni æquus virtuti atque ejus amicis 70

Quin ubi se a volgo & scena in secreta remorant

Virtus Scipiadæ & mitis sapientia Læli;

Nugari cum illo, & discincti ludere, donec

Decoqueretur olus, soliti. quicquid sum ego, quamvis

Infra Lucili censum ingeniumque; tamen me 75

Cum

Tre O my Son, I am afraid that you are not, long-liv'd, that some great Courtier, who is now your Friend, will cast such a cold Look upon you, that you won't survive it. *Hor.* But why do you think so? When * *Lucilius* led the Way in this sort of Writing, and had the Courage to unmask the World, and shew Men such as they really were, not what they falsly appear'd to be Nay, when *Metellus* and *Lupus* were so severely reprov'd, did *Lælius,* or he who justly took his Sirname from his having laid † *Carthage* in Ruins; did these great Men take any Offence at the Freedom of his Wit? Nor were *Lupus* and *Metellus* the only Persons that fell under his Censure, he inveigh'd against all the great Men of *Rome*; neither Rich nor Poor, of what Tribe soever (Virtue and her Followers only excepted) cou'd escape his Reflections: On the contrary, the valiant *Scipio,* and the wise and gentle ‡ *Lælius,* when they withdrew themselves from Crowds and Business to Privacy and Retirement, us'd to trifle and divert themselves with him, while their Herbs and Roots were boiling for Supper I do not pretend to compare my self with him; whether you regard his Wit, Quality, or Estate, he is much my Superior, but whatever I am, even Envy her self shall confess thus much, that I have convers'd

Good Men have no Reason to be afraid of Satire.

* See the Note on *Lucilius,* Sat x Book 1

† *Carthage,* the chief City of *Africa,* upon the Coast of *Barbary,* near *Tunis,* built, as 'tis thought, by *Dido,* was taken and burnt by *Scipio Africanus Minor* A U C 608. There remains nothing now of this glorious Town, which was once esteem'd the Third of the *Roman Empire,* but the Ruins, which are very considerable

‡ *Lælius,* a *Roman* Orator, so famous for his Wisdom, that he was nam'd, *The Wise, Tully* often mentions him, much to his Advantage.

and

Cum magnis vixiſſe invita fatebitur uſque
Invidia ; & fragili quærens inlidere dentem,
Offendet ſolido : niſi quid tu, docte Trebati,
Diſſentis. Equidem nihil hinc diffingere poſſum
Sed tamen ut monitus caveas, ne forte negoti   80
Incutiat tibi quid ſanctarum inſcitia legum
Si mala condiderit in quem quis carmina, jus eſt
Judiciumque Eſto: ſi quis mala ſed bona ſi quis
Judice condiderit laudatus Cæſare? ſi quis
Opprobriis dignum laceraverit, integer ipſe?   85
Solventur riſu tabulæ. tu miſſus abibis.

SATIRA II.

QUÆ *virtus & quanta, boni, ſit vivere*
       parvo,
(Nec meus hic ſermo eſt ; ſed quæ præcepit Ofellus
Ruſticus, abnormis Sapiens, craſſaque Minerva)
Diſcite, non inter lances menſaſque nitentis ;
Cum ſtupet inſanis acies fulgoribus, & cum   5
Adclinis falſis animus meliora recuſat :

and liv'd in Friendship with the greatest Men;
and therefore whatever Occasions she shall industriously lay hold on to blast my Reputation,
the Attempt shall turn to her own Disadvantage.

THESE are the Motives which encline me
to *Satire,* which I cannot but pursue, unless
you in your Wisdom, O learned *Trebatius,* shall
advise me to the contrary. *Tre.* To deal plainly, I have nothing to object against what you
say; however, take this Caution with you,
that you may'nt get into a Scrape, for want of
knowing what the * Laws wisely ordain; remember that there is one to this Effect: If any
Man write ill Verses against another, an Action
lies against the Poet. *Hor.* Very well, *If any
Man write ill Verses*; but, what if they are good
ones? What if *Cæsar* commends them? If a
Poet, of an unblemish'd Reputation, falls upon
one who deserves Infamy, what then? *Treb.*
Why then the Judges will only laugh at the Information, and dismiss it, and you who are
prosecuted, will be sent about your Business.

* By the *Law* of the 12 *Tables,* he who said or writ
any thing to the Prejudice of any Man's Reputation,
was to suffer Death.

SATIRE II.

GENTLEMEN, if you are desirous of *The*
learning the Advantages of a temperate *great Ad-*
Life, come and examine this Truth with me, *vantages*
when your Stomachs are empty, for that only *perate*
is the proper Season; not when you sit surround- *Life.*
ed with Dainties, when your Eyes are dazzled
with the Pomp of Luxury, and your deluded
Reason chooses the worse, and neglects the better. (I do not speak this of my self, what I now
advance is the Doctrine of *Ofellus,* who, tho'
un-

Verum hic impransi mecum disquirite. Cur hoc?

Dicam, si potero. male verum examinat omnis

Corruptus judex. leporem sectatus, equove

Lassus ab indomito; vel (si Romana fatigat   10

Militia adsuetum græcari) seu pila velox,

Molliter austerum studio fallente laborem,

Seu te discus agit, pete cedentem aera disco·

Cum labor expulerit fastidia; siccus, inanis

Sperne cibum vilem· nisi Hymettia mella Fa-

   lerno,   15

Ne biberis, diluta. foris est promus, & atrum

Defendens piscis hiemat mare   cum sale panis

Latrantem stomachum bene leniet unde putas, aut

Qui partum? non in caro nidore voluptas

Summa, sed in teipso est. tu pulmentaria quære   20

Sudando pinguem vitiis albumque neque ostrea,

Nec scarus, aut poterit peregrina juvare lagois.

uninstructed in the Schools of the Philosophers, was neverthelefs a very wife and honeft Man) But why muft we learn this Fafting? I will give you my Reafons: A corrupt Judge is no proper Perfon to determine what is Right. Go hunt the Hare, ride the great Horfe, or, if this Difcipline be too hard for you, who have accuftomed your felf to the more effeminate *Grecian* Way of living, make a Party at Quoits, or play with the * Balloon; your Intenfenefs on the Diverfion will render the Fatigue infenfible to you. When Labour and Exercife have fharpen'd your Appetite, and remov'd the Qualms you languifh'd under, you may defpife, if you pleafe, plain wholefome Food, and refufe to drink *Falernian* Wine, if it be not foftned with *Hymettian* Honey I dare be bold to fay, that under thefe Circumftances, if the Butler be abfent, and the Storms and Winds render Fifhing impracticable, a little Bread and Salt will then fatisfy a gnawing Stomach Now, from whence do you think this Satisfaction proceeds? The Pleafure you take in eating depends not on the Dainties, but on your felf Labour and Exercife make every Thing a Ragoo; but to thofe who are cloy'd and furfeited with high Feeding, even Oyfters and Ortelans are taftelefs and infipid

---

* The Antients had four Sorts of Balls 1 The *Follis*, or *Balloon* , which they ftruck with their Arms guarded with a wooden Bracer, if the *Balloon* was little, they us'd only their Fifts, 2 The *Pila Trigonalis*, which was like our *Tennis*-Balls, to play with this, three Perfons ftood in a Triangle, ftriking it round one to the other, he that let it fall firft was the Lofer 3. *Paganica*, a Ball ftuff'd with Feathers. 4. *Harpaftum*, a harder Kind of Ball, which they play'd with, dividing into two Companies, and ftriving to throw it thro' one another's Goals, which was the conquering Caft

Vix tamen eripiam, posito pavone, velis quin
Hoc potius quam gallina tergere palatum,
Corruptus vanis rerum; quia veneat auro   25
Rarà avis, & picta pandat spectacula caudâ.
Tamquam ad rem attineat quicquam, num vesceris
    ista,
Quam laudas, pluma? cocto num adest honor idem?
Carne tamen quamvis distat nihil, hac magis illa;
Inparibus formis deceptum te patet. esto.   30
Unde datum sentis, lupus hic, Tiberinus, an alto
Captus hiet? pontisne inter jactatus, an amnis
Ostia sub Tusci? laudas insane, trilibrem
Mullum; in singula quem minùas palmenta necesse est.
Ducit te species, video. quo pertinet ergo   35
Proceros odisse lupos? quia scilicet illis
Majorem natura modum dedit, his breve pondus.
Jejunus raro stomachus volgaria temnit.
Porrectum magno magnum spectare catino

Vellem,

I DO not expect to prevail fo far (fo fond are Men of Superfluities) but that when Peacock and Fowl are fet upon the Table, you will rather gratify your Palate with the Peacock. 'Tis indeed a rare and coftly Bird; the Beauty of its Tail is very delightful; but what is that to the Goodnefs of it? Can you eat thofe Feathers which you fo much admire? or does its Beauty continue after it is boiled? 'Tis plain therefore that you are deluded with the Appearances of Things; for in Reality, there is not the leaft Difference between Peacocks and other ordinary Fowls But granting this: How can you pretend to diftinguifh by your Tafte, whether the Pike you are now eating, was taken in the Sea, or in frefh Water? If in frefh Water, whether it was caught at the Mouth of the *Tiber*, or between the Bridges? I muft deal frankly with you, thefe Things to me are unconceivable You commend a Mullet of three Pound Weight; how ridiculous is this, when you muft cut it to Pieces, before you can eat it? Why do you admire it purely for its Bignefs? and yet at the fame time if a well-grown Pike be ferv'd up at Table, you exprefs your Diflike of it, and what is the Reafon, but that Pikes are naturally large, and Mullets little?

A Stomach that is feldom empty, loaths the moft common ordinary Food, but, fays the Glutton, it delights me to fee a prodigious Mullet ferv'd up in a prodigious *Difh, fuch a one is a
fit

---

* The *Romans* in their Entertainments were very fond of ufing great Difhes Sylla had one of maffy Silver of an hundred Pound Weight Pliny tells us, that at that time there were above 500 fuch Difhes in
Rome.

Vellem, ait Harpyiis gula digna rapacibus at vos 40
Præsentes, Austri, coquite horum obsonia. quanquam
Putet aper rhombusque recens, mala copia quando
Ægrum sollicitat stomachum; cum rapula plenus
Atque acidas mavolt inulas necdum omnis abacta
Pauperies epulis regum · nam vilibus ovis, 45
Nigrisque est oleis hodie locus haud ita pridem
Galloni præconis erat acipensere mensa
Infamis quid? tum rhombos minus æquora alebant?
Tutus erat rhombus, tutoque ciconia nido,
Donec vos auctor docuit prætorius. ergo 50

fit Companion for * *Harpies* But, O ye
South Winds, come and taint the Meat of thefe
rapacious Mortals! Yet why do I implore your
Affiftance? The Boar and Turbot, how frefh
foever, are naufeous to them, their Stomachs
are cloy'd with over-much Plenty, infomuch
that having eaten as long as they cou'd, they
are forc'd to have Recourfe to Turnips and Sa-
lads to reftore their Appetite

B u t, Thanks to Heaven, the Rich fometimes feed as coarfly as others, even Eggs and
black Olives, than which nothing is more common, find a Place at their Tables It is but of
late Years, when † *Gallonius* had a Sturgeon
ferv'd up at his Table, that the People exclaim'd
againft it as an unpardonable Extravagance; and
why did they do fo? did not the Sea afford at
that Time as many Turbots as now?

B o t h the Stork and Turbot were fecure
enough, till *Sempronius Rufus* brought 'em into
Repute; who, when he ftood to be *Prætor,*

Rome They proceeded at laft to fuch an Height of
Extravagance, that in the Time of *Claudius,* one *Dru-
fillanus Rotundus* had a Difh call'd *Promulfis,* which
weigh'd above 500 ℔ and *Vitellius* had one of that prodigious Bignefs, that it was call'd *Minerva*'s Buckler

---

* *Harpies,* fabulous Monfters, fo call'd from the
Greek αρπαζω, to fnatch, or ravifh, they were faid to
dwell in Iflands partly by Sea, and partly by Land,
they are feign'd to be Fowls with a Virgin's Face, and
Bear's Ears, their Bodies like Vultures, and their Hands
like hooked Talons, *Virgil, Æneid* III mentions three
of them, *Aello, Ocypite* and *Celæno*
    *Virginei volucrum Vultus, fædiffima Ventris
    Proluvies, uncæque manus, & pollida femper
    Ora fame*
† *Gallonius,* a Perfon fo infamous for his Gluttony, that
his Name became a Proverb, and was generally us'd to
fignify a Man that minded nothing but his Belly

K   was

Si quis nunc mergos suavis edixerit assos;
Parebit pravi docilis Romana juventus.

    Sordidus a tenui victu distabit, Ofello
Judice. nam frustra vitium vitaveris illud,
Si te alio pravus detorseris. Avidienus,   55
Cui Canis ex vero ductum cognomen adhæret,
Quinquennis oleas est, & silvestria corna;
Ac, nisi mutatum, parcit defundere vinum; &
Cujus odorem olei nequeas perferre (licebit
Ille repotia, natalis, aliosve dierum   60
Festos albatus celebret) cornu ipse bilibri
Caulibus instillat, veteris non parcus aceti

    Quali igitur victu sapiens utetur, & horum
Utrum imitabitur? hac urget lupus, hac canis, aiunt.
Mundus erit, qua non offendat sordibus, atque 65
In neutram partem cultus miser   hic neque servis,
Albuci senis exemplo, dum munia didit,

                                       Sævus

was rejected by the People upon the Account of his Gluttony; and fhou'd any one now maintain that roafted Cormorants eat very delicioufly; the *Roman Youth* are fo addicted to Luxury, that they foon wou'd put the Doctrine in Practice

In *Ofellus*'s Judgment, there is a mighty Difference between a fordid and frugal Life, to what Purpofe are we careful in fhunning one Extream, if we run into another? Thus *Avidienus* (who was nick-nam'd the Dog, and not without Reafon) feeds on wild Cornels and Olives that are five Years old, the Wine which he offers to the Gods, is fowre, his Oil ftinks abominably, even that which he ufes on the greateft Feftivals, or when cloath'd in * White he celebrates his Nuptials, or regales his Friends on the Day of his Nativity, is no better, and yet he pours it upon his Colworts out of his large Horn-Crewet, and takes Care to add Vinegar enough to them

What Diet muft a wife Man then make ufe of? Which of thefe Examples ought he to follow? Keep the Mid-way, both Extreams are equally dangerous, he muft be fo clean as not to give Offence, and as he ought not to run into Excefs, fo on the other Hand he muft not be too frugal and fparing in his Entertainments He muft not imitate old *Albucius*, who was fo exact when he treated his Friends, that he appointed his Servants their particular Pofts, which if any one neglected, he was fure of being pu-

---

* The *Romans* always wore white Gowns on Holy Days, and publick Feftivals, the Difference between the *Toga Alba* and *Toga Candida* was this, the firft was the natural Colour of the Wool, the other an artificial White.

Sævus erit, nec sic ut simplex Nævius, unctam
Convivis præbebit aquam   vitium hoc quoque magnum.

   Accipe nunc, victus tenuis quæ, quantaque secum 70
Adferat in primis valeas bene. nam variæ res
Ut noceant homini, credas, memor illius escæ
Quæ simplex olim tibi federit at simul affis
Miscueris elixa, simul conchylia turdis;
Dulcia se in bilem vertent, stomachoque tumul-
 tum   75
Lenta feret pituita vides, ut pallidus omnis
Cæna desurgat dubia? quin corpus onustum
Hesternis vitiis animum quoque prægravat una,
Atque adfligit humo divinæ particulam auræ
Alter, ubi dicto citius curata sopori   80
Membra dedit, vegetus præscripta ad munia surgit.
Hic tamen ad melius poterit transcurrere quondam;
Sive diem festum rediens advexerit annus,
Seu recreare volet tenuatum corpus. ubique
Accedent anni, & tractari mollius ætas   85
Inbecilla volet tibi quidnam accedet ad istam,
Quem puer & validus præsumis, mollitiem? seu
Dira valetudo inciderit, seu tarda senectus

   Rancidam aprum antiqui laudabant non quia
    nasus
Illis nullus erat; sed, credo, hac mente, quod hospes 90
Tardius adveniens vitiatum commodius, quam

                                                 In-

nifh'd Neithei muft he be fo carelefs as *Næ-vius*, who ferv'd his Guefts with gieafy Water This Extravagance is as blameable as the other

Now learn the Advantages of a temperate Life I begin with that of Health, which is much impaii'd by Variety of Meats Reflect with your felf how much bettei you aie, when you eat but one Sort, but when Fifh and Fowl, ioaft and boil'd aie blended togethei, the gieat-eft Part of 'em tuins to Cholei, wh'ch, mixing with Phlegm, puts the Stomach into Dif-oidei Obfeive how pale a Man comes fiom a Table fet out with great Vaiiety; nay, when the Body is ovei-chaig'd with the Exceffes of the foregoing Evening, the Mind, that Particle of divine Breath, is made heavy, and, as it were, immers'd in Mattei Whereas the fober temperate Man, after having taken a flight Re-paft, lays himfelf fecurely down to fleep, and rifes in the Moining with Strength and Vigour to his accuftomed Labouis. Befides, this ab-ftemious Man leaves room to exceed a little fometimes, and feed bettei than ordinarv, whether it be on fome annual Feftival, oi to help his Appetite, when he finds it falling off, and himfelf decaying, or when infirm old Age begins to come upon him, which iequires a foftei and more tendei Treatment But, if in the Stiength and Prime of Life, you give your felf up to an eafy delicate Way of Living, what will you do in the Time of Sicknefs and old Age?

Our wife Forefathers us'd to commend the Flefh of a Boar, which had a mufty Tafte, not that they had not Nofes as well as we, but they thought, as I fuppofe, that in cafe a Fiiend came fome Days after it was dreft, it was bet-

Integrum edax dominus consumeret. hos utinam inter
Heroas natum tellus me prima tulisset
    Das aliquid famæ, quæ carmine gratior aurem
Occupat humanam? grandes rhombi, patinæque   95
Grande ferunt una cum damno dedecus. adde
Iratum patruum, vicinos, te tibi iniquum,
Et frustra mortis cupidum; cum deerit egenti
As, laquei pretium. Jure, inquit, Trausius istis
Jurgatur verbis ego vectigalia magna,   100
Divitias habeo tribus amplas regibus Ergo,
Quod superat, non est melius quo insumere possis?
Cur eget indignus quisquam, te divite? quare
Templa ruunt antiqua Deûm? cur, improbe, caræ
Non aliquid patriæ tanto emetiris acervo?   105
Uni nimium tibi recte semper eunt res.
O magnus posthac inimicis risus! uterne

Ad

ter that he fhould have fome of it, tho' a little
rank, than that the Mafter himfelf fhould eat it
all, when frefh and good   I wou'd to God it
had been my Fate to have liv'd in thofe early A-
ges of the World, when fuch good and honourable Men were in Being

AGAIN, as to Reputation, have you any
Regard for that ? No Poetry or Mufick is more
exquifitely charming than for a Man to hear
himfelf well fpoken of; and can you be ignorant that Turbots and other coftly Difhes, befides the Expence, entail a Blemifh upon your
good Name ? Add to this, that fuch Extravagancies will draw upon you the Difpleafure of
your Relations Your Neighbours are incens'd,
and you become uneafy and infupportable to
your felf; in vain, in vain will you wifh for
Death, when your Neceffity will be fo great,
that you won't have wherewith to purchafe a
Halter, to put an End to your Mifery

Go (perhaps the Glutton will fay) read thefe
Lectures to the wretched *Traufius,* he, poor
Man, has Occafion for them, but as for me, I
have a large and plentiful Eftate, as much as
will defray three King's Expences   If this be
your Cafe, why do you not find out fome bet-
ter Way to difpofe of what you have to fpare?
Why are fo many Men of Merit opprefs'd with
Poverty, and you fo rich ? Why do the antient
Temples of the Gods lie all in Ruin ? Wretch
that you are, why do you not facrifice fome
Part of your Treafure to the Good of your
Country? Can you imagine that you only of
all Mankind are deftin'd to enjoy a conftant
Profperity ? O fhou'd your happy Fortune
change, with what Scorn and Derifion wou'd

K 4   your

Ad cafus dubios fidet fibi certius? hic qui

Pluribus affuerit mentem corpufque fuperbum;

An qui contentus parvo metuenfque futuri, 110

In pace, ut fapiens, aptarit idonea bello?

   Quo magis his credas   puer hunc ego parvus Ofellum

Integris opibus novi non latius ufum,

Quam nunc accifis videas metato in agello

Cum pecore & gnatis fortem mercede colonum, 115

Non ego, narrantem, temere edi luce profefta

Quicquam, præter olus fumofæ cum pede pernæ

Ac mihi feu longum poft tempus venerat hofpes,

Sive operum vacuo gratus conviva per imbrem

Vicinus; bene erat, non pifcibus urbe petitis, 120

Sed pùllo atque hædo. tum penfilis uva fecundas

Et nux ornabat menfas, cum duplice ficu

Poft hoc ludus erat cupa potare magiftra.

Ac venerata Ceres, ita culmo furgeret alto,

Ex-

your Enemies infult you , how wou'd they triumph over your Misfortunes ?

AGAIN, in Times of Danger and Difficulty, which of the two, think you, is moft capable of providing for his own Security? he who has brought upon his Mind, and his pamper'd Body, many artificial Wants, or he who has led a frugal Life, who fearing the worft, has, like a wife Man, as it were in Times of Peace provided for War

THAT what I have faid may make the greater Impreffion on your Minds, give me Leave to tell you, that when I was young, I knew this *Ofellus* perfectly well, and that he obferv'd the fame Frugality and Temperance and Moderation in his profperous Circumftances, as he now does in a meaner Condition

YOU may fee this honeft Farmer in his little Field, feeding his Flock, and fpeaking thus unto his Children .

COLWORTS and Bacon were my conftant Food upon every ordinary Day, unlefs the Rules of Civility oblig'd me to act otherwife   But if a good old Friend, whom I had not feen for a long Seafon, came to make me a Vifit ; or if by Chance a Neighbour ftept in, to pafs away an Hour or two in rainy Weather, I bid them welcome   And even then I did not fend to *Rome* for Fifh, but I treated my Friends with a Kid and Pullet ; Nuts, Figs, and Raifins were my fecond Courfe   Dinner being over, we drank what we pleas'd, and offer'd Libations to the Goddefs * *Ceres,* that our Corn might en-

* *Ceres,* the Daughter of *Saturn* and *Ops,* fhe was the firft who taught Men how to till the Ground and fow Corn   They who wou'd know more of the Mythology of *Ceres,* will do well to confult the 6th Tome *de la Bibliotheque Univerfelle,* where this Fable is explain'd at large.

creafe,

Explicuit vino contractæ feria frontis.   125

Sæviat atque novos moveat fortuna tumultus;

Quantum hinc inminuet? quanto aut ego parcius,
   aut vos,

O pueri, nituistis, ut huc novus incola venit?

Nam propriæ telluris herum natura neque illum,

Nec me, nec quemquam statuit. nos expulit ille;   130

Illum aut nequities aut vafri inscitia juris,

Postremum expellet certe vivacior heres

Nunc ager Umbreni sub nomine, nuper Ofelli

Dictus erat   nulli proprius; sed cedit in usum

Nunc mihi, nunc alii quocirca vivite fortes,   135

Fortiaque adversis opponite pectora rebus.

SATIRA III.

*S*I *raro scribes, ut toto non quater anno*
   Membranam poscas, scriptorum quæque retexens,
Iratus tibi, quod vini somnique benignus
Nil dignum sermone canas . quid fiet? at ipsis

creafe, and Harvefts ripen; in Hopes of which the fpritely Wine made us gay and cheerful.

LET Fortune execute her Rage upon me, I defie her Malice, fhe cannot reduce me to a lower State Tell me, O my Sons, Whether I or You have lived the worfe, fince this new Inhabitant feiz'd on my Revenues? I call him an Inhabitant; for Nature has appointed neither him, nor me, nor you, to be real Proprietors of what we call our own He has turn'd me out, and the Time will come, when, either by his Debaucheries, or thro' his Ignorance of the Quirks of the Law, he himfelf fhall be expell'd: But if none of thefe happen, his furviving Heir will moft certainly eject him This Farm, which now goes by *Umbrenus's* Name, was once in my Poffeffion, but no one can properly call any thing his own, the Profits of it are mine, and yours, and his It concerns us, therefore, to quit our felves like Men, and to be above the Power of Misfortune

SATIRE III.

Damafippus and *Horace.*

Dam IF you'll write fo feldom, as not to call for Paper four Times in a Year, but confume your Time in correcting your Verfes, and in fretting at your felf, that, by fleeping and drinking overmuch, you do nothing confiderable What will be the Confequence? You retired into the Country, to avoid being prefent

The Poet is here accus'd of being lazy

at

Saturnalibus huc fugisti sobrius. ergo   5
Dic aliquid dignum promissis incipe nil est
Culpantur frustra calami, inmeritusque labor at
Iratis natus paries Dis atque poetis.
Atqui voltus erat multa & praeclara minantis,
Si vacuum tepido cepisset villula tecto   10
Quorsum pertinuit stipare Platona Menandro,

Eupolin

at the Feast of * *Saturn*; now you are at Leisure, be just to your Promise, and produce
something extraordinary Come, Sir, begin
What? Have you nothing to say? In vain you
lay the Fault upon your Pen; What have the
Walls been guilty of, that they shou'd feel the
Effects of your Fury? You seem'd to threaten,
that when you were free from Cares and Trouble, and quietly settled in some little warm
Cottage, then great Matters might be expected
from you If not; to what Purpose did you
incumber your self with † *Plato* and ‡ *Menander?*

Why

* The Original of this Festival is unknown. *Macrobi-
us* tells us, that it was celebrated in *Italy* long before the
Building of *Rome* As to the Manner of the Solemnity,
besides the Sacrifices and other Parts of publick Worship,
there were several lesser Observations which deserve to
be taken Notice of As, first, the Liberty which was given
to Servants of being very free with their Masters; this
was done in Memory of the Liberty enjoy'd under *Saturn*, when the Names of Servant and Master were unknown to the World Besides this, they sent Presents to
one another among Friends No War was to be pro-
claim'd, no Offender executed The Schools kept a Va-
cation, and nothing but Mirth and Freedom were to be
met with in the City They kept at first only one Day,
which was the 14th of the ʌalends of *January*, but the
Number was afterwards encreas'd to Three, Four, Five,
and, some say, Seven Days

† *Plato*, the Chief of the *Academick* Sect, born at
Athens in the 87th *Olympiad*, he was *Socrates*'s Scholar,
under whom he made considerable Improvements in
Moral Philosophy He was so desirous of Knowledge,
that he travell'd into *Egypt*, where he attain'd the Knowledge of the *Jewish* Religion Several Fathers of the
Church, by observing the Conformity of his Doctrine
with that of the Old Testament, have given him the
Title of the *Athenian Moses*

‡ *Menander*, a Comick Poet of *Athens*, born in the
109th *Olympiad*, he is said to be the Prince of New
Comedy, *Plutarch* prefers him to *Aristophanes* both for
Judgment and Stile, he wrote 108 Comedies which are
ll lost, excepting some Citations from antient Authors.

See

Eupolin Archilocho? comites educere tantos?

Invidiam placare paras, virtute relicta?

Contemnere, miser vitanda est inproba Siren

Desidia; aut quicquid vita meliore parasti   15

Ponendum æquo animo Di te, Damasippe, Deæque

Verum ob consilium donent tonsore. sed unde

Tam bene me nosti? Postquam omnis res mea Janum

Ad medium fracta est; aliena negotia curo,

Excussus propriis. olim nam quærere amabam,   20

Quo vafer ille pedes lavisset Sisyphus ære;

Quid

Why were [a] *Eupolis* and [b] *Archilochus* made your Companions? Why did you bring their Works down with you? Do you think to appeale the Malice of your Enemies by leaving off writing? But you are miltaken, you will only be delpiled for it You mult either reloive to banilh Idlenels, that beautiful Inchantrels, or quietly renounce the Reputation you have gain'd by your Performances. *Hor* May the Gods, *Damalippus*, lend you a good [c] Barber for the Advice you have given me, but, prithee Man, How came you to know lo much of me and my Behaviour? *Dam*. Since I ltock-jobb'd away my Fortune with the Bankers, who live in the Middle of [d] *Janus*'s Street, having little or no Bulinels of my own, I now mind other People's. Formerly I traffick'd in every thing that was antient. It was my Bulinels to find out, Whether a Ciltern of *Corinthian* Brals was lo antient as that *Silyphus* might have walh'd

See his Fragments publilh'd by *Le Clerc*, with Dr. *Bentley*'s Remarks.

[a] *Eupolis* See *Sat*. IV *Book* I

[b] *Archilochus*, a Greek *Iambick* Poet, born at *Paros*, in the 3d *Olympiad*, he was lo Satirical upon *Lycambes*, who having promis'd him his Daughter, marry'd her to another, that he caus'd him to hang himlelf

[c] It was ulual with the Philolophers to wear long Beards, upon which they let no ordinary Value Our Poet, therefore, in return to *Damalippus* for his kind Inltructions, very handlomly ridicules him in wilhing him a good Barber.

[d] —— —— *Poltquam omnis res mea Janum Ad medium fracta elt* —— Near the Temple of *Janus* there was a Street which took the lame Name, inhabited for the molt part by Bankers and Ulurers, it was very long, and divided by the different Manner of *Janus Summus*, *Janus Medius*, and *Janus Imus*.

Quid sculptum infabre, quid fusum durius esset:

Callidus huic signo ponebam millia centum.

Hortos egregiasque domos mercarier unus

Cum lucro noram: unde frequentia Mercuriale 25

Imposuere mihi cognomen compita. Novi;

Et miror morbi purgatum te illius. Atqui

Emovit veterem mire novus; ut solet, in cor

Trajecto lateris miseri capitisve dolore·

Ut lethargicus hic cum sit pugil, & medicum ur-

guet. 30

Dum ne quid simile huic, esto ut libet O bone, ne te

Frustrere   insanis & tu, stultique prope omnes,

Si quid Stertinius veri crepat; unde ego mira

Descripsi docilis præcepta hæc, tempore quo me

Solatus jussit sapientem pascere barbam, 35

Atque a Fabricio non tristem ponte reverti.

Nam, male re gesta, cum vellem mittere operto

Me capite in flumen, dexter stetit, &, Cave faxis

Te quicquam indignum pudor, inquit, te malus angit,

Insanos qui inter vereare insanus haberi. 40

in it; whether this Statue was carv'd by a mafter-ly Hand; or that caft with all the Softnefs that the Mould might give it: I was skilful enough to fet an immenfe Price upon a choice Statue: I often bought fine Houfes and Gardens, and fold them to Advantage, infomuch that where-ever I went, I was call'd by the People *Mercury's Favourite.*

Hor. I know it very well, and am much fur-priz'd to find you cur'd of fo defperate a Ma-lady.

Dam. 'TWAS a defperate one indeed, but another of a different Nature has happily re-mov'd it; thus the Head-ach and Pleurify do frequently change Places, and fettle in the Sto-mach; and a Man that has a Lethargy does often grow frantick and beat his Phyfician

Hor. So you do not beat me, be as frantick as you pleafe.

Dam O good Sir, you quite miftake your felf; both you and all other Fools are mad, or * *Stertinius* is not to be believ'd. 'Twas from him that I learn'd thefe excellent Precepts; 'twas he that advis'd me to let my Beard grow, as a diftinguifhing Mark of Wifdom and Pru-dence; he it was that perfuaded me to go away from *Fabritius's* Bridge, in fuch a Temper and Difpofition of Mind as became a Philofopher. *Accord-ing to the Opinion of the Sto-icks, all Men are mad in fome De-gree or other.* For you muft know, that my Affairs going ve-ry ill, I went thither with an Intent to plunge my felf headlong into the River, when, as good Luck wou'd have it, *Stertinius* came to me, and diffwaded me from committing fo infamous an Action; Why, faid he, fhou'd you be fo fear-ful of being reputed a Mad-man, by thofe who are mad themfelves?

* *Stertinius,* a *Stoick* Philofopher.

L   LET

Primum nam inquiram, quid fit furere . hoc fi erit
 in te
Solo ; nil verbi, pereas quin fortiter, addam
 Quem mala ftultitia, & quemcunque infcitia veri
Cæcum agit, infanum Chryfippi porticus & grex
Autumat hæc populos, hæc magnos formula reges, 45
Excepto fapiente, tenet. nunc accipe quare
Defipiant omnes, æque ac tu, qui tibi nomen
Infano pofuere. velut filvis, ubi paffim
Palantis error certo de tramite pellit,
Ille finiftrorfum, hic dextrorfum abit ; unus utrique 50
Error, fed varius inludit partibus   hoc te
Crede modo infanum ; nihilo ut fapientior ille,
Qui te deridet, caudam trahat. eft genus unum
Stultitiæ, nihilum metuenda timentis ; ut ignis,
Ut rupis fluviofque in campo obftare queratur   55
Alterum & huic varium & nihilo fapientius, ignis
Per medios fluviofque ruentis   clamet amica
Mater, honefta foror, cum cognatis pater, uxor,
Hic foffa eft ingens, hic rupes maxima , ferva ·
Non magis audierit, quam Fufius ebrius olim, 60
Cum Ilionam edormit, Catienis mille ducentis,

Mater,

LET us firſt conſider what Madneſs is, which being once ſtated, if, upon the Enquiry, you are found to be the only Mad-man, you may drown your ſelf with my Conſent Now according to the Opinion of * *Chryſippus* and his Followers, every one that is ignorant of the Truth, and is led away by vitious Paſſions, is really mad This Definition extends it ſelf to all Mankind, the Wiſe only excepted As for the Reaſons, why thoſe, who call you a Madman, are mad themſelves, take them in their Order.

As when two Men have loſt themſelves in paſſing thro' a Wood, the one takes to the Right, and t'other to the Left, both go wrong, but they do it by different Ways; ſo it is with Mankind, he who laughs at you, makes one himſelf in the Fool's Dance.

THERE are two Soits of Madneſs which particularly deſerve to be expos'd The one is of thoſe who feign to themſelves imaginary Dangers ; who cry out in Confuſion, that Rocks, Rivers, and Fires, obſtruct their Paſſage, when they are walking on the Plain. The other Sort is quite contrary to this, but not leſs extravagant , I mean thoſe who run headlong thro' Fire and Water, who, notwithſtanding the Admonitions of their Friends, and the kind Entreaties of their Parents and Relations, to have ſome Regard to their own Preſervation, and to conſider the Danger they are in, are as deaf to their Perſuaſions, as the Actor *Fuſius*, who, playing the Part of *Ilione* ſleeping, got drunk, and ſlept ſo profoundly, that when † *Catienus*, and

---

* *Chryſippus* See *Sat* III *Book* I
† This *Catienus* play'd the Ghoſt of *Polydorus*, who was Son to *Ilione*

twelve

Mater, te adpello, *clamantibus.* huic ego volgus
Errori similem cunctum insanire docebo

    Insanit veteres statuas Damasippus emendo
Integer est mentis Damasippi creditor? esto   65
Accipe, quod numquam reddas mihi, si tibi dicam;
Tune insanus eris, si acceperis? an magis excors
Rejecta praeda, quam praesens Mercurius fert?
Scribe decem a Nerio   non est satis. adde Cicutae
Nodosi tabulas centum, mille adde catenas   70
Effugiet tamen haec sceleratus vincula Proteus.
Cum rapies in jus malis ridentem alienis,
Fiet aper, modo avis, modo saxum, &, cum volet,
    arbor

Si male rem gererere insani, contra bene sani est ·
Putidius multo cerebrum est (mihi crede) Perilli   75

Dictantis,

twelve hundred Spectators cry'd out together, *O Mother, come to my Assistance*, they were not able to awake him.

I proceed to shew, that the Generality of Mankind are infected with this Kind of Madness

DAMASIPPUS's Folly is in buying antient Statues , and is not he as great a Fool, who sells them upon Trust, or lends him Money to buy them ? If I shou'd say, I will give you Credit for such a Sum of Money, and never expect to be paid, Wou'd it be Madness in you to accept it? Wou'd it not be a greater Folly to neglect so favourable and unexpected an Opportunity of enriching your self? If a Man, who was going to lend his Money to one of a broken Fortune, should say, Here, sign a Note for the Receipt of such or such a Sum from my Banker *Nerius* This Note won't hold him fast, and if he add to it all the Securities which the knotty-pated *Cicuta* can invent , if he tie him down with a thousand Chains, yet the Knave, like another * *Proteus*, will break thro' them all and escape When you arrest and seize him, he will laugh so immoderately at you, as to set every one about you a laughing; he will be a Boar, or a Bird, a Stone, or a Tree , in short, he will be ever changing his Shape, and appear in what Form he pleases , so that you know not where to have him

IF a Man is esteem'd to be in his Senses, or out of them, from the good or ill Management of his Affairs , believe me, *Perillius*'s Brains were much more out of Sorts than yours, when

* *Proteus*, the Son of *Neptune*, King of *Ægypt* , he could transform himself into all Manner of Shapes , his Name, in this Place, is very happily apply'd to an insolvent Debtor, who uses a thousand Tricks and Artifices to elude his Creditor.

he

Dictantis, quod tu numquam refcribere poffis.

Audire, atque togam jubeo componere, quifquis
Ambitione mala, aut argenti pallet amore,
Quifquis luxuria, triftive fuperftitione,
Aut alio mentis morbo calet * · huc propius me, 80
Dum doceo infanire † omnis, vos ordine adite.

Danda eft ellebori multo pars maxima avaris ·
Nefcio an Anticyram ratio illis deftinet omnem.
Heredes Staberi fummam incidere fepulcro ;
Ni fic feciffent, gladiatorum dare centum 85
Damnati populo paria, atque epulum arbitrio Arri, &
Frumenti quantum metit Africa Sive ego prave,
Seu recte ; hoc volui. ne fis patruus mihi Credo
Hoc Staberi prudentem animum vidiffe Quid ergo
Senfit, cum fummam patrimoni infculpere faxo 90

---

* The Author here puts into *Stertinius's* Mouth four Heads of Difcourfe, as fo many Species of Madnefs, *Ambition, Avarice, Luxury,* and *Superftition,* to which he adds another general one, without any other Name than that of *alius mentis morbus* He begins to treat of Avarice, *v* 82 of Ambition, *v* 165 of Luxury, *v.* 224 of Love, *v.* 247. and of Superftition, *v* 281 which he finifhes at *v.* 295 And therefore thofe (as fome there are) who would change the Places of the feveral Parts of this *Satire,* feem not fufficiently to have attended to this Divifion of it, given us by the Author himfelf

† Read *omnes vos.*

Heredes

he drew up the Note for that Money which you can never repay him.

O ye that are led away by Ambition! or that are given to Covetousness! ye that are luxurious, profuse, or superstitious! or that languish under any other Distemper of the Mind! draw near inOrder, and listen, while I prove, that you all are mad

I declare, in the first Place, that the Covetous, above all others, stand in need of *Hellebore*, the whole Produce of * *Anticyra* will hardly suffice them   *Staberius* in his Will oblig'd his Executors to inscribe upon his Monument a Detail of his Riches   In Case of Failure, they were liable to the Penalty of diverting the People with two hundred † *Gladiators*, to make such an Entertainment as *Arrius* shou'd approve, and to distribute as much Corn among them as all *Africa* affords in one Harvest. *Whether what I have commanded be well or ill*, says *Staberius*, *'tis nothing to you, I am not your Heir, nor is it your Business to censure my Actions.* I believe that *Staberius* had his Reasons for what he did. *Dam* What Reasons cou'd he have, in Willing the Particulars of his Estate to be inscrib'd upon

All Men are mad, but the Covetous are more mad than others

___

* There were two *Anticyras*, one in *Phocis*, near the Gulph of *Corinth*, the other was near Mount *Oeta* in *Theffaly*   The best *Hellebore* grew in the last, but the Inhabitants of the former were more skilful in preparing it

† The Heathens had a Custom of killing Persons at the Funerals of Great Men, fancying the Ghosts of the deceas'd to be render'd propitious by human Blood   They afterwards contriv'd to soften this Barbarity with the specious Shew of voluntary Combat   To this Purpose they train'd up their Captives in the Knowledge of Arms, whom, upon the Day appointed for the Sacrifices to the departed Ghost, they oblig'd to maintain a mortal Encounter at the Tombs of their Friends   The first Shew of *Gladiators* was exhibited at *Rome* by *M* and *D Brutus*, upon the Death of their Father, A U. C 490.

L 4   his

Heredes voluit ? Quoad vixit, credidit ingens
Pauperiem vitium, & cavit nihil acrius · ut, si
Forte minus locuples uno quadrante periret,
Ipse videretur sibi nequior ; (omnis enim res,
Virtus, fama, decus, divina humanaque, pulchris 95
Divitiis parent ; quas qui construxerit, ille
Clarus erit, fortis, justus. Sapiensne? Etiam & rex,
Et quicquid volet) hoc, veluti virtute paratum,
Speravit magnæ laudi fore. Quid simile isti
Græcus Aristippus, qui servos projicere aurum 100
In media jussit Libya, quia tardius irent
Propter onus segnes ? uter est insanior horum ?
Nil agit exemplum, litem quod lite resolvit
Si quis emat citharas, emtas comportet in unum,
Nec studio citharæ, nec Musæ deditus ulli ; 105
Si scalpra & formas non sutor ; nautica vela

Aversus

his Monument? *Ster.* I will tell you. While he liv'd, he accounted Poverty the worst of Evils, and consequently endeavour'd industriously to avoid it; insomuch that he wou'd have look'd upon himself as a wicked Fellow, had he died but a Farthing poorer than he might have done His Opinion was that all Things in this World give Place to Money, Virtue, Honour, Glory, and Things Divine as well as Humane. So that he who has a large Stock of it, is Honourable, Couragious, Just, Wise, and even a King, or whatever he pleases.

Now *Staberius* imagin'd that Ages to come wou'd regard his Acquisitions as the just Effects of his Wisdom and Virtue How unlike to him was * *Aristippus* the *Grecian*; who, upon his Servants complaining, as they journey'd thro' *Libya*, that the Money they carried was too heavy for them, order'd 'em immediately to throw it away

Now which of these Two think you was the maddest?

Dam. One doubtful Case won't clear up another *Ster* If one that has no Skill in Musick shou'd purchase a Parcel of Guittars and Lutes; if a Man that is nothing of a Shoemaker shou'd stock himself with Paring-knives and Lasts, or, having no Inclination for Traffick, shou'd buy Sails and Anchors and Tack-

---

* *Aristippus,* the Founder of the *Cyrenaick Sect,* was the Disciple of *Socrates*, he liv'd about the 66th *Olympiad*. He made no Scruple to frequent the Courts of Princes, keep his Mistresses, and fare deliciously, answering those that tax'd him on that Account, that, if it were not a good thing to feast and eat well, People wou'd not practise it on their Holy Festivals. He was an ingenious witty Man, and extreamly happy in his Repartees.

ling

Aversus mercaturis: delirus & amens
Undique dicatur merito. qui discrepat istis,
Qui nummos aurumque recondit, nescius uti
Compositis, metuensque velut contingere sacrum? 110
Si quis ad ingentem frumenti semper acervum
Projectus vigilet cum longo fuste; neque illinc
Audeat esuriens dominus contingere granum;
Ac potius soliis parcus vescatur amaris
Si, positis intus Chii veterisque Falerni 115
Mille cadis, nihil est, tercentum millibus, acre
Potet acetum: age, si & stramentis incubet unde-
Octoginta annos natus, cui stragula vestis,
Blattarum ac tinearum epulæ, putrescat in arca;
Nimirum insanus paucis videatur; eo quod 120
Maxima pars hominum morbo jactatur eodem.

Filius aut etiam hæc libertus ut ebibat heres,
Dís inimice senex, custodis, ne tibi desit?
Quantulum enim summæ curtabit quisque dierum,
Unguerc si caulis oleo meliore, caputque 125
Cœperis inpexa fœdum porrigine? quare,
Si quidvis satis est, perjuras, surripis, aufers
Undique? tun' sanus? populum si cædere saxis
Incipias, servosve tuo quos aere pararis;

Insanum

ling for Shipping, the People wou'd juftly account him mad; and what is he better, who,
not knowing how to employ his Money, lays
it up in Hoards, and thinks it little lefs than Sacrilege to touch it?

IF a Man, arm'd with a huge great Club,
fhou'd ftand watching all Day a large Heap of
Corn, and yet not dare to touch a Grain,
though never fo hungry; if rather than do
fo, he choofes to feed on ordinary Herbs. If,
notwithftanding his Cellars are fill'd with Pipes
of good Old *Chian* and *Falernian* Wine, this
covetous Wretch drinks none but what is
fowre If, being near Eighty Years of Age,
he fleeps upon Straw, while his Beds and Blan-
kets lie rotting in a Cheft, and are an excellent
Banquet for the Moths and Worms: If this
Mifer feems frantick only to a few, 'tis becaufe
the greateft Part of Mankind are themfelves infected with his Diftemper.

ABOMINABLE Wretch! thus to abufe
the Bounty of Heaven; doft thou hoard up
thy Money for fear of Want, that thy Son,
or perhaps thy Slave, whom thou conftituteft
thine Heir, may fpend it on his Debaucheries?
How little would every Day take off from your
Poffeffions, if you would ufe better Oil for your
Colworts, and for anointing your Head too,
which for want of it is fcurfy and filthy? If
Nature is fatisfied with fo fmall a Pittance, why
do you forfwear your felf? To what End is this
filching? Why do you pillage and plunder
others? And as for you, (*addreffing himfelf to
another of his Hearers*) do you think your felf
in your Senfes? Shou'd you fling Stones at Peo-
ples Heads, or endanger the Lives of the Slaves
you have bought, wou'd not the very Boys and
Girls

Infanum te omnes pueri, clamentque puellæ.   130

Cum laqueo uxorem interimis, matremque veneno,

Incolumi capite es? quid ni? neque enim hoc facis

   Argis,

Nec ferro ut demens genetricem occidis Oreftes.

An tu reris eum occifa infaniffe parente?

Ac non ante malis dementem actum Furiis, quam 135

In matris jugulo ferrum tepefecit acutum?

Quin, ex quo eft habitus male tutæ mentis Oreftes,

Nil fane fecit quod tu reprehendere poffis

Non Pyladen ferro violare, aufufve fororem eft

Electram: tantum maledicit utrique, vocando 140

Hanc furiam, hunc aliud, juffit quod fplendida bilis.

   Pauper Opimius argenti pofiti intus & auri,

Qui Veientanum feftis potare diebus

Campana folitus trulla vappamque profeftis,

Quondam lethargo grandi eft oppreffus; ut heres 145

Jam circum loculos & clavis lætus ovanfque

Curreret. hunc medicus multum celer atque fidelis

Excitat hoc pacto. menfam poni jubet, atque

Effundi faccos nummorum, accedere pluris   150

Ad numerandum. hominem fic erigit. addit & illud;

Ni tua cuftodis, avidus jam hæc auferet heres.

                              Men'

Girls pronounce you mad? Can you pretend to enjoy your Reason, and yet be guilty of such execrable Crimes, as to strangle your Wife, and poison your Mother? I know what you wou'd say, that the Fact was not committed at * *Argos*, that your Mother was not slain like † *Clytemnestra*, who fell by the Sword of her Son *Orestes* Do you think that he run mad after the Murder; and that he was not distracted when he plung'd his Dagger into her Breast? Even from the Time that you suppose him mad, he did nothing for which you can justly reprehend him, he never attempted to kill his Friend *Pylades*, or his Sister *Electra*; 'tis true, that, in his Fits, he call'd her *Fury*, and gave him ill Language, but that was all

IT happen'd one Day that the Miser *Opimius* (who, notwithstanding his many Heaps of Gold and Silver, was so sordidly Covetous, that, on a Festival, he drank nothing but *Veientan* Wine out of a nasty Earthen Pot, at other times, that which was flat and insipid serv'd his Turn) was seiz'd with a Fit of a Lethargy; his Heir immediately, o'erjoy'd at the Accident, fell to rifling his Pockets to find his Keys An honest faithful Physician, who was call'd in upon this Occasion, brought him quickly to Life again, after this manner. He forthwith order'd a Table to be brought, and several Bags of Money to be pour'd out upon it, then he appointed diverse Persons to count it, by these Means he rais'd *Opimius* to Life again, crying out to him at the same Time, If you don't look out sharp after your Money, your

* *Argos*, a Noble and Antient City of *Peloponnesus*.
† *Clytemnestra*, see Sat. I. Book I.

greedy

Men' vivo? Ut vivas igitur, vigila: hoc age.
   Quid vis?
Deficient inopem venæ te, ni cibus atque
Ingens accedit stoma:ho fultura ruenti.
Tu cessas? Agedum, sume hoc ptisanarium oryzæ. 155
Quanti emtæ? Parvo. Quanti ergo? Octussibus.
   Eheu!
Quid refert, morbo, an furtis pereamve rapinis?
   Quisnam igitur sanus? Qui non stultus Quid
     avarus?
Stultus & insanus. Quid? si quis non sit avarus;
Continuo sanus? minime. Cur, Stoice? Dicam. 160
Non est cardiacus, Craterum dixisse putato,
Hic æger. recte est igitur, surgetque? negabit:
Quod latus, aut renes morbo tentantur acuto.
Non est perjurus, neque sordidus. inmolet æquis
Hic porcum Laribus. verum ambitiosus & au-
   dax.   165

Naviget

greedy Heir will carry it off with him. *What, while I am alive?* says the Old Man. Yes, reply'd the Physician, and therefore if you design to live, beftir your self, and take what I prescribe *What would you have me to do?* Why, Sir, said the *Doctor,* your Strength will fail you; you will certainly die without some Nourishment; you must take a good Cordial to strengthen your Stomach : Come, Sir, all Delays are dangerous; drink this *Ptisane But what will it cost?* The Price is inconsiderable. *But pray how much?* Two Shillings, says the Physician ; *alas!* crys *Opimius, What availeth it me, whether I am ruin'd by my Distemper, or by the Rapine and Thievery of others?* Dam. Who then is a Man in his Senses? *Ster* He that is not a Fool *Dam* But what is the covetous Man? *Ster.* A Madman and a Fool. *Dam.* But what if a Man be not covetous, is he therefore in his Senses? *Ster.* No such Matter *Dam.* Prithee, Stoick, why? *Ster.* I'll tell you This Patient, says *Craterus,* is not sick at his Stomach Is he therefore well? May he rise with Safety? By no means, says the Doctor ; because he has a Pleurify in his Side, or is troubled with Gravel in his Reins. This Man perhaps is neither perjur'd nor covetous; let him offer a Pig to his * Houshold Gods for fo considerable a Blessing; but then he is bold, rash and ambitious. If this Cafe

---

* *Lares,* the Houshold Gods of the *Romans,* and other *Heathen Nations,* whose Images they kept in their Houses They were divided into Publick and Private, the Publick being suppos'd to take Care of, and to be Protectors of Cities, People and Highways, as the Private of particular Houses and Families They had Feasts kept in Honour of them, and Temples built to them.

be

Naviget Anticyram. quid enim differt, balatróne

Dones quicquid habes, an numquam utare paratis?

   Servius Oppidius Canusî duo prædia, dives

Antiquo censu, gnatis divíſſe duobus

Fertur, & hoc moriens pueris dixiſſe vocatis   170

Ad lectum: Poſtquam te talos, Aule, nuceſque

Ferre ſinu laxo, donare, & perdere vidi;

Te, Tiberi, numerare, cavis abſcondere triſtem ·

Extimui, ne vos ageret veſania diſcors ;

Tu Nomentanum, tu ne ſequerere Cicutam.   175

Quare per Divos oratus uterque Penatis,

Tu cave ne minuas, tu ne majus facias id,

Quod ſatis eſſe putat pater, & natura coercet.

Præterea, ne vos titillet gloria, jure-

Jurando obſtringam ambo. uter ædilis, fue-

   ritve   180

Veſtrum

be fo, away with him to *Anticyra*; for what Difference is there, whether a Man confume his Eftate on Players and Flatterers, or never make ufe of it?

OPPIDIUS, who was what one might in former Days have called a wealthy Man, had two good old Farms at *Canufium* *, which he divided between his two Sons; when he lay upon his Death-bed he call'd both of 'em to him, and addrefs'd them thus I have obferv'd, my *Aulus*, that you, when a Child, were very carelefs and negligent of your Play-things, you either loft them, or gave them away; but you, my *Tiberius*, acted quite the contrary; you counted your Nuts, and with an Air of Anxiety were follicitous to hide them in fome private Place Thefe different Difpofitions have occafion'd your Father abundance of Concern I am fore afraid, my deareft Children, left you both be poffefs'd with a different Madnefs; left you, my *Aulus*, fhou'd be like *Nomentanus*, and you, *Tiberius*, be fo void of Senfe, as to imitate the miferable covetous *Cicuta* I adjure you both by my Houfhold Gods, that you, *Aulus*, do not leffen your Eftate, and that you, *Tiberius*, do not encreafe it 'Tis your Father's Opinion that you have enough, and that you ought not to exceed thofe Bounds which Nature has prefcrib'd I will, moreover, that you take an Oath, never to give up your felves a Sacrifice to Glory and Ambition, if either of you be † *Ædile*

M   or

---

† *Ædilis*, an Officer created to affift the *Tribunes* in the Care of Temples and publick Edifices, in infpecting the publick Stores of Corn and other Provifions, in fupervrfing all the Commodities fold in the Market, and

Veſtrum prætor, is inteſtabilis & ſacer eſto
In cicere atque faba bona tu perdaſque lupinis,
Latus ut in circo ſpatiere, & aeneus ut ſtes;
Nudus agris, nudus nummis, inſane, paternis?
Scilicet ut plauſus, quos fert Agrippa, feras tu, 185
Aſtuta ingenuum volpes imitata leonem

    Ne quis humaſſe velit Ajacem, Atrida,   vetas
      cur?

Rex ſum: nil ultra quære plebeius. & æquam
Rem imperito at ſi cui videor non juſtus; multo
Dicere, quod ſentit, permitto. Maxime regum, 190
Di tibi dent capta claſſem deducere Troja.

Ergo

or * *Prætor*, may the Curse of his Father fall heavy upon him, and may he be incapable of making a Will, and of enjoying the Privileges of a Freeman. Why fhou'd you wafte and confume your Goods in fruitlefs Donations? Why fhou'd you madly deprive your felf of the Land and Money which your Father left you, only that you may walk in State in the *Circus*, or have a brazen Statue erected to your Memory? Why fhou'd you vainly affect thofe Applaufes which † *Agrippa* receiv'd from the People of *Rome* ? This is altogether as ridiculous, as when the Fox affected to pafs for the Lion.

W H Y, ‡ *Agamemnon*, did you iffue out an Order, forbidding any Man at his Peril to bury ᵃ *Ajax* ? *Aga*. Becaufe I am a King. It is not for you who are a ᵇ Plebeian, to ask me a Reafon for what I do. Befides, the Command was juft, and if any one thinks otherwife, he may fafely fpeak his Mind. *Ster*. Greateft of Kings, may the *Gods* facilitate your taking of *Troy*, and may your Navy, crown'd with Succefs, meet with

and in punifhing Delinquents in all Matters concerning Buying and Selling, there were at firft but Two, but the Number was afterwards encreafed to Six.

* *Prætor*, fee *Sat* V *Book* I.

† *Marcus Vipfanius Agrippa*, the intimate Friend and Son-in-Law of *Auguftus*, he was the greateft General of his Time, and one of the moft confiderable Men that *Rome* ever had, tho' of mean Parentage.

‡ The Son of *Atreus*, Captain-General of the *Greeks* in their Expedition againft *Troy*.

ᵃ *Ajax*, a Famous Commander in the fame Expedition.

ᵇ Notwithftanding what Dr *Bentley* fays, I think it fhould be read *Quero*, and the whole Sentence be fuppofed fpoken, not by *Agamemnon*, but the Queftioner: If it be read *quære*, *Agamemnon* here forbids him to ask Queftions, which yet he permits him to do in the next Verfe.

a hap-

Ergo confulere, & mox refpondere licebit?

Confule   Cur Ajax heros ab Achille fecundus

Putrefcit, totiens fervatis clarus Achivis.

Gaudeat ut populus Priami Priamufque inhu-

  mato,   *195*

Per quem tot juvenes patrio caruere fepulchro?

Mille ovium infanus morti dedit, inclutum Ulixen

Et Menelaum una mecum fe occidere clamans.

Tu cum pro vitula ftatuis dulcem Aulide natam

Ante aras, fpargifque mola caput, improbe, fal-

  fa;   *200*

Rectum animi fervas? quorfum? infanus quid enim

  Ajax

Fecit? cum ftravit ferro pecus, abftinuit vim

Uxore & gnato, mala multa precatus Atridis:

Non ille aut Teucrum, aut ipfum violavit Ulixen.

Verum ego, ut hærentis adverfo litore navis   205

a happy and prosperous Voyage in its Return to *Greece*. With your Majesty's Permission, I shall take the Liberty to propose some Questions, and to make my Replies to the Answers you give me. *Aga* With all my Heart *Ster.* Why does *Ajax*, that celebrated Heroe, who so often preserv'd the *Grecian Army*, and was next in Valour to *Achilles* himself, lie rotting above Ground ? Is it that *Priam* and the *Trojans* may exult, to see that Heroe lie naked and expos'd, by whose good Sword so many of their best and bravest Warriours were depriv'd of the Benefit of being buried with their Ancestors ? *Aga* No such thing I assure you; 'tis because he ran mad, and slew in his Fury a whole Flock of Sheep, crying out, at the same time, that he had kill'd *Ulysses*, *Menelaus*, and my self *Ster* And what were you, when, instead of a Heifer, you sacrific'd the lovely charming *Iphigenia* upon the Altar at * *Aulis* ? Was you right in your Senses? [or *in your right Mind* ?] *Aga* Pray explain your self *Ster.* *Ajax* in a Fit of Madness slew only a few Sheep, and what is that? He offer'd no Violence to his Wife or Son, 'tis true, in his Fury he let fall some unbecoming Imprecations against You and *Menelaus* ; but for *Teucer* and *Ulysses*, whom he mortally hated, he never attempted to do them any Mischief *Aga* But as for me, my View was only to get my Fleet out of a hostile Port, where it was detain'd by contrary Winds, and for that End I, like a prudent General, endeavour'd

---

* *Aulis*, a City of *Bœotia*, situated upon the Streight of *Negropont*, famous for a Harbour belonging to it, where *Agamemnon*, *Achilles*, *Ulysses*, and all the *Grecian Captains* rendezvouz'd, before they set Sail for *Troy*.

to

Eriperem, prudens placavi sanguine Divos.

Nempe tuo, furiose   Meo, sed non furiosus.

Qui species alias, veri scelerisque tumultu

Permixtas, capiet, conmotus habebitur. atque

Stultitiane erret, nihilum distabit, an ira   210

Ajax, cum immeritos occidit, desipit, agnos

Tu, prudens scelus ob titulos cum admittis inanes,

Stas animo? & purum est, vitio tibi cum tumi-
dum est cor?

Si quis lectica nitidam gestare amet agnam;

Huic vestem, ut gnatæ, paret, ancillas, paret au-
rum;

Rufam aut Posillam adpellet, fortique marito 215

Destinet uxorem , interdicto huic omne adimat jus

Prætor, & ad sanos abeat tutela propinquos.

Quid? si qui gnatam pro muta devovet agna,

Integer est animi? ne dixeris ergo ubi prava 220

Stultitia, hic summa est insania qui sceleratus,

Et furiosus erit quem cepit vitrea fama,

Hunc circumtonuit gaudens Bellona cruentis

Nunc,

to appeafe the Gods with Blood   *Ster.* Mad
Prince, fay 'twas with your own Blood, that
you endeavour'd to appeafe them   *Aga.* Yes,
with my own, but that proves not I was mad.
Ster He who forms to himfelf falfe Ideas of
Things, and in Actions of a mix'd Nature is
not able to diftinguifh that which is innocent
from that which is criminal, will be efteem'd
Mad, and it will be all one whether his Errour
arifes from Folly or Anger   If *Ajax* without
Difpute was mad, in flaying fo many innocent
Sheep; are you in your Senfes, when, out of a
vain Defire of Glory, you, like a prudent General (as you fay) commit fo execrable a Wickednefs ?   Can all be right with you, when your
Heart is fwell'd with the Vice of Ambition?
Shou'd a Man bear a Lamb about with him in
a Chariot, richly drefs'd, and attended with a
fuitable Equipage, as if fhe were his Daughter;
fhould he call her his little Dear, and feek out a
proper Husband for her, the Prætor would take
away from him all Power of managing his
Eftate, and give the Care of That and his Perfon
to his fober Relations. And what if a Man, inftead of a Lamb, fhou'd facrifice his Daughter?
Is he in his Wits? Do not offer to fay fo   Folly joyn'd with Impiety is Madnefs in Perfection; 'tis impoffible for any one to be Wicked,
and at the fame Time not to be Mad I dare be
bold to fay, that *Bellona,* who delights in Blood
and Slaughter, hath thunder'd that Mortal out
of his Senfes, who greedily thirfts after honourable Titles, which are as frail and brittle as the
Glafs it felf.

Nunc, age, luxuriam & Nomentanum arripe
    mecum ·

Vincet enim ftultos ratio infanire nepotes.   225

Hic fimul accepit patrimoni mille talenta,

Edicit, pifcator uti, pomarius, auceps,

Unguentarius, ac Tufci turba inpia vici,

Cum fcurris fartor, cum Velabro omne macellum

Mane domum veniant qui cum venere fre-
    quentes,   230

Verba facit leno Quicquid mihi, quicquid & ho-
    rum

Cuique domi eft, id crede tuum; & vel nunc pete,
    vel cras

Accipe, quid contra juvenis refponderit æquus.

Tu nive Lucana dormis ocreatus, ut aprum

Cœnem ego · tu pifcis hiberno ex æquore verris · 235

Segnis ego, indignus qui tantum poffideam aufer;

Sume; tibi decies . tibi tantundem tibi triplex,

Unde uxor media currit de noÇe vocata.

Filius Æfopi deti aÇam ex aure Metellæ

(Scilicet ut decies folidum abforberet) aceto   240

Diluit infignem baccam qui fanior, ac fi

Illud idem in rapidum flumen jaceretvc cloacam?

Quinti

IF we proceed to confider the luxurious Luxury Man, Reafon will tell you that he is as mad as and Intemperance the reft. As foon as *Nomentanus* had got into his Hands a thoufand * Talents, which were another left him by his Father, he immediately gives Or-Kind of der, that all the Fruiterers, Perfumers, Cooks, Madnefs. Poulterers, Fifhmongers, Butchers, Bawds, Pimps, and Buffoons, fhould attend him at his Levy the next Morning. Accordingly they meet The Pimp, being the moft eloquent Man in the Company, makes a Speech for the reft · *Sir,* fays he, *whatever I or my Friends are poffefs'd of, is entirely at your Service; you may command it when you pleafe* Now obferve the Anfwer which this wife young Gentleman returns to this Addrefs. Honeft Huntfman, fays he, I am very fenfible of your good Services; you lie booted all Night in the *Lucanian* Snow, to kill a Boar for my Supper. You, Fifherman, notwithftanding the tempeftuous Seafon, provide Fifh for my Table, whilft I, unworthy of fo great a Bleffing, indulge my felf in Sloth and Idlenefs; 'tis very reafonable, that you fhou'd both be Partakers with me of my prefent Fortune; here, Huntfman, take an Hundred Pounds; there's as much for you, Fifherman; but you, my dear Friend, turning himfelf to the Procurer, fhall have three times that Sum.

BUT thefe Extravagancies are nothing in Comparifon of that of young *Æfop,* who took a very valuable Pearl from the Ear of *Metella,* and diffolv'd it in Vinegar, that at one Draught he might fwallow the Worth of a Million of Sefterces Now was not this Action altogether as mad, as if he had thrown it into the River, or the Common-Sewer?

* A Talent is worth of our Money, 187 *l.* 10 *s*

THE

Quinti progenies Arri, par nobile fratrum,
Nequitia & nugis pravorum & amore gemellum,
Luscinias soliti inpenso prandere coemtas ·   245
Quorsum abeant? sanin' creta, an carbone notati?

   Ædificare casas, plostello adjungere mures,
Ludere par inpar, equitare in arundine longa,
Si quem delectet barbatum; amentia verset.
Si puerilius his ratio esse evincet amare;   250
Nec quicquam differre, utrumne in pulvere, trimus
Quale prius, ludas opus, an meretricis amore
Sollicitus plores : quæro, faciasne quod olim
Mutatus Polemon? ponas insignia morbi,
Fasciolas, cubital, focalia ; potus ut ille   255
Dicitur ex collo furtim carpsisse coronas,
Postquam est inpransi correptus voce magistri?
Porrigis irato puero cum poma, recusat ·
Sume, Catelle ; negat . si non des, optet. amator

Exclusus

THE Sons of *Arrius* were true Brothers in every thing that was foolish and extravagant; so great was their Profusion, that they frequently bought Nightingales at an excessive Price, to gratify their Luxury. What are your Thoughts of such Men as these? Are they in their Senses? Will you absolve 'em, and rank 'em with the Wise, or condemn 'em for their Follies?

IF a Man in Years shou'd make Clay Houses, The Folly have a little Chariot drawn by Mice, ride upon of Love. a Hobby-horse, or play at Even or Odd, wou'd not every one that saw him pronounce him mad? Now if it appears, that it is much more child-ish for a Man to be in Love, and that there is no Difference between building Castles (which Boys generally do at three or Four Years of Age) and sighing and whining for a jilting Mistress; if this excellent Truth be clearly prov'd, let me ask you, Will you do what *Polemon* did, when he was made a Convert? Will you lay aside the Marks of your Distemper, I mean, your foppish Dress? as he, tho' drunk, is said to have stolen his Garland unobserv'd off from his Head, when he grew wise upon hearing the Discourse of the temperate Philosopher * *Xenocrates?*

IF you offer a little Child some Apples when he is angry, he'll be sure to refuse 'em. Take them, my Dear, no, he won't, but if you say he shan't have 'em, then he'll cry for 'em immediately.

---

* *Xenocrates,* a Philosopher of *Chalcedon,* the Disciple of *Plato,* he govern'd the School of *Athens* for 25 Years, he was sent Ambassador by the *Athenians* to *Philip* of *Macedon,* and afterwards to *Antipater,* in which Employ-ment he shew'd an extraordinary Prudence and Modera-tion. He was succeeded in his School by *Polemon.*

I   THIS

Exclusus qui distat? agit ubi secum, eat, an non, 260
Quo rediturus erat non arcessitus; & hæret
Invisis foribus · Ne nunc, cum me vocat ultro,
Accedam? An potius mediter finire dolores?
Exclusit; revocat   redeam? non, si obsecret ecce
Servus non paullo sapientior · O here, quæ res 265
Nec modum habet neque consilium, ratione modoque
Tractari non volt in amore hæc sunt mala bellum,
Pax rursum hæc si quis tempestatis prope ritu
Mobilia, & cæca fluitantia sorte, laboret
Reddere certa sibi; nihilo plus explicet, ac si 270
Insanire paret certa ratione modoque
Quid? cum Picenis excerpens semina pomis,
Gaudes, si cameram percusti forte; penes te es?
Quid? cum balba feris annoso verba palato,

Ædificante

THIS is juft the Cafe of a puleing Lover *, when his Miftrefs has forbid him her Houfe; tho' he knows very well that he fhall return thither uninvited; and that, notwithftanding his Proteftations never more to enter her Doors, he cannot help hankering about 'em; yet being defir'd, he pretends to debate the Matter with himfelf, whether he will fee her again or not: No, fays he, I won't go tho' fhe calls me; I am refolv'd henceforward to put an End to my Sufferings; fhe has turn'd me out of Doors, and now fhe calls me back again, and fhall I return? No, tho' even fhe herfelf fhall come and entreat me But obferve that the Servant is not a little wifer than his Mafter Sir, fays he, Reafon and Moderation are not to be made ufe of in thofe Cafes, which will not admit of them. 'Tis natural in Love, for War and Peace to fucceed each other; and he that endeavours to fix thofe things, which depend upon the Humour and Caprice of Fortune, which, like the Tides and Tempefts, are always changing and in continual Agitation, will fucceed no better, than if he attempted to be mad by Rule and Reafon

You are ftrangely delighted, if you hit the Ceiling with the Kernel of an Apple; Are you in your Wits? when, forgetting your Age, you affect to lifp and fpeak Half-words, the better to ingratiate your felf with your Miftrefs; Are you more in your Senfes than the Man that

---

* Thefe eight Verfes are taken from *Terence's Eunuchus*, *Act* I. *Scene* I which our Poet has very happily imitated Mr *Afcham* (in his fecond Book teaching the ready Way to the *Latin* Tongue) fpeaking of the Ufe of turning Profe into Verfe, fays, that *Horace* has fo turn'd the Beginning of *Terence's Eunuchus*, that he can never compare thefe two Places together, and not admire them, *p* 125.

builds

Ædificante casas qui sanior? adde cruorem 275
Stultitiæ, atque ignem gladio scrutare. modo, inquam,
Hellade percussa; Marius cum praecipitat se,
Cerritus fuit? an conmotæ crimine mentis
Absolves hominem, & sceleris damnabis eundem,
Ex more inponens cognata vocabula rebus? 280
    Libertinus erat, qui circum compita siccus
Lautis mane senex manibus currebat, &, Unum
(Quid tam magnum? addens) unum me surpite
   morti,
Dis etenim facile est, orabat; sanus utrisque
Auribus atque oculis, mentem, nisi litigiosus, 285
Exciperet dominus, cum venderet. hoc quoque volgus
Chrysippus ponit fecunda in gente Meneni.

Jupiter,

builds Houfes of Mud? To this Folly of Love add the Cruelty which is often the Effect of it, by which a bad Jobb is made a much worfe one, and (as the Proverb has it) a * Sword is put into a Mad-man's Hands. What think you of *Marius*, who, having kill'd his Miftrefs *Hellas*, threw himfelf headlong from the Top of a fteep Rock, Was he not diftracted? Or denying him to be mad, will you condemn him as a wicked Man, and, according to your ufual Cuftom, give Names to Things which differ in Appearance, but are in Effect the fame?

THERE was an Old Man, who before he had drank any thing, and after he had regularly wafh'd his Hands, us'd to run about the Streets in a Morning, crying out, O ye Gods, grant that I may never die, 'tis a fmall thing for you to make one Man immortal

THIS Man cou'd both fee and hear perfectly well, but if any Mafter were to fell him, unlefs he delighted in being litigious, he cou'd not warrant him found and perfect; he ought to except his Underftanding.

ALL thefe different Sorts of People are rank'd by *Chryfippus* in the large and numerous Family of the † *Meneny*

---

* Πῦρ μαχαίρα μὴ σαλεύειν, ftir not up the Fire with a Sword, that is, we ought not to inflame Perfons who are already at Variance. See *Dacier's* Life of *Pythagoras*, Symbol the 5th

† The Family of the *Meneny* was one of the moft confiderable among the *Romans*, it receiv'd no ordinary Luftre from *Menenius Agrippa*, who triumph'd o'er the *Sabines*, and was particularly famous for appeafing a very dangerous Infurrection, by that celebrated Apologue of the Members of the Body declaring War againft the Belly. This Family, in the Time of *Horace*, was fall'n to Decay, infomuch that there remain'd but one Perfon of it, who was little better than a Fool.

GREAT

Jupiter, ingentis qui das adimiſque dolores,
Mater ait pueri menſis jam quinque cubantis,
Frigida ſi puerum quartana reliquerit ; illo   290
Mane die, quo tu indicis jejunia, nudus
In Tiberi ſtabit Caſus medicuſve levarit
Ægrum ex præcipiti , mater delira necabit
In gelida fixum ripa, febrimque reducet.
Quone malo mentem concuſſa? timore Deorum. 295

Hæc mihi Stertinius, ſapientum octavus, amico
Arma dedit, poſthac ne conpellarer multus.
Dixerit inſanum qui me, totidem audiet ; atque
Reſpicere ignoto diſcet pendentia tergo.

Stoice, poſt damnum ſic vendas omnia pluris ; 300
Quam me ſtultitiam (quoniam non eſt genus unum)
Inſanire putas? ego nam videor mihi ſanus.
Quid ? caput abſciſſum manibus cum portat Agave
Gnati infelicis, ſibi tum furioſa videtur ?
Stultum me fateor (liceat concedere veris)   305
Atque etiam inſanum · tantum hoc ediſſere, quo me
Ægrotare putes animi vitio. Accipe . primum

Ædificas ;

GREAT *Jupiter*, faith the Mother, who The Folly
giveft and takeft away our Pains, (her Son lying and Mad-
ill of a Quartan Ague, which had held him five nefs of
Months) if my Boy get free of his Diftemper, perftiti-
he fhall ftand in the Morning naked in the *Tiber*, ous
the next Faft-Day Now when Chance, or the
Phyfician, fhall occafion his Recovery, this de-
lirious Mother will be fure to bring the Fever
again and kill her Son, by putting him into
the cold River *Dam* What ftrange and unaccountable Madnefs did poffefs her? *Ster.* She
was over-fuperftitious

Dam to *Hor*

THESE are the Arms which *Stertinius* the
Eighth Wife Man furnifh'd me with, that for
the future I might be reveng'd upon all thofe
that attack me. Whoever henceforward fhall
call me Mad-man, I fhall return him the fame
Compliment, and defire him to look into that
Part of the Wallet which is behind him. *Hor*
In Recompence for your former Loffes, may
you now fell every thing for treble Advantage.
But pray let me know, fince there are feveral
Sorts of Madnefs, which you think I labour
under , for to tell you the Truth, I think that
I am right in my Senfes *Dam.* Did * *Agave*
think her felf mad, when fhe carrv'd her unhappy Son's Head about with her, which fhe
her felf had cut off? *Hor* Well, to make an
ingenuous Confeffion, I am a Fool and a Mad-
man too ; but what do you take to be my particular Diftemper of Mind? *Dam* I will tell

---

* *Agave*, the Daughter of *Cadmus* and *Hermione*, Wife
of *Echion* the *Theban*, by whom fhe had *Pentheus*, who,
defpifing the Myfteries of *Bacchus*, was torn Limb from
Limb by his Mother, in the midft of her *Bacchanalian*
Fury.

N   you,

Ædificas; hoc eft, longos imitaris, ab imo
Ad fummum totus moduli bipedalis   & idem
Corpore majorem rides Turbonis in armis   310
Spiritum & inceffum. qui ridiculus minus illo?
An quodcumque facit Mæcenas, te quoque verum eft,
Tantum diffimilem, & tanto certare minorem?
Abfentis ranæ pullis vituli pede preffis,
Unus ubi effugit, matri denarrat, ut ingens   315
Belua cognatos eliferit. illa rogare,
Quantane? num tantum, fufflans fe, magna fuiffet?
Major dimidio Num tantum? cum magis atque
Se magis inflaret; Non, fi te ſuperis, inquit,
Par eris. hæc a te non multum abludit imago   320
Adde poemata nunc, hoc eft, oleum adde camino;
Quæ fi quis fanus fecit, fanus facis & tu
Non dico horrendam rabiem Jam define. Cultum
Majorem cenfu Teneas, Damafippe, tuis te.
Mille puellarum, puerorum mille furores   325
O major tandem parcas infane minori.

SATIRA

you, in the first Place you build, that is, you are hardly two Foot high, and yet vainly affect to appear as tall as others; when * *Turbo* is in Arms, you laugh at his haughty Strut, and think it not at all agreeable to so little a Body as his is · But is not your Behaviour full as ridiculous? Because *Mæcenas* does a Thing, must you therefore do it, who are so very unlike him, and so very unfit to rival him? An Ox by Chance trod on some young Frogs in the Absence of the old one One that escap'd told his Dam, that a great hugeous Beast trod upon his Brethren, and crush'd them to Pieces. How big was he, said the old one? Was he as big as I am, swelling her self? Bigger by half cries the young one. What, was he so big? reply'd the Dam, swelling her self still bigger and bigger. Oh! Mother, said the Son, forbear your swelling, for you can never be as big as he was, tho' you burst your self with straining

SEE your Character in this Fable, in which your Picture is drawn to the Life; add to this your Inclination to Poetry, which, consider'd with your other Vices, is like throwing Oil into the Fire; tho' I must confess, that, if ever a Poet was not mad, you are not I say nothing how subject you are to Passion *Hor* I entreat your Silence *Dam* Nor of your Extravagance in your Cloaths, which is much greater than your Estate will bear, nor of your Love to— *Hor* Good Dear *Damasippus*, confine your self to a Detail of your own Faults, and be not so severe upon me who am but a Youngster in Comparison of you

* *Turbo*, a Gladiator of small Stature, but very courageous

SATIRA IV.

UNDE, & quo Catius ? Non est mihi tempus
  aventi
Ponere signa novis præceptis ; qualia vincant
Pythagoran, Anytique reum, doctumque Platona.
Peccatum fateor, cum te sic tempore lævo
Interpellarim. sed des veniam bonus, oro.   5
Quod si interciderit tibi nunc aliquid, repetes mox :

            Sive

SATIRE IV.

Horace and *Catius*.

Hor. **CATIUS**, whence come you? whither Precepts so fast? *Cat* I have not Leisure to to be ob- talk with you at present; I am contriving how serv'd in I may make proper Images in my Mind, the making a Feast. better to retain some new Precepts, in comparison of which those of * *Pythagoras*, † *Socrates*, ‡ and *Plato*, are not to be mention'd *Hor.* I beg your Pardon for interrupting you so unseasonably; I was infinitely in the wrong for doing so, but, if any thing has escap'd you for the present, you are so particularly happy both

---

* *Pythagoras*, a Philosopher of *Samos*, the Author of the *Italian* Sect, to avoid the Tyranny of *Polycrates*, he left his Country and return'd to *Crotona*, a Town in that Part of *Italy* which is call'd *Magna Græcia*, where he had a considerable Share in the Government He understood many Sciences, especially the *Mathematicks*, and was the first that took upon him the Title of Philosopher. He liv'd in the Reign of *Tarquinius Superbus*, and not in that of *Numa*, as is generally believ'd, A U C 240.

† *Socrates*, the Disciple of *Anaxagoras*, who, notwithstanding his great Inclination to Study, was not wanting upon Occasion to give signal Proofs of his Courage, in fighting in Defence of his Country: He was possess'd of the whole Train of Vertues, to which he had so habituated himself, that they became natural to him His Thoughts of God were awful and rational, he derided the Plurality of the Heathen Deities, upon which Account being accus'd of Impiety by *Anytus* and *Melitus*, he was condemn'd to Death by the *Athenians* in the 95th *Olympiad*, being 70 Years of Age.

‡ *Plato*, see Book II. *Sat.* III.

Sive est naturæ hoc, sive artis, mirus utroque
Quin id erat curæ, quo patto cuncta tenerem;
Utpote res tenuis, tenui sermone peractas.
Ede hominis nomen, simul & Romanus an hospes 10
Ipsa memor præcepta canam· celabitur auctor.

 Longa quibus facies ovis erit, illa memento,
Ut succi melioris, & ut magis alma rotundis,
Ponere. namque marem cohibent callosa vitellum
Caule suburbano, qui siccis crevit in agris,   15
Dulcior· inriguo nihil est elutius horto.
Si vespertinus subito te oppresserit hospes;
Ne gallina malum responset dura palato,
Doctus eris vivam musto mersare Falerno
Hoc teneram faciet pratensibus optima fungis 20
Natura est   aliis male creditur ille salubris
Æstates peraget, qui nigris prandia moris
Finiet, ante gravem quæ legerit arbore solem.
Aufidius forti miscebat mella Falerno,
Mendose. quoniam vacuis committere venis   25
Nil nisi lene decet. leni præcordia mulso
Prolueris melius. si dura morabitur alvus;
Mitulus & viles pellent obstantia conchæ,
Et lapathi brevis herba; sed albo non sine Coo.

Lubrica

in a natural and artificial Memory, that you will easily recover it. *Cat.* No such thing, I assure you; I was then thinking what Method to pitch upon, the better to retain them The Maxims are fine and curious, and the Expressions have an Air of Delicacy in them *Hor.* Pray, who is the Author ? Is he a *Roman,* or a *Foreigner?* *Cat* No Names I beseech you, as for the Precepts, I'll repeat them, if you please

WHEN you would bring Eggs to Table, remember to make Choice of the long ones, they taste better, and are more nourishing than the round ones, because their Shells have a Male Yolk in them.

THE Colworts that grow in Fields that are never water'd, are sweeter than those which grow in the Gardens without the City-walls, which are tasteless and insipid by being too often water'd

IF a Stranger come upon you unexpectedly in the Evening, and you design to treat him with a Fowl for Supper, to prevent its being tough, dip it while alive in new *Falernian* Wine, and it will eat extreamly tender

THE best Mushrooms grow in the Meadows, the rest are dangerous

LET him who wou'd be healthy in Summer, eat ripe Mulberries after Breakfast, which were gather'd before the Heat of the Day

'TWAS *Aufidius's* Practice to mingle Honey with rough *Falernian* , but in this he was mistaken, for nothing but soft Wine ought to be drunk fasting . The best Draught for the Stomach is soft Wine mix'd with Honey.

IF you are costive, eat Limpins and Cockles; Sorrel mix'd with white *Coan* Wine is an excellent Remedy.

ALL

Lubrica nascentes implent conchylia lunæ   30
Sed non omne mare est generosæ fertile testæ.
Murice Baiano melior Lucrina peloris.
Ostrea Circæis, Miseno oriuntur echini
Pectinibus patulis jactat se molle Tarentum
Nec sibi cœnarum quivis temere arroget artem, 35
Non prius exacta tenui ratione saporum
Nec satis est cara piscis averrere mensa,
Ignarum quibus est jus aptius, & quibus assis
Languidus in cubitum jam se conviva reponet
Umber, & iligna nutritus glande, rotundas   40
Curvet aper lances carnem vitantis inertem
Nam Laurens malus est, ulvis & arundine pinguis.
Vinea submittit capreas non semper edulis.

Fecundæ

ALL Shell-fish are best when the Moon is increasing, but they are not equally good in all Places   The Muscles of the [a] *Lucrine Lake* are much to be preferr'd to the [b] *Baian Murret;* [c] *Circe* has the best Oysters, [d] *Misenum* excells in Crawfish, and the luxurious [e] *Tarentines* do justly boast of their large Cockles.

LET no one pretend to understand fine Eating, unless he knows to Perfection the different Taste of each sort of Meat, and how it ought to be dress'd   'Tis not sufficient for a Man to provide the best Fish at a very great Price, unless he knows which Sort is best to be stew'd, and which, if it were roasted wou'd make the Guests, tho' already satisfy'd, upon seeing them, fall to again with a fresh Appetite

THEY who dis-relish all flabby Meat, should serve up the wild Boar that feeds on Acorns in the *Umbrian* Forest; the Boars of *Laurentum*, which are fatted in Fenny Marshy Grounds, are not near so good

THE Kids, which feed on nothing but Vines, are not fit to be eaten

WHEN a Hare that is so young as not to be past breeding, is serv'd up at Table, if you're

---

[a] The *Lucrine Lake*, famous for its great Plenty of excellent Fish, was between *Baia* and *Puteoli*

[b] *Baia*, a Noble Delicious Town in *Campania*, famous for many stately Villas and Country-Seats, which were round about it, it is parted from *Puteoli* by an Arm of the Sea, about Three Miles in Length, over which the Emperor *Caligula* built a Bridge.   It is now fall'n to Decay.

[c] *Circe*, a little Town and Promontory in *Campania*, not far from *Baia*.

[d] *Misenum*, a little Town and Promontory in *Campania*, not far from *Circe*.

[e] *Tarentum*, see Book I. Sat. VI.

a Man

Fecundæ leporis sapiens sectabitur armos

Piscibus atque avibus quæ natura & foret ætas, 45

Ante meum nulli patuit quæsita palatum.

Sunt quorum ingenium nova tantum crustula pro-
    mit

Nequaquam satis in re una consumere curam

Ut si quis solum hoc, mala ne sint vina, laboret ·

Quali perfundat piscis securus olivo   50

Massica si cælo subpones vina sereno ,

Nocturna, si quid crassi est, tenuabitur aura,

Et decedet odor nervis inimicus . at illa

Integrum perdunt lino vitiata saporem

Surrentina vafer qui miscet fæce Falerna   55

Vina, columbino limum bene colligit ovo

Quatenus ima petit volvens aliena vitellus

Tostis marcentem squillis recreabis & Afra

Potorem cochlea . nam lactuca innatat acri

Post vinum stomacho: perna magis, ac magis
    hillis   60

Flagitat inmorsus refici quin omnia mavolt,

Quæcumque inmundis fervent adlata popinis.

Est operæ precium duplicis pernoscere juris

Naturam. Simplex e dulci constat olivo.

At pingui miscere mero muriaque decebit,   65

Non alia quam qua Byzantia putuit orca:

Hoc

a Man of an exquisite Palate, carve a Wing for your self

I WAS the first who cou'd distinguish by the Taste the several kinds of Birds and Fishes; I cou'd also tell what Age they were of.

SOME content themselves with having found out a new sort of Patees, but to employ all ones Care about one thing, is not sufficient; 'tis, as if a Man shou'd be careful to provide good Wine, and at the same Time be utterly negligent what kind of Oil his Fish is drest with

IF your Massick Wine be thick, set it out of Doors at Night in the Serene, and it will fine it Besides, the Smell of it, which is so bad for the Nerves, will go off But if you strain it thro' Linnen, it will lose its Strength, and become flat and insipid

HE that mingles *Surrentinian* Wine with the Lees of *Falernian*, must remember to fine it down with a Pigeon's Egg; the Yolk will draw all the thick Part to the Bottom

WHEN you have lost your Stomach with hard Drinking, eat roasted Shrimps, or *African* Cockles; some say Lettice is good, but they are mistaken, it swims in the Stomach, turns sowre, and is not easily digested Sausages and Bacon are excellent Things to restore a lost Appetite; even the Meat which is sold at the Cooks Shops, how nasty soever, is much better than Lettice

IT is worth ones while to be nicely inform'd in the Nature of Sauces, of which there are two Sorts, Simple and Compound The Simple is made of pure sweet Oil only; the Compound is best made of new Wine and the Caveare, which comes from * *Byzantium,* and grows to

---

† Non aliâ, quàm *quæ Byzantia* putruit orcâ.

3

its

Hoc ubi confusum sectis inferbuit herbis,
Corycioque croco sparsum stetit ; insuper addes
Pressa Venafranæ quod bacca remisit olivæ.
Picenis cedunt pomis Tiburtia succo :   70
Nam facie præstant. Venucula convenit ollis ·
Rectius Albanam fumo duraveris uvam.
Hanc ego cum malis, ego fæcem primus & allec,
Primus & invenior piper album cum sale nigro
Incretum puris circumposuisse catillis   75
Inmane est vitium, dare millia terna macello,
Angustoque vagos piscis urguere catino
Magna movet stomacho fastidia ; seu puer unctis
Tractavit calicem manibus, dum furta ligurrit
Sive gravis veteri crateræ limus adhæfit   80
Vilibus in scopis, in mappis, in scobe, quantus
Consistit sumtus ? neglectis, flagitium ingens.

Ten'

its proper Degree of Decay in Jars; to these you must add Herbs cut small, and set all together on the Fire; as soon as it boils, put in a little Saffron, and then pour upon it the right *Venafrian* Oil

THE Apples of * *Tivoli* are fairer and more beautiful than those of † *Ancona*, but not so juicy The *Venusian* Grapes must be preserv'd in Pots, those of *Alba* are best dried in the Smoke.

I WAS the first who invented the Fashion of serving up these Apples and Grapes in little Dishes; I was also the Author of the delicious Sauce now so much in Request; 'tis an agreeable Mixture of *Anchovies*, *Vinegar*, *White-Pepper* and *Salt*

'TIS a horrible Crime to lay out a large Sum at Market, and afterwards serve up your Fish in a Dish that is too little for them It turns a Man's Stomach to have Wine given him in a nasty Glass, which the Valet has handled with his greasy Fingers, which but just before he dipt in the Sauce Nor is an antient Family-Cup with Dirt, as it were, incorporated into it, less disagreeable. 'Tis no great Expence to provide your selves with Whiting, Brooms and Rubbing-Cloths, but to be without them is a Crime of the highest Nature

---

* *Tivoli*, a Town in *Campania*, Latin Authors call it *Tibur*, 'tis about 15 Miles from *Rome*, it is much visited by Travellers for its Paintings, Antiquities, Fountains, Palaces and Gardens, which make it one of the finest Places in *Italy*.

† *Ancona*, a considerable City in *Italy*, seated on the Adriatick Sea, belonging to the Pope, the Emperor *Trajan* built the Harbour, and adorn'd it with a Triumphal Arch, which is still remaining.

I

Is

Ten' lapides varios lutulenta radere palma,

Et Tyrias dare circum inlota toralia veſtis ;

Oblitum, quanto curam ſumtumque minorem   85

Hæc habeant, tanto reprehendi juſtius illis,

Quæ niſi divitibus nequeant contingere menſis ?

Docte Cati, per amicitiam Divoſque rogatus,

Ducere me auditum, perges quocumque, memento.

Nam quamvis memori referas mihi pectore cun-

   cta ;   *90*

Non tamen interpres tantundem juveris adde

Voltum habitumque hominis ; quem tu vidiſſe bea=

   tus

Non magni pendis, quia contigit   at mihi cura

Non mediocris ineſt, fontis ut adire remotos,

Atque haurire queam vitæ præcepta beatæ.

S A T I R A

Is it fitting to sweep a Floor of Mosaick Work with dirty Brooms? or to spread a Purple Carpet on a Couch that is not clean? The less Care and Expence there is in these Things, the Fault is the greater, and is more taken notice of by Persons of a good Taste, than if you had been wanting in providing those Dainties, which are only expected at Great Men's Tables.

Hor. O learned *Catius!* I adjure you by the Gods, and by that intimate Friendship with which you honour me, that you carry me where I may hear these Oracles, how distant soever the Place may be. For tho' you repeat them all with a wonderful Exactness, yet forasmuch as you are only an Interpreter, they do not leave so strong an Impression, as if I heard them from the Author himself.

I DEPEND upon you to give me a Sight of this incomparable Man, his Air and Aspect will increase my Satisfaction; you esteem this as nothing, because you have enjoy'd it, but with me 'tis a Matter of no small Importance, who desire with Passion to go as far as to this very Fountain of Science, and to furnish my self with such excellent Precepts, as conduce so much to the Happiness of Life.

SATIRE

SATIRA V.

*H*OC *quoque, Tiresia, præter narrata, pe-*
    tenti
Responde · quibus amissas reparare queam res
Artibus atque modis quid rides? Jamne, dolose,
Non satis est Ithacam revehi, patriosque penatis
Aspicere? O nulli quicquam mentite, vides, ut 5
Nudus inopsque domum redcam, te vate neque
    illic
Aut apotheca procis intacta est, aut pecus atqui
Et genus & virtus, nisi cum re, vilior alga est.
  Quando pauperiem missis ambagibus horres;
Accipe, qua ratione queas ditescere turdus, 10
Sive aliud privum dabitur tibi ; devolet illuc,
Res ubi magna nitet domino sene dulcia poma,
Et quoscumque feret cultus tibi fundus honores,

Ante

SATIRE V.

* *Ulysses* and † *Tiresias.*

Ulys BESIDES what you have already told The Way
me, *Tiresias*, I beg to be inform'd by to get an
you, how I may repair my broken Fortunes : Estate.
What makes you smile ? *Tir* Is it not enough,
thou subtle Fellow, to return to * *Ithaca*, and
see again your Houshold Gods ? *Ulys* Great
Prophet, whose Oracles always prove true; you
see that I am returning home indeed, as you
prophesy'd, but in a naked and indigent Condition : And you are sensible, that at home the
Suitors have devoured all my Cattle, and my
Corn, and other Provisions · And you know,
Tiresias, that Virtue and Nobility without an
Estate, are not worth a Rush *Tir* Since you
deal roundly and plainly with me, and give me
to understand that you are afraid of Poverty ·
Take Courage, Man, I will tell you a Secret
how to grow rich If any one makes you a
Present of wild Fowls, or of any thing else that
is rare and extraordinary, send it immediately to
some old rich Man who has no Children. If
your Garden produces any thing that is excellent, let him be sure to taste it first, even in

---

* *Ulysses*, King of *Ithaca*, an Island in the *Ionian* Sea,
a famous Commander at the Siege of *Troy*, where he continu'd Ten Years, and was Ten Years more wandring
about the Seas, before he return'd to his Kingdom, he
was kill'd, thro' a Mistake, by *Telegonus* his Son by *Circe*.

† *Tiresias*, a famous blind Soothsayer,

Pre-

Ante Larem gustet venerabilior Lare dives :

Qui quamvis perjurus erit, sine gente, cruentus 15

Sanguine fraterno, fugitivus ; ne tamen illi

Tu comes exterior, si postulet, ire recuses.

Utne tegam spurco Damæ latus ? haud ita Trojæ

Me gessi, certans semper melioribus Ergo

Pauper eris Fortem hoc animum tolerare jubebo, 20

Et quondam majora tuli. tu protenus, unde

Divitias, ærisque ruam, dic, augur, acervos.

Dixi equidem, & dico captes astutus ubique

Testamenta senum   neu, si vafer unus & alter

Insidiatorem præroso fugerit hamo, 25

Aut spem deponas, aut artem inlusus omittas.

Magna minorve foro si res certabitur olim ;

Vivet uter locuples sine natis, inprobus, ultro

Qui meliorem audax vocet in jus, illius esto

Defensor   fama civem causaque priorem 30

Sperne ; domi si natus erit, fecundave conjunx

Quinte, puta, aut Publi, (gaudent prænomine molles

Auriculæ)

Preference to the * *Lares* themfelves.   Is he a
Fugitive or perjur'd Perfon ? Is he of a mean
and ignoble Family ? Has he murder'd his Bro-
ther ? What of all this ? If he defires your
Company, never fcruple the Matter, but give
him the Wall and go along with him   *Ulyf.*
What ! Muft I walk Side by Side with [or
Cheek by Jowl with] the infamous *Demetrius?*
I behav'd my felf quite otherwife at *Troy*, there
I always contended with thofe that were my
Betters   *Tir* Then you will die a Beggar.
Ulyf Well, I will make my ftout Soul bear this
too patiently; it has formerly born much greater Evils ; but pray, good Prophet, go on to inform me, how I may grow rich   *Tir* I have
already told you, and do tell you again, that
you muft dexteroufly infinuate your felf into the
Affections of old Men, that they may put you
in their Wills , and tho' one or two be too
cunning for you, and efcape the Bait, be not
difcourag'd, but continue to put my Precepts in
Practice   In a Trial at Bar, let the Matter of
it be little or great, be fure to be on his Side
who is rich and childlefs, notwithftanding that
he be a very wicked Fellow, and brings a litigious Suit againft an honeft worthy Man , if
the other Party be marry'd, if he has Children,
or is like to have any, never trouble your felf
with the Juftice of his Caufe, or with the Character of the Man, 'tis not worth your while to
meddle with it

WHEN you make your Court to the old
rich Man, call him *Quintus,* or *Publius*   The
Slave's Ears love to be tickled with fuch Names
as belong only to *Roman* Citizens ; tell him that

---

* *Lares;* See *Sat* III. *Book* II

his

Auriculæ) *tibi me virtus tua fecit amicum.*

Jus anceps novi : caufas defendere poffum :

Eripiet quivis oculos citius mihi, quam te   35

Contemtum caffa nuce pauperet. hæc mea cura eft,

Ne quid tu perdas, neu fis jocus ire domum, atque

Pelliculam curare jube. fi cognitor ipfe.

Perfta, atque obdura ; feu rubra Canicula findet

Infantis ftatuas, feu pingui tentus omafo   40

Furius hibernas cana nive confpuet Alpis

Nonne vides (aliquis cubito ftantem prope tangens

Inquiet) ut patiens, ut amicis aptus, ut acer?

Plures adnabunt thunni, & cetaria crefcent.

Si cui præterea validus male filius in re   45

Præclara fublatus aletur; ne manifeftum

Cælibis obfequium nudet te, leniter in fpem

Adrepe officiofus, ut & fcribare fecundus

Heres ; & fi quis cafus puerum egerit Orco,

In

his Vertue, and a thousand other prevailing good
Qualities, have made you his Friend; that you
understand the most intricate Points of the Law;
that you are very successful in pleading; and
that you will sooner suffer your Eyes to be torn
out, than see him defrauded, tho' it be but of
a Nut-shell; that it shall be your particular
Care that no Man ridicule him, or do him the
least Injury. This said, you may persuade him
not to trouble himself any further, but to go
home, and take Care of his Health, adding
withal, that you will take the whole Care of
the Cause upon you Then you must be sure to
be indefatigably industrious; you must persevere
and force your Way thro' all Obstacles whatsoever, tho' the Heat or Cold be never so excessive; or (to speak in the Stile of the fat-
gutted _Furius_) whether the Heat of the Dog-
star rends in twain the speechless Statues, or
Jove in Winter spits down hoary Snow upon
the _Alpine_ Mountains Do you not observe,
(saith one of the Standers-by to another, jog-
ging his Elbow) how incredibly diligent this
Man is; How eager he is in the Service of his
Friends ? With what Zeal does he plead, and
how careful is he to omit nothing which may
be serviceable to his Interest ? This is the Way
to draw Fish to your Net; by this Means your
Ponds will never be empty.

THAT it may not appear that you make
your Court only to rich old Batchelors, find
out somebody who has a Son as well as a large
Estate, but let it be such a Son as is of a weak-
ly Constitution; and wind your self by Degrees
into the Father's Favour, that he may appoint
you his second Heir, that in Case his Son die,

you

In vacuum venias. perraro hæc alea fallit.   50
Qui testamentum tradet tibi cumque legendum,
Abnuere, & tabulas a te removere memento
Sic tamen, ut limis rapias, quid prima secundo
Cera velit versu solus, multisne coheres,
Veloci percurre oculo plerumque recoctus   55
Scriba ex quinque viro corvum deludet hiantem,
Captatorque dabit risus Nasica Corano

   Num furis, an prudens ludis me, obscura canendo?
O Laertiade, quicquid dicam, aut erit, aut non
Divinare etenim magnus mihi donat Apollo   60
Quid tamen ista velit sibi fabula, si licet, ede

   Tempore quo juvenis Parthis horrendus, ab alto
Demissum genus Ænea, tellure marique
Magnus erit; forti nubet procera Corano
Filia Nasicæ, metuentis reddere soldum   65
Tum gener hoc faciet tabulas socero dabit, atque
Ut legat orabit . multum Nasica negatas
Accipiet tandem, & tacitus leget , invenietque

you may come in for the Whole. This Artifice seldom fails.

IF any one offers you his Will to peruse, be sure to refuse it; but do it however in such a Manner, as to steal a Look over the second Line of the first Page, that you may know whether you are sole Heir, or whether others are join'd with you

IT frequently happens, that an old cunning * Notary, like *Æsop's* Fox who cheated the Crow, disappoints those Persons who think themselves sure of being his Heirs; and how subtle soever *Nasica* may be, he only gives an Occasion to *Coranus* to laugh at him *Ulys* Are you really inspir'd, or do you delude me with ambiguous Predictions? *Tir.* Hear me, *Ulysses*, every thing that I foretell will be, or will not, *Apollo* has given me the Art of Divination. *Ulys* If then it be lawful, pray explain the Meaning of the Story you told me of *Nasica* and *Coranus* *Tir.* 'Tis this When a young Prince, the Terror of the *Parthians*, who derives his Pedigree from the Great *Æneas*, shall be equally powerful both by Sea and Land; it shall come to pass, that the covetous *Nasica*, who never lov'd to pay his Debts, shall give his Daughter in Marriage to the valiant *Coranus*, in Hopes of being Heir to his Estate *Coranus*, being acquainted with *Nasica's* Design, after some Time gives him his Will to peruse; *Nasica* at first declines it, but being at length prevail'd upon, he reads it over to himself, and finds to his Confusion, that *Co-*

---

* *Scriba ex quinque viro* In the *Roman* Colonies, there were several inferior Magistrates call'd *Quinque Viri*, they who had gone thro' these Offices, had a Right to be Publick Notaries, whose Business it was to take an Account of the Proceedings in the Courts of Judicature.

ranus

Nil fibi legatum, præter plorare, fuifque.

Illud ad hæc jubeo: mulier fi forte dolofa,   70

Libertufve fenem delirum temperet; illis

Accedas focius : laudes, lauderis ut abfens.

Adjuvat hoc quoque   fed vincit longe prius ipfum

Expugnare caput fcribet mala carmina vecors?

Laudato fcortator erit? cave te roget. ultro   75

Penelopam facilis potiori trade. putafne,

Perduci poterit tam frugi tamque pudica,

Quam nequiere proci recto depellere curfu?

Venit enim (indignum) donandi parca juventus,

Nec tantum veneris, quantum ftudiofa culinæ. 80

Sic tibi Penelopa frugi eft. quæ, fi femel uno

De fene guftarit tecum partita lucellum,

Ut canis a corio numquam abfterrebitur uncto.

    Me fene quod dicam factum eft. anus improba
      Thebis

Ex teftamento fic eft elata   cadaver   85

Unctum oleo largo nudis humeris tulit heres ·

Scilicet, elabi fi poffet mortua; credo,

Quod nimium inftiterat viventi cautus adito.

Neu defis operæ, neve inmoderatus abundes.

Difficilem & morofum offendes garrulus ultro. 90

Non etiam fileas. Davus fis comicus; atque

Stes

ranus had left him and his Daughter nothing but an unexhauftible Fund of Grief and Sorrow.

I have yet fomewhat more to fay upon this Subject. When you perceive an old doating rich Fellow to be entirely govern'd by his Man, or Maid-Servant, affociate your felf with them, commend them to their Mafter, and they in return will not be wanting in your Commendations. This Method of proceeding is very fuccefsful; but it will avail you more to gain a perfonal Intereft in him. If you find that he has an Inclination to Poetry, do not neglect to extol his Verfes, tho' never fo bad. I will tell you what happen'd when I was an Old Man: A malicious Woman died at * *Thebes,* who by her Will order'd her Heir to anoint her with Oil, and to carry her naked Body upon his Shoulders to her Funeral Pile. She made this Order, as I fuppofe, with Defign that when dead, fhe might flip out of his hands, who had never ftirr'd from her while fhe was living.

IT concerns you much to obferve a ftrict and prudent Conduct, as you muft be careful not to neglect them, fo on the other hand, you muft be equally careful, that you do not tire them with your Importunities. Men in Years are fickle and morofe, they hate nothing fo much as a prating Fellow; but it does not follow, that you muft therefore be eternally filent. The Example of *Davus* in the Comedy, is very worthy of your Imitation; you muft affect a Reverential Pofture, with your

---

* *Thebes,* a very magnificent City of *Greece* in *Bœotia,* which was utterly demolifh'd by *Alexander* the Great: It was afterwards repair'd, or rather built by *Caffander* the Son of *Antipater,* it is now an inconfiderable Borough call'd *Stives,* fubject to the *Turks.*

Head

Stes capite obſtipo, multum ſimilis metuenti.

Obſequio graſſare: mone, ſi increbruit aura,

Cautus uti velet carum caput · extrahe turba

Oppoſitis humeris. aurem ſubſtringe loquaci. 95

Importunus amat laudari ? donec Ohe jam !

Ad cælum manibus ſublatis dixerit, urgue; &

Creſcentem tumidis infla ſermonibus uti em.

Cum te ſervitio longo curaque levarit;

Et certum vigilans, Quartæ eſto partis Ulixes, 100

Audieris, heres   Ergo nunc Dama ſodalis

Nuſquam eſt ? unde mihi tam fortem, tamque fide-
   lem ?

Sparge ſubinde   &, ſi paullum potes inlacrimare,
   eſt

Gaudia prodentem voltum celare   ſepulcrum

Permiſſum arbitrio, ſine ſordibus exſtrue funus 105

Egregiè factum laudet vicinia   ſi quis

Forte coheredum ſenior male tuſſiet, huic tu

Dic, ex parte tua ſeu fundi, ſive domus ſit

Emtor, gaudentem nummo te addicere   ſed me

Imperioſa trahit Proſerpina. vive, valeque 110

SATIRA

Head inclining a little on one fide; you muft
conquer him by your Civility; if the Wind
blows hard, fee that his precious Head be cover'd If he is in a Crowd, fhoulder all about
you, till you have brought him fafe out of it.
If he loves to talk much, hear him patiently.
If he delights in his own Commendations, be
lavifh in his Praifes; and be fure that you never
leave off extolling him, till, lifting up his
Hands to Heaven, he fays it is enough When
by his Death you fhall at length be freed from
this tedious Service, and, being broad-awake,
fhall hear that *Ulyffes* is Heir to the fourth of
his Eftate, then do not fail to fill the Houfe
with Lamentations, crying out in a mournful
and paffionate Tone, *Demetrius* is no more, the
beft Friend that I had in the World is dead
where fhall I find another Friend fo generous
and faithful as *Demetrius* was? This done, if
poffible, fhed a Flood of Tears; 'tis requifite
alfo to difguife your Joy under a fad and melancholy Afpect If his Interment be committed
to your Care, let it be fumptuous and magnificent, that all the Neighbours may commend
the Pomp and Splendour of it, and if it fo
happen, that any of the Co-Heirs is fomething
Antient, and has a Confumptive Cough, apply
your felf to him, fay, that you are willing to
fell your Part of the Inheritance, be it in Land
or Houfes, for what he pleafes But imperious
* *Proferpine* calls me back to my Abode Live
and be happy.

* *Proferpine,* the Daughter of *Ceres,* and Wife to *Plu-
to,* whom the Poets feign'd to be King of Hell.

SATIRE

SATIRA VI.

HOC erat in votis   modus agri non ita mag-
    nus,
Hortus ubi, & tecto vicinus jugis aquæ fons,
Et paullum silvæ super his foret. auctius atque
'Di melius fecere   bene est. nil amplius oro,
Maia nate,   nisi ut propria hæc mihi munera
    faxis.   5
Si neque majorem feci ratione mala rem,
Nec sum facturus vitio culpave minorem:
Si veneror stultus nil horum, O si angulus ille
Proximus accedat, qui nunc denormat agellum!
O si urnam argenti fors quæ mihi monstret! ut
    illi,   10
Thesauro invento qui mercenarius agrum
Illum ipsum mercatus aravit, dives amico
Hercule: si, quod adest, gratum juvat   hac prece
    te oro,
Pingue pecus domino facias, & cetera præter
Ingenium; utque soles, custos mihi maximus
    adsis.   15

Ergo

SATIRE VI.

A LITTLE Farm, and a pleasant clear Spring, a Garden and a Grove were the utmost of my Wishes; the Gods in their Bounty have exceeded my Hopes, and I am contented. O * *Mercury*, I desire nothing more than that these Blessings may be continu'd to me. If I have neither increas'd my Estate by any base dishonest Practices, nor lessen'd it by Debauchery, If I trouble Heaven with no idle Petitions; if I am not always wishing, that that little Spot of Ground which wou'd make my Garden so uniform and regular, were added to my Possessions; that Fortune wou'd conduct me to some hidden Treasure, as once she did a labouring Hind, who, having † *Hercules* for his Friend, found so much Gold, that he purchas'd the Field which he was ploughing for a-nother If then I make no unnecessary Prayers, if I am easy and satisfied with my present Condition; Continue, I beseech thee, thy wonted Goodness and Protection to me, and grant that my Cattle may be Fat, and that they and all things else belonging to me may be heavy, except my Understanding.

---

* *Mercury*, the Son of *Jupiter* by *Maja*, the Patron of the Poets, the Disposer of Riches, and God of the Fields. He is the same with *Sylvanus*

† *Hercules* the Son of *Jupiter* by *Alcmena*, he was appointed to be *Mercury's* Associate in the Distribution of Riches.

WHEN,

Ergo ubi me in montis & in arcem ex Urbe removi,

Quid prius inlustrem Satiris Musaque pedestri?

Nec mala me ambitio perdit, nec plumbeus Auster,

Autumnusque gravis, Libitinæ quæstus acerbæ.

Matutine pater, seu Jane libentius audis,   20

Unde homines operum primos vitæque labores

Instituunt (sic Dís placitum) tu carminis esto

Principium. Romam sponsorem me rapis: Eia,

Ne prior officio quisquam respondeat, urgue

Sive Aquilo radit terras, seu bruma nivalem   25

Interiore diem gyro trahit, ire necesse est.

Postmodo, quod mî obsit, clare certumque locuto,

Luctandum in turba, & facienda injuria tardis

Quid tibi vis, insane, & quam rem agis? impro-
     bus urguet

Iratis precibus tu pulses omne quod obstat,   30

Ad Mæcenatem memori si mente recurras.

.

Hoc

WHEN, leaving *Rome*, I retire to my little Castle upon a Hill, how can I better employ my Time than in writing *Satires*, in a Stile that comes nearer to Prose than Verse? In this my Solitude, the Charms of Ambition are not able to move me; I find no Inconvenience from the Southern Winds; the sickly Autumn, which is so beneficial to the * Undertakers, affects me not.

[side note: The Benefit and Advantages of a Country Retirement.]

O Father of the Morning! or rather *Janus*, if that Name delights thee more; thou, who presidest at the Birth of all Things, and from whom, by the Decree of Heaven, Men are wont to implore a Blessing on their Labours, be thou propitious to my present Undertaking.

[side note: The Trouble and Fatigue of a City-Life.]

YOU hurry me to *Rome* to be Surety for my Friend. Make haste, say you, lest another prevent you in so humane an Action: Let it Rain or Snow, go I must, tho' the Days be short, and the cold North Wind blows dreadfully boisterous, yet no Excuse will be admitted. Having declar'd my self his Bail, in a very loud distinct Voice, which I may probably repent of hereafter, the next Difficulty is, how to get thro' the Crowd. I push those before me, for not going faster. What wou'd this Fellow have, what, are you mad? Surely you are in mighty Haste, says an impudent Fellow, who liberally bestows his Curses upon me; what, cries he, must you throw down all before you, because you have made an Appointment with *Mæcenas*?

---

* *Libitina*, a Goddess who had a Temple at *Rome*, wherein was kept whatsoever was necessary to Funeral Solemnities, which was bought or borrow'd of the *Libitinarij* as every one had Occasion.

I   THIS

Hoc juvat, & melli eſt; ne mentiar. at ſimul
  atras

Ventum eſt Eſquilias; aliena negotia centum

Per caput & circa ſaliunt latus.   Ante ſecundam

Roſcius orabat ſibi adeſſes ad Puteal cras   35

De re communi ſcribæ magna atque nova te

Orabant hodie meminiſſes, Quinte, reverti.

Inprimat his cura Mæcenas ſigna tabellis.

Dixeris, Experiar Si vis, potes, addit, & inſtat.

Septimus octavo propior jam fugerit annus,   40

Ex quo Mæcenas me cœpit habere ſuorum

In numero · dumtaxat ad hoc, quem tollere rheda

Vellet, iter faciens, & cui concredere nugas

Hoc genus, Hora quota eſt? Threx eſt Gallina Sy, o
  par:

Matutina parum cautos jam frigora mordent   45

Et quæ rimoſa bene deponuntur in aure.

Per totum hoc tempus, ſubjectior in diem & horam

Invidiæ noſter ludos ſpectaverit una.

Luſerit in campo Fortunæ filius, omnes.

Frigidus

THIS laft Expreffion pleafes me, it is Nuts to me, I own, for it is a Folly to diffemble: But this is not all; as foon as ever I reach the *Ef-quilias,* I am prefently befet with a thoufand Suitors. *Rofcius,* faith one, defires you wou'd not fail of being before Eight at the * *Prætor's Tribunal.* The Secretaries (fays another) de-fir'd me to put you in Mind of coming to Town to Day upon fome publick Bufinefs that is new and of great Importance · A third preffes me to get *Mæcenas* to fign his Papers; if I fay, that I will ufe my beft Endeavours, he immediately replies, that I can do it if I pleafe; Sir, I conjure you to give me your Affiftance.

IT is now near Eight Years fince *Mæcenas* firft honour'd me with his Friendfhip, with no other Defign, than to take me with him in his Coach, when he went into the Country, to pafs away his leifure Hours, with asking and anfwering little Trifling Queftions; as, what is it a Clock? Is the *Thracian Gladiator* as brave as the *Syrian?* The Mornings begin to be cold, they feel it to Purpofe, who do not cloath themfelves accordingly, with many other Things of the like Importance, which one may fafely truft with a Blab-Tongue   From that Time I have been more and more envied; this *Horace,* fay they, is Fortune's Favourite, laft Night he was at the Play with *Mæcenas;* Ye-

* The *Romans,* when a Thunder-bolt fell upon a Place without a Roof, took fpecial Care to have a Co-ver built over it, which they call'd *Puteal,* this had the Name of *Puteal Libonis,* fee *Epift* 19 *Book* I. and *Scri-bonium Puteal,* it being erected by *Scribonius Libo,* by order of the Senate. The *Prætor's* Tribunal, ftanding juft by, is often fignified in Authors by the fame Ex-preffion

P   fterday

Frigidus a Roftris manat per compita rumor ·   50
Quicumque obvius eft, me confulit ; O bone, (nam te
Scire, Deos quoniam propius contingis, oportet)
Numquid de Dacis audifti? Nil equidem Ut tu
Semper eris derifor ! At omnes Di exagitent me,
Si quicquam Quid? militibus promiffa Tri-
  quetra   55
Prædia Cæfar, an eft Itala tellure daturus?
Jurantem me fcire nihil miratur, ut unum
Scilicet egregii mortalem altique filenti
  Perditur hæc inter mifero lux , non fine votis,
O rus, quando ego te afpiciam ? quandoque lice-
  bit,   60
Nunc veterum libris, nunc fomno & inertibus horis,
Ducere follicitæ jocunda oblivia vitæ ?

O quando

sterday they perform'd their Exercises together in the * *Field* of *Mars* If the Report of any ill News be spread about the City, I am presently accosted by all that meet me   Sir, say they, you live at Court, you are acquainted with the Emperor's Ministers, hear you nothing of the † *Dacians?* Nothing at all, Sir What will you be always mocking [fooling] us? May I die, if I know any Thing Will the the Distribution of Lands, which *Cæsar* has promis'd to his Soldiers, be in ‡ *Sicily* or *Italy?* I protest to them, that I know nothing of these Matters: they wonder at it, and say to themselves, that I am an excellent Man in keeping a Secret

THUS it is, that I waste away the Day; not without a thousand Prayers and Wishes . O my dear Farm, when shall I see you? When shall I have it in my Power, agreeably to put all Thoughts of Business out of my Head, by spending my Time one while in reading old Authors, and another while in dozing and trifling away the Hours? O delicious Bean, thou near

The Sweets and Pleasures of a Country Life.

---

* The *Campus Martius* was a large open Field lying near the *Tiber*, for which reason it is sometimes call'd *Tiberinus*, it was nam'd *Martius*, from its being confecrated by the old *Romans* to the God *Mars*, here the young Noblemen learn'd the Use of all Sorts of Arms, here they constantly exercis'd themselves in running Races, either with Chariots, or with single Horses

† The *Dacians* are the Inhabitants of *Hungary, Transylvania, Valachia,* and all *Moldavia*, all these are contain'd in the Limits of the antient *Dacia*

‡ *Sicily*, the greatest and most fertile Island in the *Mediterranean Sea*, it was of old joyn'd to *Italy*, but was separated by an Earthquake, or the beating of the Sea, 'tis call'd in Latin *Triquetra*, from its Triangular Form

Relation

O quando faba Pythagoræ cognata, simulque
Uncta satis pingui ponentur oluscula lardo?
O noctes, cenæque Deûm! quibus ipse meique   65
Ante Larem proprium vescor, vernasque procacis
Pasco libatis dapibus · cum, ut cuique libido est,
Siccat inæqualis calices conviva, solutus
Legibus insanis · seu quis capit acria fortis
Pocula; seu modicis uvescit lætius. ergo   70
Sermo oritur, non de villis domibusve alienis,
Nec male necne Lepos saltet. sed quod magis ad nos
Pertinet, & nescire malum est, agitamus; utrumne
Divitiis homines, an sint virtute beati ·
Quidve ad amicitias, usus rectumne trahat nos: 75
Et quæ sit natura boni, summumque quid ejus.
Cervius hæc inter vicinus garrit anilis
Ex re fabellas. si quis nam laudat Arelli
Sollicitas ignarus opes; sic incipit. Olim
Rusticus urbanum murem mus paupere fertur   80
Accepisse cavo, veterem vetus hospes amicum;

Asper,

Relation to the *Great* * *Pythagoras,* when shall I enjoy you? When shall I feed upon Herbs and sweet Bacon? O charming Evenings! O ravishing Entertainments! with which the Gods might recreate themselves. With these, in the Presence of my Houshold Deities, I regale my Friends, and give my saucy Servants what is left at my Table This is our Way and Manner of living; we are under no Constraint of drinking to Excess, here every one is free to fill as he pleases, be it more or less

IN our Conversation we concern not our selves with other Men's Affairs; we never enquire, whether *Cæsar's Mimick* dances well, or ill. Our Thoughts are employ'd on more useful Matters, such as all wise Men are concern'd to know We debate with our selves whether Vertue or Riches do most conduce to the Happiness of Life; whether Reason or Interest should principally direct us in the Choice of our Friends; What is the Nature of that which we call Good, and what is the Chief Good.

MY Neighbour *Cervius* diverts us now and then with a pleasant old Tale, that is much to the Purpose, as we talk of these Things. For Instance, shou'd any one, that is ignorant of the Cares and Anxieties which attend upon Riches, commend *Arellius's* great Estate; he presently cries, I will tell you a Story.

ONCE upon a Time a City-Mouse made a Visit to an old Acquaintance in the Country, by whom he was very kindly receiv'd. The

---

* *Pythagoras* was of Opinion that the Bean was form'd out of the same Corruption as Man, and at the same Time. See his Character, *Book* II. *Sat* IV.

Asper, & attentus quæsitis; ut tamen artum

Solveret hospitiis animum. quid multa? neque ille

Sepositi ciceris, nec longæ invidit avenæ

Aridum & ore ferens acinum, semesaque lardi 85

Frusta dedit, cupiens varia fastidia cena

Vincere tangentis male singula dente superbo:

Cum pater ipse domus palea porrectus in horna

Esset ador loliumque, dapis meliora relinquens.

Tandem urbanus ad hunc, Quid te juvat, inquit,

    amice,   90

Prærupti nemoris patientem vivere dorso?

Vis tu homines urbemque feris præponere silvis?

Carpe viam (mihi crede) comes   terrestria quando

Mortalis animas vivunt sortita, neque ulla est

Aut magno aut parvo leti fuga. quo, bone, circa, 95

Dum licet, in rebus jocundis vive beatus

Vive memor, quam sis ævi brevis.   Hæc ubi dicta

Agrestem pepulere, domo levis exsilit   inde

Ambo propositum peragunt iter, urbis aventes

Mœnia nocturni subrepere   jamque tenebat 100

Nox medium cæli spatium, cum ponit uterque

In locuplete domo vestigia   rubro ubi cocco

Tincta super lectos canderet vestis eburnos;

                                   Multaque

Country-Moufe was of a careful frugal Temper, yet very free in his Entertainments   In
fhort, the beft Peafe and Oats, which for a
long Time had been hoarded up, were immediately produc'd, to thefe were added a dry'd
Raifin and fome Scraps of Bacon, which
were probably the Relicks of a Country Feaft.
This Variety of Meat was ferv'd up in Order,
with Defign, if poffible, to give a new Appetite to his delicate Gueft, who feem'd to touch
every Thing with an Air of Difdain , all this
while the Mafter of the Houfe, ftretch'd at
length upon frefh clean Straw, made fhift to
feed on Tares and Chaff, leaving the beft Pro-
vifion for his Friend   At laft, the City-Moufe
being much diffatisfied with his Entertainment,
fpoke in this manner

" How can you endure, my dear Friend,
" faid he, to live on the Top of this craggy
" Mountain? Do you not think, that Cities
" and Men are preferable to this barren defo-
" late Wildernefs? If you do, go along with
" me , all Terreftrial Beings are fubject to
" Mortality, alas! my Friend, Death cannot
" be avoided, both the Great and Small, and
" all muft die ; let us therefore be mindful of
" the Shortnefs of our Being, let us live while
" Life is continu'd to us, and gratify our felves
" with every Thing that is pleafing

THE Country-Moufe, being charm'd with
this Difcourfe, was eafily perfuaded to leave
his Cell   They both fet forward on their
Journey together, defigning by Night to reach
the City.   They arriv'd about Midnight, and
took up their Quarters in a ftately Palace,
where the Purple Coverings on the Ivory Beds
made a glorious Appearance, but nothing

pleas'd

Multaque de magna superessent fercula cena,

Quæ procul exstructis inei anthesterná canistris. 105

Ergo ubi purpurea porrectum in veste locavit

Agrestem; veluti succinctus cursitat hospes,

Continuatque dapes. necnon verniliter ipsis

Fungitur officiis, prælibans omne quod adfert

Ille cubans gaudet mutata sorte, bonisque   110

Rebus agit lætum convivam: cum subito ingens

Valvarum strepitus lectis excussit utrumque.

Currere per totum pavidi conclave; magisque

Exanimes trepidare, simul domus alta Molossis

Personuit canibus. tum rusticus, Haud mihi

     vita   115

Est opus hac, ait, & valeas: me silva cavusque

Tutus ab insidiis tenui solabitur ervo.

SATIRA

pleas'd our Travellers better than the Remains of an excellent Supper, which lay heap'd in Baskets, one upon another   The City-Mouse, who understood good Breeding perfectly well, had no sooner plac'd his Country-Companion on a Purple Carpet, but, like a good and diligent Host, he plied him with Variety of the choicest Meats, and at the same Time perform'd the Office of a Servant, in tasting every Thing that was laid before him. The Country-Mouse, as he lay upon the Tapestry, was strangely overjoy'd at so happy and unexpected a Change of his Condition, he did all he cou'd to express his Satisfaction; when on a sudden the Door flew open with so terrible a Noise, that they both scamper'd from the Bed they lay upon.   They ran about the Room half distracted with Fear, to encrease their Terror, the Mastiff Dogs made the House to shake with their Barking.   The Country-Mouse, being a little recover'd from his Fright, was in Haste to be gone; at Parting he told his City Friend, that this Noisy Way of living was by no means agreeable to him, that he wish'd him well, that for his Part, he was going again to his little Cell, where, tho' I feed, said he, on Tares and Vetches, yet I lead a Life secure from Danger, which does more than compensate the Loss of your good Cheer.

SATIRE

SATIRA VII.

JAMDUDUM auʃculto; *& cupiens tibi*
      dicere ʃervus
Pauca, reformido Davuʃne? Ita, Davus, ami-
      cum
Mancipium domino, & frugi, quod ʃit ʃatis   hoc
      eʃt,
Ut vitale putes Age, libertate Decembri
(Quando ita majores voluerunt) utere · naria.   5
      Pars hominum vitiis gaudet conʃtanter, & urguet
Propoʃitum pars multa natat, modo recta capeʃʃens,
Interdum pravis obnoxia. ʃæpe notatus
Cum tribus annellis, modo læva Priʃcus inani,
Vixit inæqualis, clavum ut mutaret in horas ·   10
Ædibus ex magnis ʃubito ʃe conderet, unde
Mundior exiret vix libertinus honeʃte:

Jam

SATIRE VII.

Davus and *Horace.*

Dav. HAVING heard you, Sir, a confiderable Time with a great deal of Patience, I paffionately defire to change a few Words with you, but being your Servant I durft not take fo great a Liberty. *Hor* Is it you, *Davus?* *Dav* Yes, *Davus*, your Slave that loves his Mafter, and as to wafting his Goods is free enough from that, that is, not to fuch a Degree as to make you fufpect him of being fhort-liv'd. *Hor* Well, Sir, You may enjoy the Freedom of the prefent * Solemnity, our Fathers allow'd it, come, fpeak your Mind. *Dav* The greateft Part of Mankind are conftantly Vicious, they perfevere in Wickednefs, and are always the fame, others again are ftrangely changeable and inconftant; like thofe who fwim up and down a River, they float as it were, between Good and Evil, one while they are Vertuous, then again they are Vicious.

'TIs obferv'd of *Prifcus*, that he fometimes wears three Rings on his Finger, fometimes he has none; he knows not what he would be at; fometimes he appears in a Magiftrate's Robe, and then prefently again in an ordinary Habit. Sometimes he leaves his ftately Houfe, and takes a Lodging in fuch a Hole, as a cleanly Freed-man would blufh to be feen coming out

A Servant reprimands his Mafter for his unfettled Temper, and for feveral other Vices to which he was fubject.

---

* *Saturnalia.* See Book II. *Sat.* III.

of.

Jam mœchus Romæ, jam mallet doctus Athenis

Vivere. Vertumnis, quotquot sunt, natus iniquis.

Scurra Volanerius, postquam illi justa cheragra 15

Contudit articulos, qui pro se tolleret atque

Mitteret in phimum talos, mercede diurna

Conductum pavit, quanto constantior idem

*In vitiis, tanto levius miser, ac prior** ille*

Qui jam contento, jam laxo fune laborat.   20

    Non dices hodie, quorsum hæc tam putida ten-
      dant,

Furcifer? Ad te, inquam.   Quo pacto, pessime?
    Laudas

Fortunam & mores antiquæ plebis; & idem,

Si quis ad illa Deus subito te agat, usque recuses:

Aut quia non sentis, quod clamas, rectius esse; 25

Aut quia non firmus rectum defendis, & hæres,

Nequicquam cœno cupiens evellere plantam.

Romæ rus optas: absentem rusticus Urbem,

Tollis ad astra levis. si nusquam es forte vocatus

. Ad cenam, laudas securum olus; ac, velut us-
    quam   30

Vinctus

of. He is a Debauchee at *Rome*, and at *Athens* a Philosopher, he is in all Things so inconsistent, that one would think he was born at the Change of the Moon

VOLANERIUS the Buffoon, being lame with the Gout, (which his Intemperance had justly brought upon him) hir'd a Servant to take up the Dice and throw 'em in his stead. The more steady such a Man as that is in Vice, the less miserable, and the more preferable is his Condition than that Man's, who is sometimes vicious, sometimes virtuous, and (as it were) walks one while on the straight Rope, another while on the slack one

Hor SIRRAH, you had best tell me what it is you mean by these Reflections? *Dav.* They are meant of you. *Hor* As how, Rascal? *Dav* You extol the happy Condition of our Ancestors, you commend their Temperance and Chastity and Moderation; and yet should some Divinity require you to live as they did, you would refuse to do so; either because you do not believe what you say to be true, or that you are not steddy in your Resolutions You are still the same, notwithstanding you pretend the contrary; you stick fast in the Mire, and vainly endeavour to pluck your Feet out of it. When you are at *Rome*, you are all for the Country; when in the Country, then nothing so pleasant as a City Life. When no one has invited you to Supper, then you say, that you love to eat in Quiet, and enjoy your Liberty; then

Vinctus eas, ita te felicem dicis amasque,
Quod nusquam tibi sit potandum. jusserit ad se
Mæcenas serum sub lumina prima venire
Convivam; Nemon' oleum fert ocius? ecquis
Audit? cum magno blateras clamore, fugisque 35
Mulvius & scurræ, tibi non referenda precati,
Discedunt. etenim fateor me, dixerit ille,
Duci ventre levem nasum nidore supinor:
Imbecillus, iners, si quid vis; adde, popino.
Tu, cum sis quod ego, & fortassis nequior, ultro 40
Insectere, velut melior? verbisque decoris
Obvolvas vitium? quid, si me stultior ipso
Quingentis emto drachmis deprenderis? aufer
Me voltu terrere· manum stomachumque teneto.
Non sum mœchus, ais neque ego, hercule fur, ubi
      vasa   45
Prætereo sapiens argentea tolle periclum,
Jam vaga prosiliet frenis natura remotis.
Tune mihi dominus, rerum imperiis hominumque
Tot tantisque minor? quem ter vindicta quaterque

Imposita

then you pretend, that whenever you go abroad, 'tis fore against your Inclinations; but if *Mæcenas* sends for you to Supper, tho' it be late, and the Company be just ready to fit down to Table; then, Where's the Oil! quickly: Does no-body hear? Thus you fill the House with Uproar, and make all the Haste you can to *Mæcenas's Mulvius* and others, who hang upon you, are oblig'd to sneak away without Supper; I dare not say what they wish you on that Occasion. Perhaps some one will tell me (and I confess it to be true) that I am a Glutton, that I am a smell-Feast, that I am Slow, Lazy, what you will, nay, that I am a Haunter of the Stews. Now supposing all this to be true, if you are as bad as my self, or perhaps worse, why shou'd you reprimand me, as if you were better, who disguise the Baseness and Deformity of your Vices, by I know not what specious glittering Names? Nay, perhaps you will be found to be a greater Fool than your humble Servant that cost you but Fifty Crowns Lay aside, I beseech you, that surly Countenance, refrain your Passion, and keep your Hands to your self.

You say you are no Adulterer; nor am I a Thief, when I am so wise as to keep my Hands off from Plate, as I go by But take away the Danger of Punishment, and Nature will shew it self in both of us, when its Restraints are remov'd Are you fit to be my Master who have so many Passions and Men for your Masters? The *Prætor* with his * Wand may give you your

The Slavery of being Vicious.

---

* The Ceremony of Manumission was in the following Manner The *Slave* was brought before the *Prætor* by his *Master,* who laying his Hand upon his Servant's Head, said to the *Prætor, Hunc Hominem liberum esse volo,*

3 upon

Imposita haud umquam misera formidine privet? 50

Adde super, dictis quod non levius valeat · nam

Sive vicarius est, qui servo paret, uti mos

Vester ait; seu conservus · tibi quid sum ego?
  nempe

Tu, mihi qui imperitas, aliis servis miser; atque

Duceris, ut nervis alienis mobile signum.   55

  Quisnam igitur liber? Sapiens . sibi qui impe-
    riosus;

Quem neque pauperies, neque mors, nec vincula
  terrent;

Responsare cupidinibus, contemnere honores

Fortis; & in seipso totus; teres atque rotundus,

Externi ne quid valeat per læve morari;   60

In quem manca ruit semper fortuna potesne

Ex his, ut proprium, quid noscere? quinque ta-
  lenta

Poscit te mulier, vexat, foribusque repulsum

Perfundit gelida rursus vocat eripe turpi

Colla jugo . Liber, liber sum, dic age non quis 65

Urguet enim dominus mentem non lenis, & acris

Subjectat

your Freedom as often as he pleases, but it is not in his Power to deliver you from your Fears.

WHAT I am going to say farther, is of no less Weight and Importance than the former: For if he who is under the Direction of a Slave, be he an Underling (as you Masters call him); or be he a Fellow-Slave; then what am I to you? For you who command me, are a down-right Slave to others, and have no more Power over your self than a Puppet which moves by Springs and Wires *Hor* Who then is free? *Dav* The Man that is wife; he who governs himself with an absolute Power, whom neither Poverty, nor Death, nor Chains, are able to affright, who has the Courage to bridle his Passions, and despise Honour; whose Happiness depends only upon himself: Who gathers himself, like a Hedge-Hog, into so round a Shape, that no outward Accident can reach him. In short, upon whom the Attempts of Fortune are unsuccessful Do you know your self, Sir, by any Part of this Character? Your Mistress teazes you to give her Five Talents; she tires you with her Importunities; shuts you in her Passion out of Doors, throws Water upon you, then cooling a little, she calls you back again For Shame, for Shame, deliver your self from so infamous a Bondage, and say, I am free But alas, it is not in your Power to do so,

The Description of a Freeman.

upon which he let him go out of his Hand, then the *Prætor*, laying a Rod upon his Head called *Vindicta*, said, *Dico erm liber im esse more Quiritum* After this, the *Lictor* with the *Prætor's* Rod struck the Servant several Blows on the Head, Face and Back, and nothing now remain'd but to receive a Cap in token of Liberty, and to be enroll'd among the Freemen, with the Reason of his obtaining that Favour.

Q a cruel

Subjectat lasso stimulos, versatque negantem.

Vel cum Pausiaca torpes, insane, tabella;

Qui peccas minus atque ego, cum Fulvi Rutubæque

Aut Placideiani contento poplite miror   70

Prælia, rubrica picta aut carbone, velut si

Re vera pugnent, feriant, vitentque moventes

Arma viri? nequam & cessator Davus: at
    ipse

Subtilis veterum judex, & callidus audis.

Nil ego, si ducor libo fumante · tibi ingens   75

Virtus atque animus cenis responsat opimis?

Obsequium ventris mihi perniciosius est cur?

Tergo plector enim: qui tu inpunitior illa,

Quæ parvo sumi nequeunt, obsonia captas?

Nempe inamarescunt epulæ sine fine petitæ;   80

Inlusique pedes vitiosum ferre recusant

Corpus. an hic peccat, sub noctem qui puer uvam

Furtiva mutat strigili? qui prædia vendit,

Nil

a cruel Mafter keeps you under, the Tyrant Paffion rides you with Spurs till you are tir'd, and turns you which way he pleafes, whether you will or no

Again, When you gaze upon a Piece of * *Paufias*'s, with a Sort of Ecftafie, why are you more to be excus'd than I am, when I gaze on the Prize-fightings of † *Fulvius*, *Rutuba*, or *Placideianus*, which are drawn in Charcoal fo exactly to the Life, with all their feveral Motions and Geftures, that you wou'd think you faw them fighting? Tho' the Folly is the fame, yet you pafs for a mighty Critick in the Paintings of the Antients, but *Davus* is a Rafcal, Loiterer, and what not! I am prefently call'd Rogue, if I follow the Scent of a good fmoaking Cake; but are you, with all your mighty Virtue and Refolution, able to refift the Temptation when invited to fome delicious Supper? 'Tis more dangerous indeed for me to indulge my Appetite, becaufe I am fure of being whipt; but are not you punifhed too, for being fo fond of Difhes that can't be had for a fmall Expence? You find that continual Feafting brings Bitternefs along with it at laft, and your Body is fo pamper'd and bloated, that its tottering Feet cannot fupport it If your Foot-boy by Night fteals a Comb, and trucks it away for a Bunch of Grapes, is he guilty of a Fault? and does the

---

* *Paufias*, a famous Painter of *Sicyone*, the Difciple of *Pamphylus*, Contemporary with *Apelles*

† It was cuftomary, when any Perfon defign'd to oblige the People with a Fight of *Gladiators*, to fet up Bills in publick Places, giving an Account of the Time, Number, and other Circumftances, befides thefe Bills, they fet up great Pictures reprefenting the Manner of the Fight, and the Effigies of fome of the moft celebrated *Gladiators*, whom they intended to bring upon the Theatre

Man

Nil servile gulæ parens habet? adde, quod idem
Non horam tecum esse potes, non otia recte　85
Ponere; teque ipsum vitas fugitivus & erro,
Jam vino quærens, jam somno fallere curam·
Frustra　nam comes atra premit, sequiturque fu-
　　gacem.
　　Unde mihi lapidem? Quorsum est opus? Unde
　　　sagittas?
Aut insanit homo, aut versus facit Ocius hinc te　90
Ni rapis, accedes opera agro nona Sabino.

SATIRA VIII.

UT Nasidieni juvit te cena beati?
　　Nam mihi convivam quærenti, dictus here
　　illic
De medio potare die. Sic, ut mihi numquam

Man who fells his Eftate to gratify his Palate, do nothing mean and fervile? Befides, Can you bear being alone, tho' it be but for an Hour? Know you how to employ that little Time that lies upon your Hands? Like an idle Vagabond you fly from your felf, you try to drive away Care fometimes with Drinking, fometimes with Sleeping, but all to no Purpofe, the unwelcome Companion preffes you hard, you cannot fly from it *Hor* Where fhall I find a Stone? *Dav* At whom wou'd you throw it? *Hor* O that I had an Arrow! *Dav* My Mafter is either mad, or making Verfes. *Hor* Villain, be gone; if you ftay but a Moment, I will fend you forthwith to thofe eight Slaves, who are now working at my Farm.

SATIRE VIII.

Horace and * *Fundanius.*

Hor. I SENT you Yefterday an Invitation, and Word was brought me, that you went out about One, to take a Repaft with the happy † *Nafidienus*, pray how did you like your Enter-

A Defcription of a Feaft.

---

* *Fundanius,* an excellent Comedian. See *Book* I *Sat* X.
   N B. † Notwithftanding that *Dacier* and others have fuppos'd this *Nafidienus* to have been a rich, but fordid miferly *Roman,* and that this Feaft fhews his Temper, yet nothing in this Satyr fhews it, unlefs the Expreffions be forc'd and turn'd from their natural Senfe, as they are by *Dacier* for that Purpofe. He was a rich Coxcomb, and the Raillery of the Satyr turns upon his

Q 3

cha-

In vita fuerit melius. Dic (si grave non est)

Quæ prima iratum ventrem placaverit esca.   5

In primis Lucanus aper. leni fuit Austro

Captus, ut aiebat cenæ pater; acria circum

Rapula, lactucæ, radices, qualia lassum

Pervellunt stomachum, siser, allec, fæcula Coa.

His ubi sublatis, puer alte cinctus acernam   10

Gausape purpureo mensam perterfit, & alter

Sublegit quodcumque jaceret inutile, quodque

Posset cenantis offendere, ut Attica virgo

Cum sacris Cereris, procedit fuscus Hydaspes

Cæcuba vina ferens; Alcon, Chium maris expers 15

Hic herus; Albanum, Mæcenas, sive Falernum

Te magis adpositis delectat, habemus utrumque

Divitias miseras! sed quis cenantibus una,

Fundani, pulchre fuerit tibi, nosse laboro.

Summus ego, & prope me Viscus Thurinus, &

infra   20

(Si

Entertainment? *Fun* I was never better pleas'd
in all my Life. *Hor.* If it be not too much
Trouble, pray tell me what was the first Dish
brought upon the Table *Fun* The first was
a *Lucanian* Boar, which, as the Master of the
Feast inform'd us, was taken in Time, when
little or no South Wind was stirring; it was
garnish'd with Roots, Radishes, Lettice and
Skerrets, which are excellent Things to sharpen
the Appetite; the Sauce was Anchovies dissolv'd
in the Lees of *Coan* Wine The first Course
being remov'd, a Servant came in and wip'd the
Maple Table with a Purple Napkin, while another was employ'd in removing every thing
which lay in the Way, and might be offensive
to the Guests at Supper When this was done,
his Black, *Hydaspes*, like an *Athenian* Virgin
carrying the Vessels of the Goddess *Ceres*, with
a solemn Majestick Pace, enter'd the Room,
bringing *Cæcuban* Wine along with him; *Alcon* follow'd with some *Chian* that had no Mixture of Sea-Water in it Upon this our Host
said to *Mæcenas*, Sir, If *Albanian* or *Falernian*
Wines please you better than these upon the
Table, we have both *Hor* What a ridiculous rich Fellow this is! But I long to know
who were the Company at this Feast, where
you were made so much of, *Fundanius Fun.*
I lay at the Top of one * Bed, *Viscus
Thurinus*

characterizing and commending all his Dishes, and his
being at a great Expence to make a Feast, where every
thing was ill-judg'd and ill-pair'd, both the Dishes and
the Guests

* The Beds on which the *Romans* lay down to eat,
were usually of the same Shape and Make, and did generally hold no more than three Persons. Over these
they threw a kind of Quilt stuff'd with Feathers, call'd

Q 4

Cul-

(*Si memini*) *Varius*; *cum Servilio Balatrone*
Vibidius, *quos Mæcenas adduxerat umbras:*
Nomentanus erat super ipsum; *Porcius infra*,
Ridiculus totas simul absorbere placentas.
Nomentanus ad hoc, qui, si quid forte lateret,   25
Indice monstraret digito nam cetera turba,
Nos inquam, cenamus avis, conchylia, piscis,
Longe dissimilem noto celantia succum ·
Ut vel continuo patuit, cum passeris assi, &
Ingustata mihi porrexerat ilia rhombi.   30
Post hoc me docuit melimela rubere, minorem
Ad lunam delecta. quid hoc intersit, ab ipsa
Audieris melius. tum Vibidius Balatroni;

Nos,

Thurinus was next to me, and if I remember right, *Varius* was below him; on another Bed lay *Mæcenas* with *Balatro* and *Vibidius*, whom he brought along with him · The laſt had on it *Nomentanus* and *Porcius*, with *Nasidienus* lying between them. *Porcius*'s Buſineſs was (it ſeems) to make us laugh at his ſwallowing down whole Cuſtards at a Mouthful : But *Nomentanus*'s was this, If there was any Rarity which no body took Notice of, to point to it with his Finger, and make the Company obſerve it. For we, I mean the reſt of the Company, in all the Fowl and Fiſh which we ate of, found a Taſte very different from what we were acquainted with ; which he ſoon ſhew'd me by helping me to ſome of the Row of roaſted Plaiſe and of Turbot, ſuch as I had never taſted before He afterwards acquainted me with a conſiderable Secret ; the Apples of Paradiſe, ſaid he, are reddeſt when the Moon's in her Decreaſe ; what Advantage that is, he himſelf beſt can tell you Come on, ſaid

Culcitra On this Carpet were laid *Pulvini*, Pillows or Cuſhions for the Gueſts to lean their Backs upon.

As to the Manner of the Entertainment, the Gueſts in the firſt Place bath'd with the Maſter of the Feaſt, and then chang'd their ordinary Cloaths for the *Vestis Convivalis*, which was a light kind of Frock, the Slaves at the ſame time pull'd off their *Soleæ*, that they might not dirty the Carpet, which was commonly very rich As to their Places, the firſt Man lay at the Head of the Bed, reſting the Forepart of his Body on his left Elbow, having a Cuſhion to prop up his Back, the next Man lay with his Head towards the Feet of the firſt, from which he was guarded by the Cuſhion that ſupported his Back, which commonly reach'd to the Navel of the other Man, the reſt were diſpos'd in the ſame Manner. Being ſettled on the Beds they waſh'd their Hands, after which they were ſerv'd with Garlands of Roſes, and other Flowers; the moſt honourable Place was the middle Bed, and the Middle of that.

Vibidius,

Nos, nisi damnose bibimus, moriemur inulti:
Et calices poscit majores. vertere pallor   35
Tum parochi faciem, nil sic metuentis ut acris
Potores: vel quod maledicunt libertus; vel
Fervida quod subtile exsudant vina palatum
Invertunt Allifanis vinaria tota
Vibidius Balatroque, secutis omnibus · imi   40
Convivæ lecti nihilum nocuere lagenis
Adfertur squillas inter muræna natantis
In patina porrecta. sub hoc herus, Hæc gravida,
    inquit,
Capta est; deterior post partum carne futura
His mixtum jus est; oleo, quod prima Venafri 45
Pressit cella; garo de succis piscis Hiberi;
Vino quinquenni, verum citra mare nato,
Dum coquitur; cocto Chium sic convenit, ut non
Hoc magis ullum aliud; pipere albo, non sine aceto,
Quod Methymnæam vitio mutaverit uvam.   50
Erucas viridis, inulas ego primus amaras
Monstravi incoquere; inlotos Curtillus echinos,
Ut melius muria, quam testa marina remittit
    Interea suspensa gravis aulæa ruinas
In patinam fecere, trahentia pulveris atri   55
Quantum non Aquilo Campanis excitat agris.
Nos majus veriti, postquam nihil esse pericli
Sensimus, erigimur Rufus posito capite, ut si

                                     Filius

Vibidius, turning himself to *Balatro*, this Fellow will talk us to Death, and we shall die unreveng'd, unless we drink him dry, upon this he call'd for larger Glasses The Words were no sooner out of his Mouth, but *Nasidienus* turn'd as pale as Death; he fear'd nothing so much as your hard Drinkers, either because they are apt to take too great a Liberty in their Raillery, or because they lose all their Delicacy of Taste for choice Eating *Vibidius* and *Balatro* with their large Glasses quickly emptied the Bottles, the rest of the Company follow'd their Example, but the Bottles were little the worse for *Nasidienus* and his two Companions. Whilst the Bumpers went thus merrily round, a Lamprey, with Shrimps swimming in the Sauce, in a large great Dish, was set upon the Table · This Lamprey, said our Host, was taken with Young; when once they have spawn'd they are good for nothing; and then for the Sauce, 'tis made of the purest *Venafrian* Oil, the Pickle of a Lobster, and while it is boiling we pour in some *Italian* Wine full five Years old; but after it has once boil'd, then nothing is so good as a little *Chian* Wine, with white Pepper and some *Lesbian* Vinegar. I was the Man who found out the Secret of boiling green Roquets and Elicampane, but *Curtillus* was the first who boil'd Crawfish without washing them in fresh Water, which are better than the Cavear which is brought over in stinking Pots from *Byzantium*.

As he was going on, the Hangings fell down upon the Dish, and made a greater Dust than ever the North-Wind was known to raise in all *Campania* At first we were afraid that it was something worse, but when we saw that there was no Danger, we took Heart again. *Nasi-*

Filius inmaturus obiſſet, flere. quis eſſet
Finis, ni ſapiens ſic Nomentanus amicum   60
Tolleret? Heu, Fortuna, quis eſt crudelior in nos
Te Deus? ut ſemper gaudes inludere rebus
Humanis! Varius mappa conpeſcere riſum
Vix poterat. Balatro ſuſpendens omnia naſo,
Hæc eſt conditio vivendi, aiebat. eoque   65
Reſponſura tuo numquam eſt par fama labori
Tene, ut ego accipiar laute, torquerier omni
Sollicitudine diſtrictum; ne panis aduſtus,
Ne male conditum jus adponatur; ut omnes
Præcincti recte pueri comtique miniſtrent?   70
Adde hos præterea caſus   aulæa ruant ſi,
Ut modo; ſi patinam pede labſus frangat agaſo.
Sed convivatoris, uti ducis, ingenium res
Adverſæ nudare ſolent, celare ſecundæ.
Naſidienus ad hæc. Tibi Di, quæcumque preceris, 75
Commoda dent; ita vir bonus es, convivaque comis:
Et ſoleas poſcit. tum in lecto quoque videres

Stridere

dienus fell down upon the Bed, weeping and mourning, as if he had lost his only Son: He had continued his Lamentations, had not *Nomentanus* wisely interpos'd with some Words of Consolation Oh! Fortune, said he, thou of all the Divinities art our greatest Enemy. How thou takest a Pleasure in sporting with poor Mortals? *Varius*, tho' he put his Napkin to his Mouth, cou'd scarcely refrain from laughing; but *Balatro*, who was wont to railly every thing, immediately reply'd, 'Tis the hard Condition of human Life, that all our Joys are mix'd and unsincere: You must not expect, that Fame can ever do Justice to your Merits Why shou'd you suffer these Afflictions, to entertain others? Why shou'd you trouble and perplex your self lest the Bread be burnt, or the Sauce ill season'd? That your Servants be decently dress'd, or that they do their Duty in their several Stations? There are many other intervening Accidents which are not less afflicting . For Instance, if the Hangings shou'd fall down, as they did just now; or if a Groom shou'd come stumbling in, and break a Dish But let this be your Comfort, 'tis with a Master of a Feast, as with a General of an Army, it often happens that Adversity shews his Genius which had never been known in Prosperity May the Gods (said *Nasidienus* upon this) always hear your Prayers favourably , you are so good a Man, and a Guest so ready to excuse all Faults This said, he call'd for his * Slippers Upon this a general Whisper ran

---

* *Solea*, a Sort of Sandals without any upper Leather, so that they cover'd only the Sole of the Foot, being fastned above with Straps and Buckles They properly belong'd to the Ladies, and therefore were esteem'd as

scanda-

a

Stridere secreta divisos aure susurros.

Nullos his mallem ludos spectasse · sed illa

Redde, age, quæ deinceps risisti Vibidius dum 80

Quærit de pueris, num sit quoque fracta lagena,

Quod sibi poscenti non dentur pocula , dumque

Ridetur fictis rerum, Balatrone secundo

Nasidiene, redis mutatæ frontis, ut arte

Emendaturus fortunam deinde secuti 85

Mazonomo pueri magno discerpta ferentes

Membra gruis, sparsi sale multo non sine farre,

Pinguibus & ficis pastum jecur anseris albi,

Et leporum avolsos, ut multo suavius, armos,

Quam si cum lumbis quis edit tum pectore adusto, 90

Vidimus & merulas poni, & sine clune palumbis,

Suavis res, si non causas narraret earum, &

Naturas dominus: quem nos sic fugimus ulti,

Ut nihil omnino gustaremus; veluti si

*Canidia adflasset, pejor serpentibus * atris* 95

* I read *Afris*, for *ater* is not an Epithet for *Serpens,*
tho' *atra* be for *Vipera*, as in Od. l. 3 Book. IV. but
the *African* Serpents are often mention'd by the Poets.

Q HORA-

ran thro' the Company; nothing certainly in Nature cou'd be more diverting, 'twas a perfect Comedy.

Hor. HAD you nothing else to laugh at?

Fun. YES, truly, Ho Boys, said *Vibidius,* are the Bottles all broke, that you give me no Wine when I call for it? While we were laughing at this Jest, which *Balatro* mimick'd admirably well, *Nasidienus* return'd with a joyful Countenance, having by his Wit repair'd his Misfortune; his Boys follow'd him with a prodigious Dish, wherein was a Crane cut up and grill'd with Salt and Flower; the Liver of a white Goose who was fatted with Figs; several Wings of Hares, which (as he said) eat much the sweeter when cut off from the Loins. We had serv'd up too some over-roasted Blackbirds and Pidgeons without Rumps; all which I must confess were very excellent in their Kind, and would have been very grateful to us, if the Master had not been so confoundedly troublesome in his Lectures upon them We reveng'd our selves upon him for his tedious Harangues, in rising from the Table without touching a Morsel, as if his Victuals had been blown upon by *Canidia,* whose Breath is worse than that of an *African Serpent.*

scandalous in the other Sex Cicero exposes *Verres* and *Clodius* for wearing them, and we are inform'd by *Livy,* that the Great *Scipio* was censur'd on this very Account.

Q. HORATII
FLACCI EPISTOLARUM

LIBER PRIMUS.

EPISTOLA I.

Ad Mæcenatem.

PRIMA dicte mihi, summa dicende camena,
 Spectatum satis, & donatum jam rude,
  quæris,
Mæcenas, iterum antiquo me includere ludo
Non eadem est ætas, non mens. Veianius, armis
Herculis ad postem fixis, latet abditus agro;   5

Ne

HORACE's EPISTLES.

BOOK I.

EPISTLE I.

To MÆCENAS.

MÆCENAS, as my Verſes began, they muſt end with you   I have long ſince bid adieu to the *Muſes*, have gain'd ſome Reputation, and receiv'd my * Diſcharge. Why wou'd you bring your Poet again upon the Stage? Alas! I have more of Years, and leſs of Vigour of Mind about me   † *Vejanius* did wiſely in hanging up his Arms in *Hercules*'s Temple; he now lives quiet and retir'd in the

---

* The *Rudis* was a Mark of Favour conferr'd upon thoſe *Gladiators* that came off Conquerors, if the Perſon that obtain'd it was a Slave, it procur'd him a Diſcharge from any farther Performance in Publick, if a Freeman, it reſtor'd him to a full Enjoyment of his Liberty

† 'Twas a Cuſtom for all Perſons when they laid down any Art or Employment, to conſecrate the proper In-ſtruments of their Profeſſion to the particular Deity who preſided over it, in Conformity to which the *Gladiators*, when diſcharg'd, hung up their Arms to *Hercules*, who had a *Temple* by every *Amphitheatre*.

R   Country,

Ne populum extrema totiens exoret arena.
Eft mihi purgatam crebro qui perfonet aurem;
Solve fenefcentem mature fanus equum, ne
Peccet ad extremum ridendus, & ilia ducat.
Nunc itaqꝫ & verfus & cetera ludicra pono.   10
Quid verum atque decens, curo & rogo, & omnis in
    hoc fum.

Condo, & conpono, quæ mox depromere poffim
Ac ne forte roges, quo me duce, quo lare tuter.
Nullius addictus jurare in verba magiftri,
Quo me cumque rapit tempeftas, deferor hofpes. 15
Nunc agilis fio, & merfor civilibus undis,
Virtutis veræ cuftos, rigidufque fatelles.
Nunc in Ariftippi furtim præcepta relabor,
Et mihi res, non me rebus, fubjungere conor.
Ut nox longa, quibus mentitur amica, diefque   20
Lenta videtur opus debentibus   ut piger annus

Pupillis,

Country, and is no longer under the miſerable Neceſſity of ſupplicating the Grace and Favour of the People, when diſtreſs'd by his * Adverſary

I HEAR a Voice perpetually ſounding in my Ears, turn an old Horſe looſe, and do not any longer run Races with him, leſt he flag in the Courſe, and loſe the Glory of his former Conqueſts For this Reaſon I now take my Leave of Lyrick Verſe, and of all other trifling Amuſements whatſoever, I am now employ'd in ſearching after Truth, and what we call the *Decorum* in Life; and in this Search my whole Time is taken up Something of this Sort I am compoſing, which I may publiſh hereafter. Don't ask me what Sect or Party I am of, for I tie my ſelf down to the Tenets of no one Maſter in Philoſophy, but ſail juſt as the Stream carries me · Sometimes I am all for an Active Life, and plunge my ſelf over Head and Ears in Publick Affairs, following however the Rules of the trueſt and ſtricteſt Virtue: At other times I ſteal back again into the Precepts of † *Ariſtippus*, and preferring a pleaſant Life before a virtuous one, I try to make my Circumſtances comply with my Temper, inſtead of ſhaping my Temper to them, as I ought to do. As the Night ſeems long to an impatient Lover, whoſe Miſtreſs has deceiv'd him; as the Day ſeems ſlow to the weary Labourer who muſt work till

* When a *Gladiator* was worſted, he ſubmitted his Arms, acknowledg'd himſelf conquer'd, but this was not ſufficient to ſave his Life without the Conſent of the People, and therefore he made Application to them to pity him

† *Ariſtippus,* ſee Book II Sat III

Evening;

Pupillis, quos dura premit cuftodia matrum:
Sic mihi tarda fluunt ingrataq, tempora, quæ fpem
Confiliumque morantur agendi gnaviter id, quod
Æque pauperibus prodeft, locupletibus æque;   25
Æque neglectum pueris fenibufque nocebit.
Reftat, ut his ego me ipfe regam folerque elementis:
Non poffis oculos quantum contendere Lynceus;
Non tamen idcirco contemnas lippus inungui:
Nec, quia defperes invicti membra Glyconis,   30
Nodofa corpus nolis prohibere cheragra.
Eft quadam prodire tenus, fi non datur ultra.
Fervet avaritia, miferoque cupidine pectus?
Sunt verba & voces, quibus hunc lenire dolorem
Poffis, & magnam morbi deponere partem.   35
Laudis amore tumes? funt certa piacula, quæ te
Ter pure lecto poterunt recreare libello
Invidus, iracundus, iners, vinofus, amator;

Nemo

Evening; as the Years are heavy and tedious to a Minor who is under the Government of a ftrict Mother; no lefs tedious and irkfome are the Nights and Days and Years to me, till I can bring my felf to the fteady Practice of thofe Precepts, which, if duly obferv'd, will be equally profitable both to the Rich and Poor, but if neglected, will be equally ruinous to the Old and the Young

It remains therefore that I comfort my felf, and govern my Life by thefe following Maxims. If your Eyes are fore, will you neglect to anoint them becaufe you cannot fee as far as * *Lynceus* could? Will you refufe to be cur'd of the Gout, becaufe you defpair of † *Glycon*'s Strength? It is fome Satisfaction to have made what Progrefs we cou'd in Wifdom, when we can go no farther.

Are you given to Covetoufnefs? Do you thirft after Riches? There are Rules and Precepts which will foften the Paffion, and, in a great Meafure, take away the Diftemper. Are you defirous of Glory? There are certain Remedies, which, upon your carefully reading the Book that contains 'em, ‡ thrice over, will reftore you to your felf. The Envious and Paffionate, the Drunkard, the Debauch'd and Idle Perfon may be reform'd; nay, even the moft

---

* *Lynceus,* the Son of *Aphareus,* had fo piercing a Sight, that, if you will believe the Poets, he cou'd fee what was done in Heaven and Hell, the Ground of this Fable was, that he underftood all the fecret Powers of Nature, Celeftial and Terreftrial.

† *Glycon,* a Philofopher, who was very remarkable for his great Strength.

‡ He ridicules the Superftition of the Stoicks, who held the Number 3 to be fecret and myfterious.

Brutal

Nemo adeo ferus eft, ut non mitefcere poffit,
Si modo culturæ patientem commodet aurem.   40

Virtus eft, vitium fugere; & fapientia prima,
Stultitia caruiffe. vides, quæ maxima credis
Effe mala, exiguum cenfum, turpemque repulfam,
Quanto devites animi capitifque labore
Inpiger extremos curris mercator ad Indos,   45
Per mare pauperiem fugiens, per faxa, per ignis
Ne cures ea, quæ ftulte miraris & optas,
Difcere, & audire, & meliori credere non vis?
Quis circum pagos & circum compita pugnax
Magna coronari contemnat Olympia, cui fpes,   50
Cui fit conditio dulcis fine pulvere palmæ?

Vilius eft auro argentum, virtutibus aurum
O cives, cives, quærenda pecunia primum eft;
Virtus poft nummos. hæc Janus fummus ab imo
Prodocet, hæc recinunt juvenes dictata fenefque,   55
Lævo fufpenfi loculos tabulamque lacerto
Eft animus tibi, funt mores, eft lingua fidefque;
Sed quadringentis fex feptem millia defint;

Plebs

Brutal Nature may be tamed, if he will but patiently lend an Ear to Inſtruction

THE Beginning of Virtue is to avoid Vice, and the firſt Step to Wiſdom is not to be a Fool. Do you not obſerve what Pains of Mind and Body Men take to eſcape the two great Evils of Life, Poverty and Diſgrace? To avoid being poor, the unwearied Merchant makes a Voyage to the *Indies,* neither Rocks nor Tempeſts can obſtruct his Paſſage And won't you ſubmit to hear, and learn, and take Advice from ſuch as are able to give it, that you may be free from all Care about thoſe things, which it is a Folly to admire and long after? What Wreſtler wou'd chooſe to contend in Villages, rather than at the * *Olympick* Games, if he were ſure to carry away the Prize without any Difficulty? Silver is not to be compar'd with Gold, nor Gold with Virtue; and yet, 'tis the general Cry from one End of † *Janus* Street to the other, O Citizens! Citizens! get Money, firſt of all get Money, as for Virtue ſeek it afterwards Both Young and Old, with their Bags and Tables on their Arms, ſing conſtantly this Tune You are a Man (ſay they) of untainted Integrity, wiſe, valiant and eloquent; and yet, if you have not Four Hundred Thouſand Seſterces, if but Six or Seven Thouſand are

---

* The *Olympick* Games were inſtituted by *Hercules,* A M 2836 They were celebrated every four Years upon the Banks of *Alphæus* near *Piſa* in *Elis,* a Province of the *Peloponneſus,* theſe Games were reſtor'd by *Iphitus* 442 Years after their firſt Inſtitution, about 22 or 23 Years before the Building of *Rome* The Deſign of this Inſtitution was to accuſtom the *Young Grecians* to Running, Leaping, and other Manly Exerciſes They continu'd but five Days, the Victor was call'd *Olympionices,* and to be crown'd there, was as glorious as to triumph at *Rome.*

† See *Book* II *Sat* III.

wanting,

Plebs eris. at pueri ludentes, Rex eris, aiunt,
Si recte facies. Hic murus aheneus efto,   60
Nil confcire fibi, nulla pallefcere culpa.
Rofcia, dic fodes, melior lex, an puerorum eft
Nænia, quæ regnum recte facientibus offert,
Et maribus Curiis, & decantata Camillis?
Ifne tibi melius fuadet, qui rem facias, rem   65
Si poffis recte; fi non, quocumque modo rem;
Ut propius fpectes lacrymofa poemata Pupi:

An

wanting, notwithstanding your good Qualities, you shall still be a [a] *Plebeian* But the little Boys in their ordinary Pastimes reason much better; Do well, say they, and you shall be a King Let us regulate our Conduct by this admirable Precept; let this be our constant perpetual Security, never to do any thing which will wound our Consciences, and make us to look pale and be asham'd

Now which is better? [b] *Roscius*'s Law, or the Boy's Song, which bestows a Kingdom on those that do well? The [c] *Curij*, [d] *Camilli*, and the noblest *Romans*, sung this Song, and their Practice was accordingly. This Man persuades you all he can to get Money, that you may sit nearer to the Stage in the Play-house when [e] *Pupius*'s Plays are acted, which draw

Tears

[a] See *Book* I *Sat* I.

[b] *Lex Roscia*, the Author *L. Roscius Otho*, *Tribune* of the People, ordain'd, that none should sit in the first Fourteen Seats of the *Theatre*, unless they were worth Four Hundred Thousand Sesterces; he likewise order'd that no Freeman, or Son of a Freeman, should have the Privilege of being Knighted

[c] *M. Curius Dentatus*, a *Roman Consul*, famous for his Victories over the *Samnites*, *Sabines*, and *Lucanians*. After these Conquests he retir'd into the Country, where he was visited by the Ambassadors of the *Samnites*, as he was boiling Turnips in a Pipkin, who after some Discourse offer'd him a great Sum of Gold to go into their Interest *Curius* very generously refus'd their Offer, told them that he preferr'd his Poverty to their Riches, and that his Ambition was not to be rich, but to command those that were so

[d] *M Furius Camillus*, *Consul*, *Military Tribune* and *Dictator*, made himself famous by several considerable Victories, he deliver'd *Rome* when besieg'd by the *Gauls*, whom, about 23 Years after, he defeated a second time in the Plains of *Alba*, A U. C 387.

[e] This *Pupius* is said to have been peculiarly happy in raising the Passions, nothing now remains of his

Writings

An qui fortunæ te reſponſare ſuperbæ

Liberum & erectum præſens hortatur, & aptat?

  Quod ſi me populus Romanus forte roget, cur 70

Non, ut porticibus, ſic judiciis fruar iſdem,

Nec ſequar aut fugiam, quæ diligit ipſe vel odit,

Olim quod vulpes ægroto cauta leoni

Reſpondit, referam . Quia me veſtigia terrent,

Omnia te adverſum ſpectantia, nulla retrorſum 75

Bellua multorum eſt capitum nam quid ſequar, aut

  quem ?

Pars hominum geſtit conducere publica ſunt qui

Cruſtis & pomis viduas venentur avaras,

Excipiantque ſenes, quos in vivaria mittant:

Multis occulto creſcit res fenore verum   80

Eſto, aliis alios rebus ſtudiiſque teneri

Iidem eadem poſſunt horam durare probantes ?

Nullus in orbe ſinus Baiis prælucet amœnis,

Si dixit dives, lacus & mare ſentit amorem

Tears from the Eyes of the Spectators· He advifes you to get it lawfully, if poffible; but if that can't be done, to be fure to get it Another more friendly exhorts you to ftand up againft Fortune, and oppofe her Attempts when fhe means to opprefs you. Which of thefe two in your Opinion gives the beft Advice? If the People ask me whence it comes to pafs, that, as I frequent the fame Walks, I am not of the fame Sentiments with them: Why I do not love and hate juft as they do. My Reply is the fame which the Fox made to the fick Lion; All the Footfteps are towards your Den, and none from it; this is the thing which makes me afraid   The People is a many-headed Monfter; whom or what fhou'd I imitate? Some are fond of farming the Publick Revenues; fome endeavour with little Prefents to catch rich Widows, and old Men in hopes of inheriting their Eftate   Others again grow rich by private Ufury   All this proves no more than that many Men have many Inclinations, that one loves one thing, and another another· But can you find the Man, who for an Hour together is of the fame Mind? If a Perfon of Diftinction fay * *Baiæ* is a fweet delicious Place, in all the World there is not a fpot of Ground beyond it, in refpect of its lovely and beautiful Situation, the *Lucrine Lake* is prefently fenfible of the ardent Defires which this Man has to fettle there.   But the

Writings but thofe two Verfes which were happily preferv'd by *Acron* the *Grammarian*

> *Flebunt amici & bene noti mortem meam,*
> *Nam populus in me vivo lachrimavit fatis.*

* *Baiæ,* fee Book. II. *Sat.* IV

2   very

Feſtinantis heri : cui ſi vitioſa libido   85

Fecerit auſpicium; cras ferramenta Teanum

Tolletis fabri lectus genialis in aula eſt?

Nil ait eſſe prius, melius nil cælibe vita :

Si non eſt, jurat bene ſolis eſſe maritis.

Quo teneam vultus mutantem Protea nodo?   90

Quid pauper? viden', ut mutat cœnacula, lectos,

Balnea, tonſores; conducto navigio æque

Nauſeat ac locuples, quem ducit priva triremis.

Si curatus inæquali tonſore capillos

Occurro; rides ſi forte ſubucula pexæ   95

Trita ſubeſt tunicæ, vel ſi toga diſſidet inpar;

Rides quid mea cum pugnat ſententia ſecum;

Quod petiit, ſpernit; repetit quod nuper omiſit;

Æſtuat, & vitæ diſconvenit ordine toto;

Diruit, ædificat, mutat quadrata rotundis?   100

Inſanire putas ſollemnia me, neque rides,

Nec medici credis, nec curatoris egere

A prætore dati, rerum tutela mearum

Cum ſis, & prave ſectum ſtomacheris ob unguem

De te pendentis, te ſuſpicientis amici.   105

Ad

very next Day, if his capricious Humour gives him a Hint, then all the Cry is, Go, Workmen, carry your Tools and Materials to * *Teanum* Is he marry'd? then nothing appears so agreeable to him as a single Life Is he a single Man? Who then are so happy as they who are marry'd? What way shall I take to fix this *Proteus*, who is never the same Man? Nor is the poor Man less inconstant; he changes his Lodgings, Beds, Baths and Barbers; he hires a Boat, and grows in a little Time as weary of it, as the Great Men of their own Galleys

I F my Hair be cut away, if one side of my Cloak be longer than the other, if my Cloaths be new, and Linnen old, you presently laugh at me, but when I differ so unaccountably from my self in my Opinion, when I contemn what I lately desir'd, and again desire what I just now contemn'd, when I pull down and build up again, when I make square Things round, and round ones square, when my whole Life is high and low, up and down; then you forbear to laugh at me any longer, because so many Thousands are like me, and in all Respects as great Fools as my self Tho' my Life is a Series of Contradictions, yet in your Opinion I want no Guardian, neither do I stand in need of a Physician; and yet, *Mæcenas*, though you are as it were my tutelary Deity, you are angry with your Friend who admires you, and places his whole Dependance upon you, if but my Nails are ill cut. To conclude, the † Wise Man

---

* *Teanum*, a little Village of *Campania*, not far from *Baia*, famous for its hot Baths

† The *Stoicks* maintain'd that their Wise Man was equal to God, and that he might contend for Happiness with

Ad summam, sapiens uno minor est Jove, dives,
Liber, honoratus, pulcher, rex denique regum;
Præcipue sanus, nisi cum pituita molesta est

EPISTOLA II.

Ad Lollium.

TROJANI *belli scriptorem, maxime Lolli,*
Dum tu declamas Romæ, Præneste relegi.
Qui, quid sit pulchrum, quid turpe, quid utile,
quid non,

Planius

Man is inferiour to none but *Jupiter*; He only is free, rich, beautiful and honourable; He is King of Kings, He always enjoys his Health to Perfection, unlefs it be when he's troubled with * Flegm.

with him, our Poet is more modeft, he acknowledges God to be the only Wife Being, and that he is the Author and Giver of Wifdom.

* He ridicules the *Stoicks*, who confidently afferted, that the moft violent Diftempers were not capable of making the leaft Alteration in the Health of their Wife Men.

EPISTLE II.

To *Lollius.*

ILLUSTRIOUS *Lollius,* while you are pleading at *Rome,* I have carefully read over † *Homer* at ‡ *Prænefte,* and I cannot but fay, that he teaches us much better, and with greater Perfpicuity, what is Honourable, what

† *Homer,* fee *Book* I *Sat* X. This Poet, in refpect of his Leffons of Morality, according to the common Philofophical Divifion of *Good* into the *Pleafant, Profitable* and *Honeft,* which *Horace* here lays down, has more fully and clearly inftructed us, than the moft rigid Philofophers And therefore it is not to be wonder'd at, if *Greece,* which afterwards gave the Appellation of *Wife* to Men who fettled *fingle Sentences* of Truth, fhould give him the Title of the Father of Virtue See Mr. *Pope's Effay* on *Homer,* p 55

‡ *Prænefte,* a little Town in *Italy,* about 12 Miles from *Rome.*

Infamous,

Planius ac melius Chryfippo & Crantore dicit.

Cur ita crediderim, nifi quid te detinet, audi. 5

Fabula, qua Paridis propter narratur amorem

Græcia Barbariæ lento collifa duello,

Stultorum regum, & populorum continet æftus.

Antenor cenfet belli præcidere cauffam.

Quod Paris, ut falvus regnet vivatque beatus, 10

Cogi poffe negat   Neftor conponere litis

Inter Peliden feftinat & inter Atriden

Hunc amor, ira quidem communiter urit utrumque

Quicquid delirant reges, plectuntur Achivi

Seditione, dolis, fcelere, atque libidine, & ira, 15

Iliacos intra muros peccatur & extra

Rurfum, quid virtus, & quid fapientia poffit;

Utile propofuit nobis exemplar Ulixen:

Qui domitor Trojæ, multorum providus urbis

Et mores hominum infpexit; latumque per æquor, 20

Dum fibi, dum focius reditum parat, afpera multa

Pertulit,

infamous; what is profitable, what not, than either * *Crantor* or † *Chrysippus.* Hear what I have to offer in Defence of my Opinion The Poet in the *Iliads* describes the mad extravagant Passions with which both Kings and People were inflam'd, in the War that broke out between the *Grecians* and *Trojans*; which was occasion'd by the Love of *Paris*, and lasted so long, that the Strength of *Greece* was almost exhausted. ‡ *Antenor*, on the one Part, being willing to put an End to the War, advises that *Helen* should be sent back into *Greece*, but *Paris* declares, that, though his Happiness depended upon it, he wou'd never consent *Nestor*, on the other Side, endeavours all he can to compose the Difference between *Agamemnon* and *Achilles*; they were both extremely hot and furious; but Love, that Tyrant of the Soul, reign'd in the Heart of *Agamemnon*. Whatever Follies are acted by Princes, their Subjects suffer for 'em Seditions, Intrigues, Love, Anger and Revenge prevail both in the Camp and City. Thus far the *Iliads.*

IN the Person of *Ulysses*, the Poet sets before us an excellent Example of Courage and Wisdom; who, after the taking of *Troy*, travell'd thro' many distant Countries, where he diligently observ'd the different Customs and Manners of Mankind. In his Voyage to *Ithaca*, that he and his Soldiers might arrive there

---

* *Crantor*, an Academick Philosopher of *Solos*, and Disciple of *Xenocrates*, he writ an admirable Treatise upon Grief, which is much commended by *Cicero*. He flourish'd about the 116th *Olympiad*

† *Chrysippus*, see *Book* I. *Sat.* III

‡ See the Speeches of *Antenor* and *Paris*, Iliad. 7th. l. 348.

in

Pertulit, adversis rerum immersabilis undis.
Sirenum voces, & Circæ pocula nosti:
Quæ si cum sociis stultus cupidusque bibisset;
Sub domina meretrice fuisset turpis & excors.   25
Vixisset canis inmundus, vel amica luto sus.

    Nos numerus sumus, & fruges consumere nati,
Sponsi Penelopæ, nebulones, Alcinoique
In cute curanda plus æquo operata juventus;
Cui pulchrum fuit in medios dormire dies, &   30
Ad strepitum citharæ cessantem ducere somnum.
Ut jugulent hominem, surgunt de nocte latrones:
Ut teipsum serves, non expergisceris? atqui

in Safety, he ftruggled with a thoufand inexpreffible Difficulties, in all which he came off a Conqueror. You have heard of the * *Sirens* charming Voices, and of † *Circe's* Enchantments: Had our Heroe fo greedily drank up the fatal Poifon as his Companions did, his Return had been impoffible; he had made himfelf a Slave to an infamous Proftitute, who wou'd have transform'd him into a Dog, or Sow that lies wallowing in the Mire

THE Bulk of us Mortals are good for nothing but to eat and drink, we are like the Lovers of *Penelope,* like the Debauchees of ‡ *Alcinous's* Court, who fpend all their Time in pampering their Bodies, who glory in lying in Bed till Noon, and in lulling themfelves to Sleep at Night with Mufick.

THIEVES and Robbers take the Pains to rife at Midnight to cut Men's Throats; and won't you awake from your Slumber, to do your felf good? If you will not ufe Exercife when you are well, you'll be forc'd to do fo,

---

* *Sirens,* according to the Poets, were half Women and half Fifh, there were but Three, *Parthenope, Ligea,* and *Leucofta* , the Poets fay of them, that by the charming Sweetnefs of their Singing they ftop'd all Travellers, but *Ulyffes* by his Prudence happily efcap'd them

† *Circe,* a famous Enchantrefs, who, being banifh'd by her Subjects for poyfoning her Husband the King of the *Sarmatæ,* came to *italy,* and kept her Refidence in a Promontory call'd by her Name, fhe entertain'd *Ulyffes* when his Fleet was caft away upon her Coafts, made the Stars come down from Heaven in his Prefence, and transform'd his Companions into different Sorts of Beafts This Fable is a lively and beautiful Image of fenfual Pleafures, which change the braveft Men into Brutes.

‡ *Alcinous,* King of the *Phæaces,* a People of *Corcyra,* who were much given to Luxury and Intemperance

Si noles fanus, curres hydropicus · & ni
Pofces ante diem librum cum lumine; fi non   35
Intendes animum ftudiis & rebus honeftis,
Invidia vel amore vigil torquebere. nam cur,
Quæ lædunt oculum, feftinas demere, fi quid
Eft animum, differs curandi tempus in annum?
Dimidium facti, qui cœpit habet fapere aude :   40
Incipe qui recte vivendi prorogat horam,
Rufticus exfpectat dum defluat amnis · at ille
Labitur, & labetur in omne volubilis ævum.

Quæritur argentum, puerifque beata creandis
Uxor, & incultæ pacantur vomere filvæ.   45
Quod fatis eft, cui contingit, nihil amplius optet
Non domus, & fundus, non æris acervus & auri
Ægroto domini deduxit corpore febris,
Non animo curas. valeat poffeffor oportet,

St

to be cur'd of the *Dropſy. If betimes in the Morning, before break of Day, you do not call for your Book and Candle; if you do not ſeriouſly apply your Mind to ſome uſeful Studies or Buſineſs, Love and Envy will keep you awake, and put you to the Torture. If a Mote be in your Eye, you take it out immediately; and yet you neglect the Cure of your Mind whole Years together What a ſtrange and unaccountable Procedure is this? The Work is half done that is begun well Dare to be wiſe, begin this very Inſtant He that delays to lead a good Life, is like the Clown in the Fable, who, meeting a River in his way, ſat down on the Bank till the Stream ſhou'd paſs him, but alas! that flows and will flow on, till Time ſhall be no more.

We are follicitous to get Money, and a Wife that will bring us a numerous Offspring; we grub up our Woods, and plough the Lands, which were before untill'd, to increaſe our Eſtates. What occaſion has he, who is already bleſt with a competent Fortune, to wiſh for more? Neither Houſe nor Lands, nor Gold, nor Silver, can cure a Fever, or give ſo much as a Moment's Eaſe to a diſtemper'd Mind † A Man muſt be well both in Body and Mind

---

* *Curres Hydropicus, Celſus Book* III. *Chap* XXIII. ſpeaking of ſeveral Remedies for the Dropſy, has theſe Words *Multum ambulandum, currendum aliquando eſt.*

† *Plato* tells us, that Health, Beauty, Vigour, Riches, and all the other Things call'd *Goods,* are equally as Evil to the Unjuſt, as Good to the Juſt Agreeable to which is that excellent Saying of *Terence, Act* 1 *Scen* 2.

Hæc perinde ſunt ut illius animus, qui ea poſſidet
Qui uti ſcit, ei bona, illi, qui non utitur recte, mala

to

Si conportatis rebus bene cogitat uti.   50

Qui cupit aut metuit; juvat illum sic domus & res,

Ut lippum pictæ tabulæ, fomenta podagrum,

Auriculas citharæ collecta sorde dolentis.

Sincerum est nisi vas, quodcumque infundis, acescit.

Sperne voluptates. nocet emta dolore voluptas.   55

Semper avarus eget · certum voto pete finem.

Invidus alterius macrescit rebus opimis ·

Invidia Siculi non invenere tyranni

Majus tormentum   qui non moderabitur iræ,

Infectum volet esse, dolor quod suaserit & mens, 60

Dum pœnas odio per vim festinat inulto

Ira furor brevis est. animum rege. qui, nisi paret,

Imperat; hunc frenis, hunc tu conpesce catena.

Fingit equum tenera docilem cervice magister

Ire, viam qua monstret eques: venaticus, ex quo 65

Tempore cervinam pellem latravit in aula,

Militat in silvis catulus. nunc adbibe puro

Pectore

to tafte and enjoy the Bleffings of Life with Comfort and Satisfaction. If the Veffel be not fweet, the Wine will turn fowre. What Joy can Pictures afford that Man whofe Eyes are fore? Are Fomentations grateful to one that has the Gout? Can the fofteft Mufick be pleafing to him who has a Deafnefs in his Ear? No more can that Man, who is always wrack'd with Defires and Fears, take any Pleafure in his vaft Poffeffions.

ABSTAIN from Pleafure, it is much too dear when purchas'd with Pain. The Covetous Man is always in Want; learn therefore betimes to moderate your Defires. The envious Man fickens at his Neighbour's Profperity. Envy is one of the greateft Torments; the * *Sicilian* Tyrants, who were Mafters in all the Myftery of Cruelty, never invented any thing like it. He that knows not how to govern his Anger, will repent of what he did in the Heat of his Paffion, when he breath'd nothing but Fury and Revenge, and wifh it a thoufand Times undone. What is Anger? 'Tis a meer Madnefs, tho' of a fhort Duration. Be Mafter of this Paffion, it will either be your Tyrant or your Slave; hold it in with a Curb, or keep it under with a Chain.

THE tender Colt is eafily form'd by the fkilful Jocky to obey the Check and Motions of his Rider. The young Hound is taught to hunt in the Foreft, by being bred up to open at a Bucks-fkin trail'd up and down the Hall.

---

* No Country was fo famous for being opprefs'd with Tyrants as *Sicily* This gave Occafion to the Poet's Expreffion, who, without doubt, alludes in this Place to the *Bull* of *Phalaris*, the Cruel Tyrant of *Agrigentum*

Acquaint

Pectore verba puer; nunc te melioribus offer.
Quo ſemel eſt inbuta recens, ſervabit odorem
Teſta diu, quod ſi ceſſas, aut ſtrenuus anteis;   70
Nec tardum opperior, nec præcedentibus inſto.

EPISTOLA III.

Ad Julium Florum.

JULI Flore, quibus terrarum militet oris
   Claudius Auguſti privignus, ſcire laboro.
Thracane vos Hebruſque nivali compede vinctus;
An freta vicinas inter currentia terras;
An pingues Aſiæ campi colleſque morantur?   5
Quid ſtudioſa cohors operum ſtruit? hoc quoque curo.
Quis ſibi res geſtas Auguſti ſcribere ſumit?
Bella quis & paces longum diffundit in ævum?
Quid Titius, Romana brevi venturus in ora?

Pindarici

Acquaint your self with thefe excellent Maxims while you are young, and your Mind is
pure and uncorrupted. Now is the Time to
be taught by thofe who are wifer than your
felf. A new Veffel will a long Time preferve
fome Tincture of the Liquor, with which it
was firft feafon'd * I freely declare, that, in
the way of Virtue to which I invite you, as I
will not wait for you, if you lag behind ; fo
neither will I endeavour to tread on your Heels,
if you get before me.

* 'Tis an excellent Remark of the Emperor *Antoni-
nus,* that the Perfection of Virtue confifts in being neither too violent, nor too lazy.

EPISTLE III.

To *Julius Florus.*

I AM in Pain to know what is become of
Tiberius's Army Is it in *Thrace,* near the
frozen *Hebrus?* Is it on the *Hellefpont?* or is
he encamp'd in the fertile and delicious Plains
of *Afia?* I am no lefs follicitous to learn how
the Men of Letters fpend their Time. Who
has undertaken to write the Life and Actions of
Auguftus, and to tranfmit to future Ages the feveral Wars and Treaties of Peace, which have
been happily concluded by our mighty Emperor?
What is *Titus* doing, whofe Writings, I doubt
not, will in a little Time be in every *Roman*
Mouth? He difdains the Lakes and Rivers
where every one may drink ; to the Fountain-
head he goes, and has the Courage to draw from
that

Pindarici fontis qui non expalluit hauſtus,   10
Faſtidire lacus & rivos auſus apertos:
Ut valet? ut meminit noſtri? fidibuſne Latinis
Thebanos aptare modos ſtudet, auſpice Muſa?
An tragica deſævit & ampullatur in arte?
Quid mihi Celſus agit? monitus, multumque mo-
      nendus,   15
Privatas ut quærat opes, & tangere vitet
Scripta, Palatinus quæcumque recepit Apollo.
Ne, ſi forte ſuas repetitum venerit olim
Grex avium plumas, moveat cornicula riſum
Furtivis nudata coloribus. ipſe quid audes?   20
Quæ circumvolitas agilis thyma? non tibi parvum
Ingenium, non incultum eſt & turpiter hirtum.
Seu linguam cauſis acuis; ſeu civica jura
Reſpondere paras; ſeu condis amabile carmen.
Prima feres ederæ victricis præmia. quod ſi   25
Frigida curarum fomenta relinquere poſſes;
Quo te cæleſtis ſapientia duceret, ires.
Hoc opus, hoc ſtudium parvi properemus & ampli;
Si patriæ volumus, ſi nobis vivere cari.

                                           Debes

that whence *Pindar himself drew. Is he well? Am I sometimes in his Thoughts? Is he, with the Favour of the Muses, accommodating the *Theban*'s lofty Numbers to the *Roman Lyre*? or does he rage in the pompous swelling Strain of Tragedy? And how does *Celsus* employ himself? He has been often admonished, and must be so again, that he wou'd work upon his own Stock, and not steal from the Poems in † *Apollo*'s Library; lest the Birds return, and take their own Feathers, and he, like the Daw, being stripp'd stark naked, become the Jest of all that know him. And pray tell me what you your self are upon. What Thyme are you gathering? You are a Man of Delicacy and Politeness, you have a lofty and elevated Genius. Whether you are preparing to plead Causes at the Bar, or to give Advice as a *Civilian*; or whether, for Variety, you write some soft and pleasing Verses, you are sure of the first Prize; no one will dare to dispute it with you. But if you could be prevail'd on to forsake those cold Comforts, those poor Antidotes against the Cares of Life, you wou'd ascend up as high as Celestial Wisdom cou'd carry you · This is what we must all apply our selves to, if we desire to be well with our selves and dear to our Country

---

* *Pindar*, a *Greek* Poet, Prince of the *Lyricks*, and Native of *Thebes* in *Bœotia*. He liv'd in the 76th *Olympiad* He writ a great many Books, none of which are now remaining but the *Odes*, which he compos'd in Honour of those Persons, who won the Prize at the *Olympick*, *Isthmick*, *Pythian*, and *Nemæan* Games.

† *Bibliotheca Palatina*, a famous Library, built by *Augustus*, upon *Mount Palatine* near *Apollo*'s *Temple*, the greatest Honour which a Poet could attain to, was to have his Works and Statue made sacred, as it were, by being allowed a Place in this Library. See *Book* I *Sat.* IV.

I SHALL

Debes hoc etiam refcribere, Si tibi curæ eft, 30
Quantæ conveniat, Munatius; an male farta
Gratia nequicquam coit, & refcinditur; ac vos
Seu calidus fanguis, feu rerum infcitia vexat,
Indomita cervice feros? ubicumque locorum
Vivitis, indigni fraternum rumpere fœdus,   35
Pafcitur in veftrum reditum votiva juvenca

EPISTOLA IV.

Ad Albium Tibullum.

ALBI, noftrorum fermonum candide judex,
   Quid nunc te dicam facere in regione Pedana?
Scribere quod Caffi Parmenfis opufcula vincat?
An tacitum filvas inter reptare falubris,
Curantem quicquid dignum fapiente bonoque eft?   5
Non tu corpus eras fine peftore Di tibi formam,
Di tibi divitias dederunt, artemque fruendi
   Quid voveat dulci nutricula majus alumno?
Qui fapere, & fari poffit quæ fentiat, & cui

Gratia,

I SHALL be glad to know whether you continue your Love to *Munatius* as you ought to do; or whether the unhappy Difference between you is but imperfectly patch'd up Whatever was the Occasion of it, whether Heat of Blood, or Want of Experience, I cannot but say, that it is not fit, where-ever you are, that two such worthy honest Gentlemen, who are so nearly related, shou'd live at Variance with each other. I feed a fine young Heifer in my Grounds, which I have vow'd to offer to the Gods upon your happy Return

EPISTLE IV.

To *Albius Tibullus.*

MY Dear *Tibullus!* Thou impartial Critick of my *Satires* and *Epistles*, how do you spend your Time in the Country? Are you writing Volumes greater than * *Cassius*, or do you retire into the Woods, and employ your Thoughts as becomes a wise and virtuous Man? You don't use to be an unactive Lump The Gods have given you Beauty, you have Riches in abundance; and, which is yet a greater Happiness, you know how to enjoy them

CAN a tender Mother, who is passionately fond of her beloved Child, wish him better, than that he may have right Ideas of Things, and be Master of an easy graceful Elocution, that

* See *Book* I. *Sat* X.

he

Gratia, fama, valetudo contingat abunde,   10
Et domus, & victus, non deficiente cruména?
  Inter spem curamque, timores inter & iras,
Omnem crede diem tibi diluxiffe supremum.
Grata superveniet, quæ non sperabitur, hora.
Me pinguem & nitidum bene curata cute vises, 15
Cum ridere voles, Epicuri de grege porcum.

EPISTOLA V.

Ad Torquatum

SI potes Archiacis conviva recumbere lectis,
  Nec modica cenare times olus omne patella;
Supremo te sole domi, Torquate, manebo
Vina bibes, iterum Tauro diffusa paluftris
Inter Minturnas Sinueffanumque Petrinum. 5
Si melius quid habes, arceffe; vel imperium fer.
Jamdudum splendet focus, & tibi munda supellex.
Mitte levis spes, & certamina divitiarum,
Et Moschi cauffam cras nato Cæsare festus
Dat veniam somnumque dies impune licebit 10
Æstivam sermone benigno extendere noctem.

he may be well respected, may enjoy a perfect State of Health, and a clear unspotted Reputation; that he may feed on clean and wholsome Diet, have a good convenient House, and Money at Command? Hopes and Cares, Anger and Fears divide our Life; wou'd you be free from these Anxieties? think every Day will be your last, and then the future succeeding Hours will be the more welcome, because unexpected.

WHEN you are dispos'd to divert your self with a merry jolly Fellow, all you have to do is to make me a Visit, I am clean, fat, and in good Condition.

EPISTLE V.

To *Torquatus.*

IF you can lie on *Archias*'s Beds, and content your self with a Mess of plain Soop, let me see you in the Evening My Wine was tunn'd when *Taurus* was *Consul* the second time; 'tis of the Growth of *Minturna* and *Sinuessa*; if you have better, bring it along with you, or else take up with mine.

MY House is in Order, and all Things are ready for your Reception Lay aside vain Hopes, and the endless Desire of getting Riches, think on *Moschus*'s Cause another Time. To-Morrow is *Cæsar*'s Birth-Day; then it is allowable to sleep in the Morning, and therefore we may better spend the Evening in a lively facetious Conversation.

To

Quo mihi fortunam, ſi non conceditur uti?
Parcus ob heredis curam nimiumque ſeverus
Adſidet inſano. potare & ſpargere flores
Incipiam, patiarque vel inconſultus haberi.   15
Quid non ebrietas deſignat? operta recludit ʻ
Spes jubet eſſe ratas. ad prœlia trudit inertem,
Sollicitis animis onus eximit   addocet artis.
Fecundi calices quem non fecere diſertum?
Contracta quem non in paupertate ſolutum?   20
Hæc ego procurare & idoneus imperor, & non
Invitus: ne turpe toral, ne ſordida mappa
Corruget naris; ne non & cantharus & lanx
Oſtendat tibi te; ne fidos inter amicos
Sit, qui dicta foras eliminet; ut coeat par,   25
Jungaturque pari   Butram tibi Septiciumque,
Et, niſi cœna prior potiorque puella, Sabinum,
Detinet, adſumam   locus eſt & pluribus umbris:
Sed nimis arta premunt olidæ convivia capræ.

　　Tu, quotus eſſe velis, reſcribe; & rebus omiſſis 30
Atria ſervantem poſtico falle clientem

EPISTOLA

To what End are Riches, if we muſt not enjoy them? To deal frankly with you, that Man is a Fool, who, to enrich his Heirs, ſtarves himſelf. Crown me with Flowers, bring me Wine, brisk Wine, the ill-natur'd World may think me mad What mighty Things are done by Wine! It reveals Secrets, turns Hope into Enjoyment; it makes the Coward brave and valiant; inſtructs the Ignorant in Arts and Sciences; it inſpires the Miſerable with Joy and Gladneſs, and makes the Poor to forget his Poverty. Where is the Man, whom a free Glaſs of Wine does not make eloquent?

I my ſelf will take Care, that all Things be in Order; that the * Carpet and Napkins be clean and neat, and the Pots and Veſſels ſcower'd ſo bright, that you may ſee your Face in them. Reſt aſſur'd, that no Man ſhall be at Table, who reports abroad what is ſaid among Friends. And the Company ſhall be ſuch as is ſuitable the one to the other. *Butras* and *Septicius* will both be here, nor will *Sabinus* fail, if a better Supper and a Miſtreſs more engaging do not keep him from us There will be Room at Table for more Gueſts, but the preſent Seaſon conſider'd, it will be inconvenient to have too full a Table Let me know your Pleaſure how many you wou'd have, lay aſide Buſineſs, and while your Clients throng your Gate, ſteal out at the Back-door, and get rid of them.

---

* The *Romans* on their Beds laid a Kind of Quilt ſtuff'd with Feathers, call'd *Culcitra*, over this, in antient Times, they threw a Goat-skin, which was afterwards chang'd for the *Stragulum*, a Carpet which they ſometimes call'd *Toral*, as belonging to the *Torus*

EPI-

EPISTOLA VI.

Ad Numicium.

NIL admirari, prope res eft una Numici,
    Solaque quæ poffit facere & fervare beatum
Hunc folem, & ftellas, & decedentia certis
Tempora momentis, funt qui formidine nulla
Inbuti fpectent   quid cenfes,   munera terræ?   5
Quid, maris extremos Arabas ditantis & Indos?
Ludicra, quid, plaufus & amici dona Quiritis?
Quo fpectanda modo, quo fenfu credis & ore?
Qui timet his adverfa, fere miratur eodem
Quo cupiens pacto   pavor eft utrobique moleftus. 10
Inprovifa fimul fpecies exterret utrumque·
Gaudeat, an doleat, cupiat, metuatne; quid ad rem.
Si, quicquid vidit melius pejufve fua fpe,
Defixis oculis, animoque & corpore torpet?
Infani fapiens nomen ferat, æquus iniqui;   15
Ultra quam fatis eft, virtutem fi petat ipfam.
    I nunc, argentum & marmor vetus, æraque &
    artis

Sufpite :

EPISTLE. VI.

To *Numicius*.

THE only Way to be perfectly and constantly happy, is to admire nothing
There are those who can behold the Sun and
Stars, which move in a regular orderly Course,
and the certain invariable Succession of Seasons
without any Concern What think you then?
The Riches which the Earth and Sea produce,
Plays and Shows, Applause and Favour among
the People of *Rome*, how ought they to be regarded by us? This is certain, that he who
fears the contrary to these, admires them as
much as he who desires them. The Passion
is equally troublesome to both, they are equally affrighted at every unhop'd for, unexpected
Accident. It matters not, whether Joy or
Sorrow, whether Fear or Hope has the Possession of our Hearts, if when any thing happens
either good or ill, which was wholly unlook'd
for, we presently cast our Eyes down upon the
Ground, and grow into Statues Shew me
the Man that is wise and just, whenever he
carries his Desires too far, in straining even Virtue it self beyond its due Limits, he ceases to
be so Now, if you please, admire Riches;
gaze on the Marble Statues of your Ancestors,
doat on your curious brazen Vessels, extol the
Works of celebrated Artists, and be passionately in Love with your purple Garments adorn'd

He lays down some Rules how to make our selves happy.

T 2   with

Suſpice: cum gemmis Tyrios mirare colores:

Gaude, quod ſpectant oculi te mille loquentem

Gnavus mane forum, & veſpertinus pete tectum, 20

Ne plus frumenti dotalibus emetat agris

Mutus, & (indignum, quod ſit pejoribus ortus)

Hic tibi ſit potius, quam tu mirabilis illi

Quicquid ſub terra eſt, in apricum proferet ætas

Defodiet condetque nitentia cum bene notum 25

Porticus Agrippæ, & via te conſpexerit Appi,

Ire tamen reſtat, Numa quo devenit & Ancus.

Si latus aut renes morbo tententur acuto,

Quære fugam morbi vis recte vivere? quis non?

Si virtus hoc una poteſt dare; fortis omiſſis 30

Hoc age deliciis. virtutem verba putes, &

* Lucum ligna? cave ne portus occupet alter:

Ne Cibyratica, ne Bithyna negotia perdas;

Mille talenta rotundentur, totidem altera, porro &

Tertia ſuccedant, & quæ pars quadret acervum 35

Scilicet uxorem cum dote, fidemque, & amicos,

Et genus, & formam, regina Pecunia donat;

---

* It was uſual with the common People to attribute a kind of Divinity to Groves.

with Gems and precious Stones : Rejoyce that
the Eyes of Thousands were upon you when
you spoke in publick; go to the *Forum* early in
the Morning; return late in the Evening, left
Mutus, who had a plentiful Fortune with his
Wife, be richer than your self. How unbecoming is it, that one of so mean and obscure
a Birth shou'd be admired by you, and not
rather you be admir'd by him? O my *Numicius,*
the Things which are hidden shall in due Time
be reveal'd, and those which now appear so
pompous and magnificent shall vanish into nothing; even you, who are known by your splen-
did Equipage in *Agrippa's Portico,* and on the
Appian Road, must at last retire to that Place
where *Numa* and *Ancus* are gone before you
If you languish under any sharp Distemper,
seek immediately for a Remedy Wou'd you
live a happy and contented Life? Who wou'd
not do so? Bid a long and last Adieu to Pleasures, apply your self to Virtue, 'tis Virtue a-
lone that can make you happy But if you look
upon Virtue as an empty Name, if you laugh
at all Religion, make Haste, left another get to
Port before you, and the Profits of your Voyage come to nothing Endeavour to make up
your Estate a Thousand Talents, get another
Thousand, add a Thousand more, and then,
that the Number may be even, make them four
Thousand

   * MONEY, forsooth, is the Sovereign God- The
dess of the Universe; she creates a Man Friends, Power of
makes him Noble and Eloquent, Charming and Money.

---

   * All this Paragraph and the following ones are Iro-
nical, or rather spoken according to the Sentiments of
Numicius, not of *Horace*

Ac bene nummatum decorat Suadela Venuſque

Mancipiis locuples, eget æris Cappadocum rex.

Ne fueris hic tu chlamydes Lucullus, ut aiunt, 40

Si poſſet centum ſcenæ præbere rogatus,

Qui poſſum tot? ait tamen & quæram, & quot

  habebo,

Mittam. poſt paullo ſcribit, ſibi millia quinque

Eſſe domi chlamydum. partem, vel tolleret omnis.

Exilis domus eſt; ubi non & multa ſuperſunt 45

Et dominum fallunt, & proſunt furibus ergo,

Si res ſola poteſt facere & ſervare beatum;

Hoc primus repetas opus, hoc poſtremus omittas.

Si fortunatum ſpecies, & gratia præſtat ;

Mercemur ſervum, qui dictet nomina, lævum 50

Qui fodicet latus, & cogat trans pondera dextram

Porrigere. Hic multum in Fabia valet, ille Velina:

Cui libet is faſcis dabit, eripietque curule

Cui

Beautiful; the faireft Ladies with the greateft Fortunes are not able to withftand the powerful Addreffes of a wealthy Man   The King of *Cappadocia* had a Thoufand Slaves, but little or no Money· Be fure not to be like him 'Tis reported of *Lucullus*, that being ask'd to lend the Players a hundred Cloaks, Where, faid he, fhall I have fo many? However, I will fee what I have, and of thofe you may be fure.   Enquiry being made, he immediately fent Word, that he had Five Thoufand, and that he wou'd lend them part, or all of 'em.   That Houfe is but very ill furnifh'd, where there are not a great many fuperfluous Things, of which the Mafter knows nothing, which Rogues and Thieves may fteal away, and Nobody the wifer.

IF after all this you perfift in your Opinion, that the Happinefs of this Life confifts in Riches, endeavour to be rich; let this be your firft and laft Thought too.   If Honour and Popularity are the only Happinefs, provide your felf a * Servant, who can inform you of every Citizens Name; let him go along with you, and inftruct you by fome fecret Sign, or other, to reach your Hand to this or that Citizen thro' the Crowd   This· Man, faith he, has a very good Intereft in *Fabius*'s *Tribe*, that Man in the *Velian*; make him your Friend and you'll certainly be *Conful*, 'tis in vain for any

---

* They who ftood Candidates for any Office, us'd all the Arts of Popularity, in their Walks round the City, they took the meaneft Perfons by the Hand, and not only us'd the more familiar Terms of Father, Brother, Friend, and the like, but call'd them by their own proper Names, in this Service they had ufually a Monitor to affift them, who whifper'd every Body's Name in their Ears.

Man

Cui volet inportunus ebur   Frater, Pater, adde
Ut cuique eft ætas, ita quemque facetus adopta. 55
Si bene qui cenat, bene vivit; lucet: eamus
Quo ducit gula: pifcemur, venemur, ut olim
Gargilius · qui mane plagas, venabula, fervos
Differtum tranfire Forum Campumque jubebat;
Unus ut e multis populo fpectante referret   60
Emtum mulus aprum   crudi tumidique lavemur,
Quid deceat, quid non, obliti; Cærite cera
Digni; remigium vitiofum Ithacenfis Ulixei:
Cui potior patria fuit interdicta voluptas.
Si, Mimnermus uti cenfet, fine amore jocifque, 65
Nil eft jocundum; vivas in amore jocifque.

Vive,

Man to hope to be *Ædile* unleſs he pleaſes.
You muſt make your Addreſſes with a ſmiling
Countenance, call him Father or Brother, and
be ſo skillful as to give him that Title of Relation which his Age will beſt admit of

IF Happineſs conſiſts in good eating and
drinking, let us make it our Buſineſs, as ſoon
as Day breaks, to gratifie our Appetites; let us
mind nothing but Fiſhing and Hunting. Such
was *Gargilius*'s Way of Living, who, with
his Dogs and Horſes, Toils and Spears, affected to paſs in the Morning thro' the crowded
Forum with a Mule laden with a Boar, which
was not taken, as they imagin'd, but bought
for that Purpoſe. Let us upon a full Stomach
bathe our ſelves, what are the Rules of Decency to us? The * *Cenſor* may brand us for
infamous Perſons, he may do as he pleaſes; let
us imitate the lewd Companions of *Ulyſſes,* who
choſe to riot in unlawful Pleaſures, rather than
return to their Native Country

IF then (as *Mimnermus* pretends to maintain) there is nothing pleaſing and delightful
in Life, but Love and Raillery; let Love and
Raillery be our conſtant Entertainment Adieu,

---

* *Cærites,* a People of *Tuſcany,* who, for preſerving
the ſacred Relicks of the *Romans* when the *Gauls* had
taken the City, were dignified with the Name of *Roman Citizens,* but revolting afterwards, and being conquer'd by the *Romans,* they continu'd to them the Privilege of being Citizens, in Remembrance of their former Services, but to make 'em an Example, left o-
thers ſhou'd preſume to commit the like Crimes, they
depriv'd them for ever of the Right of Suffrage
Hence the *Cenſors* Tables, where they enter'd the
Names of ſuch Perſons as for ſome Miſdemeanour were
to loſe their Right of Suffrage, had the Name of *Cærites Tabulæ,*

Vive, vale. ſi quid noviſti rectius iſtis;
Candidus inperti. ſi non, his utere mecum.

EPISTOLA VII.
Ad Mæcenatem.

QUINQUE *dies tibi pollicitus me rure fu-*
turum,
Sextilem totum mendax deſideror. atqui,
Si me vivere vis ſanum recteque valentem;
Quam mihi das ægro, dabis ægrotare timenti,
Mæcenas, veniam   dum ficus prima calorque   5
Deſignatorem decorat lictoribus atris
Dum pueris omnis pater, & matercula pallet;
Officioſaque ſedulitas, & opella forenſis
Adducit febris, & teſtamenta reſignat.
Quod ſi bruma nives Albanis inlinet agris;   10
Ad mare deſcendet vates tuus, & ſibi parcet,
Contractuſque leget. te dulcis amice, reviſet

Cum

live well and be happy.   If you know any
better Maxims, be fo kind as to impart them:
If not, follow my Example, and make ufe of
thefe.

EPISTLE VII.

To *Mæcenas.*

My LORD,

I Promis'd to ftay but Five Days in the Coun-   The Poet
try, and tho' you was pleas'd to expect me   makes his
all *Auguft,* yet I ftill have fail'd you   If you   Excufe to
have any Regard for my Health, I muft beg of   *Mæcenas*
you to allow me the fame Liberty as you wou'd   waiting
do, in cafe I were fick; fince I fear to be fo,   upon him
while the Autumn continues.   The * Under-   accord-
takers are now full of Employment; Fathers   Promife.
and Mothers are in great Concern for their Children Befides, Attendance and Bufinefs, at this
critical Seafon, are of dangerous Confequence;
they occafion Fevers, which proving oftentimes
Mortal are the fatal Caufe of many Wills being
open'd

WHEN Winter comes on, if *Mount Alba*
is cover'd with Froft and Snow, your Poet de-
figns to retire nearer to the Sea, with a firm
Refolution to cloath himfelf warm, indulge
much, and ftudy little   As foon as the Swal-
lows and the foft Weft Winds give Notice of

---

* See *Book* II. *Sat.* VI

the

Cum zephyris, fi concedes, & hirundine prima.

   Non, quo more pyris vefci Calaber jubet hofpes,

Tu me fecifti locupletem   Vefcere fodes   15

Jam fatis eft   At tu quamtumvis tolle   Benigne.

Non invifa feres pueris munufcula parvis

Tam teneor dono, quam fi dimittar onuflus.

Ut libet   hæc porcis hodie comedenda relinques

Prodigus & ftultus donat quæ fpernit & ôdit.   20

Hæc feges ingratos tulit & feret omnibus annis.

Vir bonus & fapiens dignis aìt effe paratus?

Nec tamen ignorat, quid diftent æra lupinis?

Dignum præftabo me, etiam pro laude merentis

Quod fi me noles ufquam difcedere; reddes   25

Forte latus, nigros angufta fronte capillos

Reddes dulce loqui · reddes ridere decorum, &

Inter vina fugam Cinaræ mærere protervæ.

   Forte per anguftam tenuis nitedula rimam

Repferat in cumeram frumenti, paftaque, rurfus 30

Ire foras pleno tendebat coi pore fruftra

Cui muftela procul, Si vis, ait, effugere iftinc;

Macra cavum repetes artum, quem macra fubifti.

                                    Hac

the Spring, he will not fail to fee you again, if he hears nothing to the contrary.

All that I have is from your Bounty; how different is your Treatment from that of the *Calabrian* Inn-keeper, who entertain'd his Guefts with choaky Pears! Pray, Sir, eat, fays the Hoft   *Gueft* I have eat enough.   *Hoft* However take fome   *Gueft* You are very liberal   *Hoft* They will be no unacceptable Prefent to your Children   *Gueft* I thank you as much as if I had them   *Hoft* Do as you pleafe, Sir; what you leave fhall be given to the Hogs.

He acknowledges his Generofity, and is very thankful for his Kindnefs to him.

'Tis common for Fools to be very profufe of what they do not value; fuch Prodigals as thefe make Men ingrateful, and will always do fo: But a wife and liberal Man, who underftands Mankind, and knows the value of what he gives, declares his Prefents are for none but the deferving   I will therefore endeavour to merit your Favours; you fhall have no Occafion to think me ungrateful; but, if you wou'd always have me with you, give me back my former Strength and Vigour, my black curl'd Locks, my eafy Smile, and graceful Elocution, let me fweetly complain, as the Cups go round, of the cruel, rigorous, charming *Cinara,* who will not hear me.

Once upon a Time, a half-ftarv'd Moufe wriggled himfelf thro' a Chink into a Basket fill'd with Corn, having feafted very liberally, he endeavour'd to get out again, but in vain To whom a Weafel, who ftood leering afar off, gave this Advice; If you hope, Sir Moufe, ever to get out, you muft ftay till you're as lean as when you came in

1

I F

Hac ego ſi conpellor imagine, cuncta reſigno :

Nec ſomnum plebis laudo ſatur altilium, nec   35

Otia divitiis Arabum liberrima muto.

Sæpe verecundum laudaſti : Rexque, Paterque

Audiſti coram, nec verbo parcius abſens ·

Inſpice, ſi poſſum donata reponere lætus.

Haud male Telemachus proles patientis Ulixei ; 40

Non eſt aptus equis Ithace locus, ut neque planis

Porrectus ſpatiis, nec multæ prodigus herbæ.

Atride, magis apta tibi tua dona relinquam.

Parvum parva decent. mihi jam non regia Roma,

Sed vacuum Tibur placet, aut inbelle Tarentum 45

    Strenuus & fortis, cauſſiſque Philippus agendis

Clarus, ab officiis octavam circiter horam

Dum redit, atque foro nimium diſtare Carinas

Jam grandis natu queritur ; conſpexit, ut aiunt,

Adraſum quendam vacua tonſoris in umbra   50

Cultello proprios purgantem leniter unguis.

Demetri, (puer hic non læve juſſa Philippi

IF any one thinks fit to make the Application of this Fable to me, I am ready to refign
all my Poffeffions When I praife a Peafant's
quiet Life, 'tis not becaufe I am furfeited with
Plenty; no! my *Mæcenas,* 'tis my Love of Liberty which makes me defire it, which I wou'd
not exchange for all the Riches in *Arabia* You
have often commended me for my Modefty;
I faid in your Prefence, that you were a King
and Father to me, and in other Places I have
done you Juftice. Try me, Sir, If I am not
willing to reftore what your Bounty has given
me 'Twas an excellent Reply of young * *Telemachus,* when *Menelaus* would have prefented
him with fome fine Horfes, Sir, faid he, " I
" do not know what to do with them; there
" are no Plains in *Ithaca,* Pafture and Forrage
" are very fcarce; pray keep your Prefent, it
" is much fitter for your felf than me.

MEAN things beft become mean Men; *Ti-
bur* and *Tarentum,* the fweet and peaceful *Tibur*
and *Tarentum* delight me more than the Palaces
of *Rome*

PHILIP, a great and eminent Lawyer, as
he went home one Day from Pleading, full of
Complaints, that the *Forum* and † *Carinas* were
too diftant from each other for a Man in Years,
as he was, faw a Freed-Man in a Barber's Shop,
who was paring his Nails in a very carelefs negligent Manner. *Demetrius,* faid he, (this was
his Foot-boy, and knew how to take a Meffage

---

* *Telemachus,* the Son of *Ulyffes* by *Penelope* His
Speech to *Menelaus* in *Homer,* Odyf. Book 4. is here
very happily tranflated by our Poet, as you may fee
by comparing 'em together

† *Carinas,* a Street of *Rome* between *Mount Efquiline*
and *Mount Cælius*

Accipiebat) *abi, quære, & refer; unde domo, quis,*

Cujus fortunæ, quo sit patre, quove patrono

It, redit, & narrat, Volteium nomine Menam   55

Præconem, tenui censu, sine crimine natum,

Et properare loco & cessare, & quærere & uti,

Gaudentem parvisque sodalibus & lare curto,

Et ludis & post decisa negotia Campo.

Scitari libet ex ipso, quodcumque refers. dic   60

Ad cenam veniat. non sane credere Mena:

Mirari secum tacitus. quid multa? Benigne,

Respondet. Neget ille mihi? Negat, improbus, & te

Negligit, aut horret. Volteium mane Philippus,

Vilia vendentem tunicato scruta popello,   65

Occupat, & salvere jubet prior. ille Philippo

Excusare laborem & mercenaria vincla,

Quod non mane domum venisset; denique quod non

Providisset eum.   Sic ignovisse putato

Me tibi, si cenas hodie mecum. Ut libet. Ergo   70

Post nonam venies. nunc i, rem strenuus auge.

Ut

very well) Go, enquire, and bring me Word who that Man is; let me know his Father, Family, Condition and Patron. The Servant went and return'd in a trice, and told his Master, that the Man's Name was *Vulteius Mena,* by Profession a Cryer, of a small Estate, but of honest Parents; one who perfectly knew how to work and to be idle, to get and to spend too: He usually kept Company with none but his Equals, had a little House of his own, and, when Business was over, never scrupled to divert himself with a *Comedy,* or in taking a Walk in the *Campus Martius.* I wou'd hear what you say, from himself, said *Philip;* go, and invite him from me to Supper. *Demetrius* went, and came back and told his Master, that *Mena* was so surpriz'd at the Invitation, that he wou'd not believe him; nevertheless he return'd his Thanks in a very civil obliging Manner. What, did he refuse me, cry'd *Philip?* Sir, reply'd *Demetrius,* he either fears or neglects you.

THE next Morning *Philip* happen'd to meet him, as he was selling Frippery to the poorer People: He immediately address'd him, and bad him good Morrow. *Vulteius,* being all in Confusion at so unexpected an Honour, began to excuse himself, that the Meanness of his Trade, to which he was a Slave, prevented his waiting on him in the Morning, and that he beg'd his Pardon for not seeing him first. I will easily excuse you, said *Philip,* upon Condition that you sup with me in the Evening. *Vulteius* made Answer, that he was at his Service. I usually, said *Philip,* eat after Three; in the mean time I wou'd advise you to mind your Business, and to get what you can.

U SUPPER-

Ut ventum ad cenam est; dicenda, tacenda locutus
Tandem dormitum dimittitur. hic ubi sæpe
Occultum visus decurrere piscis ad hamum,
Mane cliens, & jam certus conviva; jubetur 75
Rura suburbana indictis comes ire Latinis.
Impositus mannis, arvum cælumque Sabinum
Non cessat laudare. videt, ridetque Philippus.
Et sibi dum requiem, dum risus undique quærit,
Dum septem donat sestertia, mutua septem 80
Promittit; persuadet, uti mercetur agellum.
Mercatur. ne te longis ambagibus ultra
Quam satis est morer; ex nitido fit rusticus, atque
Sulcos & vineta crepat mera: præparat ulmos
Immoritur studiis, & amore senescit habendi. 85
Verum ubi oves furto, morbo periere capellæ;
Spem mentita seges, bos est enectus arando;
Offensus damnis, media de nocte caballum
Arripit, iratusque Philippi tendit ad ædis
Quem simul aspexit scabrum intonsumque Philip-
    pus;
Durus, ait, Voltei, nimis attentusque videris 90

Esse

SUPPER-TIME being come, *Vulteius* went according to his Promise; he talk'd at Random of a thousand Things, and at length took Leave *Philip* perceiving that *Mena* (like a Fish that nibbles at the Bait) was constantly at his Levé, and that he was always a sure Guest at Supper, gave him an Invitation to pass the * Holidays with him in the Country Accordingly into the Country they went; *Vulteius* being mounted on an excellent Pad, cry'd out in a Rapture, Oh the sweet Air! Oh the delicious *Sabine* Fields! *Philip* was exceedingly pleas'd to see his Transports, and, as he studied his own Ease and Pleasure, immediately gave him Seven Thousand Sesterces, and promis'd to lend him as much more, provided he wou'd buy a little Farm that was near his Seat, and settle in the Country *Vulteius* accepts of *Philip*'s kind Offer, and buys the Farm. To make short of the Story, the Citizen turns Farmer, and now all his Discourse is of Vines and Furrows, and planting of Elms, He almost kills himself with Pains, and grows Old with the Pursuit after Riches But at last his Sheep were stol'n; his Kids dy'd, his Harvests were bad, his Oxen were kill'd with working too hard Being quite discourag'd with so many Losses, he rises at Midnight, mounts his Horse, and goes to *Philip* in the utmost Confusion; who seeing him make such a rough and clownish Figure, said, *Vulteius,* you take too much

---

* *Latina Indicta,* Festivals celebrated upon *Mount Alba,* in Memory of a Treaty of Peace concluded between the *Romans* and the *Hernici Volsci,* and the other People of *Latium* These Feasts continu'd four Days, the Time of their Celebration was at the Pleasure of the *Consul*

Pains,

Esse mihi   Pol me miserum, patrone, vocares;
Si velles, inquit, verum mihi ponere nomen.
Quod te per Genium dextramque, Deosque Penates,
Obsecro, & obtestor; vitæ me redde priori.   95
Qui semel aspexit, quantum dimissa petitis
Præstent; mature redeat, repetatque relicta.
    Metiri se quemque suo modulo ac pede, verum
est.

EPISTOLA VIII.

Ad Celsum Albinovanum.

CELSO gaudere & bene rem gerere Albinovano,
    Musa rogata, refer, comiti scribæque Neronis
Si quæret, quid agam, dic multa & pulchra mi-
    nantem,
Vivere nec recte, nec suaviter · haud quia grando
Contuderit vitis, oleamve momorderit æstus;   5
Nec quia longinquis armentum ægrotet in agris.
Sed quia mente minus validus quam corpore toto,
Nil audire velim, nil discere, quod levet ægrum.
Fidis offendar medicis, irascar amicis,
Cur me funesto properent arcere veterno.   10

Quæ

Pains, you are over follicitous. *Mena* reply'd, O my Patron, if you will call me by my proper Name, fay I am a poor and miferable Wretch But I conjure you by the Gods, by your own Right Hand and happy *Genius*, reftore me again to my former Condition. As foon as ever any Man has found, that the Way of Life which he has quitted is preferable to that which he is in, let him make hafte back to it, and take it up again; for this is a fure Maxim, that every one fhould examine his Capacity, and direct himfelf accordingly

EPISTLE VIII.

To *Celfus*.

GO, Mufe, to *Celfus*, *Nero*'s Secretary, you will find him among that Prince's Retinue; fay that I wifh him all Health and Happinefs. If he asks you, how I do, tell him, that after all the fair Promifes I have made, I live neither a good Life nor a pleafant one. It is not becaufe my Vines or Olives are utterly ruin'd by the Hail and Heat, nor becaufe my Flocks, who feed abroad in diftant Paftures, are in a languifhing Condition; but being diftemper'd more in Mind than Body, I cannot endure to hear of a Remedy. I chide my Friends, and am angry with them, when, like faithful Phyficians, they endeavour to awake me from my Lethargy I eagerly pur-

fue

Quæ nocuere fequar, fugiam quæ profore credam:
Romæ Tibur amem, ventofus, Tibure Romam
Poft hæc, ut valeat; quo pacto rem gerat & fe;
Ut placeat Juveni, percontare, utque cohorti:
Si dicet, Recte · primum gaudere, fubinde   15
Præceptum auriculis hoc inftillare memento;
Ut tu fortunam, fic nos te, Celfe, feremus

EPISTOLA IX.
Ad Claudium Neronem.

SEPTIMIUS, Claudi, nimirum intelligit
    unus,
Quanti me facias nam cum rogat, & prece cogit
Scilicet, ut tibi fe laudare & tradere coner,
Dignum mente domoque legentis honefta Neronis,
Munere cum fungi propioris cenfet amici;   5
Quid poffim, videt ac novit me valdius ipfo.
Multa quidem dixi, cur excufatus abirem ·
Sed timui, mea ne finxiffe minora putarer,
Diffimulator opis propriæ, mihi commodus uni

ſue what is hurtful to me, and as eagerly avoid that which is good. I am ſo inconſtant, that when I am at *Rome*, I want to be at *Tibur*; when at *Tibur*, I wiſh to be at *Rome*. Having told him all this, inform your ſelf concerning his Health ; enquire how Affairs go with him? whether he is a Favourite with the Prince and Court ? If he ſays, he is , Congratulate him upon it; and then be careful gently to remind him, that as he behaves himſelf under his good Fortune, ſo ſhall we, his Friends, behave our ſelves towards him

EPISTLE IX.

To *Claudius Nero.*

My Dear Prince,

ONE wou'd imagine, that none but *Sep-* He re*timius* knows what a Value you have for com-me ; for when he importunes, and even forces Friend me to recommend him to your Favour, as one *Septimius* worthy to attend upon your Highneſs, who to *Clau-*chooſe none but the Deſerving, when he fan-*dius*'s Facies that I have the Honour of an intimate vour. Friendſhip with you, he, forſooth, knows better than I do, the Intereſt which I have in you I us'd a great many Arguments why I ought to have been excus'd from venturing upon it; but in Truth I was afraid of being thought to repreſent your Regard for me as leſs than it is, and to diſſemble my Power with you, that I
U 4 might

Sic ego, majoris fugiens opprobria culpæ,　　10
Frontis ad urbanæ deſcendi præmia. quod ſi
Depoſitum audas ob amici juſſa pudorem;
Scribe tui gregis hunc, & fortem crede bonumque.

EPISTOLA X.

Ad Fuſcum Ariſtium.

URBIS amatorem Fuſcum ſalvere jubemus
Ruris amatores; hac in re ſcilicet una
Multum diſſimiles. at cetera pene gemelli,
Fraternis animis · quicquid negat alter, & alter:
Adnuimus pariter vetuli notique columbi,　　5
Tu nidum ſervas; ego laudo ruris amœni
Rivos, & muſco circumlita ſaxa, nemuſque
Quid quæris? vivo & regno, ſimul iſta reliqui
Quæ vos ad cælum fertis rumore ſecundo.

Utque,

might the better promote my own private Intereſt : And thus avoiding the being reproach'd
with a Crime of a worſe Sort, I ſubmitted to
put on a little Town-Aſſurance *. But if you
can excuſe the laying aſide of Modeſty, when
it is only to comply with the Commands of a
Friend, receive *Septimius* into your Retinue,
and believe me, when I aſſure you that he is a
Man of Courage and Virtue.

* I fancy that the Phraſe of *frontis urbanæ præmia*
was uſed by ſome Poet of the Age, and that *Horace*
brings it in here as a ridiculous one. A thing which
the Criticks think he has done more than once in his
Writings.

EPISTLE X.

To *Fuſcus Ariſtius.*

I WISH my Friend *Fuſcus* all imaginable He pre-
Happineſs, you love the Town and I the fers the
Country ; but let us not be the leſs dear to each Country
other, ſince in all Things elſe our Sentiments to the
are the ſame. Never two Brothers had more City.
Affection for one another. Our Harmony is
like that of two kind Turtles, who, Time out
Mind, have been Mates together You ſit upon the Neſt, while the Brooks, and Groves,
and Grottoes are my Delight The very Moment I depart from *Rome*, which you and o-
thers commend to the Skies, I am as Happy,
and as Great as an Emperor, like ſome Prieſt's
Servant,

Utque facerdotis fugitivus, liba recufo;   10

Pane egeo, jam mellitis potiore placentis.

Vivere naturæ fi convenienter oportet,

Ponendæque domo quærenda eft area primum;

Noviftine locum potiorem rure beato?

Eft, ubi plus tepeant hiemes? ubi gratior aura 15

Leniat & rabiem Canis, & momenta Leonis,

Cum femel accepit folem furibundus acutum?

Eft, ubi divellat fomnos minus invida cura?

Deterius Libycis olet aut nitet herba lapillis?

Purior in vicis aqua tendit rumpere plumbum, 20

Quam quæ per pronum trepidat cum murmure ri-

    vum?

Nempe inter varias nutritur filva columnas,

Laudaturque domus, longos quæ profpicit agros,

Naturam expelles furca, tamen ufque recurret,

Et mala perrumpet furtim faftidia victrix.   25

    Non, qui Sidonio contendere callidus oftro

Nefcit Aquinatem potantia vellera fucum,

Certius accipiet damnum, propiufve medullis;

Quam qui non poterit vero diftinguere falfum.

Quem res plus nimio delectavere fecundæ,   30

Mutatæ quatient. fi quid mirabere, pones

Invitus fuge magna licet fub paupere tecto

Reges & regum vita præcurrere amicos.

Servant, I am cloy'd with Cakes, I prefer good wholfome Bread to Sweetmeats

IN order to a pleafant delicious Life, the firft Thing to be confider'd is, where to fettle. What Place can you pitch upon that is preferable to the Country? Is there any Place where the Winters are warmer? Where a cooler Air foftens the fultry Autumn's Heat, and calms the Rage and Fury of the Lion, when the fcorching Sun is got into that Sign? Is there any Place where you can fleep more fecure from Cares? Does not the Colour and Beauty of the Grafs excel your fineft *Libyan* Marble? The Water that is forc'd into Leaden Pipes, is it purer than that of our murmuring Brooks, which run in a conftant natural Courfe? How much are thofe Seats efteem'd in *Rome*, which have a Profpect of a fort of Country within them? How do Men affect to plant Trees between the Columns of Marble of diverfe Colours, by which the nobleft Porticoes are fupported? 'Tis impoffible to make Nature change her Biafs, if you fhut her out at the Door, fhe'll come in at the Window, and by Stealth, as it were, become victorious over all your falfe irrational Difgufts. The Merchant who don't know the Cloth dyed with *Italian* Purple from the *Tyrian*, will not be more fenfibly a Sufferer, than he who cannot diftinguifh Truth from Falfhood. He that is too much elevated in Profperity, will moft certainly be dejected in an adverfe State. If you love any Thing above Meafure, the Lofs of it will grieve you Fly Greatnefs; a poor Man in a lonely Cell, as to the real Pleafures of Life, may be happier than a King and all his Nobles.

ONCE

Cervus equum pugna melior communibus herbis

Pellebat; donec minor in certamine longo　　　　35

Inploravit opes hominis, frenumque recepit ·

Sed poſtquam violens victo diſceſſit ab hoſte,

Non equitem dorſo, non frenum depulit ore.

Sic qui pauperiem veritus potiore metallis

Libertate caret, dominum vehit improbus, atque 40

Serviet æternum, quia parvo neſciet uti

Cui non conveniet ſua res, ut calceus olim

Si pede major erit, ſubvertet, ſi minor, uret.

Lætus ſorte tua vives ſapienter, Ariſti ·

Nec me dimittes incaſtigatum, ubi plura　　　　45

Cogere quam ſatis eſt, ac non ceſſare videbor

Imperat aut ſervit collecta pecunia cuique,

Tortum digna ſequi potius quam ducere funem.

　　Hæc tibi dictabam poſt fanum putre Vacunæ;

Excepto, quod non ſimul eſſes, cætera lætus.　　50

EPISTOLA

ONCE upon a Time, the Stag, having got the better of the Horse, drove him out of the Common; the Horse, to be reveng'd, implor'd Man's Assistance, and gladly suffer'd himself to be bridled But his Revenge cost him dear; for tho' by this Means he subdu'd his Enemy, yet he found afterwards that he could not get the Rider off from his Back, or the Bit out of his Mouth And thus, whosoever sells his Liberty, which is more precious than Gold, thro' the Fear of Poverty, gives up to another the Mastery of him, and is a Slave for Life, because he knows not the Art of being happy with a little. If a Man's Circumstances don't fit him, he will find them like his Shoes, if too big for his Feet, they will trip him up; if too little, they will pinch him. O *Aristius*, if you are wise, live contented with your Condition. If ever I lay up more than what is sufficient, and don't stop my Hand, I give you Leave to reprimand me Money is every Man's Master, or his Slave, but it is much better that it should follow, than lead him

P S. FROM behind the Temple of the Goddess * *Vacuna* I want nothing to compleat my Happiness, but your good Company.

---

* *Vacuna*, the Goddess of the Peasants She was very favourable and propitious to those who sought their Quiet, they celebrated her Feast in *December*.

EPISTLE

EPISTOLA XI.
Ad Bullatium.

QUID tibi visa Chios, Bullati, notaque Les-
          bos?
Quid concinna Samos? quid Crœsi regia Sardis?
Smyrna quid, & Colophon? majora minorane fa-
    ma?
Cunctane præ Campo & Tiberino flumine sordent?
An venit in votum Attalicis ex urbibus una?   5
An Lebedum laudas, odio maris atque viarum?
Scis, Lebedus quid sit. Gabiis desertior atque
Fidenis vicus: tamen illic vivere vellem;
Oblitusque meorum, obliviscendus & illis,
Neptanum procul e terra spectare furentem   10
Sed neque qui Capua Romam petit imbre lutoque
Aspersus, volet in caupona vivere; nec qui
Frigus collegit, furnos & balnea laudat,
Ut fortunatam plene præstantia vitam
Nec si te validus jactaverit Auster in alto,   15
Idcirco navem trans Ægæum mare vendas
Incolumi Rhodos & Mitylene pulchra facit, quod

                              Penula

EPISTLE XI.

To *Bullatius*.

BULLATIUS, how were you pleas'd with *Chios* and *Lesbos*? What are your Thoughts of *Samos* and *Smyrna*, of *Colophon* and *Sardis*, where the mighty *Crœfus* kept his Court? Do they exceed the common Report, or come fhort of it? Are they not all much in-feriour to *Rome*? Have they any Thing that e-quals our *Campus Martius*, or the celebrated *Tiber*? Were you not charm'd with the Cities in *Afia*? Had you not rather fettle at *Lebedos*, than expofe your felf anew to the Fatigues of Travelling by Sea and Land? *Bull* You know well enough what a Place *Lebedos* is, *Gabii* and *Fidenæ* are not fo unpeopled as that is And yet I could wifh to take up my Abode there, and to fee nothing of the raging Ocean but from a Di-ftance, forgetting all my Acquaintance, and be-ing forgotten by them *Hor.* But yet they who in travelling from *Capua* to *Rome* arrive at an Inn all wet and dirty, tho' they find it a con-venient Place, do not defire to fettle there A good Fire and a Bath may be very acceptable to one whofe Limbs are benum'd with Cold, but they do not compleat the Happinefs of Life. Becaufe you have been toft in a Tempeft at Sea, muft you therefore fell your Ship when you come to Land? If you have entirely con-quer'd your Paffions, neither *Rhodes* nor *Mity-lene*,

Penula folftitio, campeftre nivalibus auris,
Per brumam Tiberis, Sextili menfe caminus.
Dum licet, ac voltum fervat fortuna benignum, 20
Romæ laudetur Samos, & Chios, & Rhodos abfens.
Tu, quamcumque Deus tibi fortunaverit horam,
Grata fume manu; neu dulcia differ in annum.
Ut, quocumque loco fueris, vixiffe libenter
Te dicas nam fi ratio & prudentia curas, 25
Non locus effufi late maris arbiter aufert;
Cælum, non animum, mutant qui trans mare cur-
    runt;
Strenua nos exercet inertia · navibus atque
Quadrigis petimus bene vivere quod petis, hic eft,
Eft Ulubris; animus fi te non deficit æquus. 30

EPISTOLA XII.

Ad Iccium.

F*RUCTIBUS Agrippæ Siculis, quos colligis,*
    Icci,
Si recte frueris; non eft ut copia major

lene, how charming ſoever, are of any more Uſe than a Cloak in Summer, and a Silk Waſt-coat when it ſnows, *Tiber* in Winter, or a Fire in *Auguſt* While you enjoy a proſperous For-tune, and have all that you can wiſh for at your Command, if I may adviſe you, return to *Rome* · There you may be laviſh in your Pane-gyricks of *Rhodes*, *Chios* and *Samos* Be thank-ful to the Gods for the happy Moments they beſtow upon you; enjoy the preſent Pleaſures, and do not defer them to another Time. Let every Place be ſtill the ſame to you, and reſt contented wherever you are For if Reaſon and Prudence only take away Cares, it is not the happy Situation of any Town that will cure you; in vain you croſs the Seas, the Cli-mates are different, but your Mind is the ſame The Pains which we take are all to no Pur-poſe, they are a kind of laborious Idleneſs, we compaſs Sea and Land in Purſuit of Happineſs; and yet what you ſeek is at Home, it is even to be found at *Ulubræ*, if you can keep your Paſſi-ons under Subjection.

EPISTLE XII.

To *Iccius.*

IF you make a right Uſe of the Fruit you gather from the Lands which you hold of * *Agrippa* in *Sicily*, you are ſufficiently happy
Away

He advi-ſes his Friend to be con-tented with his Condi-tion.

---

* *Agrippa* having entirely defeated the Younger *Pom-pey* in a Sea-Fight near *Meſſina*, *Auguſtus* in Recompence for

X

Ab Jove donari poſſit tibi tolle querelas ·
Pauper enim non eſt, cui rerum ſuppetit uſus
Si ventri bene, ſi lateri eſt, pedibuſque tuis; nil 5
Divitiæ poterunt regales addere majus.
Si forte in medio poſitorum abſtemius, herbis
Vivis & urtica; ſic vives protenus, ut te
Confeſtim liquidus fortunæ rivus inauret:
Vel quia naturam mutare pecunia neſcit, 10
Vel quia cuncta putas una virtute minora
Miramur, ſi Democriti pecus edit agellos
Cultaque, dum peregre eſt animus ſine corpore ve-
lox?   ·
Cum tu inter ſcabiem tantam & contagia lucri

Nil

Away with Complaints; for he that wants nothing, cannot be Poor. If you are but provided for Back and Belly, and have all the Ne-
ceſſaries of Life, 'tis not in the Power of *Jove*
himſelf to make you richer   If it be true *,
that in the midſt of what you poſſeſs, you live
ſparingly and temperately upon Herbs, you will
live on ſtill after the ſame manner, even though
† Riches ſhould come rowling in haſtily upon
you; either becauſe it is not in their Power to
alter your Nature, or becauſe it is your ſettled
Opinion that theſe are not to be regarded in
Compariſon of Virtue   Do we wonder that
Democritus, when his Soul was, as it were,
gone, Abroad from his Body, to ſearch into
the Secrets of Nature, left his Field as a Prey
to his Neighbours Cattel? And is it not much
more wonderful, that, in this avaritious dege-
nerate Age, when Men, as I may ſay, infect
each other with the Love of Money, you
ſhou'd ſo entirely withdraw your Mind from
the Things of this World, as to give up your

for ſo great a Service, beſtow'd upon him ſeveral conſiderable Lordſhips in *Sicily*.

* *If it be true*, &c. This Place has hitherto been
miſunderſtood by the Commentators and Interpreters
of *Horace*, but is here ſet right by rendring *ut, tho'*, a
Senſe which is frequently given to it in good Authors,
and even in *Horace* himſelf, as might be ſhewn by Inſtances, if there were Occaſion   The 10th and 11th
Verſes are (according to this Interpretation) good Reaſons why Increaſe of Riches would not alter *Iccius*'s
Temper   But as this Paſſage is commonly underſtood,
they are no Reaſons at all for any thing ſaid before

† The Poet alludes in this Place to *Pactolus* and *Tagus*,
the one a River of *Spain*, whoſe Source is in *Caſtile* on
the Borders of *Arragon*, the other of *Libya*, now call'd
Sarabat, both celebrated by the Poets for their Golden
Sands.

X 2   ſelf

Nil parvum fapias, & adhuc fublimia cures. 15
Quæ mare conpefcant cauffæ. quid temperet an-
num:
Stellæ fponte fua, juffæne vagentur & errent
Quid premat obfcurum lunæ, quid proferat orbem ·
Quid velit & poffit rerum concordia difcors :
Empedocles, an Stertinium deliret acumen.   20
    Verum feu pifcis, feu porrum & cæpe trucidas,
Utere Pompeio Grofpho; &, fi quid petet, ultro
Defer: nil Grofphus nifi verum orabit & æquum.
Vilis amicorum eft annona, bonis ubi quid deeft.
Ne tamen ignores, quo fit Romana loco res.   25
Cantaber Agrippæ, Claudi virtute Neronis
Armenius cecidit. jus imperiumque Phraates
Cæfaris accepit, genibus minor. aurea fruges
Italiæ pleno defundit Copia cornu.

EPISTOLA

self to the sublime Study of Nature, to know
what it is that bounds the Sea, and occasions
such an agreeable Variety of Seasons, to know,
whether the Planets move of themselves, or
act in Obedience to some higher Cause? You
carefully enquire, what occasions the constant
regular Increase and Decrease of the Moon,
and what is the Nature and Power of the Ele-
ments, which, tho' always at Variance with
one another, unite together in preserving the
Universe. Whether * *Empedocles* or *Stertinius*
the *Stoick* has given the best Account of these
Matters. But whether you delight to feed on
Fish, or Onions and Garlick are your only Entertainment, afford my Friend *Grosphus* a kind
Reception. If he ask any Favour, grant him
his Request, assure your self, that *Grosphus* is
so wise and modest a Man, that he will ask you
nothing but what is very just and reasonable.
Surely Friends must be a Drug, when good
Men are suffer'd to be in Want!

I cannot conclude without acquainting you
with the present Condition of our Affairs.
Agrippa has entirely conquer'd the *Spaniards*;
Tiberius the *Armenians*, *Phraates* on his Knees
has submitted to *Cæsar*, and own'd himself his
Vassal. We have here in *Italy* a very plentiful
Harvest.

---

* *Empedocles*, a Philosopher of *Agrigentum*, now *Ger-*
genti in *Sicily*, he liv'd about the 84th *Olympiad*.

EPISTLE

EPISTOLA XIII.

Ad Vinnium.

*U*T *proficifcentem docui te fæpe diuque,*
    Augufto reddes fignata volumina, Vinni;
Si validus, fi lætus erit, fi denique pofcet:
Ne ftudio noftri pecces, odiumque libellis
Sedulus importes, opera vehemente minifter   5
Si te forte meæ gravis uret farcina chartæ,
Abjicito potius, quam quo perferre juberis
Clitellas ferus inpingas, Afinæque paternum
Cognomen vertas in rifum, & fabula fias
Viribus uteris per clivos, flumina, lamas   10
Victor propofiti fimul ac perveneris illuc,
Sic pofitum fervabis onus ne forte fub ala
Fafciculum portes librorum, ut rufticus agnum,
Ut vinofa glomus furtivæ Pyrrhia lanæ,
Ut cum pileolo foleas conviva tribulis   15
Neu volgo narres te fudaviffe ferendo
Carmina, quæ poffint oculos aurifque morari

                                    Cæfaris,

EPISTLE XIII.

To *Vinnius*.

ACCORDING to the many repeated Instructions which I gave you, before you went from me, see that you remember to deliver my Poems seal'd to *Augustus*; and that by no means you present him with them, unless he be well, in good Humour, and desirous to know the Contents of my Packet; but more especially take Care, lest by being too officious you do me a Disservice

IF you find your self overcharg'd with the Load of my Papers, throw them away, rather than stumble in *Cæsar*'s Presence; lest the Courtiers, alluding to your Father's Name, say you are an Ass, and make you the Subject of their Mirth and Raillery Use all your Strength in passing o'er the Mountains, Bogs and Rivers, and, when you come to Court, so order your self as to conceal my Poems, do not carry them under your Arm, as a Peasant carries a Lamb to the Market; or as a Guest his Cap and Slipper, when he returns from a Neighbour's Feast; or, as drunken *Pyrrhia*, who carry'd the Bottom of Yarn she had stol'n, in so publick a Manner, that the Theft was discover'd.

BUT above all, tell not every Passenger, how much you have sweated in carrying such Verses, as may possibly engage even *Cæsar* himself to hear or read 'em I conjure you, *Vin-*

X 4

Cæfaris, oratus multa prece, nitere porro
Vade, vale · cave ne titubes, mandataque frangas.

EPISTOLA XIV.
Ad Villicum Suum.

VILLICE filvarum & mihi me reddentis
　　agelli,
Quem tu faftidis habitatum quinque focis, &
Quinque bonos folitum Variam dimittere Patres;
Certemus, fpinas animone ego fortius, an tu
Evellas agro & melior fit Horatius, an ius　　5
　　Me quamvis Lamiæ pietas & cura moratur
Fratem mærentis, rapto de fratre dolentis
Infolabiliter; tamen iftuc mens animufque
Fert, & avet fpatiis obftantia rumpere clauftra
Rure ego viventem, tu dicis in Urbe beatum.　　10
Cui placet alterius, fua nimirum eft odio fors
Stultus uterque locum immeritum cauffatur inique.

In

nius, to proceed on your Journey; go, fare you well; be sure that you don't stumble and lose your Errand by the way.

EPISTLE. XIV.

To *his Bailiff.*

BAILIFF, who haft the Care of my Woods and of my Farm, the Place to which when I retire from Business, I am my self again; the Place, which, tho' you undervalue it, had antiently five Families in it, and us'd to send as many good Housekeepers up to *Varia* upon every publick Meeting Come, Bailiff, let you and I make a Trial, which of us is most industrious, you in Weeding my Fields, or I my Mind, and whether *Horace* or his Lands are best cultivated Tho' my Love to *Lamia,* who is sensibly afflicted at his Brother's Death, detains me at *Rome;* yet my Heart is with you. I long for nothing more, than to break thro' those Barriers which keep me here You place your Felicity in a City-Life, but 'tis the Country alone, that can make me happy He who envies his Neighbours Circumstances, is dissatisfied with his own We are both in the wrong to lay the Blame upon the Place were we are Alas! the Fault is in

He gives his Reasons, why he prefers the Country to the City.

---

* *Varia,* a little Village in the Country of the *Sabines,* situated between the *Tiber* and *Horace*'s Seat

the

In culpa eſt animus, qui ſe non effugit umquam.
Tu mediaſtinus tacita prece rura petebas
Nunc Urbem & ludos & balnea villicus optas. 15
Me conſtare mihi ſcis, & diſcedere triſtem,
Quandocumque trahunt inviſa negotia Romam.
Non eadem miramur. eo diſconvenit inter
Meque & te nam quæ deſerta & inhoſpita teſqua
Credis, amœna vocat mecum qui ſentit, & odit 20
Quæ tu pulchra putas formix tibi & uncta popina
Incutiunt Urbis deſiderium, video, & quod
Angulus iſte feret piper & tus ocius uva;
Nec vicina ſubeſt vinum præbere taberna
Quæ poſſit tibi, nec meretrix tibicina, cujus 25
Ad ſtrepitum ſalias teræ gravis & tamen urgues
Jampridem non tacta ligonibus arva, bovemque
Disjunctum curas, & ſtrictis frondibus exples
Addit opus pigro rivus, ſi decidit imber,
Multa mole docendus aprico parcere prato 30
Nunc age, quid noſtrum concentum dividat, audi.
Quem tenues decuere togæ nitidique capilli,
Quem ſcis inmunem Cinaræ placuiſſe rapaci,
Quem bibulum liquidi media de luce Falerni,

Cena

the Mind; and the Mind, you know, cannot
fly from it self When you were the lowest
of my Menial Servants, how often did you
pray to be my Country-Bailiff? Now you are
so, you grow weary of your Place, and desire
again to be at *Rome* You know very well,
that in this Particular I am much more constant, whenever I am forc'd away to *Rome* by
that odious Thing called Business, I go with a
sad and aking Heart. Our Inclinations are entirely different, we cannot admire one and the
same Thing Nothing is so disagreeable to you
as the Country, to you it seems a Desart; but
to me, and to those who delight in Solitude, 'tis
irresistibly charming, they and I can't endure
to live at *Rome,* but you esteem it as your only
Happiness. You long to enjoy a Bottle and a
Mistress, and that is the Reason why you wish
to be there You complain that my Lands
will sooner bring forth Frankincense and Pepper, than the generous Grape, that there is
no Publick-House to supply you with Wine;
nor kind fair Minstrel to provoke your Heavi-
ness to dance to her hoarse untuneable Voice.
You are moreover oblig'd to till the Ground,
which Time out of Mind has been neglected;
you must fodder the Oxen when loosned from
the Plough, and what is yet more, in Rainy
Weather, when you hop'd to enjoy a little
Ease, you must dam up the Rivers to prevent
Inundations

Now learn the Reasons, why you and I
cannot accord. 'Tis confess'd, that formerly I
lov'd to be Gay; fine Cloaths and powder'd
Hair were my Delight, the covetous *Cynara*
entertain'd me *gratis,* I oftentimes spent whole
Nights in drinking, but now a little Supper

Cena brevis juvat, & prope rivum somnus in
   herba.   35
Nec lusisse pudet, sed non incidere ludum.
Non istic obliquo oculo mea commoda quisquam
Limat, non odio obscuro morsuque venenat:
Rident vicini glebas & saxa moventem.
Cum servis tu urbana diaria rodere mavis   40
Horum tu in numerum voto ruis . invidet usum
Lignorum & pecoris tibi calo argutus & horti
Optat ephippia bos . piger optat arare caballus.
Quam scit uterque libens, censebo, exerceat artem.

EPISTOLA XV.
Ad C. Numonium Valam.

*Q*UÆ *sit hiems Veliæ, quod cælum, Vala,*
       Salerni,
Quorum hominum regio, & qualis via · (nam mi-
  hi Baias
Musa supervacuas Antonius . & tamen illis

                                     Me

contents me: I covet no greater Happineſs than to ſleep on the Banks of ſome peaceful Stream 'Tis no Shame for a Man to have been extravagant, but to continue ſo

WHEN I am in the Country, no Man envies my Condition, I live ſecure from poiſonous Tongues, nor does any one, that I know of, hate me in ſecret. My Neighbours ſmile when they behold me working in my Fields· You, on the contrary, want to be in Town to eat with my Footmen; They, on the other ſide, envy your Condition, and wiſh they had Horſes and Woods and Gardens, to make uſe of as they pleaſed The Ox wou'd be Saddled, and the lazy Horſe wou'd go to Plough; but 'tis my Advice, that every one ſhou'd diligently mind his own Buſineſs

EPISTLE XV.

To his Friend Vala.

IAM about to leave * *Baiæ* and its Waters; † *Antonius Muſa* adviſes me againſt them The Inhabitants are much incens'd againſt me, He deſires to be inform'd of the Conveniencies of the Place, whither he deſigns to retire for his Health.

* See *Book* II *Sat* IV.
† *Anton Muſa, Gr..an,* Phyſician to *Auguſtus,* whom he cur'd of dangerous Fit of Sickneſs by Bathing, In Recompence of which Cure the *Romans* erected a Statue to him, near that of *Æſculapius.* He was the firſt Phyſician that adviſed the Uſe of the Cold Bath.

becauſe

Me facit invisum, gelida cum perluor unda

Per medium frigus. sane murteta relinqui, 5

Dictaque cessantem nervis elidere morbum

Sulfura contemni, vicus gemit; invidus ægris,

Qui caput & stomachum subponere fontibus audent

Clusinis, Gabiosque petunt & frigida rura.

Mutandus locus est, & deversoria nota 10

Præteragendus equus Quo tendis? non mihi Cumas

Est iter aut Baias; læva stomachosus habena

Dicet eques sed equis frenato est auris in ore)

Major utrum populum frumenti copia pascat,

Collectosne bibant imbris, puteosne perennis 15

Jugis aquæ · (nam vina nihil moror illius oræ:

Rure meo possum quidvis perferre patique

Ad mare cum veni, generosum & lene requiro,

Quod

because I use the Cold Bath in the Winter
They complain of my leaving their Myrtle
Groves, and neglecting their Waters, which
by reason of their Sulphur are deservedly famous for curing of the Gout.   They cannot
bear that any sick Persons shou'd use the cold
Baths of a *Clusium* and b *Gabij*   To calm
their Resentments, I resolve to remove, and my
Horse must not stop at the usual Stages.   I
shall grow angry with him by the Way, and
turning my Bridle to the Left, shall cry, Whither
would you go? I don't design for c *Cumæ* or
Baiæ   But I shall be a Fool for talking to him,
for it is the Rein only that can make him understand me   Tell me therefore, good *Vala*, is the
Winter kind at d *Velia* and e *Salernum?* Is the
Air healthy? What sort of People are the Inhabitants, and which is the readiest Way to go
thither? Does *Velia* or *Salernum* abound most
in Corn? How is their Water? Do they keep
it in Cisterns, or have they Plenty of Wells?
As for the Wine of those Parts, I have no great
Opinion of it   I can make shift with any in
the Country, tho' never so ordinary, but when
I come to a Sea-Port Town, give me some no-

---

a *Clusium,* now *Chiusi,* a City of *Tuscany,* where
King *Porsenna* kept his Court.

b *Gabij,* a little City situate between *Præneste* and
Rome

c *Cumæ,* a small Town not far from *Baiæ,* famous
for several curious Antiquities, particularly for the
Grotto of the *Sibylla*

d *Velia,* a City of *Lucania*

e *Salernum,* now *Salerno,* a City in the Kingdom of
Naples, which was a *Roman* City and Colony call'd *Urbs
Picentorum*   The School of the Physicians which is
kept here, is deservedly famous for the great Men it has
produc'd, and for the Book of Verses known by the
Name of *Schola Salernitana*

Quod curas abigat, quod cum fpe divite manet
In venas animumque meum, quod verba mini-
 ftret,   20
Quod me Lucanae juvenem commendet amicae)
Tractus uter pluris lepores, uter educet apros;
Utra magis pifcis & echinos aequora celent,
Pinguis ut inde domum poffim Phaeaxque reverti:
Scribere te nobis, tibi nos adcredere, par eft   25
 Maenius, ut rebus maternis atque paternis
Fortiter abfumtis urbanus caepit haberi;
Scurra vagus, non qui certum praefepe teneret;
Inpranfus non qui civem dignofceret hofte;
Quaelibet in quemvis opprobria fingere faevus;   30
Pernicies & tempeftas barathrumque macelli,
Quicquid quae fierat, ventri donaret avaro
Hic, ubi nequitiae fautoribus & timidis nil
Aut paullum abftulerat, patinas cenabat unafi,
Vilis & agninae; tribus urfis quod fatis effet   35
Scilicet ut ventres lamna candente nepotum
Diceret urendos corrector Beftius idem
Si quid erat nactus praedae majoris, ubi omne
Verterat in fumum & cinerem, Non hercule miror,
Aiebat, fi qui comedunt bona cum fit obefo   40
Nil melius turdo, nil volva pulchrius ampla.
Nimirum hic ego fum · nam tuta & parvula laudo,

           Cum

ble Wine, which will drive away my Cares, infpire my Heart with Hope and Gladnefs, and make me eloquent   Are there many Hares and Boars in thefe Places? Are their Seas well ftock'd with Fifh? Have they Plenty of Cray-fifh? As I have no fmall Confidence in you, I defire to be fully inform'd in thefe Particulars, that, at my Return, I may appear as plump and healthy as if I had liv'd at *Alcinous's* Court.

MÆNIUS having fquander'd away his Eftate, fet up for a Wit, he had no conftant Eating-place, but was forc'd to dine where he cou'd : When he was hungry .he wou'd be ve-ry fcurrilous, at fuch times he fpar'd neither Friend nor Foe, all were alike to him; he was the very Ruin and Deftruction of the Market, whate'er he got, he fpent upon his Belly. When he met with little or nothing abroad, from thofe who lov'd to encourage Extravagance, or who fometimes gave him a Meal's Meat out of Fear of him, he wou'd devour as much Guts and Garbage as wou'd ferve Three Bears; and then, putting on a ferious Air, like another *Beftius,* he wou'd fay, that no *Epicure* deferv'd to live, that their Bellies fhou'd be fear'd with a red-hot Iron, as a Punifhment for their Lux-ury   At other times when he glutted himfelf with better Fare, I do not wonder (faid he) that Men fpend their Eftates in eating well; for certainly, nothing in the World can be more excellent than an Hog's Harflet, and a fine fat Thrufh   Thus it is with me   When I am forc'd to feed on coarfe homely Food, I praife a quiet frugal Life, and like a Philofo-pher feem perfectly contented with my Condi-tion; but when I fit at a great Man's Table,

Y   who

Cum res deficiunt; satis inter vilia fortis.
Verum ubi quid melius contingit & unctius; idem
Vos sapere & solos aio bene vivere, quorum   45
Conspicitur nitidis fundata pecunia villis.

EPISTOLA XVI.

Ad Quintium.

NE perconteris, fundus meus, optime Quinti,
  Arvo pascat herum, an baccis opulentet olivæ,
Pomisne, an pratis, an amicta vitibus ulmo;
Scribetur tibi forma loquaciter & situs agri
  Continui montes; ni dissocientur opaca   5
Valle   sed ut veniens dextrum latus aspiciat Sol,
Lævum decedens curru fugiente vaporet.
Temperiem laudes   quid, si rubicunda benigni
Corna vepres & pruna ferunt? si quercus & ilex
Multa fruge pecus, multa dominum juvat um-
  bra?   10
Dicas adductum propius frondere Tarentum.
Fons etiam rivo dare nomen idoneus, ut nec
Frigidior Thracam nec purior ambiat Hebrus,
Infirmo capiti fluit utilis, utilis alvo
Hæ latebræ dulces, & (jam si credis) amœnæ,   15
Incolumem tibi me præstant Septembribus horis.

Tu

who eats nothing but what is exquifitely fine;
they only, then fay I, are wife and happy, who
lay out their Money in Lands and Houfes, and
are Mafters of large and plentiful Eftates

EPISTLE XVI.

To *Quintius.*

Deareft QUINTIUS,

TO prevent your Enquiries concerning my
Farm, whether it yields me Hay or Corn
in Plenty, or whether it abounds in Olives, or
Apples, or Vines, I here fend you a Defcription
of it   'Tis pleafantly fituated between Two
Mountains, which are divided by a fruitful Val-
ley; the Right is to the Eaft, the Left to the
Weft; the Climate is exceeding temperate, it
is neither too hot, nor too cold.   Did you but
fee how my Quickfets abound with Sloes and
Cornels, how my Oaks give Plenty of Acorns
to my Cattel, and to me a fweet and delightful
Shade; you wou'd think your felf at the charming * *Tarentum*   Here is alfo a Fountain, which
is large enough to give Name to a River, not
Hebrus's Waters are purer, or cooler, it has,
over and above, this extraordinary Quality, that
it is very good for the Head and Cholick   It
is this fweet and delicious Solitude, which pre-
ferves me in Autumn from all Difeafes

*The De-
fcription
of his
Farm.*

* See *Book* I *Sat.* VI

Y 2   You

Tu recte vivis, si curas esse quod audis.

Jactamus jampridem omnis te Roma beatum

Sed vereor, ne cui de te plus quam tibi credas;

Neve putes alium sapiente bonoque beatum ·   20

Neu, si te populus sanum recteque valentem

Dictitet, occultam febrem sub tempus edendi

Dissimules, donec manibus tremor incidat unctis.

Stultorum incurata pudor malus ulcera celat

Si quis bella tibi terra pugnata marique   25

Dicat, & his verbis vacuas permulceat auris ,

Tene magis salvum populus velit, an populum tu,

Servet in ambiguo, qui consulit & tibi & Urbi,

Juppiter. Augusti laudes agnoscere possis.

Cum pateris sapiens emendatusque vocari;   30

Respondesne tuo, dic sodes, nomine? nempe

Vir bonus & prudens dici delector ego, ac tu

Qui dedit hoc hodie, cras, si volet, auferet: ut si

Detulerit fascis indigno, deripiet idem

Pone, meum est, inquit · pono, tristisque rece-

do.   35

Idem,

You are truly happy, if you endeavour to be what Men ſay you are It is a long Time ſince all *Rome* ſpoke of you, as a happy Man I am mightily afraid, that you believe what others ſay of you, rather than your ſelf; and that you think a Man may be happy tho' he be neither Wiſe nor Good. What if others are pleas'd to ſay you look well, muſt you therefore diſſemble your Fever ſo long, till the Fit ſeizes you at Supper? It is owing to a falſe and vitious Modeſty that Fools often conceal their Sores, ſo that no * Care is taken of them Shou'd any one flatter you ſo far as to ſay, that you have gain'd conſiderable Battles both by Land and Sea; and wiſh that *Jupiter*, who preſerves the City in preſerving you, may ſtill keep us in Suſpence, whether you are more zealous of the Safety of the *Romans*, or they of yours Shou'd any one, I ſay, addreſs you in this Manner, you wou'd preſently reply, that ſuch Praiſes as theſe belong only to *Auguſtus*. But when they give you the flattering Titles of Wiſe and Good, tell me, my *Quintius*, how can you take them, as if they were your Due? *Qu'n* O! very eaſily, I am pleas'd with the Character, and am as much delighted with being thought a Wiſe and Good Man, as you your ſelf can be. *Hor.* But the People who give you theſe flattering Titles, can take them away as their Fancy moves them: As they make a Man *Conſul*, and remove him at Pleaſure Come, ſay they, lay down your good Cha-

Advice concerning a happy Life

___

* *Curare ulcus* and *ſanare ulcus* differ much, the laſt ſignifies *to heal a Sore*, the firſt only *to dreſs it*, or *take Care of it.* So *Hor.* Ep l 2 Ep. 2 150 ——— Fugeres radice vel herba 'proficiente nihil curarier.

racter;

Idem, ſi clamet furem, neget eſſe pudicum,

Contendat laqueo collum preſſiſſe paternum,

Mordear opprobriis falſis, mutemque colores.

Falſus honor juvat, & mendax infamia terret

Quem, niſi mendoſum & medicandum? vir bonus

    eſt quis?   40

Qui conſulta Patrum, qui leges juraque ſervat,

Quo multæ magnæque ſecantur judice lites,

Quo res ſponſore, & quo cauſſæ teſte tenentur.

Sed videt hunc omnis domus & vicinia tota

Introrſus turpem, ſpecioſum pelle decora.   45

Nec furtum feci, nec fugi, ſi mihi dicit

Servus   Habes pretium; loris non ureris, aio.

Non hominem occidi. Non paſces in cruce corvos

Sum bonus, & frugi· renuit negitatque Sabellus

Cautus enim metuit foveam lupus, accipiterque 50

Suſpectos laqueos, & opertum miluus hamum

Oderunt peccare boni, virtutis amore.

Tu nihil admittes in te, formidine pœnæ

Sit ſpes fallendi, miſcebis ſacra profanis.

Nam de mille fabæ modiis cum ſubripis unum, 55

Damnum eſt, non facinus, mihi pacto lenius iſto.

                                             Vir

racter; it is we who gave it you: I lay it down,
but muft I do it with Grief and Dejection?
And fo, if the People fhould on the other
hand report, that I am a Thief, that I lead a
lewd and infamous Life, that I murder'd my
Father, fhall I fuffer fuch Calummes as thefe
to move me, fhall they make me turn pale, or
create in my Face the leaft Diforder? To be
pleas'd with a good Name, and to be afraid of
a bad one, when we don't deferve either, fhews
that we have Faults which ought to be corrected. Who then is a good Man? *Quin* He,
who obeys the Laws of the Senate, and invio-
lably adheres to the Rules of Juftice, who is
chofen Arbitrator in the greateft Matters;
whofe Truth and Integrity are fo well known,
that they always are fure of gaining their Caufe
for whom he appears as Witnefs. *Hor* And
yet this wife good Man you fpeak of, notwithftanding his formal fpecious Appearance of being a juft and upright Man, is known by his
Domefticks to be a Knave at the Bottom, and
is generally thought fuch by all the Neighbourhood If my Servant fay, I am no Thief, nor
did I ever defert your Service I reply, 'tis
well, you have efcap'd being whip'd I am
no Murderer; if you were, you would be cru-
cified If he continues, I am a good and vertuous Man, that I deny For the Wolf, Hawk
and Kite are afraid of the Snares which Men
lay for them They that are good, refrain from
Vice out of Love to Vertue, but you refrain
for Fear of being punifh'd Cou'd you be fure
of paffing undifcover'd, not the Temples of
the Gods wou'd then efcape you If from a
thoufand Bufhels of Beans you fteal but one,
the Damage is lefs to me, but the Crime is not

Y 4 fo

Vir bonus, omne forum quem ſpectat & omne tri-
    bunal, '

Quandocumque Deos vel porco vel bove placat,

Jane pater, clare, clare cum dixit, Apollo

Labra movet metuens audiri; Pulchra Laverna, 60

Da mihi fallere, da juſto ſanctoque videri

Noctem peccatis, & fraudibus objice nubem

Qui melior ſervo, qui liberior ſit avarus,

In triviis fixum cum ſe demittit ob aſſem,

Non video. nam qui cupiet, metuet quoque   por-
    ro   . 65

Qui metuens vivit, liber mihi non erit umquam

Perdidit arma, locum virtutis deſeruit, qui

Semper in augenda feſtinat & obruitur re.

Vendere cum poſſis captivum, occidere noli.

Serviet utiliter. ſine paſcat durus aretque   70

Naviget, ac mediis hiemet mercator in undis.

Annonæ proſit, portet frumenta penuſque

Vir bonus & ſapiens audebit dicere, Pentheu

Rector Thebarum, quid me perferre patique

Indignum

fo to you. That Oracle of the Law, whom you lately mention'd, who is fo much refpected in all the feveral Courts of Juftice; when he offers a Hog or Ox in Sacrifice, cries with a loud and audible Voice, hear me, Father *Janus*, O *Apollo* hear me! then, fhutting his Lips, he mutters to himfelf, "Beauteous *La- "verna!* grant me the Art of deceiving Man- "kind; let the World believe me Juft and "Honeft, and let all my wicked fraudulent "Practices be buried in Darknefs. And then for the Covetous Man; in what Refpects is he better than a Slave, when, in paffing the Streets, he foolifhly ftoops down to take up a Penny that is nail'd to the Ground? In Truth there is little Difference between 'em, they are both Slaves; he that is Covetous lives in Fear, and Fear and Slavery are one and the fame Thing. The Man that perpetually fatigues himfelf, and impairs his Health in heaping up Riches, is like a Soldier that has loft his Arms, and de- ferted from his Colours; he has bafely quitted the Caufe of Vertue, and is good for nothing: Whereas your Slave, fo you do not kill him, may be ferviceable to you in many Refpects; you may fell him if you pleafe, or you may employ him in feeding your Cattel, and manu- ring your Lands. In the Winter he may make a Voyage, improve your Revenues, and return home laden with Corn and Provifions for the Neceffities of Life To conclude, he only is truly Wife and Good, who (like *Bacchus* in the Tragedy) dares fay to *Pentheus* King of *Thebes*, What Punifhment will you inflict on

---

* *Laverna*, the Patronefs of Thieves, fhe had a ftately Temple at *Rome*, fhe was adored in *Greece* under the Name of *Praxidica*.

Indignum coges? Adimam bona. Nempe pecus,
 rem, 75
Lettos, argentum: tollas licet. In manicis &
Compedibus fævo te fub cuftode tenebo
Ipfe Deus, fimul atque volam, me folvet opinor,
Hoc fentit, Moriar. mors ultima linea rerum eft.

EPISTOLA XVII.

Ad Scævam.

*Q*UAMVIS, *Scæva, fatis per te tibi confu-*
 lis, & fcis
Quo tandem pacto deceat majoribus uti,
Difce, docendus adhuc quæ cenfet amiculus: ut fi
Cæcus iter monftrare velit: tamen afpice, fi quid
Et nos, quod cures proprium feciffe, loquamur. 5
  Si te grata quies & primam fomnus in horam
Delettat, fi te pulvis ftrepitufque rotarum,
Si lædet caupona; Ferentinum ire jubebo.
Nam neque divitibus contingunt gaudia folis,

Nec

me, who am innocent? *Pen.* I will take away your Goods. *Bac.* You mean my Beds and Money and Cattel; you may take them. *Pen.* I will confine you close Prisoner, load you with Irons, and appoint you a hard and cruel Goaler. *Bac.* A God, when I call, will give me a Deliverance. I suppose that he means this, *I will die.* Death is the End of all our Miseries.

EPISTLE XVII.

To *Scæva.*

THOUGH you know well enough by this Time how to behave your self among your Superiours, yet vouchsafe to learn of me, for still you are unacquainted with the Sentiments of your Friend upon this Matter: Tho' I must own that it is like a Blind Man's pretending to shew the Road; yet however see if I have not something to offer on the Subject, which you may think worth the putting in Practice. If you desire to take your Ease, and sleep till Seven or Eight in the Morning; if you cannot endure the Clattering of Coaches, nor the more tumultuous roaring Noise, which usually abounds in all Publick Houses, take my Advice and retire to * *Ferentino.* For it is not the rich Man only who is Happy; nor was he

He advises his Friend Scæva, how he ought to demean himself in the Company of great Men.

* * *Ferentino,* a small Village in *Italy,* about ten Miles from *Agnania,* which was formerly a very considerable City, but now almost ruin'd

a mi-

Nec vixit male, qui natus morienſque fefellit. 10

Si pi odeſſe tuis, paulloque benignius ipſum

Te tractare voles; accedes ſiccus ad unctum.

Si pi anderet olus patienter; regibus uti

Nollet Ai iſtippus Si ſci et regibus uti;

Faſtidi et olus, qui me notat utrius hoi um 15

Vei ba probes & facta, doce vel junior, audi

Cur ſit Ariſtippi potioi ſententia namque

Mordacem Cynicum ſic eludebat, ut aiunt;

Scurror ego ipſe mihi, populo tu · rectius hoc &

Splendidius multo eſt. equus ut me portet, alat

　rex, 20

Officium facio tu poſcis vilia rei um,

Dante minor; quamvis fei s te nullius egentem.

Omnis Ai iſtippum decuit color & ſtatus & i es,

Tentatem

a miferable one who lived and died in an obfcure Retreat   But if you defire to ferve your
Friends, and give a little more Indulgence to
your felf, frequent the Tables of the Great [a]
If [b] *Ariftippus,* faid *Diogenes,* knew how to
dine on Herbs, he wou'd not be fo often at
great Men's Tables   *Ariftippus* reply'd; if
[c] *Diogenes* knew how to make his Court to Princes,
ces, he wou'd foon difdain his Dinner of Herbs
Which of thefe two was in the right? Either
tell me your Opinion, or learn from me, who
am older than your felf, why I give my Vote
for *Ariftippus*   I divert the Great, faid *Ariftip-*
pus to the *Cynick,* and am plentifully rewarded,
you divert the common People, and have nothing for your Pains   I make my Court, and
eat with Princes, [d] you beg your Bread from
Door to Door, and tho' you pretend that you
want for nothing; yet by accepting the Alms,
you fhew your felf poorer than thofe who relieve you.   As for [e] *Ariftippus,* all Stations,
Condi-

[a] *Tables of the Great*   The Latin is *unctum,* which fignifies a Feaft, or delicious Entertainment, as in *Art.*
Poet v 422.

  Si verò eft, unctum qui recte ponere poffit

[b] See *Book* II *Sat* III

[c] *Diogenes,* a *Cynick* Philofopher born at *Sinope,*
A. U. C 341   He embrac'd a voluntary Poverty, and
liv'd in a Tub.   See the Particulars of his Hiftory and
Sayings in *Diogenes Laertius,* l 6

[d] In Cafe, fays *Epicurus,* our wife Man fhou'd be reduc'd to want the common Neceffaries of Life, yet
will he not with the *Cynicks* betake himfelf to the common Refuge of Begging, but rather undertake the In-
ftruction of others in Wifdom, and by fo doing act
according to the Dignity of his Prudence, and at the
fame time defervedly accommodate himfelf with what
he wants, from thofe that have Abundance

[e] There is no Condition that does not fit well upon a
wife Man.   For this Reafon I fhall never quarrel with
a Phi-

Tentantem majora, fere præfentibus æquum.

Contra, quem duplici panno patientia velat,   25

Mirabor, vitæ via fi converfa decebit.

Alter purpureum non exfpectabit amictum;

Quidlibet indutus celeberrima per loca vadet;

Perfonamque feret non inconcinnus utramque

Alter Mileti textam cane pejus & angui   30

Vitabit chlamydem; morietur frigore, fi non

Rettuleris pannum: refer, & fine vivat ineptus

Res gerere & captos oftendere civibus hofti,

Attingit folium Jovis & cæleftia tentat

Principibus placuiffe viris, non ultima laus eft 35

Non cuivis homini contingit adire Corinthum

Sedit, qui timuit ne non fuccederet · efto ·

Quid? qui pervenit, fecitne viriliter? atqui

Hic eft, aut nufquam, quod quærimus. hic onus
  horret,

Ut

Conditions, and Circumſtances of Life ſat well on him . He was commonly trying to mend his Fortune, yet was always contented with what it was. But on the other hand, as for that Fellow, wrapt round with Patience, and a double-breaſted Great-Coat, I mean *Diogenes,* I ſhould wonder much if any other Way of Life ſhould become him The firſt will never ſtay to put on his beſt Cloaths, but will paſs thro' Places of the greateſt Reſort with a Thread-bare Coat on his Back, and yet both Parts will become him, that of a Beau, and that of a Sloven But ſhou'd you offer a Scarlet Cloak to *Diogenes,* he wou'd ſhun it *as* he wou'd a Dog or Serpent, rather than wear it, he wou'd go in his Shirt and die with Cold Give him his Weather-beaten Cloak again, and let him ſuffer for his Folly.

To gain great Victories, and to ride in Triumph thro' the City of *Rome* with a Train of Captives, are Things ſo truly great and glorious, that they make a Man almoſt equal to the Gods Nor is it a mean and ordinary Accompliſhment to be able to pleaſe Great Men ; few there are who know how to do ſo He that doubts of Succeſs, chooſes to ſit ſtill, and not expoſe himſelf Agreed But what will you ſay of him that ſucceeds? Is he not a very gallant Man? Either here or no where the Perſon is to be found that we are enquiring after. The one is afraid that the Enterprize is too

a Philoſopher for living in a Prince, but ſhall at the ſame Time not excuſe him, if he can't content himſelf with a Cottage I ſhall not be ſcandaliz'd to behold him in the Apparel of Kings, provided he has not their Ambition *Monſieur* Evremont *in his Reflections upon the Doctrine of* Epicurus

great,

Ut parvis animis & parvo corpore majus: 40

Hic fubit, & perfert. aut virtus nomen inane eft,

Aut decus & pretium recte petit experiens vir.

    Coram rege fuo de paupertate tacentes

· Plus pofcente ferent   diftat, fumafne pudenter,

An rapias. atqui rerum caput hoc erat, hic fons. 45

Indotata mihi foror eft, paupercula mater,

Et fundus nec vendibilis nec pafcere firmus,

Qui dicit; clamat, Victum date. fuccinit alter,

Et mihi dividuo findetur munere quadra.

Sed tacitus pafci fi poffet corvus, haberet   50

Plus dapis, & rixæ multo minus invidiæque.

    Brundifium comes aut Surrentum ductus amœ-

    num,

Qui queritur falebras & acerbum frigus & imbris,

Aut ciftam effractam & fubducta viatica plorat;

Nota refert meretricis acumina, fæpe catellam, 55

Sæpe

great; that neither his Strength nor Courage is sufficient: The other boldly undertakes the Matter, and is crown'd with Success Now you must confess, that Virtue is only an empty Name, or that he who knows how to make his Address to Men of Quality, deserves both to be commended, and rewarded for it

THEY who say nothing of their Poverty before their Patron *, will get more than the Importunate and Craving And even when a Present is made you, there is a wide Difference between catching greedily at it, and receiving it modestly. This is a Precept of the highest Importance. He who says, I have a Sister unprovided of a Fortune , my Mother is poor; I cannot live on the Income of my Estate, and am so tied up, that I cannot sell it; says, in effect, Give me somewhat to subsist me Another starts up, and immediately subjoyns, Let me I beseech you, Sir, share in your Bounty. But if the Raven would eat his Meat in Quiet, he wou'd have more of it; and no one wou'd enter into Contest with him, or envy his good Fortune.

A MAN of Quality makes an Invitation to one that waited on him at his Levee, I shall be glad, Sir, says he, of your Company to *Brindes* or *Surrentum*, 'tis a sweet Place The Man replies, the Weather is cold, the Ways are bad and plashy, that his Cabinet was lately broke open, and his Money stol'n. He that expresses himself after this manner, gives us to understand what he wou'd be at, and his Reward is accordingly It is with him as with

Z Women

---

* *Their Patron.* Coram Rege *suo*, so I read, and not *suâ*, as if it were to be joyn'd with *paupertate.* If *Horace* had

said

Sæpe periscelidem raptam sibi flentis. uti mox
Nulla fides damnis verisque doloribus adsit.
Nec semel inrisus triviis attollere.curat
Fracto crure planum licet illi plurima manet
Lacrima; per sanctum juratus dicat Osirin,　　60
Credite, non ludo; crudeles, tollite claudum.
Quære peregrinum, vicinia rauca reclamat

EPISTOLA XVIII.
Ad Lollium.

*S*I *bene te novi, metues, liberrime Lolli,*
　　Scurrantis speciem præbere, professus amicum.
Ut matrona meretrici dispar erit atque
Discolor, infido scurræ distabit amicus
Est huic diversum vitio vitium prope majus,　　5
Asperitas agrestis & inconcinna gravisque.
Quæ se commendat tonsa cute, dentibus atris;

Dum

Women of the Town, who by often pretending imaginary Losses, make their real ones to
be disbeliev'd He that has once been sound-
ly laught at for relieving a Cheat, will be very
cautious that he be not couzen'd a second Time.
The impotent Vagrant may cry his Eyes out;
he may swear by *Osiris* that he is no Deceiver;
hear me ye cruel-hearted Men! instead of relieving him, the whole Neighbourhood immediately cry out upon him, Get you gone you
Rascal to those that do not know you.

* *Osiris*, the Patron of Vagrants, he is the same as
Apis and *Serapis*, by *Osiris* some understand the Sun.

EPISTLE XVIII.

To *Lollius*.

IF I know any thing of your Temper, *Lol-* He advi-
lius, you are too sincere to flatter your ses his
Friends A Friend in all his Actions and Beha- Friend
viour is as different from a Flatterer, as a vertu- get the
ous Lady, both in her Dress and Conversation, Love of
from a Woman of the Town But there is a all his
Vice quite opposite to this, which is more in- Acquain-
supportable I mean a clownish, disagreeable, tance
uncultivated Roughness of Behaviour, which

said *Coram Rege suâ*, &c then *Rex* should have signified a
King in general, but he is in this Epistle speaking of the
Arts of making Court to the Great among the *Romans*,
and Patrons were called the *Reges* of their Clients, so
Horace tells *Mæcenas*,

————*Rexq, Paterq,*
Audisti coram.————Epist. 7 V 37.

under

Dum volt libertas dici mera, veraque virtus.

Virtus est medium vitiorum, & utrimque redu-
 ctum.

Alter in obsequium plus æquo pronus, & imi 10

Derisor lecti, sic nutum divitis horret,

Sic iterat voces, & verba cadentia tollit;

Ut puerum sævo credas dictata magistro

Reddere, vel partis mimum tractare secundas.

Alter rixatur de lana sæpe caprina, & 15

Propugnat nugis armatus: Scilicet ut non

Sit mihi prima fides? &, vere quod placet, ut non

Acriter elatrem? pretium ætas altera sordet

Ambigitur quid enim? Castor sciat an Docilis plus;

Brundisium Minuci melius via ducat, an Appî 20

    Quem damnosa Venus, quem præceps alea nudat,

Gloria

under the Difguife of Virtue and plain Dealing, takes a Liberty of treating all Mankind with Infolence and Brutality.

ALL Vice confifts in Extremes, which are direct Contraries; and are either the Defect or Excefs of fome Virtue; fo that there are not only two Vices to every Virtue, but both are Extremes running counter to each other Between thefe are the Paths of Virtue, which lie ftrait forward, and like *Parallel Lines* never interfere True Virtue is the Medium between two Extremities. The Parafite is all Complaifance to the rich Man, at whofe Table he is, and is ever playing upon thofe who fit on the loweft Couch at Dinner He pays fuch a Regard even to the Nod of the Mafter of the Feaft, fo catches up his Words and repeats them, that you would think him like a School-boy faying his Leffon after his Mafter, or rather like one who acts an inferior Part in a Play, and does it in fuch a Manner as to fet off the principal Actor The other rude unconverfable Mortal, having little or no Knowledge of the World, and being over-full of himfelf, difputes about Trifles. What, fays he, fhall I not be believ'd fooner than another? Shall I not freely fpeak my Thoughts? Were I to live a hundred Years longer, on Condition I were filent, I wou'd much rather choofe to die, than be debarr'd of the Liberty of maintaining my Opinions Now what do you think was the Occafion of all this Heat? Why, 'twas only, whether *Caftor* or *Docilis* was the beft Fencer; whether the *Minucian* or *Appian* Way is the fhorter or better Way to *Brindes*

NOTHING is more common, than for a rich Man to hate thofe of his Acquaintance,

who

Gloria quem fupra vires & veftit & unguit,

Quem tenet argenti fitis inportuna famefque,

Quem paupertatis pudor & fuga, dives amicus,

Sæpe decem vitiis inftructior, odit & horret   25

Aut fi non odit, regit ; ac, veluti pia mater,

Plus quam fe fapere & virtutibus effe priorem

Volt: & ait prope vera; Meæ (contendere noli)

Stultitiam patiuntur opes   tibi parvula res eft .

Arta decet fanum comitem toga   define mecum 30

Certare Eutrapelus, cuicumque nocere volebat,

Veftimenta dabat pretiofa beatus enim jam

Cum pulchris tunicis fumet nova confilia & fpes;

Dormiet in lucem; fcorto poftponet honeftum

Officium; nummos alienos pafcet; ad imum   35

Threx erit, aut olitoris aget mercede caballum.

Arcanum neque tu fcruteris illius umquam,

Conmiffumque teges, & vino tortus & ira.

Nec tua laudabis ftudia, aut aliena reprendes

Nec, cum venari volet ille, poemata panges.   40

Gratia

who have fpent their Eftates in Play, or on Women, who are Covetous or Ambitious, or affect to live beyond their Circumftances, and choofe to do any Thing, tho' never fo difhonourable, to avoid being poor He cannot fo much as bear the Sight of them, tho' he himfelf is guilty of the fame, or greater Vices. If he does not deteft them, like a tender Mother, he advifes them to be better and wifer than himfelf. And certainly in fome Senfe, the Counfel which he gives is juft and reafonable. My Fortune, faith he, will bear me out in a thoufand Follies, you have but a fmall Income· He that lives upon another's Table (if he is wife) will cut his Coat according to his Cloth; then don't pretend to drefs at me

EUTRAPELUS, an old crafty Courtier, when any one offended him, took his Revenge in the following Manner. He prefented the Man with fine Cloaths and a fplendid Equipage, Thefe, faid he to himfelf, will fill his Mind with different Ideas, he will affect to live Great, fleep till Noon, take up Money at exceffive Intereft, and facrifice his Honour and Confcience to his Pleafures; till at laft he is forc'd to turn Gladiator and fight for a Subfiftence; or, what is as bad, hire himfelf to fome poor Gardener, to drive his Horfe laden with Cabbages to the Market

BE not over-follicitous to be made acquainted with your Friend's Secrets, but if, unask'd, he entrufts you with them, let not Wine or Provocations force you to betray him Neither cenfure others, nor commend your felf If your Friend at any Time asks you to go a Hunting, let not the Mufes be your Excufe Such a Pretence as this created a Difference be-

Z 4　　　　　　　tween

Gratia sic fratrum geminorum Amphionis atque
Zethi dissiluit, donec suspecta severo
Conticuit lyra. fraternis cessisse putatur
Moribus Amphion   tu cede potentis amici
Lenibus imperiis   quotiensque educet in agros   45
Ætolis onerata plagis jumenta canesque;
Surge, & inhumanæ senium depone Camenæ,
Cœnes ut pariter pulmenta laboribus emta:
Romanis sollemne viris opus, utile famæ,
Vitæque, & membris · præsertim cum valeas, & 50
Vel cursu superare canem, vel viribus aprum
Possis. adde, virilia quod speciosius arma
Non est qui tractet. scis quo clamore coronæ
Prœlia sustineas campestria . denique sævam
Militiam puer & Cantabrica bella tulisti   55
Sub duce, qui templis Parthorum signa refigit
Nunc; &, si quid abest, Italis adjudicat armis.

Aç

tween * *Zethus* and *Amphion* who were Twins,
nor had they ever been reconcil'd, had not *Amphion* laid aside his Musick, and comply'd with
his surly humoursome Brother.   When your
powerful Friend does but mention his Mind,
obey it as readily as if it was a Command:
When he leads out his Dogs and Horses to
the Field, let Poetry be neglected, which renders you unsociable; get up and hunt, and be
in with the formost, and enjoy with Pleasure
your Portion of the Prey.

HUNTING is a noble and generous Recreation, the *Romans* love it; 'tis Reputable and
Healthy, it makes the Limbs more pliant and
active: But above all Things, 'tis most proper
for you, who enjoy the Prime and Bloom of
Youth   No Man handles his Arms with a better Grace, in Swiftness you excel the fleetest
Hounds, and in point of Strength, the fiercest
Boars are nothing to you   With what Applause do you perform your Exercises in the
Field of *Mars?*   When you were little better
than a Boy, you made with Honour a Campaign in *Spain,* under that famous and renowned *General,* whose victorious Arms have recover'd our Banners from the *Parthian* Temples,
and, if any thing is wanting to compleat his
Glory, are now advancing to subdue the few
remaining Parts of the Universe, which refuse

---

* *Zethus* and *Amphion,* the Twin-Sons of *Jupiter* and
Antiope, their Inclinations were extreamly different,
Zethus lov'd Hunting, and *Amphion* delighted in nothing
but Musick, but as *Zethus* was of a rough and savage
Disposition, and consequently had no Ear for Musick,
he cou'd not endure that his Brother *Amphion* shou'd
play upon the Harp, he quarrel'd so often with him a-
bout it, that at last *Amphion* was oblig'd for Quietness
to bid adieu to Harmony.

Ac ne te retrahas, & inexcufabilis abftes;
Quamvis nil extra numerum feciffe modumque
Curas, interdum nugaris rure paterno. 60
Partitur lintris exercitus: Actia pugna,
Te duce, per pueros hostili more refertur:
Adverfarius est frater; lacus Hadria · donec
Alterutrum velox victoria fronde coronet.
Confentire fuis studiis qui crediderit te, 65
Fautor utroque tuum laudabit pollice ludum.

   Protenus ut moneam; (si quid monitoris eges tu)
Quid de quoque viro, & cui dicas, fæpe videto
Percontatorem fugito nam garrulus idem est
Nec retinent patulæ conmiffa fideliter aures; 70
Et femel emiffum volat inrevocabile verbum.

   Non ancilla tuum jecur ulceret ulla puerve,
Intra marmoreum venerandi limen amici:
Ne dominus, pueri pulchri caræve puellæ
Munere te parvo beet, aut incommodus angat 75
Qualem conmendes, etiam atque etiam aspice: ne
  mox
Incutiant aliena tibi peccata pudorem.
Fallimur, & quondam non dignum tradimus: ergo,
Quem fua culpa premet, deceptus omitte tueri.
At penitus notum si tentent crimina, ferves 80

Tuterifque

to submit to the *Roman* Power. It wou'd be an unpardonable Fault in you, wholly to abstain from this noble Recreation: For tho' no Man observes a just *Decorum* more strictly than your self, yet in the Country, you do not disdain to amuse your Thoughts with youthful Diversions. You divide a little Army of Boys into two Parts; each has an equal Number of Vessels You command the one, and your Brother the other; the *Lucrine* Lake serves you instead of the *Adriatick*; here you fight o'er again the Battle at * *Actium*, and never give over, till one Side is victorious This Condescension to your Brother's Inclinations will gain you Friends, and engage other Men to approve of yours. One more Piece of Advice I am to give you (if there be any Advice that you want) which is, that you be very careful of what you say of other Men, and to whom you say it Shun all inquisitive curious Persons; they are commonly Tatlers, and a Word once spoken can never be recall'd

IT concerns you also to be very cautious whom you recommend; lest you happen to be put to the Blush for the Miscarriages of others Shou'd this be your Case, (for we are all fallible, and sometimes recommend unworthy Persons) as soon as you are convinc'd that he is blameable, don't pretend to take his Part that has thus deceiv'd you· But if you are well af-

* *Actium*, a Promontory of *Epirus*, now *Capo Figulo.* Near this Place *Augustus* overcame *Marc Antony*, built the City *Nicopolis* in Memory of the Victory, instituted the *Actian* Games to be solemniz'd every five Years, and repair'd the Temple of *Apollo*, new dedicating it to *Mars* and *Neptune.* This Battle was fought A. M. 4024, about 30 Years before *Christ.*

sur'd

Tuterifque tuo fidenter præfidio: qui
Dente Theonino cum circumroditur, ecquid
Ad te post paullo ventura pericula fentis?
Nam tua res agitur, partes cum proximus ardet:
Et neglecta folent incendia fumere vires   85

    Dulcis inexpertis cultura potentis amici:
Expertus metuit. tu, dum tua navis in alto eft,
Hoc age, ne mutata retrorfum te ferat aura
    Oderunt hilarem tristes, tristemque jocofi,
Sedatum celeres, agilem gnavumque remiffi .   90
Potores liquidi media de luce Falerni
Oderunt porrecta negantem pocula; quamvis
Nocturnos jures te formidare tepores.
Deme fupercilio nubem. plerumque modestus
Occupat obfcuri fpeciem, taciturnus acerbi   95

    Inter cuncta leges & percontabere doctos,
Qua ratione queas traducere leniter ævum;
Ne te femper inops agitet vexetque cupido,
Ne pavor, & rerum mediocriter utilium fpes
Virtutem doctrina paret, naturane donet .   100

Quid

ſur'd that he is unjuſtly accus'd, ſpeak up for him, and defend him, for he relies on you as his Patron and Friend. When your Neighbour's Houſe is ſet on Fire, you run great Riſque of loſing your own; the Flames will ſpread, unleſs ſpeedily extinguiſh'd.

To attend upon the Great, ſeems pleaſant to thoſe, who know nothing of the Matter; but they who have experienc'd what it is, are afraid of engaging a ſecond Time in ſo doubtful an Employment. While your Ship enjoys a proſperous Gale, be ſure to improve ſo fair an Opportunity, leſt the Wind change, and force you back again into the Port, from whence you ſet ſail

THEY who are of a gloomy Temper, deteſt a lively and facetious Man; the lively and facetious abhor a dull and gloomy Gravity. The ſlothful Man hates him that is active, and is hated by him; they who drink hard, diſdain the Man that refuſes his Glaſs; in vain you pretend that the Vapours in the Night are very unwholſome, you muſt not be ſo uncomplying

IN Converſation put on an open and chearful Countenance, generally ſpeaking the Shamefac'd Man paſſes for a Dull one, and the Silent for a Moroſe one.

AMONG other things, do not neglect to read the Philoſophers; learn from the Wiſe the invaluable Secret how to lead an eaſie and contented Life. Let them inſtruct you how to moderate your Deſires, that the Hopes and Fears of things, that can hardly be ſaid to be profitable, may not perplex and diſturb your Felicity. They will inform you, whether Virtue is implanted in our Nature, or attainable

able

Quid minuat curas, quid te tibi reddat amicum:
Quid pure tranquillet; honos, an dulce lucellum,
An secretum iter & fallentis semita vitæ
Me quotiens reficit gelidus Digentia rivus,
Quem Mandela bibit, rugosus frigore pagus; 105
Quid sentire putas, quid credis, amice, precari?
Sit mihi, quod nunc est, etiam minus & mihi
    vivam
Quod superest ævi, si quid superesse volunt Di·
Sit bona librorum & provisæ frugis in annum
Copia   neu fluitem dubiæ spe pendulus horæ 110
Sed satis est orare Jovem, quæ ponit & aufert.
Det vitam, det opes· æquum mi animum ipse pa-
    rabo.

EPISTOLA XIX.
Ad Mæcenatem.

PRISCO si credis, Mæcenas docte, Cratino;
   Nulla placere diu nec vivere carmina possunt,
Quæ scribuntur aquæ potoribus. ut male sanos,

Adscripsit

able by Study. They will tell you what
it is which leſſens our Cares, and makes a Man
in Friendſhip with himſelf Whether Riches
or Honour, or a private Retirement, where
Life inſenſibly glides away, is the trueſt Happineſs When I ſit on the Banks of *Digentia's*
Stream (which ſupplies the Inhabitants of *Mandela* with Water) than which nothing in Nature is more refreſhing, what do you think is
the utmoſt of my Wiſhes? All that I deſire, is
quietly to poſſeſs the little I have, or even leſs,
if Heaven ſo pleaſes; and, for the Time that
is yet to come, if any Remainder is yet behind,
to live at my own Diſpoſal Let me have a
good Number of the choiceſt Books, and a
Year's Proviſion before-hand in my Barns. And
may I never be toſs'd too and fro between Hopes
and Fears of what is to happen hereafter,——
but I forbear——it is ſufficient that I ask of
Jupiter thoſe Things which he can give, or
take away Let him but grant me Life and
Riches; and I will take Care to provide my
ſelf with ſuch an Evenneſs of Temper, as that
I may enjoy his Bleſſings aright

EPISTLE XIX.

To *Mæcenas.*

Learned MÆCENAS,

IF you believe old *Cratinus,* they who drink
nothing but Water, will never make good
Poets, the Verſes they write, pleaſe only for a
Time,

Adſcripſit Liber Satyris Fauniſque poetas;
Vina fere dulces oluerunt mane Camenæ. 5
Laudibus arguitur vini vinoſus Homerus.
Ennius ipſe pater numquam niſi potus ad arma
Proſiluit dicenda. Forum putealque Libonis
Mandabo ſiccis, adimam cantare ſeveris.

  Hoc ſimul edixi; non ceſſavere poetæ 10
Nocturno certare mero, putere diurno.
Quid? ſi quis voltu torvo ferus, & pede nudo,
Exiguæque togæ ſimulet textore Gatonem;
Virtutemne repræſentet moreſque Catonis?
Rupit Iarbitam Timagenis æmula lingua; 15
Dum ſtudet urbanus, tenditque diſertus haberi.
Decipit exemplar vitiis imitabile quod ſi
Pallerem caſu, biberent exſangue cuminum.
O imitatores, ſervum pecus; ut mihi ſæpe
Bilem, ſæpe jocum veſtri movere tumultus! 20

Libera

Time; they quickly periſh, and are utterly forgotten

SINCE *Bacchus* thought fit to rank the Poets with the *Fauns and Satyrs,* the Muſes have conſtantly indulg'd themſelves with the Juice of the Grape. Even * *Homer* himſelf, as is evident from his frequent Encomiums upon Wine, was no Starter from it   Old Father † *Ennius* was likewiſe ſenſible of the good Effects of it; he never ſet himſelf to write of Battles before he had warm'd and elevated his Spirits with a Glaſs of good Wine. Let thoſe who drink nothing but Water, mind the Buſineſs of the Law; let them not dare to invoke the Muſes. I had no ſooner ſaid this in Publick, than all the Poets fell to drinking for the Laurel, Day and Night together   What if any one ſhould affect *Cato*'s rugged Air, walk without Shoes, and wear, like him, a little ſcanty Cloak, muſt it therefore follow, that he can imitate his Virtues? *Hiarbitas,* by endeavouring to emulate ‡ *Timagenes* in his Wit and Raillery, quite ruin'd himſelf. A Model that is faulty in ſome Particulars, if thoſe Faults are imitated, is oftentimes of dangerous Conſequence to thoſe who form themſelves by it   If by Chance I ſhould look pale, I'll warrant that the whole Tribe of Poets would immediately drink Cummin, that their Looks might be like mine   Ye ſervile Mortals, ye very Herd of Imitators! how often have ye ſet me a fretting, how often a laughing with your apiſh Affectations?

* See *Book* I. *Sat* X.   † See *Book* I *Sat.* IV.
‡ *Timagenes,* an Orator of *Alexandria,* was for ſome Time in great Favour with *Auguſtus,* which he fooliſhly loſt, by taking too great a Freedom with the Emperor.

Libera per vàcuum posui vestigia princeps,

Non aliena meo pressi pede. qui sibi fidit,

Dux regit examen   Parios ego primus Iambos

Ostendi Latio, numerosque animosque secutus

Archilochi, non res & agentia verba Lycamben. 25

Ac ne me foliis ideo brevioribus ornes,

Quod timui mutare modos & carminis artem.

Temperat Archilochi Musam pede mascula Sappho,

Temperat Alcæus, sed rebus & ordine dispar

Nec socerum quærit, quem versibus oblinat

*   atris,*   30

Nec sponsæ laqueum famoso carmine nectit

Hunc ego, non alio dictum prius ore, Latinus,

Volgavi fidicen juvat inmemorata ferentem

Ingenuis oculisque legi, manibusque teneri.

Scire velis, mea cur ingratus opuscula lector 35

Laudet ametque domi, premat extra limen iniquus?

Non

I was the first, who dar'd to tread in unbeaten Paths, where no Man ever set Foot before me   He that can justly depend upon himself, is fit to lead others   I was the first who attempted *Iambicks* in the *Latin* Tongue   I endeavour'd at the Numbers and Spirit of * *Archilochus*, but not his bitter Invectives, which cost *Lycambes* his Life   Nor is the Laurel less my Due for not changing his Measures, since I have happily intermix'd 'em with † *Sapphics* and ‡ *Alcaics*, which soften their Rapidity   Besides, the Subject and Manner of treating it are entirely different   In my Verses there is no Father-in-law inveigh'd against; nor any thing said so Infamous as to make a Spouse hang her self   It is much for my Glory, that I was the first who dar'd to imitate *Archilochus* in *Latin*; and as the thing was before unattempted, I shall take a particular Joy and Satisfaction in being read by Men of Quality

N o w, if you would know the Reason, why some unjust and ungrateful Persons pretend in Publick to censure my Writings, tho' they secretly admire them: 'Tis briefly this   I

---

* See *Book* II. *Sat.* III

† *Sappho*, a Poetess of the Isle of *Lesbos*, she writ nine Books of *Lyrick* Verses, and was the Inventress of that Kind of Verse which from her is call'd the *Sapphick*. She was particularly happy in the Sweetness of her Verses, in which are some Strokes of Delicacy, which are the finest and most passionate in the World 'Tis a thousand Pities, says M *Bayle*, that *Anacreon* and *Sappho* did not live together   If they had, they ought to have been Husband and Wife, that the World might have seen what would have been the Effect of two such delicate Souls   According to *Calvisius*, *Sappho* flourish'd in the Time of *Nabonassar*, A M 3341

‡ *Alcæus*, a *Lyrick* Poet of *Mitylene* in the Isle of *Lesbos*, Contemporary with *Sappho*

never

Non ego ventofæ plebis fuffragia venor
Impenfis cenarum, & tritæ munere veftis:
Non ego nobilium fcriptorum auditor & ultor,
Grammaticas ambire tribus & pulpita dignor. 40
Hinc illæ lacrimæ.   Spiffis indigna theatris
Scripta pudet recitare, & nugis addere pondus,
Si dixi; Rides, ait, & Jovis auribus ifta
Servas   fidis enim manare poetica mella
Te folum, tibi pulcher.   Ad hæc ego naribus uti 45
Formido; &, luctantis acuto ne fecer ungui,
Difplicet ifte locus, clamo, & diludia pofco.
Ludus enim genuit trepidum certamen, & iram;
Ira truces inimicitias, & funebre bellum.

EPISTOLA XX.

Ad Librum fuum.

VERTUMNUM Janumque, liber, fpectare
videris:
Scilicet ut proftes Sofiorum pumice mundus.

Odifti

never hunt for popular Applause, I difdain to treat the Mob for their Suffrages, or to purchafe their Votes with my caft off Cloaths I never hear the *Romans* repeat their Verfes, nor do I repeat mine. I don't make my Court to the Grammarians, which is the Caufe of their Rage againft me. If I fay, that I am afham'd to have my forry Lines rehears'd in the Theatre; that 'tis fetting a Value upon Things that are Trifles; you railly us, fay they; you referve your Poems for none but *Auguftus*; you fancy your felf the beft Poet of the Age, and vainly imagine that your Numbers alone are Sweet and Harmonious When they fay this, I dare not for my Life be fevere upon them, left, being provok'd, they fhould tear me in Pieces. I only reply, that the Place is not what I like, and therefore defire that we may not meet; for Contention produces Strife and Paffion; and Paffion concludes in War and Deftruction.

EPISTLE XX.

To his Book.

I FIND, my Book, that you want to be abroad; your Eyes are fix'd on * *Janus* and *Vertumnus*; you long to be neatly bound and gilt, and to lie expos'd in the Bookfellers Shops. A modeft Child delights to be under the Tuiti-

---

* Near the Statues of *Janus* and *Vertumnus*, which were plac'd in the *Tufcan* Street, there were a great many Bookfellers.

on

Odiſti claves, & grata ſigilla pudico;
Paucis oſtendi gemis, & communia laudas;
Non ita nutritus fuge quo deſcendere geſtis   5
Non erit emiſſo reditus tibi.   Quid miſer egi,
Quid volui? dices; ubi quid te læſerit, & ſcis
In breve te cogi, plenus cum languet amator
Quod ſi non odio peccantis deſipit augui,
Carus eris Romæ, donec te deſerit ætas.   10
Contrectatus ubi manibus ſoi deſcere volgi
Cœperis; aut tineas paſces taciturnus inertis,
Aut fugies Uticam, aut vinctus mitteris Ilerdam.
Ridebit monitor non exauditus   ut ille,
Qui male parentem in rupis protruſit aſellum   15
Iratus quis enim invitum ſervare laboret?
Hoc quoque te manet, ut pueros elementa docentem
Occupet extremis in vicis balba ſenectus

Cum

• on of his Parents, but you hate to be confin'd; the very Thought of being read only by a few Persons is grievous to you; you were not bred to appear in Publick, and yet you wish for nothing more Well, my Book, go where you please, but remember that when you are once set out, there is no returning. The Criticks will spend their Malice upon you; and then you will repent of what you have done, and bewail your Misfortune Even your Admirers will in a little Time grow weary of you, roll you up, and lay you aside If I am not prejudic'd thro' my Resentment of this your Folly, I will venture to prophesie that at your first Appearance in *Rome,* you will meet with a kind and civil Reception But when you shall fall into the Hands of the Vulgar, and become contemptible; they will throw you aside for a Prey to the Moths, transport you to * *Utica,* or perhaps employ you to a better purpose, in covering the Packets which go from hence to † *Lerida* How shall I then laugh at you for not following my Advice? like the Man in the Fable, who when he found that his Ass in spight of all he could do, would fall over the Precipice, e'en push'd him over For, who would take Pains to save him that will be ruin'd? I foresee likewise, that it will be your Destiny to be thumb'd by some old stammering Schoolmaster, who in the Suburbs of the City teaches

---

* *Utica,* a City of *Africa,* made famous by the Death of *Cato* the Younger, who kill'd himself in this Place.

† *Ilerda,* or *Lerida,* a City of *Catalonia* in *Spain,* in the Time of the *Romans* it was the Capital of that Part of *Spain* call'd *Tarraconensis.*

Boys

Cum tibi ſol tepidus pluris admoverit auris;
Me libertino natum patre, & in tenui re,   20
Majores pennas nido extendiſſe loqueris;
Ut quantum generi demas, virtutibus addas.
Me primis Urbis belli placuiſſe domique;
Corporis exigui, præcanum, ſolibus aptum;
Iraſci celerem, tamen ut placabilis eſſem.   25
Forte meum ſi quis te percontabitur ævum;
Me quater undenos ſciat impleviſſe Decembris,
Collegam Lepidum quo duxit Lollius anno

Q. HORATII

Boys to read. * Whenſoever the exceſſive Heat
of the Sun brings you in a large and numerous
Audience; be ſure to acquaint them, that, tho'
I was the Son of a Slave made free; yet by my
Learning I improv'd my Fortunes and advanc'd
my Condition. By this Means you will add to
my Merit, what you take from my Birth You
may tell 'em further, that I had the good Fortune to pleaſe the greateſt Men in *Rome*, both
Generals and Stateſmen, that my Stature was
ſmall; that my Hairs were grey before my
Time; that I lov'd to warm my ſelf in the
Sun, and as for my Temper, that I was ſoon
angry and ſoon pleas'd. If they ask my Age,
ſay that I was Four and Forty Years old, when
Lollius and *Lepidus* were *Conſuls.*

* The Poets recited their Verſes in Porticoes or Temples, and as theſe were cool Places, the hotter the Weather was, the more People flock'd in for Shade, and ſo
made the more numerous Audiences. *Juvenal* ſpeaks of
Auguſto recitantes menſe Poetas.

HORACE's

Q. HORATII
FLACCI EPISTOLARUM

LIBER SECUNDUS.

EPISTOLA I.
Ad Auguftum.

*C*UM tot *fuftineas & tanta negotia folus,*
 Res Italas armis tuteris, moribus ornes,
  Legibus emendes, in publica commoda peccem,
Si longo fermone morer tua tempora, Cæfar
Romulus, & Liber pater, & cum Caftore Pol-
lux,   *5*

.

            Poft

HORACE's EPISTLES.

BOOK II.

EPISTLE I.

To *Augustus.*

WHILE You bear alone the Weight of the Empire, while You protect us by the Terror of Your Arms, and make all *Italy* compleatly happy by your excellent Laws and more excellent Example, I shou'd do an irreparable Injury to the Publick, shou'd I take up your Time with a long Epistle

* R O M U L U S and † *Bacchus,* ‡ *Castor* and *Pollux,*

---

* *Romulus,* the first King and Founder of the City of *Rome,* A M 3501, was Brother of *Remus,* and Son of *Rhea-Sylvia,* the Daughter of *Numitor* He reign'd 37 Years.

† *Bacchus,* the God of Wine, Son of *Jupiter* by *Semele* See his History in the 4th Book of *Diodorus Siculus.*

‡ *Castor* and *Pollux,* two Brothers, Sons of *Jupiter* and *Leda,*

Poſt ingentia fata Deorum in templa recepti,
Dum terras hominumque colunt genus, aſpera bella
Conponunt, agros adſignant, oppida condunt;
Ploravere ſuis non reſpondere favorem
Speratum meritis. diram qui contudit Hydram, 10
Notaque fatali portenta labore ſubegit,
Conperit invidiam ſupremo fine domari.
Urit enim fulgore ſuo, qui prægravat artis
Infra ſe poſitas · extinctus amabitur idem
Præſenti tibi maturos largimur honores, 15
Jurandaſque tuum per numen ponimus aras,
Nil oriturum alias, nil ortum tale fatentes.
Sed tuus hoc populus ſapiens & juſtus in uno,
Te noſtris ducibus, te Graiis anteferendo,
Cetera nequaquam ſimili ratione modoque 20
Æſtimat , & niſi quæ terris ſemota ſuiſque
Temporibus defuncta videt, faſtidit & odit

Sic

Pollux, who were deify'd after their Decease; even these, while they were spending their Days in doing Good to Mankind, in building Cities, planting Colonies, dividing Lands, and in bringing cruel and destructive Wars to a happy Conclusion, complain'd that they did not meet with the Acknowledgments which were due to their Merits

Even * *Hercules* himself, who slew the *Hydra,* and was born to quell the Monsters of the Earth, found by fatal Experience, after all his Victories, that Envy was not to be conquer'd but by Death.

He that excells in any Art or Science, will most certainly be envy'd by those whom he excells; but when he dies, their Envy dies with him, his Rivals forget their former Hatred, and do Honour to his Memory

'Tis Your Felicity to be ador'd while living, to You we raise Altars, we swear by your Divinity, and confess that the World has never seen, nor will it ever see your Equal. But tho' the *Romans* do you Justice in preferring you to all the great Commanders, which *Greece* or *Italy* have ever produc'd; yet they do not observe the same just Measures in other Matters They are grown such immoderate Lovers of Antiquity, that they cannot bear with any thing that is modern. They are so

---

Leda, Wife to *Tyndarus,* they follow'd *Jason* to *Colchis* for the Conquest of the Golden Fleece, where they made themselves famous by the ʳˡiant Actions

* *Hercules,* Son of *Jupiter* by *Alcmena,* By the Envy of *Juno* he narrowly escap'd Death, By her he was made subject to *Lurystheus,* at whose Command he perform'd several extraordinary things, One of which was the killing the *Hydra,* a Monster with Seven Heads His Story is at large in *Ovid* and other Poets

Sic fautor veterum, ut tabulas peccare vetantes,

Quas bis quinque viri ſanxerunt, fœdera regum,

Vel Gabiis vel cum rigidis æquata Sabinis,   25

Pontificum libros, annoſa volumina vatum,

Dictitet Albano Muſas in monte locutas

Si, quia Graiorum ſunt antiquiſſima quæque

Scripta vel optima, Romani penſantur eadem

Scriptores trutina, non eſt quod multa loqua-

mur ·   30

Nil intra eſt olea, nil extra eſt in nuce duri

Venimus ad ſummum fortunæ: pingimus, atque

Pſallimus, & luctamur Achivis doctius unctis

Si meliora dies, ut vina, poemata reddit;

Scire velim, chartis pretium quotus arroget an-

nus   35

Scriptor ab hinc annos centum qui decidit, inter

Perfectos, vetereſque referri debet, an inter

Vilis, atque novos? excludat jurgia finis.

Eſt

prepossess'd in Favour of the Antients, that
they maintain, that the * Laws of the Twelve
Tables, which were enacted by the *Decemviri*,
the Treaties of Peace which our Kings concluded with the *Sabins* and *Gabij*; the Rituals
of the High-Priests; the Books of the † *Sibyls*;
and other antient Poets, are what the Muses
themselves pronounc'd upon the Top of Mount
Alba What if among the *Grecian* Writers
the most antient are the best, does it follow
that the *Latin* must be so too? They who talk
after so ridiculous a Manner, may as well persuade us, that Black is White, and White
Black

I might as justly and truly affirm that we *Romans* are arriv'd at the highest Perfection, that
we sing and paint, and perform our Exercises
much better than the *Grecians* 'Tis agreed on
all Hands that Wine is the better for being old,
if it be so with Poetry, I shall be glad to know
what Time is necessary to give a Value to a Poem? Is an Author that died a Hundred Years
ago to be rank'd among the Antients, or the
Moderns? Is he a good or bad Writer? Some
Time must be settled, or the Dispute will be

---

* The Body of the antient *Roman* Laws was collected
by the *Decemviri*, who were created for that Purpose,
from the *Grecian* Laws, A U C 301 See an Account of
'em in *Livy's* History, *Book* III *Chap* xxxiii, and xxxiv,
where he calls 'em the *Fons omnis publici privatique juris Tully* in his first Book *de Oratore*, prefers them
for their Wisdom to whole Libraries of the Philosophers

† *Sibyls*, Ten Heathen Virgins who were famous for
their Prophesies. Their Books were a Collection of
Oracles, which *Sibylla Cumana* sold to *Tarquinius Superbus* for 300 Crowns, they were lost when the Capitol was burnt in *Sylla's* Time, about 83 Years before
Christ.

endless.

Eft vetus, atque probus, centum qui perficit annos.

Quid? qui deperiit minor uno menfe, vel anno, 40

Inter quos referendus erit? veterefne poetas,

An quos & præfens, & poftera refpuat ætas?

Ifte quidem veteres inter ponetur boneftè,

Qui vel menfe brevi, vel toto eft junior anno.

Utor permiffo, caudæque pilos ut equinæ   45

Paullatim vello, & demo unum, demo & item u-

    num:

Dum cadat elufus ratione ruentis acervi,

Qui redit in faftos, & virtutem æftimat annis.

Miraturque nihil, nifi quod Libitina facravit.

Ennius & fapiens, & fortis, & alter Homerus 50

(Ut critici dicunt) leviter curare videtur,

Quò promiffa cadant, & fomnia Pythagorea.

Nævius in manibus non eft, & mentibus hæret

Pene recens? adeo fanctum eft vetus omne'poema

Ambigitur quotiens uter utro fit prior; aufert   55

Pacuvius docti famam fenis, Accius alti;

                                              Dicitur

endlefs *Rom.* The Author that died a hundred Years ago is undoubtedly Antient, and his Works are valuable *Hor* But what if he wants a Month, or a Year of the Time you mention, will you not place him among the Antients? Shall the prefent and the fucceeding Age pafs Sentence upon him as vile and contemptible? *Rom* If a Month or a Year be wanting, I fhall reckon it as nothing *Hor.* According to your Conceffion, like the Man who pluck'd off a Horfe's Tail, Hair by Hair, I firft take away one Year, then another, afterwards a Third, and fo on; till you your felf, who reckon that to be Excellent which is Antient, and think only thofe Things to be valuable, which have been confecrated by Death, fhall confefs your Miftake **ᵃ** *Ennius,* if you'll believe the Criticks, had both Senfe and Spirit, they look upon him as a fecond *Homer.* But he did not take Care to juftify the Truth of *Pythagoras's* Doctrine, by fully convincing us, that the Soul of that incomparable Poet had its Refidence in him.

ARE not the Poems even of **ᵇ** *Nævius* in every one's Hands? Nay, are they not got by Heart? So great is the Veneration which they have for Antiquity

WHEN it is difputed which of the antient Poets is the beft, **ᶜ** *Pacuvius* or **ᵈ** *Accius?* The Criticks

---

ᵃ See *Book* I *Sat* IV

ᵇ *Nævius,* the Author of feveral Latin Comedies, the firft of which was acted at *Rome,* A U C 519, being too *Satyrical,* he incurred the Difpleafure of *Metellus,* by whofe Means he was banifh'd the City, whence he retir'd to *Utica,* where he died, A U C. 551

ᶜ *Pacuvius* was Nephew to *Ennius* We have now fo little remaining of him, that it is hard to fay what advances he made in the *Roman Satire*

ᵈ *Accius,* a Tragick Writer, contemporary with *Pacuvius.*

B b

Dicitur Afrani toga convenisse Menandro.
Plautus ad exemplar Siculi properare Epicharmi:
Vincere Cæcilius gravitate, Terentius arte.

Hos

Criticks prefer the one for the Sublime, the o-
ther for his Learning 'Tis agreed that [a]*Afranius* equals [b]*Menander*, and that [c]*Plautus* imitates [d]*Epicharmus* so closely, that he never loses
him out of Sight. That [e]*Cæcilius* excels in
Weight and Matter; [f]*Terentius* in his Manners,

[...]*vius* Quintilian, Book X Chap. I. gives them both
this Character Tragœdiæ Scriptores Accius atque Pacuvius clarissimi gravitate sententiarum, verborum pondere &
auctoritate personarum Cæterum nitor & summa in exco
lendis operibus manus magis videri potest temporibus, quam
ipsis defuisse Virium tamen Accio plus tribuitur, Pacuvi-
um videri doctiorem, qui docti esse affectant, volunt

[a] *Afranius,* a *Latin* Poet, who writ several Comedies
in Imitation of *Menander*, he was a Man of Wit and
Sense *Quintilian* blames him for his scandalous Management of Amours He liv'd, according to *Vossius,*
in the 170th *Olympiad*

[b] *Menander,* a Comick Poet of *Athens,* born in the
109th *Olympiad,* he is said to have written 108 Comedies, which are all lost, some few Fragments excepted.
The Criticks prefer him to *Aristophanes,* both for his
Judgment and Stile, he was the Prince of new Comedy

[c] *Plautus,* a Comick Poet of *Sarsina* in *Italy,* who, having spent all he had on Players Apparel, was fain for
his Living to serve a Baker in turning a Hand-Mill
He died in the first Year of the 149th *Olympiad* A
great Part of his Works is lost, we have yet remaining 20 of his Comedies, he was an absolute Master of
the *Roman* Language, and was very happy in an ingenious and facetious Way of Raillery

[d] *Epicharmus,* a Poet and *Pythagorean* Philosopher of
Sicily, he compos'd several Comedies much esteem'd by
the Antients, and several other Pieces, which *Plato* is
said to have converted to his own Use

[e] *Cæcilius,* (*Statius*) a Comick Poet of *Milan,* Contemporary with *Ennius,* he writ several Comedies, which
are all lost, the Fragments of some of them are collected by *Robert Stephens*

[f] *Terentius,* a Comick Poet, born at *Carthage,* who
being a Slave at *Rome* to *Terentius Lucanus,* by his Means
got acquainted with *Scipio* and *Lælius,* by whom he was
assisted in writing his Plays. *Erasmus* tells us, that

Hos edifcit, & hos arto ftipata theatro   60

Spectat Roma potens; habet hos numeratque poetas

Ad noftrum tempus Livî fcriptoris ab ævo

Interdum volgus rectum videt. eft ubi peccat.

Si veteres ita miratur laudatque poetas,

Ut nihil anteferat, nihil illis conparet; errat: 65

Si quædam nimis antique, fi pleraque dure

Dicere cedit eos, ignave multa fatetur;

Et fapit, & mecum facit, & Jove judicat æquo.

Non equidem infector, delendave carmina Lævî

Effe

ners, Characters, and Verſification. Theſe are
the Poets, whoſe Works the *Romans* learn by
Heart ; they throng the Theatre, when their
Plays are acted ; and theſe are the only Poets
they approve, from the Times of * *Andronicus*
to the Age we live in. The People are ſometimes right in their Judgment, ſometimes in the
wrong If they are ſo infatuated in Favour
of the Antients, as to think that none of the
Moderns ſurpaſs them, or can even ſtand in
Competition with them, I muſt ſay, they are
miſtaken; but if they will allow, that their
Poems contain many obſolete Words; that
their Expreſſions are mean and low, and their
Style uneven ; I will readily join with them,
they are right in their Judgment

I WOULD by no Means be thought to take
from the Antients what is juſtly due to them;
nor do I condemn old *Lævius*'s Verſes, I know
their

there is no Author from whom we can better learn the
pure *Roman* Stile than from this Poet, and it is further
ſaid of him, that the *Romans* thought themſelves in Converſation when they heard his Comedies. He confin'd
himſelf in all his Characters within the Bounds of Nature, and that is the Reaſon that he is ſo much admir'd. Dr. *Bentley* in his Eſſay, *De Arte Terentianâ,* remarks upon this Paſſage. *Dubium eſt artemne Metricam
Poeta velit an Comicam utramq, opinor Nam in utrâq,
Noſter, tam verſuum concinnitatis, quam lucidæ rerum
diſpoſitionis, primas tenet,* p 16.

* *Livius Andronicus,* a *Grecian,* who being inſtructed
in the Manners and Decencies of the *Athenian* Theatre,
was the firſt that writ a regular Play for the *Roman*
Stage. He was made a Slave by *Livius Salinator,* who
brought him to *Rome,* and made him Tutor to his Children, which Truſt he diſcharg'd ſo well, that *Salinator*
gave him his Liberty. Being made a Freeman of *Rome,*
he added to his own Name, that of *Livius* his Maſter.
His firſt Play was acted, A.U.C. 514. All his Writings
are loſt. B b 3

Eſſe reor, memini quæ plagoſum mihi parvo   70
Orbilium dictare; ſed emendata videri
Pulchraque, & exactis minimum diſtantia, miror:
Inter quæ verbum emicuit ſi forte decorum,
Si verſus paullo concinnior unus & alter;
Injuſte totum ducit venitque poema.   75
Indignor quicquam reprehendi, non quia craſſe
Conpoſitum inlepideve putetur, ſed quia nuper ·
Nec veniam antiquis, ſed honorem & præmia poſci.
Recte necne crocum floreſque perambulet Attæ
Fabula, ſi dubitem, clament periiſſe pudorem   80
Cuncti pene patres   ea cum reprehendere coner,
Quæ gravis Æſopus, quæ doctus Roſcius egit
Vel quia nil rectum, niſi quod placuit ſibi, ducunt;
Vel quia turpe putant parere minoribus, & quæ
Inberbi didicere, ſenes perdenda fateri   85

Jam

their Value, my Master *Orbilius*, when I was a Boy, took such Care with his Ferula to explain them to me, that they will not easily be forgotten But what I am most amaz'd at, is, that they would impose them upon us for very correct Poetry

If they have some proper Words and beautiful Expressions, if here and there a Verse or Two be smoother than the rest, it is too much to buy the Poem, and cry it up for the Sake of these There is nothing that sooner moves my Indignation, than when I hear a Book condemn'd, not for its Dullness or Want of Delicacy, but purely because it was lately writ; and that Men are not content with our pardoning the Antients, unless we also prefer 'em to the Moderns If a Man shou'd but doubt whether * *Atta*'s Comedies deserv'd that Applause which they met with on the Theatre, all the old Men wou'd immediately cry out, What Impudence is this? how dare you be so bold as to censure what the famous † *Æsop*, and the more celebrated *Roscius*, have so often acted with so great Applause? This they do, either because they think nothing is Good, but that which they have been long us'd to be pleas'd with, or that they think it a Disgrace to be taught by those who are younger than themselves, and to acknowledge in their Old Age, that what they learn'd in their Youth is good for nothing

* *Atta*, a Comick *Latin* Poet, who died ten or twelve Years before *Virgil* was born, *Horace* ridicules the Lameness of his Verses, by alluding to his Name, which signifies one that cannot stand upon his Feet

† *Æsop* and *Roscius* were the most celebrated Actors among the *Romans*, *Æsop* excell'd in Tragedy, *Roscius* in Comedy.

Hc

Jam Saliare Numæ carmen qui laudat, & illud
Quod mecum ignorat, folus volt fcire videri;
Ingeniis non ille favet plauditque fepultis,
Noftra fed inpugnat, nos noftraque lividus odit
Quod fi tam Graiis novitas invifa fuiffet,   90
Quam nobis; quid nunc effet vetus? aut quid ha-
    beret,
Quod legeret tereretque viritim publicus ufus?
    Ut primum pofitis nugari Græcia bellis
Cæpit, & in vitium fortuna labier æqua;
Nunc athletarum ftudiis, nunc arfit equorum   95
Marmoris aut eboris fabros aut æris amavit:
Sufpendit picta voltum mentemque tabella.

Nunc

HE that commends the Poems of the * *Sa-ly*, which were compos'd by *Numa*, and wou'd make us believe that he understands them; (tho' neither he nor my self know any thing of them) may pretend if he pleases that he only means to do Justice to the Antients; but his real Design is against the Moderns; he envies their Merit, and does all he can to bring us and our Writings into Disgrace. Had this Humour prevail'd in *Greece*, had the *Grecians* been such implacable Enemies to every thing that was new, what Books would be extant? What could we read and study now?

WHEN the Wars, which had long troubled *Greece*, were ended, and Prosperity had introduc'd Luxury among them; one while Wrestling and Horse-races were the common Entertainment; then Sculpture and Painting by little and little gain'd upon their Affections. After some Progress in these two Arts, the Hu-

* * *

* *Salii* an Order of Priests instituted by *Numa* to preserve the Brazen Target which fell from Heaven, their great Feast was in *March*, at which Time they carry'd their sacred Charge about the City They were clad in a short Scarlet Cassock, having round them a broad Belt clasp'd with Brass Buckles, on their Heads they wore Copper Helmets. In this manner they went with a nimble Motion, keeping just Measures with their Feet, and demonstrating great Strength and Agility by the various and graceful Turns of their Body, they sung likewise as they danc'd, an Old Set of Verses call'd *Carmen Saliare*, to which our Poet alludes in this Place. It contain'd the Praises of the Heathen Deities, *Mars, Minerva, Juno, Janus*, and of *Jupiter Lucetius* (i. e) the Author of the Light As these Deities were celebrated each in his Turn, the Hymns they sung were call'd *Minervii, Junonii, Janualii*, after the Name of the Deity who was the Subject of 'em. They were in Being in *Cicero*'s Time, but the *Latin*, according to *Quintilian*, was so obscure, that the *Salii* themselves could hardly understand 'em.

Nunc tibicinibus, nunc est gavisa tragœdis :

Sub nutrice puella velut si luderet infans,

Quod cupide petiit, mature plena reliquit   100

Quid placet, aut odio est,   quod non mutabile credas ?

Hoc paces habuere bonæ, ventique secundi

    Romæ dulce diu fuit & sollemne, reclusa

Mane domo vigilare, clienti promere jura ·

Scriptos nominibus rectis expendere nummos .   105

Majores audire, minori dicere, per quæ

Crescere res posset, minui damnosa libido.

Mutavit mentem populus levis, & calet uno

Scribendi studio   puerique patresque severi

Fronde comas vincti cenant, & carmina dictant 110

Ipse ego, qui nullos me adsumo scribere versus,

Invenior Parthis mendacior ; & prius orto

Sole vigil, calamum & chartas & scrinia posco.

Navem agere ignarus navis timet   abrotonum ægro

Non audet, nisi qui didicit, dare : quod medicorum
est,

Promittunt medici   tractant fabrilia fabri   115

Scribimus indocti doctique poemata passim.

                                                Hic

mour chang'd, and nothing but Plays and Mufick pleas'd them, like Children at Nurſe,
they were ſoon diſguſted with thoſe very Pleaſures, which but juſt before they ſo paſſionately
admir'd; ſo inconſtant are we in our Inclinations and Averſions Theſe were the Effects of
Peace and Proſperity.

FOR a long Time it was the ſettled Practice
of the *Romans*, (and they took no ordinary
Pleaſure in it) to be early in the Morning up,
and at Home to give Advice to their Clients
who came to conſult them; to enquire out
good Securities for their Money, to hear their
Advice who were wiſer than themſelves; to inſtruct Young Men how to improve and manage
their Fortunes to the beſt Advantage, and to
moderate their Paſſions But alas! how ſtrangely are we chang'd from what we were! the
Itch of Poetry has tainted all Perſons; Fathers
and Sons, Young and Old crown their Temples with Laurel, and affect to write Verſes.
Even I my ſelf who have ſo often abjur'd the
Name of Poet, am in this Reſpect more Faith-
leſs than the * *Parthians*; I no ſooner awake,
but I immediately call for Pen, Ink and Paper,
tho' the Sun be not riſen

HE that is ignorant of the Art of Naviga-
tion, is afraid to take upon him to pilot a Ship;
no one dares to preſcribe Medicines to the Sick,
but he who has made them his Study · Phyſi-
cians and Artiſts apply themſelves to their proper Buſineſs, but Learned and Unlearned, all
alike make Pretences to Poetry, and verſify in
Abundance.

* The *Parthians* were particularly noted for their Dex-
terity in ſhooting behind them, as they fled.

Hic error tamen & levis hæc infania quantas
Virtutes habeat, fic collige: vatis avarus
Non temere eft animus: verfus amat, hoc ftudet
 unum.

Detrimenta, fugas fervorum, incendia ridet. 120
Non fraudem focio, puerove incogitat ullam
Pupillo · vivit filiquis, & pane fecundo:
Militiæ quanquam piger & malus, utilis urbi;
Si das hoc, parvis quoque rebus magna juvari, 125
Os tenerum pueri balbumque poeta figurat ·
Torquet ab obfcenis jam nunc fermonibus aurem:
Mox etiam pectus præceptis format amicis,
Afperitatis & invidiæ corrector & iræ.
Recte facta refert. orientia tempora notis   130
Inftruit exemplis · inopem folatur & ægrum.
Caftis cum pueris ignara puella mariti
Difceret unde preces, vatem ni Mufa dediffet?
Pofcit opem chorus, & præfentia numina fentit
Cæleftis inplorat aquas, docta prece blandus. 135
Avertit morbos, metuenda pericula pellit.
Inpetrat & pacem, & locupletem frugibus annum:

Carmine

THIS is the Folly of the prefent Age; but tho' it be a Folly, it comes attended with feveral Virtues. Did you ever know a Poet a covetous Man? His Head is employ'd in making Verfes, and he minds nothing elfe. If you tell him that his Servants are run away, that his Houfe and Goods are deftroy'd by Fire, he is unconcern'd He fcorns to defraud his Bofom-Friend; and is guilty of no unwarrantable Practice againft the Minor, that is left to his Care. Brown Bread and Peafe are his daily Food; he is indeed a very bad Soldier, but is neverthelefs a very profitable Member of the Common-wealth

The good Qualities of a Poet.

IF you will allow, that there is no Member of the Body Politick, fo mean and contemptible, but what may be ferviceable to the Publick in fome Station or other, the Poet is no inconfiderable Perfon He teaches our Children to fpeak; he moulds and forms their tender Organs, corrects their Stammering, and inures them to a clear and diftinct Pronunciation He diverts them from hearing any thing that is obfcene, he furnifhes their Minds with excellent Precepts; he breaks their Humours, and moderates their Paffions; he fings the Actions of their greateft Heroes, and relates in Verfe fuch admirable Inftances of Piety and Virtue, as will be of Ufe to fucceeding Ages He comforts the Poor and relieves the Sick If it were not for the Poet, what wou'd our young Ones do for Anthems? They offer to the Gods their Petitions in Verfe, and they are not unfuccefs-ful: In Times of Drought they pray for Rain, and their Prayers are anfwer'd They cure Difeafes, divert Calamities, and crown the Year with Peace and Plenty. In a Word, fuch is

the

Carmine Di fuperi placantur, carmine Manes.

   Agricolæ prifci, fortes, parvoque beati,

Condita poft frumenta, levantes tempore fefto 140

Corpus & ipfum animum fpe finis dura ferentem,

Cum fociis operum pueris & conjuge fidâ,

Tellurem porco, Silvanum lacte piabant,

Floribus & vino Genium memorem brevis ævi.

Fefcennina per hunc invecta licentia morem 145

Verfibus alternis opprobria ruftica fudit;

Libertafque recurrentis accepta per annos

Lufit amabiliter   donec jam fævus apertam

In rabiem cœpit verti jocus, & per honeftas

Ire domos impune minax. doluere cruento 150

Dente laceffiti   fuit intactis quoque cura

Conditione fuper communi   quin etiam lex

Pœnaque lata, malo quæ nollet carmine quemquam

Defcribi. vertere modum, formidine fuftis

Ad bene dicendum delectandumque redacti. 155

Græcia

the mighty Power of Verse, that it sooths the
Gods of Heaven and Hell; they confess its
Charms, and forget their Indignation

IT was an usual Practice with the Clowns of
old, who liv'd hard and were happy with a
little, when their Harvest was got in, to feast
themselves on Holidays; and to give their
Spirits that Repose, which they so long had labour'd to enjoy   They met together with
their Wives and Children, the Companions of
their Labours, and having first sacrific'd a Sow
to *Vesta*, and ador'd *Sylvanus* with a Libation
of Milk, they offer'd Wine and Flowers to
their *Genius*, who perpetually minds us of the
Shortness of Life

FROM hence this Custom of the Clowns in
their Turns reproaching one another with de-
faming Rhimes, which was first begun at *Fes-
cenninum*, spread thro' *Italy*; which Practice
continu'd for several Years, and was no less innocent than diverting , but at length these artless
rustick Jests degenerated into downright Railing, and several Great and Honourable Families were insolently attack'd with bitter Invectives; who not being willing tamely to pass
over such inhuman Treatment, others also who
had escap'd, interesting themselves in so publick a Grievance, petition'd for Redress   Upon this a Law was presently enacted, which forbad all Persons to fall foul upon any Man's Reputation upon Pain of Death   They soon
mended their Manners for Fear of Punishment;
they were now constrain'd to speak well of o-
thers, and to write nothing but what was in-
structive, pleasing and agreeable, whether they
wou'd or not

GREECE

Græcia capta ferum victorem cepit, & artis
Intulit agresti Latio sic horridus ille
Defluxit numerus Saturnius, & grave virus
Munditiæ pepulere. sed in longum tamen ævum
Manserunt, hodieque manent, vestigia ruris. 160
Serus enim Græcis admovit acumina chartis,
Et post Punica bella quietus quærere cœpit,
Quid Sophocles & Thespis & Æschylos utile fer-
   rent :

Tentavit

GREECE being conquer'd by the Arms of the *Romans*, fubdu'd its rough and favage Conquerors, by introducing among them the Liberal Arts, with which the *Romans* were before unacquainted Thus barbarous Language, and ill-founding Verfe, which was full of Invectives, and had been in Ufe from the Times of * *Saturn*, fell into Decay, and Elegance and Politenefs fucceeded in their Place. However, this Change was not fo perfect, but that fome Remains of their former Barbarity continu'd amongft them a confiderable Time (and we ftill fee fome Footfteps of it); for it was very late before the *Romans* apply'd themfelves to read the *Greek* Authors; it was not till after the firft † *Punic* War, (*Rome* then enjoying a perfect Peace) that they began to inquire into the Excellencies of ‡ *Thefpis*,

---

* We have no certain Light from Antiquity, by which we can difcover what this *Numerus Saturnius* was, but we may fafely conclude, that, like the *Grecian*, it was a rude and artlefs kind of Poetry, without Feet or Meafure The *Romans* had a Cuftom of reproaching each other in a fort of tumble hobling Verfe, and they anfwer'd in the fame kind of grofs Raillery, their Wit and their Mufick being of a Piece Some are of Opinion, that this *Numerus Saturnius* was the fame as the *Fefcennine*.

† *Horace* means only the firft *Punic* War, for between the end of the 1ft and the 3d, or from the Year of the City 512 to 607, flourifh'd the moft eminent Poets, efpecially Dramatick.

‡ *Thefpis*, a Tragick Poet of *Icaria*, a Town of *Attica* in *Greece*, flourifh'd *A M.* 3050 In his Time Tragedy was carry'd on by a Set of Muficians and Dancers, who fung Hymns in Praife of *Bacchus* He, that the Dancers might have fome Refpite, and the Audience fome other Diverfion, introduc'd an Actor, who, after every fecond Song, repeated fome Difcourfe upon a Tragical Subject.

C c
Æfchylus,

Tentavit quoque rem, fi digne vertere poffet,
Et placuit fibi, natura fublimis & acer ;   165
Nam fpirat tragicum fatis, & feliciter audet
Sed turpem putat infcitus metuitque lituram.
Creditur, ex medio quia res arceffit, habere
Sudoris minimum; fed habet Comœdia tanto
Plus oneris, quanto veniæ minus. afpice, Plautus, 170
Quo pacto partis tutetur amantis ephebi;
Ut patris attenti, lenonis ut infidiofi.
Quantus fit Doffennus edacibus in parafitis.

Quam

* *Æschylus*, and † *Sophocles*. Some among them attempted to tranflate their ‡ Tragedies, and they found Reafon to be pleafed with their own Performances, for the *Romans* are naturally of a lofty Genius, and very fit to write Tragedy; they are very happy in Attempts of this Kind; but this is their Misfortune, that they think it beneath them to make any Corrections

SOME are of Opinion, that 'tis a very eafie thing to write a Comedy, becaufe its Characters are low and mean, and are taken from the Vulgar, but let me affure them, that nothing in Nature is more difficult; and the Difficulty arifes from our being fo very fevere in our Criticifms upon it Confider how *Plautus* reprefented the Follies of a paffionate Lover, the Characters of a Pimp and of a covetous Father. Obferve what a meer *Doffennus* he is in defcribing a guttling Parafite, how very far his

* *Æschylus*, an *Athenian* Tragick Poet of *Eleufis*, Contemporary with *Pindar* in the 63d Olympiad He writ Sixty Six Plays, was *Victor* in Thirteen, of which Seven only are extant. He had a noble Boldnefs of Expreffion, his Imaginations were lofty and heroick, but in fome Places he is daring to Extravagance

† *Sophocles*, a Tragick Poet, born at *Athens* in the fecond Year of the 71ft Olympiad He writ 123 Tragedies, of which Seven only are extant. He was *Victor* Four and Twenty Times, he added much to the perfecting Tragedy He was a Perfon of an extraordinary Genius, *Virgil* had a great Efteem for him

Sola Sophocleo tua Carmina digna Cothurno Ecl viii v 10.

He makes in this Verfe a particular Diftinction between him and all other Tragick Poets.

‡ The moft confiderable were *Livius Andronicus*, *Ennius*, *Nævius*, *Pacuvius*, *Accius*, *Cæcilius*, *Plautus*, *Afranius*, *Terence* and *Lucilus* *Livius Andronicus* prefented his firft Dramatick Piece A U. C 514, a Year before the Birth of *Ennius*.

Chara-

Quam non adſtricto percurrat pulpita ſocco.

Geſtit enim nummum in loculos demittere, poſt hoc

Securus, cadat an recto ſtet fabula talo   175

Quem tulit ad ſcenam ventoſo gloria curru,

Exanimat lentus ſpectator, ſedulus inflat

Sic leve, ſic parvum eſt, animum quod laudis avarum

Subruit ac reficit. valeat res ludicra, ſi me   180

Palma negata macrum, donata reducit opimum.

Sæpe, etiam audacem, fugat hoc terretque poetam;

Quod numero plures, virtute & honore minores,

Indocti, ſtolidique, & depugnare parati

Si diſcordet eques, media inter carmina poſcunt 185

Aut urſum aut pugiles his nam plebecula gaudet.

Verum equiti quoque jam migravit ab aure voluptas

Omnis, ad ingratos oculos, & gaudia vana.

Quatuor aut plures aulæa premuntur in horas;

Dum fugiunt equitum turmæ, peditumq, cater-

væ ·   190

Mox trahitur manibus regum fortuna retortis

Eſſeda feſtinant, pilenta, petorrita, naves

Captivum portatur ebur, captiva Corinthus.

Characters are from being exact It is but too evident from his negligent Writing, that his principal Design was to get Money; which when he had once got, he never more concern'd himself, whether his Comedies pleas'd or not.

NOTHING is more killing to a Poet, who writes for Applause, which is always very dubious and uncertain, than to see the Spectators sit cold and unconcern'd when his Play is acting; but if they are attentive, how is he transported? So light, so small a Matter it is that sinks or raises the Spirits of him who is greedy of Praise If a Man must come off Fat or Lean, just as his Success is on the Stage, farewel Plays! may I never have any thing to do with the Theatre!

BUT there is another thing which often disheartens the most daring Poets, and that is, that the greatest Part of the Audience being Persons of no Distinction or Merit, and consequently very foolish and ignorant, will sometimes in the Middle of an Act call for the Bears or the Gladiators, and are ready to fight the Men of Quality if they offer to oppose them The common People are strangely delighted with such Sights as these, nor are the Gentry free from the Infection, who have universally forsaken the agreeable and more lasting Pleasure of the Ear, for that of the Eye, which is vain and transitory.

IT frequently happens, that the Play is interrupted for four or five Hours, and nothing is to be seen upon the Stage but a Multitude of Horse and Foot, in the utmost Confusion, after this you see a Captive Prince with his Hands behind him; next follow Chariots, Litters and Carriages, then Vessels and Cities

and

Si foret in terris, rideret Democritus ; ſeu

Diverſum confuſa genus panthera camelo,   195

Sive elephas albus volgi converterit ora :

Spectaret populum ludis attentius ipſis,

Ut ſibi præbentem mimo ſpectacula plura

Scriptores autem narrare putaret aſello

Fabellam ſurdo nam quæ pervincere voces   200

Evaluere ſonum, referunt quem noſtra theatra?

Garganum mugire putes nemus, aut mare Tuſcum

Tanto cum ſtrepitu ludi ſpectantur, & artes,

Divitiæque peregrinæ quibus oblitus actor

Cum ſtetit in ſcena, concurrit dextera lævæ   205

Dixit adhuc aliquid? nil ſane quid placet ergo?

Lana Tarentino violas imitata veneno

Ac ne forte putes me, quæ facere ipſe recuſem,

Cum recte tractent alii, laudare maligne

Ille per extentum funem mihi poſſe videtur   210

Ire poeta; meum qui pectus inaniter angit,

Irritat,

and Ivory Statues are carried in Triumph. If
* *Democritus* were living, he would laugh hear-
tily to see the People so strangely transported
at the Sight of a white Elephant, or a strange
Beast, that is a Leopard and a Camel too, he
would stare at the Spectators more than the
Actors, as most likely to give him the greatest
Diversion. He would say, that the Poets were
very ill employ'd in writing Comedies for an
ignorant Mob; 'tis like telling a Story to a
poor deaf Ass; for how can an Actor possibly
be heard, when the Theatre rings with the Cla-
mours of the People, and is nothing but Confusion? Did you but hear the Noise they make
at the Sight of the *Persian* embroider'd Habits,
with which the Players are gorgeously array'd,
you would compare it to the Roarings of the
Forest of *Garganus*, or of the *Tuscan* Sea As
soon as an Actor thus magnificently adorn'd
appears upon the Stage, they clap their *Hands*
in Admiration. Has he said any thing? Not
a Word Whence then are these Applauses?
'Tis because the Player is dress'd in Purple of
Tarentum

But left you should suspect that I am very
sparing in my Commendations of Plays, because I never pretended to write any, tho' o-
ther Poets have succeeded that way, let me declare that these are my Sentiments on the Matter That Poet seems to be a Master in his Profession, who can touch my Passions with a meer

---

* *Democritus*, a Philosopher called *Abderites*, because
he liv'd at *Abdera*, he continually laugh'd at the Weak-
ness and Vanity of Men, as designing a thousand ridiculous Things, when he believ'd that all things depended upon meer Chance, and a casual Concourse of
Atoms. He died in the 104th Olympiad

Fable,

Inritat, mulcet, falsis terroribus inplet,
Ut magus; & modo me Thebis, modo ponit Athenis.

   Verum age & his, qui se lectori credere malunt,
Quam spectatoris fastidia ferre superbi,   215
Curam impende brevem. si munus Apolline dignum
Vis conplere libris; & vatibus addere calcar,
Ut studio majore petant Helicona virentem.

   Multa quidem nobis facimus mala saepe poetae,
(Ut vineta egomet caedam mea) cum tibi librum 220
Sollicito damus, aut fesso cum laedimur, unum
Si quis amicorum est ausus reprendere versum
Cum loca jam recitata revolvimus inrevocati
Cum lamentamur non adparere labores
Nostros, & tenui deducta poemata filo ·   225
Cum speramus eo rem venturam, ut, simul atque
Carmina rescieris nos fingere, commodus ultro
Arcessas, & egere vetes, & scribere cogas.

Sed

Fable, so as to keep 'em in continual Alarms about nothing Who, like an Enchanter, can fill my Breast with Joy and Terror, provoke my Rage, and sooth me again into Kindness and Compassion, who can carry me from the Theatre, and place me at * *Thebes* or † *Athens* as he pleases.

Such Writers as these are worthy of your Regard, but, *Mighty Prince*, if you desire to fill the Library, which you have built in Honour of *Apollo*, with choice good Books; if you design to inspire the Poets with a generous Emulation to ascend the Height of Mount *Parnassus*, whose Top is always green and flourishing; let not those be neglected, who choose rather to submit their Works to the Reader's Censure, than hazard the Contempt of an insolent Spectator

We Poets indeed do often injure our selves (if I may confess a Truth which makes against my own Profession) when we present you with our Poems at unseasonable Times, when you are either weary, or busie with Affairs of State; when we are angry that a Friend is so free as to play the Critick upon one of our Verses; when without being asked, we are ever repeating the Verses which we had rehearsed in Publick; when we complain that those who read our Compositions are not sensible of the mighty Pains we have taken, and that the Beauty of our Address and Delicacy of Expression are lost upon them Lastly, when we flatter our selves, that as soon as you hear a Character of our Works, you will immediately send for us, give us good Pensions, and command us to go on.

---

* *Thebes,* a City of *Greece* in *Bœotia.*
† *Athens,* see Book I. Sat. I.

It

Sed tamen eft operæ pretium cognofcere, quàlis

Ædituos habeat belli fpectata domique   230

Virtus, indigno non committenda poetæ.

Gratus Alexandro regi Magno fuit ille

Chœrilos, incultis qui verfibus & male natis

Rettulit acceptos, regale nomifma, Philippos.

Sed veluti tractata notam labemque remittunt 235

Atramenta, fere fcriptores carmine fœdo

Splendida facta linunt idem rex ille, poema

Qui tam ridiculum tam care prodigus emit,

Edicto vetuit, ne quis fe præter Apellen

Pingeret, aut alius Lyfippo cuderet æra   240

Fortis Alexandri voltum fimulantia quod fi

Judicium fubtile videndis artibus illud

Ad libros & ad hæc Mufarum dona vocares;

Bœotum in craffo jurares aere natum

At neque dedecorant tua de fe judicia, atque 245

Munera, quæ multa dantis cum laude tulerunt,

Dilecti tibi Virgilius Variufque poetæ

Nec magis expreffi voltus per aenea figna,

Quam per vatis opus mores animique virorum

IT is worth your While to know, *Great Prince*, who is fit to record your Glorious Actions in Peace and in War, and to transmit them down to Posterity in their proper Lustre; that no mean Poet may ever be honour'd with so Noble an Employment * *Alexander* had so great an Esteem for *Chœrilus*, that he gave him a considerable Sum of Money for a very bad Poem But as Ink, when spilt, leaves a Stain behind it, so wretched Poems leave a Blemish upon those glorious Actions which they attempt to celebrate The same *Alexander*, who paid so dear for a foolish Poem, made a Law that no other Painter but † *Apelles* should attempt his Picture, and that none but ‡ *Lysippus* should design his Statue. Now if this Prince, who had so fine and excellent a Taste for Painting and Sculpture, was to be consider'd only as to his Judgment in Poetry, one would swear that he was born in the foggy stupifying Climate of *Bœotia* But you, *Augustus*, have no Reason to be asham'd of the Choice you have made of *Varius* and *Virgil*, nor of your Grace and Bounty to them. The Statuaries, 'tis confess'd, are sometimes very happy in expressing the Lines and Features of their Heroes, but the Poets express their Honourable Actions, they paint their Virtues, and draw the more

* *Alexander*, firnamed the *Great*, King of *Macedon*, having conquer'd *Darius* at *Guazamela*, Oct 1st. A M. 3620, laid the Foundation of the *Grecian* Empire

† *Apelles*, the Prince of Painters, born at *Cos*, in the 112th Olympiad

‡ *Lysippus*, a famous Statuary of *Sicyone*, he was first a Locksmith, which Trade he soon quitted to apply himself to that of a Statuary He made several Statues of *Alexander* the *Great*, and of all his most beloved Favourites, which *Metellus* brought along with him to *Rome*, after having subdued *Macedonia* to the *Roman* Empire.

charming

Clarorum adparent. nec fermones ego mallem 250

Repentis per humum, quam res conponere geftas,

Terrarumque fitus & flumina dicere, & arcis

Montibus inpofitas, & barbara regna, tuifque

Aufpiciis totum confecta duella per orbem,

Clauftraque cuftodem pacis cohibentia Janum, 255

Et formidatam Parthis, te principe, Romam

Si quantum cuperem, poffem quoque. fed neque
    parvum

Carmen majeftas recipit tua; nec meus audet

Rem tentare pudor, quam vires ferre recufent

Sedulitas autem ftulte, quem diligit, urguet, 260

Præcipue cum fe numeris commendat & arte

Difcit enim citius, meminitque libentius illud

Quod quis deridet, quam quod probat & veneratur

Nil moror officium, quod me gravat ac neque ficto

In pejus voltu proponi cereus ufquam,   265

Nec prave factis decorari verfibus opto

Ne rubeam pingui donatus munere, & una

Cum fcriptore meo capfa porrectus operta

Deferar in vicum vendentem tus & odores,

Et piper, & quicquid chartis amicitur ineptis 270

EPISTOLA

charming Beauties of their Minds to a greater Perfection

IF my Abilities were equal to my Wishes, I would lay aside this familiar Way of writing, and attempt your Great and Immortal Actions in Immortal Verse I wou'd then describe the Nations you have conquer'd, the Rivers you have pass'd, the Forts you have built on the highest Mountains, the barbarous Kings whom you have subdu'd, and the Victories you have gain'd throughout the World I would tell how you shut the Temple of *Janus*, and gave Peace to the Universe. I would sing how *Rome* grew formidable to the *Parthians* when you was Emperor, but alas! my Numbers are much too low for so great a Subject, nor have I the Vanity to engage in a Work which I am not able to perform 'Tis the Fault of many a well-meaning Man to be too officious, and to do a Disservice where he intended a Favour; and a Poet of all others, ought to be careful not to offend in this Particular, Men being more dispos'd to learn and remember that which is ridiculous, than that which merits their Praise and Commendation For my Part, I have no Regard for such Services Nor do I desire that any one, under Pretence of honouring me, shou'd represent me in Wax more deform'd than the Original; much less would I thank him for writing ill Verses in my Commendation I should blush at such a Present, and be in a terrible Consternation, lest in a little Time both my self and Poet should be laid at Length in an open Box, and carry'd to the Street where the *Romans* sell Incense, Perfumes, Pepper, and all sorts of Ware, which are usually wrapt up in impertinent Poems.

EPISTLE

EPISTOLA II.

Ad Julium Florum.

FLORE, bono claroque fidelis amice Neroni,
  Si quis forte velit puerum tibi vendere natum
Tibure vel Gabiis, & tecum fic agat, HIC &
Candidus, & talos a vertice pulcher ad imos
Fiet eritque tuus nummorum millibus octo;   5
Verna ministeriis ad nutus aptus herilis.
Literulis Græcis imbutus, idoneus arti
Cuilibet · argilla quidvis imitaberis uda.
Quin etiam canet indoctum, fed dulce bibenti·
Multa fidem promiſſa levant, ubi plenius æquo 10
Laudat venalis, qui volt extrudere, merces.
Res urguet me nulla · meo fum pauper in ære·
Nemo hoc mangonum faceret tibi non temere a me
Quivis ferret idem   femel hic ceſſavit, & (ut fit)
In fcalis latuit metuens pendentis habenæ.   15
Des nummos, excepta nihil te fi fuga lædit.
Ille ferat pretium, pœnæ fecurus, opinor
Prudens emifti vitiofum: dicta tibi eft lex:

Infequeris

EPISTLE II.

To *Julius Florus*.

Dear FLORUS,

SUPPOSE a Merchant was to fell you a
Boy that was born at * *Tivoli* or *Gabii*,
and fhould thus addrefs you. He is Fair, Beautiful, and of juft Proportion, to make but one
Word with you, give me Fifty Pounds and he
is yours, he is a very pretty tractable Boy, and
is fo diligent, that not a Motion of your Eye
can efcape him; he has learnt a little *Greek*,
and is fit for every thing, you may mould him
as you pleafe I cannot fay much as to his Judgment in Singing, but his Voice is well enough
to entertain you at your Meals over a Glafs of
Wine. I know very well that large Commendations are apt to breed Sufpicion in the Buyer;
it looks as if a Man wanted to put off his
Ware, when he commends it beyond all Meafure But I have no occafion to fell mine; tho'
I am poor, yet I owe nothing No other
Merchant would ufe you fo kindly as I do, nor
would I deal thus freely with any but your felf.
Once indeed he neglected his Duty, and, as it is
natural in fuch Cafes, hid himfelf for Fear of
being whipt; if you can pardon this fmall O-
miffion, take him, or leave him After this
Preamble, the Seller may fafely take your Money, he told you his Faults, and you were con-

* *Tivoli*, fee *Book* II. *Sat* IV

tented

Infequeris tamen hunc, & lite morairis iniqua

Dixi me pigrum proficifcenti tibi, dixi   20

Talibus officiis prope mancum: ne mei fævus

Jurgares ad te quod epiftola nulla veniret

Quid tum profeci, mecum facientia jura

Si tamen attentas? quereris fuper hoc etiam, quod

Exfpectata tibi non mittam carmina mendax? 25

Luculli miles collecta viatica multis

Ærumnis, laffus dum noctu ftertit, ad affem

Perdiderat   poft hoc vehemens lupus, & fibi &
    hofti

Iratus pariter, jejunis dentibus acer,

Præfidium regale loco dejecit, ut aiunt,   30

Summe munito, & multarum divite rerum·

Clarus ob id factum, donis ornatur honeftis,

Accipit & bis dena fuper feftertia nummûm.

Forte fub hoc tempus caftellum evertere prætor

Nefcio quod cupiens, hortari cœpit eundem   35

Verbis, quæ timido quoque poffent addere mentem.

I, bone, quo virtus tua te vocat; i pede faufto,

Grandia

tented to buy him; and yet you purfue this honeft Merchant, and unjuftly commence a Suit againft him.

THIS is juft my Cafe; when you parted from me laft, I gave you to underftand that I was an idle lazy Fellow, and that I hated above all things to write Letters: I took thefe Precautions to prevent your being angry, if you heard not from me; but I find they were to little Purpofe; all that I can fay to juftify my felf fignifies nothing; you likewife complain of my Neglect, in not fending you the Verfes according to my Promife

A SOLDIER that ferv'd in * *Lucullus*'s Army, who had undergone a great many Hardfhips in getting a little Money, was robb'd, as he flept, of all that he had. The Thought of his Lofs made him almoft diftracted; like a famifh'd Wolf, he was mad with himfelf, and no lefs enrag'd againft the Enemy. In a Word, he attack'd a little Fort, took it Sword in Hand, and found therein a confiderable Booty. Having made himfelf famous by fo gallant an Action, he was, as he deferv'd, very liberally rewarded Some Time after, his General, having a Mind to be Mafter of another Fort, which he defign'd to level with the Ground, addrefs'd the fame Soldier in very moving Terms, fuch as were capable of infpiring a Coward with Bravery and Refolution. " Go, faid he, " my Soldier, where your Courage calls you; " go and conquer, and expect a Recompence

---

* *Lucullus*, a Perfon of great Wealth, Valour and Eloquence, he was chofen Conful to carry on the War againft *Mithridates*, whom he foon forc'd to abandon his Kingdom, and betake himfelf to his Son-in-Law *Tigranes* King of *Armenia.*

" great

Grandia laturus meritorum præmia · quid ftas?

Poft hæc ille catus, quantumvis rufticus, Ibit,

Ibit eo quo vis, qui zonam perdidit, inquit　　　40

　　Romæ nutriri mihi contigit, atque doceri

Iratus Graiis quantum nocuiffet Achilles.

Adjecere bonæ paullo plus artis Athenæ ·

Scilicet ut poffem curvo dignofcere rectum,

Atque inter filvas Academi quærere verum.　　　45

Dura fed emovere loco me tempora grato;

Civilifque rudem belli tulit æftus in arma, ·

Cæfaris Augufti non responfura lacertis.

Unde fimul primum me dimifere Philippi,

Decifis humilem pennis, inopemque paterni　　　50

Et laris & fundi, paupertas inpulit audax

Ut verfus facerem fed, quod non defit, habentem

Quæ poterunt umquam fatis expurgare cicutæ,

Ni melius dormire putem, quam fcribere verfus?

Singula de nobis anni prædantur euntes;　　　55

Eripuere jocos, venerem, convivia, ludum;

Tendunt

" great as your Merits " Why do you not go? The Soldier, tho' a Peasant, made this smart Reply, Let him go on the Attack who has lost his Money.

It was my Felicity to be educated at *Rome*, where I read *Homer's Iliads* From thence I went to *Athens*, where I made a farther Improvement, being taught to distinguish Right from Wrong; and in my Conversation with the *Academicks* in their Groves, to enquire after Truth The Violence of the Times soon forc'd me to leave this agreeable Retirement; I was carried away by the Tide of the Civil Wars, raw and unskill'd in Arms as I was, and was enter'd into that Party which fought against *Augustus*, but without Success Our Army being routed at the Battle of * *Philippi*, I betook my self to a shameful Flight. My Fortunes were then in a low Condition, my Wings were clipt, I had no Inheritance either in Land or Houses. Under these hard Circumstances, Poverty, which is always bold and daring, put me upon trying my Faculty in Poetry, but now I am possess'd of a competent Fortune, it would be an unaccountable Madness in me, when I may quietly enjoy my self, to disturb my Brains with making Verses I was formerly of a gay and chearful Temper, Love and Pleasure were my constant Entertainment But now, what a wonderful Alteration has Time made in me! Age has taken from me all Relish of Mirth and Women, Feasts and Plays, even my Passion for the Muses is almost extinct, 'tis

---

* *Philippi,* a City of *Macedon*, near this Place *Pompey* was defeated by *Cæsar*, A U C 706, and *Brutus* and *Cassius* were overcome by *Augustus* and *Marcus Antonius,* 712

with

Tendunt extorquere poemata quid faciam vis?

Denique non omnes eadem mirantur amantque

Carmine tu gaudes hic delectatur iambis

Ille Bioneis sermonibus, & sale nigro   63

Tres mihi conviva prope dissentire videntur,

Poscentes vario multum diversa palato.

Quid dem? quid non dem? renuis quod tu, jubet

  alter.

Quod petis, id sane est invisum acidumque duobus.

   Praeter cetera, me Romae poemata censes 65

Scribere posse, inter tot curas totque labores?

Hic sponsum vocat, hic auditum scripta, relictis

Omnibus officiis: cubat hic in colle Quirini,

Hic extremo in Aventino; visendus uterque ·

Intervalla vides humane commoda verum   70

Pura sunt plateae, nihil ut meditantibus obstet.

Festinat calidus mulis gerulisque redemtor .

Torquet nunc lapidem, nunc ingens machina tig-

  num

Tristia robustis luctantur funera plaustris.

Hac rabiosa fugit canis, hac lutulenta ruit sus. 75

I nunc, & versus tecum meditare canoros.

Scriptorum chorus omnis amat nemus, & fugit

  urbis,

Rite cliens Bacchi somno gaudentis & umbra:

Tu me inter strepitus nocturnos atque diurnos

              3

                                          Vis

with no small Difficulty that I preserve some Remainder of it. Be so kind as to tell me what I must do   But there is another thing which gives me a great Aversion to Poetry, I mean Men's different Tastes about it   One is for *Lyricks,* another for *Iambicks,* a third is pleas'd with nothing but *Satire*; and how is it possible to gratify them all? Here are three Guests of different Palates, what must I do for your Satisfaction? That which pleases him, displeases you; and that which you like, is equally distastful to the other two   Besides all this, how do you think it possible for a Man to write Verses at *Rome,* in the midst of so much Hurry and Business? One asks me to be Surety for him; another desires I would lay aside Business, and hear him repeat his Poetry   The one dwells on *Mount Quirinal,* the other on the *Aventine,* a considerable Distance from each other, and yet both must be visited   You will possibly reply, that the Streets are free, and that there I have Liberty enough for Meditation   Yes truly, they are very commodious; here you meet a Builder posting along with his Mules and Porters; there creaks an Engine; here Carmen and Mourners that attend at Funerals encounter each other; there a mad Dog comes foaming along, or a nasty Sow all over Mire runs gruntling by you, and bespatters you as she passes.   Let those make Verses here that can; the Sons of *Apollo* hate nothing so much as a City-Life, like *Bacchus,* the God whom they adore, they love the Fields and Woods and Forests, and rejoice to sleep in cooling Shades. Why then wou'd you have me attempt to write in the midst of so much Noise and Clamour? Alas! here is no such thing as Quietness   Day

and

Vis canere, & non tacta ſequi veſtigia vatum. 80

Ingenium, ſibi quod vacuas deſumſit Athenas,

Et ſtudiis annos ſeptem dedit, inſenuitque

Libris & curis, ſtatua taciturnius exit

Plerumque, & riſu populum quatit   hic ego re-

ram

Fluctibus in mediis & tempeſtatibus Urbis,   85

Verba lyræ motura ſonum connectere digner?

   Frater erat Romæ conſulti rhetor, ut alter

Alterius ſermone meros audiret honores

Gracchus ut hic illi, foret huic ut Mucius ille.

Qui minus argutos verſat furor iſte poetas?   90

Carmina conpono, hic elegos · mirabile viſu

Sacratumque novem Muſis opus, aſpice primum

Quanto cum faſtu, quanto molimine circum-

Spectemus, vacuam Romanis vatibus ædem.

Mox etiam (ſi forte vacas) ſequere, & procul

audi,   95

Quid

and Night the Confusion is the same; how then can I hope to tread in the unbeaten Steps of the antient Poets, and to sing like them? If it very often happens that a Person, who has spent Seven Years at *Athens*, (which is one of the finest Retirements in the World, and most proper for Study) and done nothing all that Time but pored upon Books, appears abroad at last as mute as a Statue, and is laugh'd at by the People for his Taciturnity; would it not be more ridiculous in me who live in a perpetual Hurry, and am surrounded as it were with Storms and Tempests, to tune my Numbers to the *Lyrick* Strain?

THERE were two Brothers at *Rome*, the one a Lawyer, the other a Rhetorician, who continually prais'd each other. The Orator call'd the Lawyer * *Mutius*; the Lawyer in Return for so fine a Compliment, said that the Orator was a second † *Gracchus*. Do not we Poets do the same? I write *Odes*; another writes *Elegies*, and we both declare, that they cannot be equal'd Observe, if you please, with what Vanity and Confidence we cast our Eyes round *Apollo*'s Temple, a Work truly wonderful and sacred to the Muses, intimating by our Looks, that no *Latin* Poet will ever be there, till our Poems are consecrated, by being plac'd in it. If you are at Leisure, come a little nearer and

---

* Q *Mutius Scævola*, a famous Lawyer and *Roman* Consul, Governor of *Asia*, he compos'd many Works, and had the Reputation of an accomplish'd Orator Cicero calls him the most Eloquent of all the Lawyers, and the best Lawyer of all the Orators He was murder'd during the Wars between *Marius* and *Sylla*, A U. C. 672.

† *Gracchus*, the Son of *Titus Sempronius Gracchus*, by the Celebrated *Cornelia* Daughter of *Scipio*, He was a Person of rare Parts and admirable Eloquence.

listen

Quid ferat, & quare fibi nectat uterque coronam

Cædimur, & totidem plagis confumimus hoftem,

Lento Samnites ad lumina prima duello.

Difcedo Alcæus puncto illius: ille meo quis?

Quis nifi Callimachus? fi plus adpofcere vifus; 100

Fit Mimnermus, & optivo cognomine crefcit.

Multa fero, ut placem genus irritabile vatum,

Cum fcribo; & fupplex populi fuffragia capto.

Idem, finitis ftudiis, & mente recepta,

Obturem patulas inpune legentibus auris. 105

Ridentur mala qui conponunt carmina. verum

Gaudent fcribentes, & fe venerantur, & ultro,

Si taceas, laudant; quicquid fcripfere, beati.

At qui legitimum cupiet feciffe poema,

Cum tabulis animum cenforis fumet honefti: 110

Audebit

liften to our Verfes; and learn why every one lays claim to the Bays   We are nothing but Flattery: If at any Time we act the Critick, we do it in a foft and gentle Manner; like the [a] *Samnite* Gladiators, who will fight a whole Day without being wounded.   He protests that I am a fecond [b] *Alcæus*; in Return to his Civilities, I call him [c] *Callimachus*; and left that Title fhould not be fufficient, I fay he's [d] *Mimnermus*, a Title extreamly pleafing to him.

THE Poets are a Sort of People eafily provok'd; and therefore when I write and defign to engage the Suffrages of the Multitude, I endure any thing, to keep them in Temper: But now, having bid Adieu to Poetry, and enjoying again the Ufe of my Reafon, I am fully refolv'd to liften no longer to their tedious Repetitions.

NOTHING certainly is more ridiculous than for a Man to write ill Verfes; but Poets for the moft Part are fo ftrangely delighted with their Productions, that they admire and adore them, if you fay nothing in their Commendation, they themfelves will praife them; how wretched foever their Poetry be, they, happy Men, are fatisfied with it

HE that would write a perfect Poem, muft act the Critick upon himfelf; he muft retrench

[a] A Sort of Gladiators call'd *Samnites*, who fought with Foils inftead of Swords

[b] *Alcæus*, fee Book I *Epift* XIX

[c] *Callimachus* an excellent *Greek* Poet of *Cyrene*, in great Favour with *Ptolemæus Philadelphus*.   He writ many *Hymns*, *Elegies*, and *Epigrams*, fome of which are now extant, and not many Years fince publifh'd by the Learned *Mademoifelle le Fevre*, with Notes and Remarks full of ufeful and folid Learning.

[d] *Horace* prefers him here to *Callimachus* for his fine and florid Stile.

a

Audebit quæcumque parum splendoris habebunt,
Et sine pondere erunt, & honore indigna ferentur,
Verba movere loco. quamvis invita recedant,
Et versentur adhuc intra penetralia Vestæ
Obscurata diu populo bonus eruet, atque   115
Proferet in lucem, speciosa vocabula rerum,
Quæ priscis memorata Catonibus atque Cethegis
Nunc situs informis premit & deserta vetustas:
Adsciscet nova, quæ genitor produxerit usus
Vehemens, & liquidus, puroque simillimus am-
    ni,   120
Fundet opes, Latiumque beabit divite lingua ·
Luxuriantia conpescet · nimis aspera sano
Levabit cultu virtute carentia tollet
Ludentis speciem dabit, & torquebitur, ut qui
Nunc Satyrum, nunc agrestem Cyclopa move-
    tur   125
Prætulerim scriptor delirus inersque videri,
Dum mea delectent mala me, vel denique fallant,
Quàm sapere, & ringi fuit haud ignobilis Argis,
Qui se credebat miros audire tragœdos,
In vacuo lætus sessor plausorque theatro   130
Cetera qui vitæ servaret munia recto
More; bonus sane vicinus, amabilis hospes,
Comis in uxorem, posset qui ignoscere servis,
Et signo læso non insanire lagenæ:

Posset

a great many Words, which have neither
Strength nor Beauty in them, whatever reluctance he finds to do so; nor must he be hasty
in publishing his Works He must revive some
significant Words us'd heretofore by *Cato* and
Cethegus, which for many Years have been utterly abandon'd, purely for their Antiquity;
nor must he neglect those modern Terms,
which Custom has introduc'd among us He
must be strong, yet clear, and adorn and enrich
the *Roman* Language; just as a River by its
Crystal Streams gives Plenty to the Country.
He must retrench whatever is superfluous;
smooth and polish what appears to be rough;
and lay aside every thing that is flat and insipid.
He must spare no Pains, and yet appear to be easy
and natural, like a skilful Player, he must imitate all Humours; he must personate the *Satyr*,
and then again the *Cyclops*, as Occasion shall require For my Part, I had rather be accounted a very dull and impertinent Author, provided I am pleas'd with what I write, and am
unacquainted with my own Imperfections, than
be wise at this Rate

THERE was an eminent Citizen of *Argos*,
who wou'd frequently sit alone in the Theatre,
and fancy himself present at some excellent
Tragedy, and clap and hum, and express his
Satisfaction, as if the Play had been really acted. This one Thing excepted, in all other Matters, he discharg'd his Duty like a prudent
Man; he was a good Neighbour, a kind
Husband · He was free and liberal in his Entertainments, he would often pass over his Servants Faults, and not fall into a Passion when he
found a Bottle of Wine unseal'd. In a Word,
he had Sense enough to avoid a Precipice,

or

Poſſet qui rupem & puteum vitare patentem. 135

Hic ubi cognatorum opibus curiſque refeЄtus

Expulit elleboro morbum bilemque meraco,

Et redit ad ſeſe · Pol me occidiſtis, amici,

Non ſervaſtis, ait; cui ſic extorta voluptas,

Et demtus per vim mentis gratiſſimus error   140

Nimirum ſapere eſt abjeЄtis utile nugis,

Et tempeſtivum pueris concedere ludum:

Ac non verba ſequi fidibus modulanda Latinis,

Sed veræ numeroſque modoſque ediſcere vitæ

Quocirca mecum loquor hæc, tacituſque recor-

      dor.   145

Si tibi nulla ſitim finiret copia lymphæ;

Narrares medicis quod quanto plura paraſti,

Tanto plura cupis, nulline faterier audes?

Si volnus tibi monſtrata radice vel herba

Non fieret levius, fugeres radice vel herba   150

Proficiente nihil curarier audieras, cui

Rem Di donarint, illi decedere pravam

Stultitiam &, cum ſis nihilo ſapientior, ex quo

Plenior es, tamen uteris monitoribus iſdem?

At ſi divitiæ prudentem reddere poſſent,   155

Si cupidum timidumque minus te; nempe ruberes,

Viveret in terris te ſiquis avarior uno.

Si

or pass by a Well, if he met one in his Way. His Friends and Relations, who spar'd for nothing that might do him good, gave him a lusty Dose of *Hellebore*, which brought him to himself As soon as he was sensible of his Recovery, O my Friends! said he, what have you done? You have not cur'd, but kill'd me; you have taken away the only Pleasure of my Life; which by your Remedies is now forc'd from me.

WISDOM consists in laying aside Trifles, and in leaving to young Men those Diversions which best become their Age and Condition: 'Tis better for a Man to learn how to live, to be Regular and Uniform in all his Actions; than to spend his Time in unprofitable Amusements, in composing Songs for the *Roman* Lyre When I am alone, I often make these Reflections to my self. If you had such a Thirst upon you, as could not be allay'd; wou'd not you lay open your Case to a Physician? And why will you not confess, that the more you have, the more you desire? If any one should recommend some Root or Herb for a Wound that you have, and it should give you no Ease, you wou'd forbear to apply that Root or Herb to your Wound, because it has prov'd ineffectual You have heard from the Philosophers, that when the Gods have given a Man Riches, they take away Folly; and yet you find that your large Possessions have not made you the wiser Why will you listen to such Deceivers? If Riches could add to your Wisdom and Prudence, cou'd they dissipate your Fears, and moderate your Passions, you wou'd then have Reason to be asham'd, shou'd any other Man be more covetous than your self If

what

Si proprium est, quod quis libra mercatus & ære
    est;

Quædam (si credis consultis) mancipat usus;

Qui te pascit ager, tuus est: & villicus Orbi, 160

Cum segetes occat tibi mox frumenta daturas,

Te dominum sentit. das nummos; accipis uvam,

Pullos, ova, cadum temeti. nempe modo isto

Paullatim mercaris agrum, forsasse trecentis,

Aut etiam supra, nummorum millibus emtum 165

Quid refert, vivas numerato nuper an olim?

Emtor Aricini quondam Veientis & arvi

Emtum cenat olus, quamvis aliter putat   emtis

Sub noctem gelidam lignis calefactat aenum.

Sed vocat usque suum, qua populus adsita certis 170

Limitibus vicina refigit jurgia   tamquam

Sit proprium quicquam, puncto quod mobilis horæ

Nunc prece, nunc pretio, nunc vi, nunc morte su-
    prema

Permutet dominos, & cedat in altera jura

Sic, quia perpetuus nulli datur usus, & heres 175

Heredem alternis, velut unda supervenit undam,

Quid vici prosunt, aut horrea? quidve Calabris

Saltibus adjecti Lucani? si metit Orcus

Grandia cum parvis, non exorabilis auro.

Gemmas, marmor, ebur, Tyrrena sigilla, ta-
    bellas,   180

Argentum, vestis Gætulo murice tinctas,

what we buy and pay for is our own, if it be true, as the Lawyers tell us, that the Use of some Things gives a Man a Right and Title to them; then the Field from whence you have your Subsistence, may be said to be yours; and when *Orbius*'s Bailiff harrows the Clods, which will supply you with Corn in Harvest, he does in effect acknowledge you his Master You pay your Money, and in Exchange you receive Grapes and Wine, Eggs and Pullets, and thus by Degrees you purchase that Farm, which was sold for above two Thousand Pounds Pray where is the Difference between your paying for what you have, or living upon what you formerly paid for ? He that purchased the *Arician* and *Veientian* Fields, buys the Herbs he eats, tho' he will not believe it. He has not so much as one poor Faggot to boil his Pot with, but what he pays for; and yet he calls all the Land his own, till you come to the Poplar, which serves for a Boundary, to prevent Disputes between him and his Neighbours. As if any thing could properly be call'd our own, which by Sale or Death, by Consent or Violence, can in an Instant change its Master, and become another's. The Hope of enjoying any thing for ever, is vain and fruitless, Heirs succeed Heirs, as one Wave follows close upon another To what Purpose then should we make new Purchases? Why should we multiply Farms and Manors, since cruel Death, that inexorable Tyrant, (who will not be brib'd with Sums of Gold) mows down both Great and Small alike, without Distinction

THERE are many in the World, who have neither Jewels nor Plate, nor purple Garments; who have neither Pictures nor Marble, nor Ivory

ry

Sunt qui non habeant; eft qui non curat habere.

Cur alter fratrum ceffare, & ludere, & ungui

Præferat Herodis palmetis pinguibus; alter

Dives & inportunus, ad umbram lucis ab ortu 185

Silveftrem flammis & ferro mitiget agrum:

Scit Genius, natale comes qui temperat aftrum,

Naturæ deus humanæ, mortalis in unum-

Quodque caput, voltu mutabilis, albus & ater.

Utar, & ex modico, quantum res pofcet, acervo 190

Tollam. nec metuam, quid de me judicet heres,

Quod non plura datis invenerit. & tamen idem

Scire volam, quantum fimplex hilarifque nepoti

Difcrepet, & quantum difcordet parcus avaro.

Diftat enim, fpargas tua prodigus, an neque fum-
   tum

Invitus facias, nec plura parare labores;   195

Ac potius, puer ut feftis Quinquatribus olim,

Exiguo

ry Statues; and there are others, who never trouble themselves about 'em. Whence comes it to pass, that of the two Brothers in the Play, one shall prefer his Ease and Pleasure to * *Herod's* Estate, the other, tho' rich, shall toil and moil from Morning to Evening, in improving his Lands and burning the Stubble? This Secret is known to none but our *Genius,* who governs the Star that presides at our Nativity; he is the God of our human Nature; he influences our Actions, and lives and dies with us, he changes according to our different Circumstances, He is white or black, happy or unhappy. I will therefore prudently enjoy my self, and take from the little Estate I have, what is sufficient to supply my Necessities; nor will I be concern'd, what my Heir shall say of me, when he shall find, that I have added nothing to the Bounty of my Friends   Nor will I neglect to observe the Difference between a frugal and a covetous Man, between one that is truly liberal, and one that is extravagant   The Difference indeed is very considerable, he may be justly tax'd with Prodigality, who wastes his Fortune, and squanders away his Money   But he who spends it wisely and freely, who thinks he has enough, and does not toil for more, but sweetly enjoys himself and Friend, and makes as much as he can of Life, (as the School-Boys do of † *Minerva's* Festival, whose Duration is short,)

---

* *Herod,* sirnam'd the *Great,* Son of *Antipater,* an *Idumæan,* was made by *Antony* Governor of *Judæa,* in which Government, *Antony* being defeated at *Actium,* he was afterwards confirm'd by *Augustus*

† *Festa Quinquatria,* the Feasts of *Minerva* commenc'd on the 19th of *March,* and ended the 23d, during this Solemnity the Boys and Girls pray'd to *Minerva* for

Exiguo gratoque fruaris tempore raptim.

Pauperies immunda procul procul absit ego utrum

Nave ferar magna an parva, ferar unus &
      idem   200

Non agimur tumidis velis Aquilone secundo;

Non tamen adversis ætatem ducimus Austris

Viribus, ingenio, specie, virtute, loco, re,

Extremi primorum, extremis usque priores

Non es avarus abi. quid? cetera jam simul isto 205

Cum vitio fugere? caret tibi pectus inani

Ambitione? caret mortis formidine & ira?

Somnia, terrores magicos, miracula, sagas,

Nocturnos lemures, portentaque Thessala rides?

Natalis grate numeras? ignoscis amicis?   210

Lenior & melior fis accedente senecta?

Quid te exemta levat spinis de pluribus una?

Vivere si recte nescis, decede peritis.

Lusisti satis, edisti satis, atque bibisti.

Tempus abire tibi est ne potum largius æquo 215

Rideat & pulset lasciva decentius ætas.

Q HORATII

short,) is the liberal Man   Let me but be free
in a sordid Poverty; it matters not whether
I sail in a little Pinnace, or in a larger Vessel.
My Gales are neither prosperous nor adverse; if
in Strength and Beauty, Wit and Virtue, Fortune and Condition I am excell'd by others;
there are those whom I excel.

To be free from Covetousness is no ordinary
Perfection; but what is become of your other
Vices? have you stifled the Flames of Pride and
Ambition? Have you conquer'd your Passions?
Have you surmounted the Fear of Death?
Have you acquir'd such a Presence of Mind, as
to laugh at Dreams and Magick Terrors? Are
you fearless of Monsters, Ghosts and Prodigies,
so frequent in *Thessaly*? Can you seriously reflect on the Years you have liv'd with Satisfaction? Are you dispos'd to pardon the Failings of
your Friends? Are you less passionate, are you
milder and better as your Years increase? What
will it avail you to pull out one Thorn, while
many more remain behind? Will the taking
out that one asswage your Pain? If you know
not how to act as you ought, give Place to
those who are wiser than your self; you have
eat and drank and enjoy'd your Share of the
Pleasures of Life; 'tis high Time to retire, lest
by drinking to Excess, you Expose your self to
the gay young Men; who may indulge their
Passions with a better Grace.

Wisdom and Learning, to this Custom *Juvenal* alludes,
Sat. X.

Eloquium & famam Demosthenis & Ciceronis
Incipit optare, & totis Quinquatribus optat

At the same Time the Boys carried their Masters their Fee,
which was called *Minerval*

HORACE's
ART OF
POETRY
Done into ENGLISH.

Ludentis Speciem dabit, & torquebitur.

Lib. 2. Epift. l. 124.

Q. HORATII

ARS POETICA.

*H*UMANO *capiti cervicem pictor equinam*
Jungere si velit, & varias inducere plu-
mas
Undique collatis membris, ut turpiter atrum
Desinat in piscem mulier formosa superne;
Spectatum admissi risum teneatis amici?　　5
Credite, Pisones, isti tabulæ fore librum
Persimilem, cujus, velut ægri somnia, vanæ
Fingentur species; ut nec pes, nec caput uni
Reddatur formæ. Pictoribus atque poetis
Quidlibet audendi semper fuit æqua potestas :　10
Scimus, & hanc veniam petimusq; damusq; vi-
cissim.

Sed

HORACE's
Art of POETRY.

SHOULD a * *Painter* attempt a Med-
ley Piece, with the Head of a Woman, and the Neck of a Horfe; fhould
he continue to draw it with various
Limbs taken from Beafts of a different Kind,
cover it with Feathers, and compleat his
Work with the Tail of a Fifh; wou'd not all
that faw it contemn the Performance?

BELIEVE me, Gentlemen, that Poem is
as ridiculous, whofe Thoughts and Parts, like
fick Mens Dreams, have no Connexion with,
or Relation to each other   If it be faid, that
Painters and Poets affume to themfelves a Privilege of drawing and fancying what they pleafe;
We grant they do fo   We both mutually give

---

* We ought to take a great deal of Care, not to fall
into the whimfical Defign of that Painter, who, being to draw the Picture of *Helen*, whom he defigned to
reprefent perfectly beauteous, refolv'd to give her all
the Graces, which he had heard commended in the
faireft Perfons   He chang'd her Lips into Coral, Cheeks
into Rofes, Eyes into Suns, and unskilfully joining them
together, made a Figure like this of *Horace*   Mr *de la
Valterie* in his Effay of the true and falfe Beauty of ingenious Writings.

and

Sed non ut placidis coeant inmitia ; non ut

Serpentes avibus geminentur, tigribus agni.

　Inceptis gravibus plerumque & magna professis,

Purpureus, late qui splendeat, unus & alter　　15

Adsuitur pannus. cum lucus & ara Dianæ,

Et properantis aquæ per amœnos ambitus agros,

Aut flumen Rhenum, aut pluvius describitur arcus

Sed nunc non erat his locus　& fortasse cupressum.

Scis simulare . quid hoc, si fractis enatat exspes 20

Navibus, ære dato qui pingitur ? amphora cœpit

Institui, currente rota, cur urceus exit ?

Denique sit quidvis, simplex dumtaxat & unum

Maxima pars vatum, pater & juvenes patre digni,

Decipimur specie recti　brevis esse laboro,　　25

Obscurus fio · sectantem lenia nervi

Deficiunt animique　professus grandia turget

Serpit

and take this Liberty· But then some Regard must be had to Nature; the mild and gentle Part of the Creation must not be coupled with the savage and cruel Is there any Union between *Birds* and *Serpents*, or can *Lambs* and *Tigers* accord together?

In an *Epick Poem*, the Beginning is often pompous and magnificent, and promises much; the Poet excells in many beautiful Descriptions, the *Grove* and *Temple* of the Goddess *Diana*, a purling *Stream* gliding thro' the Meadows, the *Rhine* and *Rainbow* are admirably express'd; but, like fine Purple Patches in a Garment, they are generally misplac'd. Suppose you know how to draw a Cypress-Tree, will not he lose his Money and Expectations, who shall employ you to paint a Shipwreck, to paint him contending with Storms and Tempests, and swimming to the Shore on a broken Piece of the shatter'd Vessel? When you set out in so lofty a Manner, why make you so trifling and insipid a Conclusion? In a Word, let your Subject be what it will, take Care it be * simple and entirely the same

We who set up for Poets, are generally deceiv'd in taking the Shadow for the Body, the Appearance of Truth, for Truth it self, by endeavouring to be short, I grow obscure, by endeavouring to smooth and polish my Numbers, I destroy the Strength and Spirit of † 'em.
Some,

---

* *N.B.* Simplicity is the Perfection of every Work, and is an Ornament even to Beauty it self

† *Longinus*, who next to *Aristotle* was the greatest Critick among the *Greeks*, in his 27th Chapter ϖεὶ ὕψυς, has judiciously preferr'd the *sublime Genius that sometimes errs,* to *the indifferent one that makes few Faults, but seldom or*

Serpit humi tutus nimium timidusque procellæ

Qui variare cupit rem prodigialiter unam,

Delphinum silvis adpingit, fluctibus aprum. 30

In vitium ducit culpæ fuga, si caret arte

Æmilium circa ludum faber, unus & unguis

Exprimet, & mollis imitabitur ære capillos;

Infelix operis summa   quia ponere totum

Nesciet. hunc ego me, si quid conponere curem, 35

Non magis esse velim; quam naso vivere pravo,

Spectandum nigris oculis nigroque capillo.

Sumite materiam vestris, qui scribitis, æquam

Viribus; & versate diu, quid ferre recusent,

Quid valeant humeri cui lecta potenter erit res, 40

Nec facundia deseret hunc, nec lucidus ordo

Ordinis hæc virtus erit & venus, aut ego fallor;

Ut jam nunc dicat, jam nunc debentia dici

Pleraque differat & præsens in tempus omittat.

Some, by affecting a lofty Stile, run into Bombast. Others again are so wretchedly cautious, that thro' Fear of a Storm they servilely creep along the Shore   Others delight in a monstrous Variety; draw *Boars* in *Seas* and *Dolphins* in *Woods.*   Thus the carefully avoiding some Faults, where Judgment is wanting, is oftentimes the Means of falling into greater

'Tis possible that a Statuary may excell all others in graving the Nails, and in imitating the Softness and Beauty of the Hair; and yet know not how to finish his Work   Were I to compose a Poem, I would no more be thought to resemble this Artist, than I would appear in Publick with fine black Eyes and Hair, and a flat or wry Nose

POETS must be sure to know themselves, to understand the Strength and Vigour of their Genius, lest haply they launch beyond their Depth   He that chooses a Subject proportionable to his Parts, will neither be wanting in Method nor Eloquence

Now, if I mistake not, the Force and Beauty of Method consist, sometimes in saying what was proper to be said, sometimes in postponing a great many Things, which, tho' pertinent to the Subject, may for the present be better omitted.

---

never rises to an Excellence   He compares the *first* to a Man of large Possessions, who has not Leisure to consider of every slight Expence, but is careful of the Main   On the other Side, he likens the *Mediocrity* of *Wit* to one of a mean Fortune, who manages his Store with extreme Frugality, but thro' Fear of being Profuse, never arrives to the Magnificence of Living   This kind of *Genius*, says Mr. *Dryden,* writes so correctly, that he is neither to be blam'd, nor prais'd.

In verbis etiam tenuis cautusque serendis, 45
Hoc amet, hoc spernat, promissi carminis auctor.
Dixeris egregie, notum si callida verbum
Reddiderit junctura novum si forte necesse est
Indiciis monstrare recentibus abdita rerum;
Fingere cinctutis non exaudita Cethegis 50
Continget: dabiturque licentia sumta pudenter.
Et nova factaque nuper habebunt verba fidem; si
Græco fonte cadent, parce detorta. quid autem
Cæcilio Plautoque dabit Romanus, ademtum
Virgilio Varioque? ego cur adquirere pauca, 55
Si possum, invideor? cum lingua Catonis & Enni
Sermonem patrium ditaverit, & nova rerum
Nomina protulerit. licuit, semperque licebit
Signatum præsente nota procudere nummum.
Ut silvis folia privos mutantur in annos; 60
Prima cadunt ita verborum vetus interit ætas,
Et juvenum ritu florent modo nata vigentque.
Debemur morti nos, nostraque. sive receptus

Terra

It is moreover required of Poets, that they be very nice and cautious what Words they make use of Happy is he, who, by the Skilfulness of his Composition, can make a vulgar Word appear a new one If the Subject you treat of be deep and abstruse, some Term may be us'd of your own inventing, such as the antient Warlike * *Romans* knew nothing of, provided this Liberty be manag'd with Discretion They, generally speaking, succeed the best, which are deduc'd from the *Grecian Language* , but then their Derivations must be easie and natural, not forc'd and constrain'd Where is the Justice, to condemn those Things in *Virgil* and *Varius*, which we approve in *Plautus* or *Cæcilius* ? Why am I envy'd for endeavouring to embellish my Native Tongue, when *Cato* and *Ennius*, by the many new Names they have given to Things, have so considerably enrich'd it ? Men ever had, and will always have the Liberty of making new Words, such as are agreeable to the Genius and Taste of the Age they live in

As the Leaves of Trees fall away in Autumn, and are succeeded by others at the returning Spring, so it is with Words , the Old decay and are forgotten, and New ones rise up and flourish, and have all the Charms and Graces of Youth Both we and our Works are subject to Fate ; if the *Lucrine Lake* is now

---

* The antient *Romans* wore their Gowns after this Manner ——The Lappet of the Gown which us'd to be brought up to the Left Shoulder, being drawn thence, was cast off in such a Manner upon the Back, as to come round short to the Breast, and there fasten in a Knot, which Knot tuck'd up the Gown, and made it shorter and straiter

Terra Neptunus claſſis Aquilonibus arcet,

Regis opus; ſteriliſve palus prius aptaque remis 65

Vicinas urbis alit, & grave ſentit aratrum :

Seu curſum mutavit iniquum frugibus amnis,

Doctus iter melius   mortalia cuncta peribunt;

Ne dum ſermonum ſtet honos, & gratia vivax.

*Multa renaſcentur, quæ jam cecidere; cadentque,*70

Quæ nunc ſunt in honore vocabula. ſi volet uſus,

Quem penes arbitrium eſt, & jus, & norma lo-
    quendi

Res geſtæ regumque ducumque, & triſtia bella

Quo ſcribi poſſent numero, monſtravit Homerus.

Verſibus inpariter junctis querimonia primum, 75

Poſt etiam incluſa eſt voti ſententia compos

Quis tamen exiguos elegos emiſerit auctor,

Grammatici certant, & adhuc ſub judice lis eſt.

Archilochum proprio rabies armavit iambo.

Hunc

made a Harbour and Protection to the *Roman* Navy from the Fury of the North-winds; (a Work so stupendous, that none but *Cæsar* was able to effect it) if the Fens, where Boats were row'd in former Ages, are now so drain'd that they are plow'd and sow'd, and yield Corn in great Plenty to the neighbouring Cities; if the rapid *Tiber*, which so often over-flow'd the Fields and Meadows, now takes a milder and more gentle Course; I say, if such Changes as these happen to such considerable Things as Lakes, Fens and Rivers, then all Things must perish, and there are little Hopes that Words should always preserve their Grace and Beauty. If Custom pleases, Custom the absolute Master of Language, the Sovereign Judge and Rule of Speech, many Words that have been long dead, shall revive and flourish; and many that are now in the highest Esteem, shall be buried in Oblivion

HOMER was the first who taught us in *Heroicks* to sing of Wars, and mighty Generals; to sing the immortal Deeds of Kings in Numbers as immortal A complaining Grief was at first express'd in unequal Measures; but of late this Sort of * Verse has been us'd to describe the Success of happy Lovers, and the like We are yet in the Dark who the Person was that invented the *Pentameter*; the *Grammarians* maintain warm Contests about it, but the Matter is not yet determin'd

RAGE and Indignation first arm'd *Archilochus* with his own *Iambicks*, which were imme-

---

* *Elegy*, by the Quality of its Name, says *Rapin*, is destin'd to Complaints, and therefore its Character should be doleful. But afterwards it was us'd in Subjects of Tenderness, as in *Love-matters*, and the like.

diately

Hunc focci cepere pedem grandefque cothurni,   80
Alternis aptum fermonibus, & popularis
Vincentem firepitus, & natum rebus agendis.
Mufa dedit fidibus Divos, puerofque Deorum,
Et pugilem victorem, & equum certamine primum,
Et juvenum curas, & libera vina referre.   85
Defcriptas fervare vices operumque colores,
Cur ego fi nequeo ignoroque, poeta falutor ?
Cur nefcire, pudens prave, quam difcere malo?
Verfibus exponi tragicis res comica non vult ·
Indignatur item privatis ac prope focco   90
Dignis carminibus narrari cena Thyeftæ
Singula quæque locum teneant fortita decentem
Interdum tamen & vocem Comœdia tollit,
Iratufque Chremes tumido dilitigat ore.

Et

dlately receiv'd upon the Theatre, as being moft proper both for the *Tragick* and *Comick* Strain. The *Iambick* is peculiarly adapted to * Conveifation, in Difcourfe we naturally run into it; it commands Attention, filences the Noife of the Pit and Galleries, and, of all others, is moft fit for Action.

THE *Lyrick Mufe* delights in a lofty elevated Subject; fhe fings of Gods and God-like Men; fhe fings of Crowns that were won at the *Olympicks*; fhe defcribes the pleifing Joys of Wine, and the more pleafing Lovers Cares

IF I know not how to obferve thefe Rules; if I am ignorant with what kind of Stile, and in what Meafures this or that Subject ought to be exprefs'd, why am I honour'd with the Name of Poet? Why am I faluted as fuch, when through a foolifh affected Modefty I perverfly refolve to continue ignorant rather than learn of others?

THE Writers of *Comedy* exprefs their *Characters* in an eafie familiar Converfation-Stile; but the pompous Strain is peculiar to Tragedy. The Feaft of † *Thyeftes* difdains a low and humble Verfe, which is only proper to the *Comick* Mufe Each Subject muft be treated in fuch a Stile as is fuitable to it; not but that in *Comedy* it is fometimes neceffary to ufe a high and elevated Tone; ‡ *Chremes* in a Paffion foams and

rages,

---

* *Ariftotle* and *Cicero* both obferve, that it is difficult to fpeak either *Greek*, or *Latin*, without making *Iambicks*

† The Hiftory of *Thyeftes* eating his own Children, who were murder'd by his Brother *Atreüs*, is here put by the Poet for all Sorts of Tragedies, who judicioufly remarks, it being fo extremely cruel and barbarous in every Circumftance, that it muft be told, not reprefented.

‡ *Non, fi ex capite fis meo natus item, ut aiunt Minervam effe ex Jove, ea caufa magis patiar, Clitipho,*

flagitiis

Et tragicus plerumque dolet sermone pedestri   95
Telephus aut Peleus : cum pauper & exsul uterque
Projicit ampullas, & sesquipedalia verba,
Si curat cor spectantis tetigisse querela.
Non satis est pulchra esse poemata ; dulcia sunto,
Et quocunque volent, animum auditoris agunto 100
Ut ridentibus adrident, ita flentibus adflent
Humani voltus si vis me flere, dolendum est
Primum ipsi tibi . tunc tua me infortunia lædent.

Telephe,

rages; and so likewise in *Tragedy*, when the Poets describe the Passion of Grief, they usually lay aside their swelling Words; * *Peleus* or *Telephus* being banish'd from his Country, and reduc'd to a poor and indigent Condition, must tell his Miseries in a natural Manner, if he expects that those, who hear his Complaints, shou'd be affected with 'em.

Nor is it enough that their Expressions be correct, unless they be moving, they must know how to raise and work which Passion they please† We are apt to imitate the Actions of others; as they laugh, or mourn, so do we. If you wou'd therefore have me weep, you must weep your self; then, *Telephus*, I shall

---

flagitiis tuis me infamem fieri. Ter Heauton. *Act* 5. *Scen* 4.

* *Longinus* lays this down for a Rule in writing Tragedy, that a Pompous, Lofty, Stately Stile is very improper when we seek to move the Pity of others. Nothing is more ridiculous than to endeavour to be eloquent on such an Occasion. It is a fine Observation of *Aristotle*'s, that the Opinions, Manners, and Passions of Men are obscur'd by sounding pompous Phrases, hard Metaphors, and elaborate Expressions.

† As we may observe, that one who yawns makes another also yawn, and as our seeing others laugh, provokes also Laughing in us After the same Manner, what Passion soever we exhibit in our selves, the same steals insensibly upon those we speak to, while their Mind, attending to the Words they hear, is not aware of the subtle Spirit's Motions, that, by a Kind of Contagion, rise and swell in their Hearts According to which natural Inclination in all Men, the Master of Poets, and excellent Observer of Mens Humour, said passing well,

Si vis me flere, dolendum est, Primum ipsi tibi

Sir *Kenelm Digby*, of the *Operations of the Soul.* p 35.

feel

Telephe, vel Peleu, male si mandata loqueris,

Aut dormitabo, aut ridebo. tristia mæstum 105

Voltum verba decent ; iratum, plena minarum ;

Ludentem, lasciva ; severum, seria dictu

Format enim natura prius nos intus ad omnem

Fortunarum habitum ; juvat, aut inpellit ad iram,

Aut ad humum mærore gravi deducit & angit . 110

Post effert animi motus interprete lingua

Si dicentis erunt fortunis absona dicta,

Romani tollent equitesque patresque cachinnum

Intererit multum, Divusne loquatur an heros ;

Maturusne senex, an adhuc florente juventa 115

Fervidus ; & matrona potens, an sedula nutrix ,

Mercatorne vagus, cultorne virentis agelli ;

Colchus, an Assyrius ; Thebis nutritus, an Argis.

Aut

feel the Weight of your Calamities; and be as
sensible of 'em as if they were my own. But
if you act your Part unskilfully, instead of com-
passionating your Misfortunes, I shall fall a
Sleeping, or Laughing

Our Words must change with the Subject; in Painting of Sorrow, let our Expressions be mournful; in describing of Joy, let
'em be gay and lively Anger requires a
threatning Stile, and what is grave does best
agree with serious Things

Nature fashions the Mind to every Condition, and writes the Change of our Fortunes
in our Countenance; it aids, inclines, and ex-
cites us to Anger; it tortures, dejects, and
brings us even to the Ground with Care and
Sorrow, and the Tongue is, as it were, the
Soul's Interpreter in expressing those Passions
which we feel within us If then our Words
and Fortunes disagree, we become a Jest to all
good Judges.

It is a Matter of Importance to observe the
different Characters of the Actors A * *God*
and a *Hero* must not say the same Things; there
is a mighty Difference between the Conversation of a *Lady of* † *Quality* and her *Woman*;
between an experienc'd Wise Old Man and a
hot-brain'd Fellow, who is in the Prime and
Vigour of his Youth If a *Merchant*, or *Far-*
mer, a Native of *Colchos*, or *Assyria*, a *Theban*

---

* It was usual with the antient Tragedians to introduce the Gods upon the Stage, as is evident from several Passages in *Æschylus, Sophocles* and *Euripides*

† *Matrona Potens*, a Lady of Quality The Poet had
undoubtedly in View *Euripides's Hippolytus*, where *Phæ-*
dra and her Nurse discourse together, but in a very
different Manner.

Aut famam sequere, aut sibi convenientia finge,
Scriptor. Homereum si forte reponis Achillem; 120
Inpiger, iracundus, inexorabilis, acer,
Jura neget sibi nata, nihil non arroget armis.
Sit Medea ferox invictaque, flebilis Ino,
Perfidus Ixion, Io vaga, tristis Orestes.

   Si quid inexpertum scenæ conmittis, & audes 125
Personam formare novam ; servetur ad imum
Qualis ab incepto processerit, & sibi constet.

Difficile

or an *Argian* appears upon the Stage, let his Difcourfe be fuch as becomes his Country, Age and Condition

IN reprefenting any Perfon, follow the common Report of the World; if you feign a Character, fay nothing but what is confiftent with it.

IF you defcribe *Achilles*, let his Character be the fame as *Homer* gives him, when he contends for his beautiful Captive with *Agamemnon* · Paint him Active and Paffionate, Haughty and Inexorable; let him fancy himfelf above all Laws, and fwear that his Sword fhall do him Juftice Let [a] *Medea* be cruel and implacable, [b] *Ino* muft weep, ' *Ixion* be perfidious, let [d] *Io* be a Wanderer, and let *Oreftes* appear in the higheft Diftraction

IF you have the Courage to write a Play on a Subject never yet attempted, if the Characters you form are New, take Care they be

---

[a] *Medea* being flighted by *Jafon*, who efpoufed *Creufa*, Daughter of *Creon*, King of *Corinth*, was fo enraged, that fhe flew both Father, Daughter, and the two Children which *Jafon* had by her

[b] *Ino* being married to *Athamas*, who had a Son by a former Wife, pretended an Oracle which requir'd him to be offer'd in Sacrifice to *Jupiter*, upon which *Athamas* growing diftracted, flew her eldeft Son, and had alfo kill'd her, and her other Boy, had fhe not thrown herfelf into the Sea with the Infant in her Arms, the Lamentations of a Mother on fuch an Occafion cannot but be exceeding forrowful.

[c] *Ixion* diffembling his Anger at *Deioneus*'s taking away his Horfes, invited him to an Entertainment, and by a Trap-Door made him to fall down into a Furnace, where he was prefently confum'd

[d] *Jupiter* being in Love with *Io*, the better to conceal her from *Juno*, chang'd her into a Cow, but the Goddefs, perceiving the Cheat, fent a Gad-Bee, who tormented her to fuch a Degree, that at laft fhe threw herfelf into the Sea

Uniform,

Difficile est proprie communia dicere . tuque

Rectius Iliacum carmen deducis in actus,

Quam si proferres ignota indictaque primus. 130

Publica materies privati juris erit, si

Non circa vilem patulumque moraberis orbem ;

Nec verbum verbo curabis reddere fidus

Interpres ; nec desilies imitator in artum,

Unde pedem proferre pudor vetet aut operis lex. 135

   Nec sic incipies, ut scriptor Cyclius olim ·

FORTUNAM Priami cantabo, & nobile bellum

Quid dignum tanto feret hic promissor hiatu ?

Parturiunt montes nascetur ridiculus mus

Quanto rectius hic, qui nil molitur inepte . 140

DIC MIHI, Musa, virum, captæ post mœnia
    Tiojæ,

Qui mores hominum multorum vidit, & urbis.

Non fumum ex fulgore, sed ex fumo dare lucem

Cogitat, ut speciosa dehinc miracula promat,

Antiphaten, Scyllamq, & cum Cyclope Charyb-

din. 145

Nec

Uniform, and always the fame But I muft tell you, 'tis difficult to excel in any new Subject, you had better choose fome common Argument contain'd in *Homer*, than depend on any thing of your own Invention, tho' that which you publifh was never known or mention'd before. Another's Work may be eafily made yours, if you carefully avoid too exact a Tranflation, if (like fome fervile Imitators) you follow not too clofely your Author's Method with which every one is acquainted; nor put your felf under fuch Reftraints, by reprefenting every Circumftance of the Action, as you can't honourably extricate your felf, without doing Violence to the Laws of Tragedy. Nor muft you begin like that impertinent Poet,

* *I fing* Troy's *Noble War and* Priam's *Fate.*

Now what is the Iffue of thefe mighty Pretences? The Mountains are in Labour, and the Product is a foolifh and ridiculous Moufe. How much better does *Homer*, that excellent Poet, begin his *Odyffes?*

Mufe, fpeak the Man, who fince the Siege of Troy, *So many Towns, fuch Change of Manners faw*

He imitates the Fire, which begins at firft with a little Smoak, and kindles by Degrees into a glorious Flame; his Beginning is plain and uniform, but he afterwards furprizes you with feveral bright and admirable Incidents; the Story of *Antiphates, Scylla, Charybdis,* and the Monfter *Polyphemus,* have all a peculiar Beauty in 'em. He did not like *Antimachus,* who, in

---

* This was the Beginning of *Mævius*'s Poem on the *Trojan* War, which contain'd the Hiftory of *Priam,* from the Day of his Birth to the Day of his Death, for which Reafon *Horace* here calls him *Poeta Cyclius.*

Nec reditum Diomedis ab interitu Meleagri,
Nec gemino bellum Trojanum orditur ab ovo:
Semper ad eventum festinat; & in medias res,
Non secus ac notas, auditorem rapit. & quæ
Desperat tractata nitescere posse, relinquit · 150
Atque ita mentitur, sic veris falsa remiscet,
Primo ne medium, medio ne discrepet imum.

Tu, quid ego & populus mecum desideret, audi;
Si fautoris eges aulæa manentis, & usque
Sessuri, donec cantor, Vos plaudite, dicat. 155
Ætatis cujusque notandi sunt tibi mores,
Mobilibusque decor, maturis dandus & annis.
Reddere qui voces jam scit puer, & pede certo
Signat humum; gestit paribus colludere, & iram
Colligit ac ponit temere, & mutatur in horas. 160
Inberbus juvenis, tandem custode remoto,
Gaudet equis canibusque, & aprici gramine campi;
Cereus in vitium flecti, monitoribus asper,
Utilium tardus provisor, prodigus æris,
Sublimis, cupidusq, & amata relinquere pernix. 165
Converfis studiis, ætas animusque virilis
Quærit opes & amicitias, inservit honori;
Conmisisse cavet quod mox mutare laboret.

Multa

his Poem on the Return of *Diomed*, began his
Adventures from the Death of *Meleager*; nor
does he begin the *Trojan War* with *Leda*'s Eggs,
but haftens on to the principal Action, and
makes his Audience to pafs over every Thing that
precedes it, with which he fuppofes 'em already
acquainted. He choofes no *Epifodes* but what
will beautify and embellifh his Poem, and judicioufly rejects what is incapable of Improvement. In a Word, his Fictions are fo ingenious, Truth and Falfhood are fo aptly mix'd
and blended together, that all the Parts are entirely of a Piece, and confpire in a pleafing and
graceful Uniformity.

I F Poets would have the Spectators ftay the
Play out, till the Curtain is let down, and the
Actor takes his Leave of them with a *Plaudite*,
let them hear what I and every Auditor expect.

T H E *Manners* of every particular Age muft
be carefully obferv'd, and fuch a Character given as is fuitable to the Young and the Old

A C H I L D that can but juft fpeak and walk,
delights to play among his Equals; he is foon
angry, and as foon appeas'd, and is feldom of
the fame Mind an Hour together.

A R A W wild Youth, being newly freed
from his Tutor's Care, is mighty fond of Dogs
and Horfes; Hunting and Racing are his Delight; he is prone to Vice, impatient of Re-
proof; he is proud, carelefs, extravagant, loving
and inconftant

A R R I V'D at Manhood he has different Inclinations; now he bends his Mind to improve
his Fortune, to cultivate the Friendfhip of the
Great and Powerful, and preferve a clear and
unfpotted Reputation; he is very careful not to
do any thing of which hereafter he may have
Caufe to repent.   W H A T

Multa senem circumveniant incommoda; vel quod

Quærit, & inventis miser abstinet, ac timet

uti, 170

Vel quod res omnis timide gelideque ministrat,

Dilator, spe lentus, iners, pavidusque futuri;

Difficilis, querulus, laudator temporis acti

Se puero, castigator censorque minorum.

Multa ferunt anni venientes commoda secum, 175

Multa recedentes adimunt: ne forte seniles

Mandentur juveni partes, pueroque viriles.

Semper in adjunctis, ævoque morabimur aptis.

Aut agitur res in scenis, aut acta refertur:

Segnius irritant animos demissa per aurem, 180

Quam quæ sunt oculis subjecta fidelibus, & quæ

Ipse sibi tradit spectator non tamen intus

Digna geri promes in scenam: multaque tolles

Ex oculis, quæ mox narret facundia præsens·

Ne pueros coram populo Medea trucidet; 185

Aut humana palam coquat exta nefarius Atreus,

Aut

WHAT a Multitude of Evils attend old Age? In the Decline of Life, how careful are we to heap up Money, which we dare not touch or make ufe of on the moft preffing Occafions? An Old Man is generally cold and timorous in all his Undertakings; he is flow to Hope, full of Delays, and afraid of what may happen; he is morofe, and full of Complaints; he is always commending the happy Times when he was a Young Man; and is ever cenfuring and finding Fault with the prefent Generation

As we grow up, Time brings along with it many Advantages, which forfake us, when Life declines A Boy muft not have the Ambition of a Man, nor a Man the Cares and Infirmities of Age. Regard muft be had to that which is effential to every Character, nor muft any thing be faid but what is proper to it

IN every Play fome Things are acted, fome related The former have much the Advantage of the latter; the Things which we hear affect us lefs than the Things we * fee, which make the ftronger Impreffion on our Minds, becaufe the Spectator reprefents 'em to himfelf, but notwithftanding this Advantage, there are feveral Things which are better related than acted on the Stage *Medea* muft not murder her innocent Children, nor *Atreus* prepare his inhuman Feaft, in the Prefence of the Audience. How fhocking wou'd fuch a Spectacle be? It is alfo

---

* Human Nature (fays *Garth*, in his Dedication of *Ovid*'s *Metamorphofes*, to her Royal Highnefs) is always more affected with what it fees, than what it hears of, and as thofe Ideas, which enter by the Eye, find the fureft Paffage to the Heart, fo the more the Object, whatever it be, feems defirable to the One, the longer it continues in the other.

ridiculous

Aut in avem Procne vertatur, Cadmus in anguem.

Quodcumque ostendis mihi sic, incredulus odi.

Neve minor, neu sit quinto productior actu

Fabula, quæ posci volt, & spectata reponi. 190

Nec Deus intersit, nisi dignus vindice nodus

Inciderit . nec quarta loqui persona laboret

   Actoris partes chorus, officiumque virile

Defendat · neu quid medios intercinat actus,

Quod non proposito conducat & hæreat apte. 195

Ille bonis faveatque & consilietur amice,

Et regat iratos, & amet pacare tumentis

Ille dapes laudet mensæ brevis, ille salubrem

Justitiam, legesque, & apertis otia portis:

Ille tegat commissa, Deosque precetur & oret, 200

Ut redeat miseris, abeat fortuna superbis.

Tibia non, ut nunc orichalco juncta, tubæque

ridiculous to fee *Progne* chang'd into a Swallow, *Cadmus* into a Serpent. I hate to fee fuch Things upon the *Stage*, they are Idle and Romantick.

* I F you expect that your Play fhould pleafe the Town, it muft confift of Five Acts, neither more nor lefs

L E T not a God be brought upon the Stage, but upon a great and extraordinary Occafion, an Occafion worthy of Him, and in one Scene never let four Actors difcourfe together.

T H E † *Chorus* fupplies the Place of an Actor, the Part he plays is as confiderable as the reft; nothing muft be fung between the Acts but what conduces to the bringing on the Plot, or is effential to it 'Tis the Bufinefs of the *Chorus* to declare its felf in Favour of Virtue and its Adherents, and to give 'em Advice; to calm the Paffionate, and footh 'em into Temper; to favour the Innocent, to commend Sobriety, Temperance, Juftice, and the Pleafures which flow from Peace and Tranquillity; to keep the Secrets committed to its Truft, and to pray and befeech the immortal Gods to change the prefent Courfe of Things, to pull down the Proud, and to exalt the Meek and Humble.

W H E N the Stage was in its Infancy, the Mufick was different from what it is now; the

---

* Mr. *Dryden* tells us, that 'tis a Queftion whether the firft *Roman Drama*'s were divided into Acts, and that it is very probable that they were not admitted into Comedy till the *Chorus* was filenc'd

† The *Chorus*, according to *Hedelin*, was a Company of Actors reprefenting thofe Perfons who either were, or were fuppofed to be prefent, where the Bufinefs was faid to be tranfacted, at firft it was nothing elfe but a Company of Muficians, finging and dancing in Honour of *Bacchus*, but was afterwards regulated by *Thefpis*, who is generally honour'd with the Title of the firft Tragedian.

Æmula; sed tenuis simplexque foramine pauco,
Aspirare & adesse choris erat utilis, atque
Nondum spissa nimis conplere sedilia flatu 205
Quo sane populus numerabilis, utpote parvus
Et frugi castusque verecundusque coibat
Postquam cœpit agros extendere victor, & urbem
Laxior amplecti murus, vinoque diurno
Placari Genius festis inpune diebus; 210
Accessit numerisque modisque licentia major.
Indoctus quid enim saperet liberque laborum;
Rusticus urbano confusus, turpis honesto?
Sic priscæ motumque & luxuriem addidit arti
Tibicen, traxitque vagus per pulpita vestem: 215
Sic etiam fidibus voces crevere severis,
Et tulit eloquium insolitum facundia præceps;
Utiliumque sagax rerum, & divina futuri,
Sortilegis non discrepuit sententia Delphis.

Carmine

Pipe then in Use was plain and simple, not a-
dorn'd with Brass, nor did it Rival the Trum-
pet in Size. Its Sound was shrill, and its Holes
were few; this at that Time was fitted to the
Chorus, and was large enough to be heard all
over the Theatre; then, when the Theatre was
not so spacious as now, when the Crowd was
so small that one might number it, and the Audience was a plain, frugal and modest one.

But as our Ancestors grew famous for their
Conquests, which oblig'd 'em to extend the
narrow Bounds of the City, and make the
Walls wider; the *Romans* began, especially on
Festivals, to give themselves a Loose to Luxury
and Intemperance, nor were they afraid of be-
ing punish'd for it, then it was that Musick and
Poetry grew more licentious   For what else
could be expected from a Multitude of idle il-
literate Villagers being made Citizens, than that
Vice and Ignorance should corrupt their former
Simplicity of Manners? Hence it came to pass
that those who play'd on the Flute, added to
the antient Musick a particular Gesture, and
a Luxury which appeared in their sweeping the
Theatre with long Trains to their Gowns.
And hence too, those who play'd on the
Harp, added new Notes to that Instrument,
which before was grave and solemn: The Stile
of their Tragedies ran hastily into a false and
swelling Eloquence; and the Moral Sentences of
the Plays, which were wont to contain good
Advice upon Points of Importance, or to give
their Judgment upon Things future, were express'd with such an affected Obscurity, that
they might have passed for Oraculous Answers
deliver'd at *Delphos*

Carmine qui tragico vilem certavit ob hircum, 220
Mox etiam agrestis Satyros nudavit, & asper
Incolumi gravitate jocum tentavit. eo quod
Inlecebris erat & grata novitate morandus
Spectator functusque sacris, & potus, & exlex.
Verum ita risores, ita conmendare dicacis 225
Conveniet Satyros, ita vertere seria ludo;
Ne quicumque Deus, quicumque adhibebitur heros
Regali conspectus in auro nuper & ostro,
Migret in obscuras humili sermone tabernas.
Aut, dum vitat humum, nubis & inania cap-
      tet. 230
Effutire levis indigna Tragœdia versus,
Ut festis matrona moveri jussa diebus,
Intererit Satyris paullum pudibunda protervis.

Non

THE Poets who firſt attempted Tragedy,
(when a vile Goat was the ſole Reward of thoſe
who writ beſt) in a very little Time brought
naked Satyrs on the Stage, who made Jeſts on
each other, but ſtill the Majeſty of Tragedy
was preſerv'd　This they did to pleaſe the
lawleſs drunken Mob, when they came from
ſacrificing; theſe Antick Geſtures and pleaſing Novelties, being the only Means to make
'em ſit ſtill while the Play was acting.　But
then theſe merry jeſting Satyrs muſt be judici-
ouſly introduc'd, and the Tranſition from what
is ſerious to Farce ſo artfully manag'd, that if
a God or Hero tread the Stage, the ſame Perſon who before was gorgeouſly array'd in Tiſ-
ſue or Purple, muſt not afterwards ſo demean
his Character, as to talk like a Mechanick:
Nor, to avoid ſuch poor Expreſſions, muſt he
ſoar aloft beyond the Clouds, and ſpeak nothing
but Bombaſt

THIS Kind of *Tragedy* diſdains whatever is
trifling and indecent; its *Satyrs* are different
from other *Satyrs* who are generally debauch'd;
like a Woman of Character, who, tho' ſhe
does not make Dancing her Profeſſion, will ne-
vertheleſs not ſcruple to comply with ſo Religious a Rite upon a ſolemn * Occaſion

WERE I to write a † Satirical Piece, I
wou'd

---

* It was uſual for Ladies of the firſt Quality to walk or
dance round the Altars in a grave majeſtic Manner, during the Time that the Prieſts were offering Sacrifice,
with a Torch in their Hands　Thus *Virgil* repreſents
Dido, Æneid IV. ver 62.

———*Ante ora Deum pingues ſpatiatur ad aras.*

† The Satire here mention'd was a kind of Poem between Tragedy and Comedy, it was neither ſo grave
and ſublime as the one, nor ſo low as the other　It
was invented by *Pritmas*, who, as *Horace* obſerves, liv'd

Non ego inornata & dominantia nomina solum
Verbaque, Pisones, Satyrorum scriptor amabo. 235
Nec sic enitar tragico differre colori,
Ut nihil intersit, Davusne loquatur & audax
Pythias emuncto lucrata Simone talentum,
An custos famulusque Dei Silenus alumni
Ex noto fictum carmen sequar. ut sibi quivis 240
Speret idem; sudet multum, frustraque laboret
Ausus idem. tantum series juncturaque pollet:
Tantum de medio sumtis accedit honoris
Silvis deducti caveant, me judice, Fauni,
Ne velut innati trivius, ac pene forenses,   245
Aut nimium teneris juvenentur versibus umquam,
Aut immunda crepent ignominiosaque dicta.
Offenduntur enim, quibus est equus, & pater, & res;
Nec, si quid fricti ciceris probat & nucis emtor,
Æquis accipiunt animis, donantve corona   250

Syllaba

wou'd not choofe to have none but vulgar and
plain Words; nor would I affect to make the
Stile of it fo different from that of Tragedy,
but that I wou'd take Care to obferve a Difference between the Character of *Silenus* the Governor and faithful Companion of *Bacchus*, and
that of a *Davus* and *Pythias*, the one a cunning
Servant, and the other a confident Waiting-
Woman, who fool'd honeft *Simo* out of his
Money. No, I would choofe a known and
common Subject, which I would difpofe in fo
natural a Manner, that every one who reads it
may prefently think he can write the fame; but
when he fhall dare to try the Experiment, he
will find it a Work of mighty Difficulty; he
will find to his Sorrow, that all his Toil and
Sweat and Labour were vain and fruitlefs So
great is the Force of Method and Connexion,
that 'tis almoft incredible, how they beautify a
mean and ordinary Subject

As Satyrs are fuppos'd to be bred in the
Woods, let 'em talk like Satyrs, not like Citizens of *Rome*. Verfes that have Tendernefs and
Paffion, how well foever they may be receiv'd
from the Gay and Young, are very ridiculous
when fpoke by them, and as I would not have
'em appear polite, fo neither muft their Words
be immodeft or obfcene: Perfons of Condition
will take Offence at fuch Liberties; and tho'
they may poffibly pleafe the Rabble, yet
fure I am that they will never be approv'd of by
Men of Quality.

some Time after *Thefpis*. Vid p. 373. None of thefe
Pieces are now preferv'd, but the *Cyclops of Euripides*.
The *Fabulæ Atellanæ* were writ by *Romans* in Imitation
of 'em.

Syllaba longa brevi subjecta vocatur Iambus,

Pes citus · unde etiam Trimetris adcrescere jussit

Nomen Iambeis, cum senos redderet ictus

Primus ad extremum similis sibi   non ita pridem,

Tardior ut paullo graviorque veniret ad auris, 255

Spondeos stabilis in jura paterna recepit

Commodus & patiens; non ut de sede secunda

Cederet aut quarta socialiter   hic & in Acci

Nobilibus trimetris apparet rarus, & Enni.

In scenam missus cum magno pondere versus,   260

Aut operæ celeris nimium curaque carentis,

Aut ignoratæ premit artis crimine turpi.

Non quivis videt inmodulata poemata judex.

Et data Romanis venia est indigna poetis.

Idcircone vager, scribamque licenter? ut omnis 265

Visuros peccata putem mea, tutus & intra

Spem veniæ cautus? vitavi denique culpam,

Non

AN *Iambick* confifts of a fhort and long Syllable, fix of which make a pure *Iambick*; but
tho' they ftrike the Ear fix feveral Times, yet
by Reafon of their Swiftnefs, they make but
three Meafures, and are therefore call'd *Trimeters*. It is not long fince the *Iambicks* were contented to admit the *Spondees* into their Society,
that the Majeftick Gravity of the one might
temper and allay the Rapidity of the other.
This Affociation was made upon Condition,
that the *Iambicks* fhould always maintain their
Right to the fecond and fourth Places But
Plautus and * *Ennius*, notwithftanding their
Numbers are fo much admir'd, have very rare-
ly obferv'd this Rule of keeping the *Iambicks*
in the fecond and fourth Place. Tho' the load-
ing the Vèrfe with too many *Spondees* is a certain Argument either of the Poet's Ignorance
of the Rules of Art, or of his Negligence and
Over-haftinefs in Compofing.

THERE are very few who are Judges of the
Beauty and Harmony of Numbers; the *Romans* are too kind and indulgent to the Poets.
What then? fhall I write in a loofe and ram-
bling Manner, and obferve no Rules? Tho'
every one fees and cenfures my Faults, fhall I
think my felf fafe, becaufe I am fure of obtaining Pardon? I avoid the committing any Errors, but is this the Way to raife a Reputation?

---

* The Metres of *Ennius*, *Cæcilius*, *Plautus* and *Terence*,
are very mean and not to be followed, they writing in
an Age when all Kind of *Poetry* among the *Latins* was
very imperfect, which being obferv'd by *Virgil* and *Horace*, they, by imitating *Homer*, *Euripides*, and others,
brought *Poetry* to as great Perfection in *Latin*, as it is in
the *Greek*. Our *Poet* therefore in this Place, *propter Carmen Iambicum*, recommends young Students to their
Imitation

Non laudem merui. vos exemplaria Græca
Nocturna versate manu, versate diurna.
At vestri proavi Plautinos & numeros &   270
Laudavere sales; nimium patienter utrumque,
Ne dicam stulte, mirati. si modo ego & vos
Scimus inurbanum lepido seponere dicto,
Legitimumque sonum digitis callemus & aure.

  Ignotum Tragicæ genus invenisse Camenæ   275
Dicitur & plaustris vexisse poemata Thespis
Qui canerent agerentque, peruncti fæcibus ora.
Post hunc personæ pallæque repertor honestæ
Æschylos & modicis instravit pulpita tignis,
Et docuit magnumque loqui nitique cothurno   280
Successit vetus his Comœdia, non sine multa
Laude   sed in vitium libertas excidit, & vim
Dignam lege regi   lex est accepta: chorusque
Turpiter obticuit, sublato jure nocendi.
Nil intentatum nostri liquere poetæ :   285
Nec minimum meruere decus   vestigia Græca
Ausi deserere, & celebrare domestica facta,

Vel

If you wou'd excel in Writing well, read over carefully the *Greek Originals*, read them Day and Night.

YOUR Anceſtors were ſtrangely in Love with *Plautus*; they prais'd his Wit, and admir'd his Numbers; but if you and I know how to diſtinguiſh Wit from Punning, or have any Judgment in Verſification, we cannot but wonder at their Simplicity.

THESPIS is ſaid to have invented Tragedy, a new Kind of Poetry, which before his Time was unknown to the *Grecians*; it is ſaid too that he carried the Players about in a Cart, and taught 'em to ſing, and daub their Faces with the Lees of Wine.

AFTER him came *Æſchylus*, who built a little Theatre, and brought in the Uſe of the Mask *, and the decent long flowing Veſt; he was the firſt who taught the Actors to dreſs, ſpeak and move gracefully.

NEXT follow'd the old Comedy, which was receiv'd with great Applauſe; but it degenerated by Degrees, till at laſt it grew ſo licentious and abuſive, that the Magiſtrates were forc'd to make a Law to ſuppreſs it. Thus the Chorus, having loſt its Power of ſlandering honeſt Men, in a ſcandalous Manner ſilenc'd it ſelf.

THE *Roman* Poets have left nothing unattempted; but in this Particular they deſerve our Praiſe, that diſdaining to borrow from the *Grecian* Store, they found at Home fit Subjects for

---

* The *Perſona* of the *Antients* was not like ours, which conceals the Face only, it came over the whole Head, and had always a Peruque faſten'd on it, such as was ſuitable to the Perſon whom they were to repreſent.

their

Vel qui Prætextas, vel qui docuere Togatas.
Nec virtute foret clarifve potentius armis,
Quam lingua, Latium; ſi non offenderet unum- 290
Quemque poetarum limæ labor & mora vos, ô
Pompilius ſanguis, carmen reprehendite, quod non
Multa dies & multa litura coercuit, atque
Præfectum decies non caſtigavit ad unguem.
Ingenium miſera quia fortunatius arte 　　　　295
Credit, & excludit ſanos Helicone poetas
Democritus; bona pars non unguis ponere curat,
Non barbam. ſecreta petit loca, balnea vitat
Nanciſcetur enim pretium nomenque poetæ,
Si tribus Anticyris caput inſanabile numquam 300
Tonſori Licino conmiſerit. ô ego lævus,
Qui purgo bilem ſub verni temporis horam!

Non

their Mufe, both in their * Tragedies and Comedies. Would they but be perfwaded to correct, refine and polifh their Numbers, the *Ro-*
mans wou'd be no lefs famous for their Poetry,
than they are for their Victories.

ILLUSTRIOUS *Pifos,* the worthy Off-
fpring of the Glorious † *Numa,* reject thofe
Verfes that are made in Hafte; which have neither been often perus'd nor corrected, which
want both Care and Time and Study to bring
'em to Perfection

IT was *Democritus*'s Opinion, that Nature
contributed more than Art to the making of a
Poet; in Confequence of which, he efteem'd
none truly fuch, but thofe only who had a
Tincture of Madnefs in 'em Upon this, a great
many are fo intoxicated as to renounce all Clean-
linefs and Converfation, and to affect Retirement; they imagine themfelves eftablifh'd Poets,
if they never go to *Licinus* the Barber to have
their Heads fhav'd; whofe frantick Lunacy no
Hellebore can cure. What a Fool am I, to
phyfick every Spring for the Choler which I

---

* The *Drama*'s prefented at *Rome* were divided in general into *Palliata* and *Togata,* the firft were *Grecian,* the
fecond *Roman,* the *Comedies* properly *Roman* were of
feveral Sorts, the *Togata* were acted by Perfons of the
lower Rank, the *Prætextata* by Perfons of Quality, fuch
as had the Liberty of wearing the *Prætexta,* or purple
Gown, this laft has fo near a Refemblance of the *Gre-*
cian Tragedy, that I thought it proper to tranflate it fo
by way of Diftinction.

† *Numa Pompilius* was fecond King of the *Romans,*
who had fo great an Opinion of his Virtue, that they
immediately chofe him to fucceed *Romulus,* A. U C. 40.
Rimer fays, that till this King's Time the *Romans* had
Verylittle either of *Religion* or *Poetry* among 'em 'Tis
probable that for this Reafon the Poet takes Notice that
the *Pifos* were defcended from him,

Non alius faceret meliora poemata verum
Nil tanti est ergo fungar vice cotis, acutum
Reddere quæ ferrum valet, exsors ipsa secandi 305
Munus & officium, nil scribens ipse docebo;
Unde parentur opes; quid alat formetque poetam;
Quid deceat, quid non; quo virtus, quo ferat error.
Scribendi recte, sapere est & principium & fons.
Rem tibi Socraticæ poterunt ostendere chartæ; 310
Verbaque provisam rem non invita sequentur.
Qui didicit patriæ quid debeat, & quid amicis;
Quo sit amore parens, quo frater amandus & hospes;
Quod sit conscripti, quod judicis officium, quæ
Partes in bellum missi ducis, ille profecto　　315
Reddere personæ scit convenientia cuique
Respicere exemplar vitæ morumque jubebo
Doctum imitatorem, & vivas hinc ducere voces.
Interdum speciosa locis, morataque recte
Fabula, nullius veneris, sine pondere & arte, 320
Valdius oblectat populum meliusque moratur,
Quam versus inopes rerum nugæque canoræ
Graiis ingenium, Graiis dedit ore rotundo
Musa loqui, præter laudem nullius avaris.
Romani pueri longis rationibus assem　　325

　　　　　　　　　　　　　　　　　Discunt

am fubject to! Were it not for this, none wou'd
have excell'd me in the Art of Poetry. But the
Honour is not worth the Pains; I had rather
teach others how to be Poets, than be one my
felf   As the Whetftone ferves to fharpen the
Razor, tho' it cannot cut, fo, without Writing, I may dictate to others how they ought to
write, how they may furnifh themfelves with
Matter; I may tell what forms and improves a
Poet; what is becoming, what not; what are
Faults, what Excellencies

GOOD Senfe is the Source of Writing well;
in *Socrates*'s *Morals* you'll be fure to find it;
and when once the Matter is duly prepar'd,
Words will naturally come after.

HE who knows the Duties of Civil Life,
what we owe to our Country, Parents, Brethren, Friends and Strangers; who knows how
Judges, Senators and Generals ought to act in
their feveral Employments, is beft able to give
fuch Thoughts and Behaviour to every Character, as are moft proper and agreeable to it
Every wife, judicious Poet fhould clofely and
narrowly confider and examine the different
Manners and Inclinations of Mankind, that the
Copies he draws may be according to Nature.
In a Play, where there are fome common Places well touch'd up, and fome Moral Sentences
that are Juft, tho' the Fable has no Manner of
Beauty, tho' Strength and Art are both wanting, yet it fhall divert and pleafe an Audience
more than trifling Verfes that have Numbers,
but no Senfe in them.

THE *Greeks* had all the Graces of Eloquence,
they were Witty and Polite, and Fame was the
only End of their Ambition; but as for Us,
our Youth are bred up in a different Manner,
they

Difcunt in partis centum diducere.   Dicas,
Filius Albini, fi de quincunce remota eft
Uncia, quid fuperet? poterat dixiffe, Triens. Eu!
Rem poteris fervare tuam redit uncia . quid fit?
Semis. an, hæc animos ærugo & cura peculi   330
Cum femel imbuerit, fperamus carmina fingi
Poffe linenda cedro, & levi fervanda cupreffo?

Aut prodeffe volunt, aut delectare poetæ;
Aut fimul & jocunda & idonea dicere vitæ
Quicquid præcipies, efto brevis   ut cito dicta   335
Percipiant animi dociles, teneantque fideles.
[Omne fupervacuum pleno de pectore manat.]
Ficta voluptatis cauffa fint proxima veris:
Ne, quodcumque volet, pofcat fibi fabula credi;
Neu pranfæ Lamiæ vivum puerum extrahat alvo.
                                                        340

Centuriæ feniorum agitant expertia frugis;
Celfi prætereunt auftera poemata Ramnes
Omne tulit punctum, qui mifcuit utile dulci,
Lectorem delectando, pariterque monendo.
Hic meret æra liber Sofiis, hic & mare tranfit, 345
Et longum noto fcriptori prorogat ævum.
Sunt delicta tamen, quibus ignoviffe velimus:

                                                        Nam

they learn Arithmetical, not Poetical Numbers.
Tell me *Albinus,* take one Ounce from Five,
what remains? Why don't you answer? The
Boy replies, Four　Oh the fine Child! He
knows how, I'll warrant, to keep what he has;
but if to the Five you add one Ounce, what
then is the Number? the Boy answers, Six.
When once their Minds are tainted with such
mean and ignoble Ideas, can any Thing that
is Great, Generous and Noble be expected
from them? Can Verses writ by Persons thus
educated, lay Claim to Immortality?

POETS should either please or instruct, or
rather both　Let the Rules you lay down be
short and clear, such Precepts are sooner com-
prehended and more easily retain'd. If your
Design be only to please, let your Fictions put
on a Face of Truth, let 'em resemble it as much
as possible, never pretend to impose upon
our Faith, or to bring a Child alive upon the
Stage, which has been murder'd and devour'd
by Canibals. Old Men like none but Moral
Plays, and if too grave, they displease the
Young; but that * Poet can never fail of Success, whose Pieces are so agreeably compos'd,
that they please and instruct at the same Time.
The Booksellers Shops will be crowded with Cu-
stomers for such excellent Poems, they will pass
the Seas with Admiration, and bestow an eternal Fame upon their Authors

YET there are Faults which in pure good
Nature we ought to pass over; a String may

---

* The simple and unchangeable Beauty of Virtue is
not always sure to reach our Souls. 'Tis not enough
that we are shewn the Truth, she must be represented
to us under such Colours as may make her lovely and
desirable.

Nam neque chorda sonum reddit, quem volt manus
    & mens ;
Poscentique gravem persæpe remittit acutum ·
Nec semper feriet, quodcumque minabitur, arcus. 350
Verum ubi plura nitent in carmine, non ego paucis
Offendar maculis, quas aut incuria fudit,
Aut humana parum cavit natura quid ergo est ?
Ut scriptor si peccat idem librarius usque,
Quamvis est monitus, venia caret , ut citharœdus 355
Ridetur, chorda qui semper oberrat eadem :
Sic mihi qui multum cessat, sit Chœrilos ille,
Quem bis terve bonum, cum risu miror ; & idem
Indignor, quandoque bonus dormitat Homerus.
Verum operi longo fas est obrepere somnum.   360
Ut pictura, poesis : erit quæ, si propius stes,
Te capiat magis , & quædam, si longius abstes .
Hæc amat obscurum ; volet hæc sub luce videri,
Judicis argutum quæ non formidat acumen :
Hæc placuit semel ; hæc decies repetita placebit 365
O major juvenum, quamvis & voce paterna
Fingeris ad rectum, & per te sapis ; hoc tibi dictum

Tolle

Jar, tho' the Instrument be touch'd by a Master in Musick; the most expert Archer cannot
always hit the White: If therefore a Poem be
elegantly writ, if there are a thousand Beauties in it, if the Design, Thought, Conduct and
Expressions be such as proceed from a true Genius of Poetry, 'tis unmanly to snarl at a few
slight Faults, which thro' Negligence have
been committed, Faults for which the Frailty
of our Nature is a just Excuse.   What Faults
then are they which ought not to be pardon'd?
As an *Amanuensis,* who commits the same Error, tho' often told of it, is without Excuse;
or, as a Musician exposes himself to the Laughter of the Company, who is always out at the
same Note, yet is always playing it : So it is
with Poets, he who is guilty of many Absur-
dities, is to me another *Chœrilus* If by Chance
a bright Thought or two fall from him, I
naturally admire 'em, tho' I despise him; but
when *Homer,* the excellent *Homer,* is faulty, it
grieves me to the Heart, tho' in a long *Heroick
Poem,* Errors of little or no Importance ought
to pass uncensur'd.

POETRY and Painting have so near and close
a Resemblance to each other, that in Effect
they are both the same.   There are some Pictures which please at a Distance , others, the
nearer you look upon 'em, delight the more
Some love the Shade, others again appear best
in the Light, and challenge the sharpest and
most piercing Eye of the skilfullest Artist, just
so it is with Poems, some please for a Time,
some always please

BUT, Noble *Piso,* tho' your Father's Precepts
and your own Experience have made you wise,

Tolle memor · certis medium & tolerabile rebus

Recte concedi : consultùs juris, & actor

Caussarum mediocris ; abest vii tute diserti   370

Messallæ, nec scit quantum Cascellius Aulus ;

Sed tamen in pretio est : mediocribus esse poetis

Non homines, non Dí, non concessere columnæ.

Ut gratas inter mensas symphonia discois,

Et crossum unguentvm, & Sardo cum melle pa-

     pavei

Offendunt , poterat duci quia cena sine istis : 375

Sic animis natum inventumque poema juvandis,

Si paullvm summo decessit, vergit ad imum

    Ludei e qui nescit, campestiibus abstinet aimis

Indoctusque pilæ, discive, tiochive, quiescit, 380

Ne spissæ iisum tollant inpune coionæ

Qui nescit, veisus tamen audet fingere Quid ni ?

Liber & ingenuus, piæfiitim census equestiem

Summam nummoium, vitioque iemotus ab omni

Tu nihil invitâ dices faciesve Minervâ ·   385

Id tibi judicium est, ea mens si quid tamen olim

Scripseiis, in Mæci descendat judicis auiis,

Et patiis, & nostios, nonumque piematui in

    annum,

Membi ans

yet let me defire you to remember this Sentence A Mediocrity is allowable in fome Profeffions ; a Counfellor, or a Lawyer, tho' he has neither *Meffala*'s Eloquence, nor has read half fo much as the learned *Cafcellius*, may neverthelefs be in great Efteem. But neither Gods, nor Men, nor *Columns will admit of it in Poetry For as bad Mufick, or Perfumes not well fcented, take off from the Grace and Delicacy of a Feaft, offend the Guefts, and might more difcreetly have been fpar'd ; fo Poetry, whofe End is to pleafe and delight, muft ftand or fall according to this Rule, If it is not fublimely good, 'tis fcandaloufly ill

HE who has never inur'd himfelf to the Sports and Exercifes which are perform'd in the *Campus Martius*, who neither knows how to tofs the Ball, manage the Hoop, or play at Quoits, wifely refrains from making a Party at any of thofe Paftimes for Fear of being hifs'd and laugh'd at by the Mob But every bold pretending Fool, tho' at the fame Time he knows nothing of the Matter, lays Claim to Poetry I am free, well born, have a good Eftate, my Reputation is fair and unfpotted, what have you, or any one to fay againft my writing Verfes ? But, Learned *Pyfo*, you have a true and difcerning Judgment, you know which Way your Talent lies, and underftand your felf better than to act againft Nature, but if ever it fhould be your Fate to write, let *Mecius*, or your Father, examine your Productions, or let me perufe 'em ; be fure not to let 'em fee the Light till Time and Care have

---

* The Advertifements of Books juft publifh'd were pafted upon Columns.

H h 2   ripen'd

Membranis intus positis. delere licebit
Quod non edideris: nescit vox missa reverti. 390
    Silvestris homines sacer interpresque Deorum
Cædibus & victu fœdo deterruit Orpheus;
Dictus ob hoc lenire tigris rabidosque leones.
Dictus & Amphion, Thebanæ conditor arcis,
Saxa movere sono testudinis, & prece blanda 395
Ducere quo vellet. fuit hæc sapientia quondam,
Publica privatis secernere, sacra profanis;
Concubitu prohibere vago, dare jura maritis;
Oppida moliri; leges incidere ligno.
Sic honor & nomen divinis vatibus atque 400
Carminibus venit. post hos insignis Homerus,
Tyrtæusque mares animos in Martia bella
Versibus exacuit. dictæ per carmina fortes,

Et

ripen'd 'em to Perfection; while they lie in your Study you may correct and alter 'em as you please, but when once publish'd, they can never be recall'd.

ORPHEUS, the first inspir'd Poet, dissuaded Men from Rage and Cruelty, civiliz'd their Manners, and taught 'em to live friendly and sociably together   Hence it is feign'd, that by the Charms and Power of his Numbers the Lions and Tigers chang'd their Nature, and laid aside their Savageness. *Amphion* too is said to have built the Walls of *Thebes* by the Power of his Musick; the Sounds of his Lyre were so perswasive, that the Stones inanimate danc'd to his Numbers, and moved as he directed 'em.

IN former Ages Poets were the only Instructors of the World; they were the first who taught Mankind to distinguish between publick and private Good, between Things that were sacred, and those that were ordain'd for Civil Use   They instituted Marriage, forbad all lawless and promiscuous Love; they taught their Fellow-Creatures to build Cities, and enacted wise and useful Laws   By this Means both Poetry and Poets were in great Esteem.

THE next that appear'd were *Homer* and * *Tyrtæus*, who by their bold and martial Numbers inspir'd their Countrymen with a Noble Ardour, and urg'd 'em on to warlike Atchievements.   The sacred Oracles and the Secrets of Nature were reveal'd in Verse.   Some by their

---

* *Tyrtæus*, a Poet and Musician of *Athens*, some say of *Miletum*, was chosen by the Advice of the Oracle to be General of the *Lacedemonians* in their War against the *Messenians*   This *Tyrtæus* so animated the Soldiers with some Verses he made on that Occasion, that the *Lacedemonians*, tho' before worsted in several Encounters, won the Day.

Muse

Et vitæ monstrata via est, & gratia regum
Pierius tentata modis, ludusque repertus, 405
Et longorum operum finis   ne forte pudori
Sit tibi Musa lyræ solers, & cantor Apollo.

   Natura fieret laudabile carmen, an arte,
Quæsitum est ego nec studium sine divite venâ,
Nec rude quid possit video ingenium : alterius
   sic 410
Altera poscit opem res, & conjurat amice.
Qui studet optatam cursu contingere metam,
Multa tulit fecitque puer; sudavit & alsit;
Abstinuit venere & vinq. qui Pythia cantat
Tibicen, didicit prius, extimuitque magistrum 415
Nec satis est dixisse, Ego mira poemata pango :
Occupet extremum scabies. mihi turpe relinqui est,
Et, quod non didici, sane nescire fateri.
Ut præco, ad merces turbam qui cogit emendas;
Adsentatores jubet ad lucrum ne poeta 420
Dives agris, dives positis in fenore nummis
Si ucio est, unctum qui recte ponere possit,
Et spondere levi pro paupere, & eripere artis
Litibus implicitum, mirabor, si sciet inter-
Noscere mendacem verumque beatus amicum. 425
Tu seu donaris, seu quid donare voles cui;
Nolito ad versus tibi factos ducere plenum

                                    Lætitiæ

Mufe have gain'd the Love and Favour of Kings, and Poetry had a Part in all the Plays and Shows that were invented to refresh the Mind when wearied with Busines; then blush not, *Pifo*, to make your Court to *Apollo* and the *Mufes*

'TIS a common Question, whether Art or Nature makes a Poet I am of Opinion that neither Art without Nature, nor Nature without Art can effect the Thing, they mutually stand in Need of each others Assistance

HE who is ambitious of winning the Prize at the *Olympick* Games, must inure himself betimes to Toil and Labour; he must accustom himself to Heat and Cold, and renounce the Joys of Wine and Love Was ever Musician distinguish'd for his playing well upon the *Flute*, who had not first learn'd the Grounds of his Art under some wise and able Master? But now every Scribler impudently boasts, that he's wonderfully happy in his Compositions, Shame take all those that write ill Verses, I shou'd be sorry to be of their Number, or to confefs my Ignorance of an Art which I never understood

A Poet of Condition, who has a large Estate, and Money at Command, takes oftentimes as much Pains to provide himself Flatterers, as a Crier does to bring People together to a Sale of Goods Moreover, if he's dispos'd to make Entertainments, to be Surety for his poor and indigent Friends, and to employ his Interest in their Behalf when in Distress, I shall greatly wonder if such a Man is so happy as to distinguish a Friend from a Flatterer

NEVER read your Verses before any Perfon whom either by some kind Present or Promise you have engag'd to be your Friend, he will

Lætitiæ. clamabit enim, Pulchre, bene, rette;

Pallescet; super his etiam stillabit amicis

Ex oculis rorem, saliet; tundet pede terram. 430

Ut qui conducti plorant in funere, dicunt

Et faciunt prope plura dolentibus ex animo: sic

Derisor vero plus laudatore movetur.

Reges dicuntur multis urguere culullis,

Et torquere mero, quem perspexisse laborant, 435

An sit amicitia dignus. si carmina condes,

Numquam te fallant animi sub volpe latentes

Quintilio si quid recitares, Corrige sodes

Hoc, aiebat, & hoc. melius te posse negares,

Bis terque expertum frustra? delere jubebat, 440

Et male ter natos incudi reddere versus.

Si defendere delittum, quam vertere, malles;

Nullum ultra verbum, aut operam insumebat ina-

nem,

Quin sine rivali teque & tua solus amares

Vir bonus & prudens versus reprehendet iner-

tis,   445

Culpabit duros, incomtis adlinet atrum

Transverso calamo signum; ambitiosa recidet

Ornamenta; parum claris lucem dare coget;

Arguet

cry aloud in the Fulnefs of his Joy, How fine, how excellent is this! He will feem to fwoon at every Line, Tears will ftand in his Eyes for Pleafure, he will dance, and ftrike his Foot upon the Ground. As they who are hir'd to mourn at Funerals, wring their Hands, and make much greater Lamentations than thofe who truly and inwardly mourn; fo a Flatterer affects to appear more mov'd than a fincere well-meaning Friend

THEY fay that Kings, before they honour any Perfon with their Friendfhip, ufe to try and prove and examine him throughly, and to unmask, as it were, his Soul, by plying him briskly with full Bowls of Wine If ever you write, be fure to take Care that no defigning Flatterers deceive you.

WERE you to confult *Quintilius Varus*, he wou'd impartially tell you your Faults; he wou'd frankly fay, this and this Verfe muft be corrected: If you anfwer'd you cou'd not, that you had often endeavour'd to do fo, but without Succefs; he would then advife you to blot 'em out, and go to the Forge again for others in their room. But if he finds you proud and obftinate, more difpos'd to defend and juftify your Faults than to correct 'em, without making more Words, he would leave you to admire your beloved Self, and to adore your Favourite Poems without Fear of a Rival.

AN honeft fincere impartial Friend, if your Lines want Spirit, or if your Numbers are unharmonious, will boldly and frankly tell you of it : He will blot out thofe Verfes that are rough and unpolifh'd, lop off all fuperfluous Beauties; this he'll fay is obfcure, and needs Illuftration; this is ambiguous, and muft be

2 fet

Arguet ambigue dictum ; mutanda notabit ;
Fiet Aristarchus non dicet, Cur ego amicum 450
Offendam in nugis ? hæ nugæ seria ducent
In mala derisum semel, exceptumque sinistre
Ut mala quem scabies aut morbus regius urguet,
Aut fanaticus error, & iracunda Diana ;
Vesanum tetigisse timent fugiuntque poetam, 455
Qui sapiunt. agitant pueri, incautique sequuntur.
Hic, dum sublimis versus ructatur, & errat,
Si veluti merulis intentus decidit auceps
In puteum, foveamve, licet, Succurrite, longum
Clamet, io cives: non sit qui tollere curet 460
Si curet quis opem ferre, & demittere funem ;
Qui scis, an prudens huc se projecerit, atque
Servari nolit ? dicam : Siculique poetæ
Narrabo interitum. Deus inmortalis haberi
Dum cupit Empedocles, ardentem frigidus Ætnan.

set in a clearer Light; he will act the Part of
* *Ariſtarchus*, and criticiſe upon every Syllable,
nor fear to loſe your Friendſhip for Trifles:
They are indeed but Trifles, but may prove of
ſerious Conſequence to you, when once by their
Means you are made ridiculous.

A ſenſeleſs Poet in a raging Fit is generally
more dreaded by all wiſe Men than one that is
frantick, or is infected with the Plague, Lepro-
ſy or Jaundice, he is follow'd indeed by Boys
and Fools who make him their Diverſion While
he is mouthing his lofty Verſes, and Strolling
about, if by Chance (as it ſometimes happens
to a Bird-catcher when he is thinking on nothing but his Black-birds) he falls into a Well
or a Ditch, he might cry till his Heart ak'd
before any one wou'd offer to help him out.
Shou'd any compaſſionate charitable Perſon
throw down a Rope and endeavour to aſſiſt
him, ſome wou'd poſſibly ſay, How know you
that he did not fall in on Purpoſe, and that he
does not deſire to continue there? I will tell
you how a Poet of *Sicily* died *Empedocles*,
that the People might take him for a God,
leapt into *Ætna*'s burning Flames Let Poets

---

* *Ariſtarchus* of *Samos*, a Critick of great Reputation, Contemporary with *Callimachus* and *Crates* He
commented on moſt of the *Greek* Poets, publiſh'd a correct Edition of *Homer*, reſtored ſome Verſes to their former Reading, rejected others as not being genuine, writ
nine Books of Animadverſions upon him, and took ſo
much Care to make this Performance juſt and accurate,
that Antiquity was ſo prepoſſeſs'd in his Favour upon
this Account, that every candid and judicious Critick
was call'd *Ariſtarchus*, and the contrary a *Zoilus*, one
who much about the ſame Time, writ a fooliſh ill-natur'd injudicious Criticiſm againſt *Homer* He flouriſh'd
under *Ptolemy Philometor*, who made him *Præceptor* to his
Son *Euergetes*, in 158th *Olympiad*, A.U C. 606

deſtroy

Infiluit. fit jus liceatque perire poetis. 465
Invitam qui fervat, idem facit occidenti
Nec femel hoc fecit; nec fi retractus erit jam,
Fiet homo, & ponet famofæ mortis amorem.
Nec fatis adparet, cur verfus factitet, utrum 470
Minxerit in patrios cineres, an trifte bidental
Moverit inceftus: certe furit, ac velut urfus
Objectos caveæ valuit fi frangere clathros,
Indoctum doctumque fugat recitator acerbus.
Quem vero arripuit, tenet, occiditque legendo, 475
Non miffura cutem, nifi plena cruoris, hirudo.

F I N I S.

deſtroy themſelves, if they pleaſe; 'tis as great an Injury to ſave a Man againſt his Will, as it is to murder him; beſides, he has done ſo more than once; cou'd you take him out alive, he wou'd not be like other Men, he wou'd ſtill be ambitious of dying in a remarkable Way. And you don't know for what Crime he is puniſh'd, when this Spirit of Poetry poſſeſſes him; whether it be for his having defil'd his Father's Monument, or his having ſacrilegiouſly remov'd the Bounds of ſome conſecrated Place; but ſo it is, that like a furious Beaſt broke looſe from his Den, this eternal Rhimer puts all he meets to Flight, whether Learned or Unlearn-ed, without any Diſtinction. If he ſeizes on any one, like Leaches who never quit their Hold till they are ready to burſt with Blood, without the leaſt Compaſſion or Remorſe, he reads him to Death with his nauſeous Repe-titions.

F I N I S.

BOOKS Printed for W. MEARS *at the* Lamb, F. CLAY *at the* Bible, *and* D. BROWNE *at the* Black Swan *without* Temple-Bar

THE Works of *Horace* in *Latin* and *English*, in Two Volumes; the *English* Version, by Mr. *Creech*. The Fifth Edition.

Great Britain's Vade Mecum· Containing 1 A concise Geographical Description of the World, with an Enquiry into the Nature, Quality and principal Commodity of each Country. 2. The several Counties of *England* and *Wales* particularly described; an Account of their valuable Products, Market-Towns, Market-Days, Chief Fairs, &c With a short View of Trade in general, &c. The whole of universal Use to Persons of all Ranks in Town and Country; particularly to Country Gentlemen, Travellers, Lawyers, Merchants, Tradesmen, Builders, Gaugers, &c

The Gentleman's Library, containing Rules for Conduct in all Parts of Life, written by a Gentleman.

Walsingham's Manual, or prudential Maxims for Statesmen and Courtiers, with Instructions for Youth, Gentlemen and Noblemen. The Second Edition.

71

INDEX.

A

	Page
ACCIUS	369
Actium	347
Ædilis	161
Æſop	375
Æſchylus	387, 437
Afranius	371
Agrippa	163, 305
Agamemnon	163
Ajax	ibid.
Alcæus	355
Alfenus Varus	35
Alexander	395
Alcinous	259
Ambition, the Folly of it	163
Amphion	345, 469
Anxur	55
Anticyra	151
Ancona	189
Anger, the Neceſſity of ſubduing it	263
Antonius Muſa	317
Appij Forum	53
Apelles	395
Ariſtophanes	37
Aricia	53
Archilochus	143
Ariſtippus	153, 333
Attendance upon Great Men, very troubleſome	349
Atta	375
Aulis	165

B

	Page
Baia	185, 251
Balloon	125
Bari	65
Beds, an Account how the *Romans* lay upon them	231
Beneventum	61
Bibliotheca Palatina	267
Brunduſium	65

C

	Page
Callimachus	409
Celſus	103

Camillus

INDEX.

	Page
Camillus	249
Campus Martius	211
Canusium	63
Capua	59
Castor	363
Cato	353
Carthage	121
Catullus	103
Censor	69
Ceres	137
Cærites	281
Cæcilius	371
Chrysippus	33
Childhood	443
Chorus	447
City-Life	207
Circe	259
Clazomene	81
Country-Life	211, 295, 313
Comedy	41, 433
Comedians	37
Conversation	45, 213
Contentment	305
Covetousness, the Excuses Men make for it, 5. The ill Effects of it, 7. The Description of a Covetous Man	9
Crantor	257
Cumæ	319
Custom	431

D

Dacians	211
Death not to be avoided	215
Democritus	307, 391
Diogenes	333
Discontent	1
Dishes	127
Divination	93
Draco	33

E

Education	47, 75, 403
Elegy	431

Empedocles

INDEX.

Empedocles   Page 309
Ennius   43
Epicharmus   371
Estate, the Way to get one   193
Extreams to be avoided   13, 15

F

Failings. Men are very apt to overlook their own, and to censure and condemn the same in others 21. We ought to excuse 'em 23. No Man without some or other   27
Ferentino   331
Feronia   55
Fescennine   383, 385
Festa Quinquatria   417
Flattery   399
Formia   57
Free-Man   225
Friends, how they ought to behave themselves towards each other 25. A good Friend the greatest of Blessings   57
Fundi   ibid.
Frog   179

G

Gallonius   129
Gladiators   151
Glory   69
Glycon   245
Gnatia   65
Gracchus   407
Greatness   77

H

Happiness   275, 297
Harpies   129
Hecate   89
Hercules   205, 265
Herod   417
Homer   107, 255
Heroicks   431

I

Iambicks   431, 433
Ilerda   359
Impertinent   91
Ingenuus   67
Inconstancy   219, 253
Ino   439

I i   *Jupiter*

I N D E X.

Jupiter   Page 439
Ixion   ibid.

L

Laberius   101
Lares   159
Laverna   329
Laws why inftituted 31. The *Roman* Laws by whom collected   367
Legion   73
Lælius   121
Libertinus   67
Libitina   207
Longinus   435
Love, the Folly of it 171. How to gain the Love of others   335
Lucilius   37, 101
Lucrine-Lake   185
Luxury   169
Lucullus   401
Lynceus   245
Lysippus   395

M

Madnefs, all Men affected with it   145
Malice   47
Manhood   443
Manumiffion   223
Mæcenas   3
Mænius   13
Menenii   175
Mercury   205
Menander   141, 371
Medea   439
Method   441
Money   153, 277
Moufe, City and Country   213
Mutius   407

N

Nature not to be refifted   119, 299
Nævius   369
Nomentanus   13

O

Old Age   133, 445
Olympick Games   247
Orpheus   469

P

Pacuvius   369

INDEX.

Pantolabus   Page 87
Parthians   379
Paſſions   263, 435
Pauſias   227
Petillius   47
Philippi   403
Pilum   115
Pindar   267
Plato   141
Plautus   371
Poet, who may be ſaid to deſerve that Character 41.
    What Qualifications are requiſite to form one 101,
    409. The Danger of provoking a Poet 119. Much
    given to drinking 353. His good Qualities   381
Praiſes of good Judges only valuable   111
Præneſte   255
Prætor   57
Proteus   149
Proſerpine   203
Pupius   249
Puteal   209
Pythagoras   R   181, 213
Reputation   135
Riches, the Uſe of them 11. How to grow Rich 193
Roſcia Lex   249
Roſcius   375
Romulus   363
Rudis   241
Rubi   S   63
Salernum   319
Salii   377
Sappho   355
Satire, few are pleas'd with it 39. Unknown to the
    Grecians 109. Good Men have no Reaſon to be
    afraid of it   121
Saturnalia   141
Saturnius Numerus   385
Servius Tullius   67
Secrets not to be revealed   343
Siſyphus   25
Sinueſſa   57
Siſenna   83
                       Sicily

INDEX.

Sicily   Page 211, 263
Sirens   259
Sibyls   367
Socrates   181
Solea   237
Sophocles   387
Stag and the Horse   301
Superstition   177

T

Tarentum   79
Tabulæ votivæ   117
Temperance   123
Teanum   253
Terentius   371
Thebes   201, 393, 469
Thespis   385, 453, 457
Tigellius   21
Tillius   71
Timagenes   353
Time, the Alterations it makes in us   403
Tisiphone   89
Tiresias   193
Tivoli   189
Toga virilis   19
Trivicus   63
Tragedy   435, 451
Translation   441
Tyrtæus   469

V

Vacuna   301
Velia   319
Virtue to be regard d more than Birth   67
Virgil   21, 105
Vice, the Slavery that attends it   223
Ulysses   193, 257
Uniformity   441, 443

W

Wine   315
Words

X

Xenocrates   171

Y

Youth   443

Z

Zethus   345